# Understanding
## global social policy

# Understanding Welfare: Social Issues, Policy and Practice

Published in association with the Social Policy Association and Social Policy Subject Benchmark compliant, this series helps students understand the causes of and responses to social issues. Each textbook provides chapter-specific summaries, questions for discussion, illustrative boxes and diagrams to help understanding as well as full bibliographies.

## Also in the series:

*Understanding human need (Second edition)*
By **Hartley Dean**

*Understanding 'race' and ethnicity (Second edition)*
Edited by **Sangeeta Chattoo**, **Karl Atkin**, **Gary Craig**
and **Ronny Flynn**

*Understanding the mixed economy of welfare
(Second edition)*
Edited by **Martin Powell**

*Understanding social security (Third edition)*
Edited by **Jane Millar** and **Roy Sainsbury**

*Understanding the cost of welfare (Third edition)*
By **Howard Glennerster**

*Understanding health and social care (Third edition)*
By **Jon Glasby**

Find out more at
**policy.bristoluniversitypress.co.uk/
understanding-welfare-social-issues-policy-
and-practice-series**

# Understanding
# global social policy

Third edition

Edited by Nicola Yeates and Chris Holden

First edition published in 2008, Second edition published in 2014, Third edition published in Great Britain in 2022 by

Policy Press, an imprint of
Bristol University Press
University of Bristol
1–9 Old Park Hill
Bristol
BS2 8BB
UK
+44 (0)117 954 5940
bup-info@bristol.ac.uk

Details of international sales and distribution partners are available at policy.bristoluniversitypress.co.uk

British Library Cataloguing in Publication Data
A catalogue record for this book is available from the British Library

ISBN 978-1-4473-5803-9 hardcover
ISBN 978-1-4473-5804-6 paperback
ISBN 978-1-4473-5805-3 ePub
ISBN 978-1-4473-5806-0 ePdf

Cover design: Qube Design Associates, Bristol
Front cover image: www.jupiterimages.com

Bristol University Press and Policy Press use environmentally responsible print partners

Printed and bound in Great Britain by CMP, Poole

# Contents

# Detailed contents

# List of tables, figures and boxes

## Tables

## Figures

## Boxes

# List of abbreviations

| | |
|---|---|
| ACFTA | African Continental Free Trade Area |
| ASEAN | Association of Southeast Asian Nations |
| AU | African Union |
| BAME | Black, Asian and and minority ethnic |
| BASIC | Brazil, South Africa, China, India |
| BIAC | Business and Industry Advisory Committee to the OECD |
| BIT | bilateral investment treaty |
| BMGF | Bill & Melinda Gates Foundation |
| BPfA | Beijing Platform for Action |
| BRICS | Brazil, Russia, India, China and South Africa |
| CAT | Convention Against Torture, and Other Cruel, Inhuman or Degrading Treatment or Punishment |
| CCT | conditional cash transfer |
| CEDAW | Convention on the Elimination of All Forms of Discrimination Against Women |
| CEO | chief executive officer |
| CETA | Comprehensive Economic Trade Agreement |
| COP | Conference of the Parties |
| CPD | Commission on Population and Development |
| CPTPP | Comprehensive and Progressive Agreement for Trans-Pacific Partnership |
| CRC | Convention on the Rights of the Child |
| CSO | civil society organisation |
| CSR | corporate social responsibility |
| CSW | Commission on the Status of Women |
| DAWN | Development Alternatives for Women for a New Era |
| EBF | Extra Budgetary Fund |
| EC | European Commission |
| ECB | European Central Bank |
| ECJ | European Court of Justice |
| ECOSOC | United Nations Economic and Social Council |
| EEC | European Economic Community |
| EFA | Education For All |
| EP | European Parliament |
| ERT | European Round Table of Industrialists |
| ETUC | European Trade Union Confederation |
| EU | European Union |
| FAO | Food and Agriculture Organization |
| FCTC | Framework Convention on Tobacco Control |

| | |
|---|---|
| FDI | foreign direct investment |
| FOE | Friends of the Earth |
| GATS | General Agreement on Trade in Services |
| GATT | General Agreement on Tariffs and Trade |
| GAVI | Global Alliance for Vaccines and Immunizations |
| GCF | Green Climate Fund |
| GDI | gross domestic income |
| GDP | gross domestic product |
| GenU | Generation Unlimited |
| GFC | global financial crisis |
| GFMD | Global Forum on Migration and Development |
| GHG | greenhouse gas |
| GHPPP | global health-related public–private partnership |
| GIJI | Global Institute for Justice in Innovation |
| GMR | Global Monitoring Report |
| GNI | gross national income |
| GNP | gross national product |
| GSP | global social policy |
| GST | Global Social Trust (solitary fund) |
| GUF | global union federation |
| HAI | HelpAge International |
| HDI | Human Development Index |
| HiAP | Health in All Policies |
| HIF | Health Impact Fund |
| IAE | International Accredited Entities |
| IBRD | International Bank for Reconstruction and Development (World Bank) |
| ICC | International Chambers of Commerce |
| ICCPR | International Covenant on Civil and Political Rights |
| ICEF | International Children's Emergency Fund, now known as UNICEF |
| ICERD | International Convention on the Elimination of All Forms of Racial Discrimination |
| ICESCR | International Covenant on Economic, Social and Cultural Rights |
| ICPD | International Conference on Population and Development |
| ICRMW | International Convention on the Rights of Migrant Workers |
| ICT | information and communication technology |
| IDA | International Development Association (World Bank) |
| IDWF | International Domestic Workers' Federation |
| IFC | International Finance Corporation (World Bank) |
| IFI | international financial institution |

| | |
|---|---|
| IGO | intergovernmental organisation |
| IHR | International Health Regulations |
| IIASA | International Institute of Applied Systems Analysis |
| ILC | International Labour Conference |
| ILO | International Labour Organization |
| ILOSTAT | International Labour Organization Statistics |
| IMF | International Monetary Fund |
| INGO | international non-governmental organisation |
| INSTRAW | International Research and Training Institute for the Advancement of Women |
| IO | international organisation |
| IOM | International Organization for Migration |
| IPCC | International Panel on Climate Change |
| IPR | intellectual property right |
| ISDS | investor–state dispute settlement |
| ITUC | International Trade Union Confederation |
| IUF | International Union of Food, Agricultural, Hotel, Restaurant, Catering, Tobacco and Allied Workers |
| IWHC | International Women's Health Coalition |
| IWRM | integrated water resources management |
| LaDC | landlocked developing country |
| LeDC | least developed country |
| LGBTQI | lesbian, gay, bisexual, transgender, queer and intersex |
| LoN | League of Nations |
| MDG | Millennium Development Goal |
| MFN | most favoured nation |
| MPI | Multidimensional Poverty Index |
| MSF | Médecins Sans Frontières |
| NAFTA | North American Free Trade Agreement |
| NCD | non-communicable disease |
| NDC | nationally determined contribution |
| NEET | 'not in education, employment or training' |
| NGO | non-governmental organisation |
| NHS | National Health Service (UK) |
| OECD | Organisation for Economic Co-operation and Development |
| OSAGI | Office of the Special Advisor on Gender Issues and the Advancement of Women |
| PISA | Programme of International Student Assessment |
| PISA-D | Programme of International Student Assessment for Development |
| PPPs | public–private partnerships |
| PPP | purchasing power parity [used in Chapter 8 only] |

| | |
|---|---|
| R&D | research and development |
| RBF | Regular Budgetary Fund |
| SADC | Southern African Development Community |
| SAP | structural adjustment programme |
| SARS | severe acute respiratory syndrome |
| SDG | Sustainable Development Goal |
| SDH | social determinants of health |
| SEWA | Self Employed Women's Association |
| SIDS | small island developing states |
| SME | small or medium-sized enterprise |
| SMEunited | European Association of Craft, Small and Medium-Sized Enterprises (formally known as UEAPME) |
| SOE | state-owned enterprise |
| SPF | Social Protection Floor |
| SPIAC-B | Social Protection Inter-Agency Cooperation Board |
| SPL | societal poverty line |
| SRHR | sexual and reproductive health and rights |
| TAA | Trade Adjustment Assistance |
| TFN | transnational feminist network |
| TJM | Trade Justice Movement |
| TNC | transnational corporation |
| TPP | Trans-Pacific Partnership |
| TRIPS | Trade-Related Aspects of Intellectual Property Rights |
| TTC | transnational tobacco company |
| TTIP | Transatlantic Trade and Investment Partnership |
| TUAC | Trade Union Advisory Committee to the OECD |
| UBI | universal basic income |
| UDHR | Universal Declaration of Human Rights |
| UEAPME | European Association of Craft, Small and Medium-Sized Enterprises (also known as SMEunited) |
| UHC | universal health coverage |
| UK | United Kingdom |
| UN | United Nations |
| UNAIDS | United Nations Programme on HIV/AIDS |
| UNDESA | United Nations Department of Economic and Social Affairs |
| UNDP | United Nations Development Programme |
| UNDRIP | United Nations Declaration on the Rights of Indigenous Peoples |
| UNEP | United Nations Environment Programme |
| UNESCO | United Nations Educational, Scientific and Cultural Organization |
| UNFCCC | United Nations Framework Convention on Climate Change |

| | |
|---|---|
| UNFPA | United Nations Population Fund |
| UNGA | United Nations General Assembly |
| UNHCR | United Nations High Commissioner on Refugees |
| UNICE | Union of Industrialists and Confederation of Employers (now BusinessEurope) |
| UNICEF | United Nations Children's Fund |
| UNIFEM | United Nations Development Fund for Women |
| UN-OHRLLS | United Nations Office of the High Representative for the Least Developed Countries, Landlocked Developing Countries and Small Island Developing States |
| UNRISD | United Nations Institute for Social Development |
| UN Women | United Nations for Gender Equality and the Empowerment of Women |
| USA | United States of America |
| USAID | United States Agency for International Development |
| USMCA | US–Mexico–Canada Agreement |
| USP2030 | Global Partnership for Universal Social Protection to Achieve the Sustainable Development Goals |
| WDM | World Development Movement |
| WEDO | Women's Environment and Development Organisation |
| WEF | World Economic Forum |
| WESODATA | World Employment and Social Outlook Data (ILO) |
| WHA | World Health Assembly |
| WHO | World Health Organization |
| WIEGO | Women in Informal Employment: Globalizing and Organizing |
| WMO | World Meteorological Organization |
| WSF | World Social Forum |
| WTO | World Trade Organization |
| WWF | World Wildlife Fund |
| YEN | Youth Employment Network |

# Acknowledgements

All edited collections are works of collaboration, and this one is no different. We thank all of the contributors for their excellent chapters, their enthusiasm for a third edition of the book, their thoughtful engagement with our feedback and comments, and their speedy response to our queries. Many of the authors of this edition of *Understanding global social policy* are contributors to the previous two editions, while others have joined for this third round. All are highly appreciated colleagues, distinguished experts in their areas, and we have enjoyed working with them in the context of this third edition.

All the chapters have been thoroughly reviewed by ourselves, other authors, and external reviewers at different stages of the process. The book has benefited from the comments arising from the anonymised peer review process. We thank the authors for providing their comments on draft chapters by other contributors. As authors of Chapter 5, 'Theorising global social policy', we have greatly appreciated their supportive engagement with our ideas under development.

We would like to thank the copyright holders of chapter figures for permission to reproduce them. Should any have been overlooked, please contact us and we will rectify any errors at the earliest opportunity.

We are appreciative of The Open University's School of Social Sciences and Global Studies Research Fund for financially supporting some of our work on this book.

The commissioning, editorial and production team at the Policy Press have, as ever, been a delight to work with. We thank Laura Vickers-Rendell, Emma Cook, Amelia Watts-Jones, Millie Prekop and Dawn Rushen for their timely support, delivered with clarity and purpose.

Since the publication of the second edition, one of our contributors, Bob Deacon, sadly passed away. A key figure in global social policy, his contributions to the field are sorely missed. At the same time, we are pleased to involve a younger generation of global social policy scholars to contribute to this edition, and to work with colleagues to author chapters who may not have previously identified with global social policy. Such ongoing dialogues have been very productive for us all and have helped to refresh, develop and expand this edition of the book. We look forward to many cross-disciplinary, intergenerational and international dialogues continuing well into the future.

# Notes on contributors

**Roger Dale** is Emeritus Professor of Sociology of Education at the University of Bristol, UK. Roger has written extensively on the state and education, with a particular focus on education governance. He has also published seminal papers on globalisation and education and was founding editor, with Susan Robertson, of the journal *Globalisation, Societies and Education*.

**Kevin Farnsworth** is Reader in Social Policy at the University of York, UK. His research interests focus on the exercise of power by business and labour on governments, especially with regard to social policy. He is author of *Corporate power and social policy* (Policy Press, 2004), *Social versus corporate welfare* (Palgrave, 2012), and co-editor (with Zoe Irving) of *Social policy in challenging times: Economic crisis and welfare systems* (Policy Press, 2015) and *Social policy in times of austerity: Global economic crisis and the politics of welfare* (Policy Press, 2015)

**Ross Fergusson** is Professor of Social Policy and Youth Policy at The Open University, UK. His research interests are in socially excluded young people, the relationships between social policy and youth criminal justice, and youth unemployment internationally. His recent books are *Global youth unemployment: History, governance and policy* (with Nicola Yeates, Edward Elgar, 2021) and *Young people, welfare and crime: Governing non-participation* (Policy Press, 2016). His other recent publications include 'International organizations' involvement in youth unemployment as a global policy field and the global financial crisis', in K. Martens, D. Niemann and A. Kaasch (eds) *International organizations in global social governance* (Palgrave Macmillan/Springer, 2021).

**Chris Holden** is Reader in International Social Policy at the University of York, UK, where he is Director of the Centre for Research in Comparative and Global Social Policy. He has published widely on the relationships between the global economy, transnational corporations and health and social policy. He is co-editor of *The global social policy reader* (with Nicola Yeates, Policy Press, 2009) and a former co-editor of *Social policy review* (2009–11). He is Chair of the Editorial Board for the *Journal of Social Policy* and is a member of the International Advisory Board of the journal *Global Social Policy*. He is a former member of the Executive Committee of the UK Social Policy Association (2004–11).

**Meri Koivusalo** is Professor of Global Health at Tampere University, Finland. Her educational background is in medicine, with a PhD and MSc in Public Health. She has a wide research focus – from epidemiology to the commercialisation of health systems, public participation, intersectoral policy influence and assessment, and health and trade. Her current research interests and focus include the platform economy, health and commercial policy issues, and common global health policy interests and regulatory challenges across countries. She is a former editor of *Global Social Policy* (2005–10).

**Lutz Leisering** is Emeritus Professor of Social Policy in the Faculty of Sociology, Bielefeld University, Germany. He holds a PhD from the London School of Economics and Political Science, an MPhil in Sociology from Bielefeld University and in Mathematics from Bonn University. He works on social protection in Europe and the Global South, with a focus on old age security, social assistance, international organisations and the ideational foundations of social policy. His recent books include *The global rise of social cash transfers* (Oxford University Press, 2019) and *One hundred years of social protection: The changing social question in Brazil, India, China, and South Africa* (Palgrave Macmillan, 2021). He is a board member of HelpAge Germany (HAD) and a representative of HAD in the Global Partnership for Universal Social Protection and in the Open-Ended Working Group on Ageing at the United Nations.

**Sophie Mackinder** is Lecturer in Global Social Policy and International Development at the University of York, UK. Her research interests are in the field of global governance, in particular the impact of intergovernmental actors on social protection, fragile states and refugee settlements in the Global South. Her recent publications include 'Ideas, institutions and the World Bank: The social protection and fragile states agendas' (*Global Policy*, 2020), and 'Tracing the institutional barriers to the integration of the fragile states and social protection agendas within the World Bank' (*Journal of International and Comparative Social Policy*, 2020). Her most recent research examines the impact of engagement with the private sector in refugee settlements in the Global South on refugee welfare and livelihoods.

**Rianne Mahon** is Distinguished Research Professor with the Department of Sociology and Anthropology at Carleton University, Canada. She has published numerous articles and chapters on various topics – industrial policy, labour market restructuring, childcare politics and the redesign of social policy at the local, national and global scales. Rianne has co-edited numerous books, including *After 08: Social policy and the global financial crisis* (with G. Boychuk and S. McBride, UBC Press, 2015), *Achieving the social development goals: Global governance challenges* (with S. Dalby and S. Horton, Routledge, 2019), and she has co-authored *Advanced introduction to social policy* (with D. Béland, Edward Elgar, 2016). Her current work focuses on the gendering of global governance, with a particular focus on transnational care chains.

**Robert O'Brien** is Professor of Political Science and former Director of the Institute on Globalization at McMaster University, Canada. His teaching and research interests are in the fields of international political economy, global governance, global civil society and the political economy of climate change. His most recent research book is *Labour internationalism in the Global South* (Cambridge University Press, 2019). His co-authored textbook *Global political economy: Evolution and dynamics* is now in its sixth edition and has been translated into Bangla, Chinese, Greek and Turkish. Robert is a founding and consulting editor of the online open access *Global Labour Journal* and former co-editor of the journal *Global Social Policy* (2005–10). He is also Fulbright Canada Research Chair in Public Diplomacy, University of Southern California, 2021–22.

**Eeva Ollila**, MD, is a specialist in public health and Associate Professor in Health Policy at Tampere University, Finland. She currently works as Chief Medical Officer for the Cancer Society of Finland. She has previously worked at the Finnish Ministry of Social Affairs and Health, the World Health Organization, the European Commission as a civil servant, and as a researcher at the National Research and Development Centre for Welfare and Health and Department of Public Health of the University of Helsinki. She has published on a range of global health policy issues, including pharmaceutical policies, tobacco policies, population, health and development, public–private partnerships and commercial interests in public health policy-making.

**Theo Papaioannou** is Professor of Politics, Innovation and Development at The Open University and Director of the Innogen Institute (University of Edinburgh and The Open University), UK. His background is in social and political thought. Theo has researched and published extensively in the areas of global justice and the politics of technological innovation and development. His recent publications include: 'The idea of justice in innovation: Applying non-ideal political theory to address questions of sustainable public policy in emerging technologies' (*Sustainability*, 2021), 'Reflections on the entrepreneurial state, innovation and social justice' (*Review of Evolutionary Political Economy*, 2020) and *Inclusive innovation for development: Meeting the demands of justice through public action* (Routledge, 2018).

**Nicola Piper** is Professor of International Migration and was founding Director of the Sydney Asia Pacific Migration Centre at the University of Sydney, Australia. In 2018, the British Academy awarded her a Global Professor Fellowship, hosted by Queen Mary University of London in the UK, where she will be conducting research until December 2022. As a political sociologist, her research interests focus primarily on global labour mobility, global and regional migration governance, advocacy politics and migrant rights issues, about which she has published extensively. She is (co-)chief editor of the *Global Social Policy* journal and editor of the book series Asian Migration with Routledge.

**Susan Robertson** is Professor of Sociology of Education at the Faculty of Education, University of Cambridge, UK. Susan has published widely on the globalising and regionalising of education policies as a result of transformations of the national state, and the construction of education as a services sector. She is founding editor and currently co-editor of the journal *Globalisation, Societies and Education*.

**Jeremy J. Schmidt** is Associate Professor of Geography at Durham University, UK. He is the author of *Water: Abundance, scarcity, and security in the age of humanity* (New York University Press, 2017) and co-editor of *Water ethics: Foundational readings for students and professionals* (with P. Brown, Island Press, 2010). His research focuses on the social dimensions of water, land and energy, with particular attention to the ethics and politics of human impacts on the planet. In 2015 he received an Impact Award (Talent Category), the highest recognition granted by the Social Sciences and Humanities Research Council of Canada.

**Carolyn Snell** is Reader in Social Policy based in the Department of Social Policy and Social Work at the University of York, UK. Carolyn's career began with a degree in Politics and English Literature and was followed by an MA and PhD in Social Policy. Following this she held a research post at the Stockholm Environment Institute working on the social and public policy dimensions of transport policies. Since 2011 Carolyn's research and publications have largely focused on the relationship between energy, climate change and social policy in the UK, with a particular interest in fuel poverty. Carolyn's most recent research has focused on the social implications of the zero carbon transition. Carolyn leads the UK Social Policy Association's 'Climate Justice and Social Policy' group.

**Nicola Yeates** is Professor of Social Policy in the Department of Social Policy and Criminology at The Open University, UK. She has taught and published widely on a range of matters in global social policy, notably regarding world-regional social policy, global migrations, and global health and social care labour forces. Her work has been widely reprinted and translated. She was an editor-in-chief of the journal *Global Social Policy* (2005–10), and is a member of its International Advisory Board. She is sole editor of two previous editions of *Understanding global social policy* (Policy Press, 2008, 2014), and co-editor of *The global social policy reader* (with Chris Holden, Policy Press, 2009). Her most recent books are *Global youth unemployment: History, governance, policy* (with Ross Fergusson, Edward Elgar, 2021) and *International health worker migration and recruitment: Global governance, politics and policy* (with Jane Pillinger, Routledge, 2019).

# 1

# Introducing global social policy

## Nicola Yeates and Chris Holden

### Overview

This chapter introduces global social policy as a field of academic study and as a political practice of social actors. It sets out the essence of a globalist approach to social policy, briefly traces the development of global social policy in academic analysis, and draws attention to its changeable, differentiated and co-determined nature. The chapter introduces key topics, themes, issues and debates taken up in the book, together with key developments in recent years that have shaped global social policy. Finally, it provides a brief guide to using this book, a summary of the key points covered in the chapter, and suggestions about how to keep up to date with developments in this fast-moving field.

### Key concepts

Global social policy; globalisation; methodological transnationalism; methodological nationalism

## Introduction

Global social politics, policies and programmes of social action have a potent influence on domestic social policy, the terms of social development and the condition of human welfare around the world. They affect the everyday lives of billions of people in myriad ways, impact on individual and collective subjectivities, shape major social institutions, frame policy responses and influence welfare outcomes in ways that, although not always immediately perceptible, are nevertheless highly significant.

Building on the successes of the first and second editions of *Understanding global social policy* (Yeates, 2008, 2014), this third edition provides an up-to-date, comprehensive and accessible collection of research-based student-facing chapters that bring alive and illuminate key issues, themes and debates in contemporary **global social policy** (GSP). This edition, like previous ones, provides an introductory overview of GSP as a field of academic study and as a political practice of social actors. It is concerned with the 'what', 'who', 'why' and 'how' of GSP. The chapters span a wide range of areas and issues, uncovering the multifaceted scope of GSP, why it is needed, what and who is involved in making it, how it is enacted, what its consequences and impacts are, and what challenges lie ahead. This edition contains a mix of updated chapters from previous editions as well as newly commissioned ones, written by world-leading scholars in GSP.

The remainder of this chapter introduces the book as a whole. It discusses the significance of the prefix 'global' and what this implies. It distinguishes key features of GSP as a field of academic study and research and as political practice. After a brief introduction of each of the chapters, it concludes with a summary of key points, guidance on using the book, questions for further discussion and further resources.

## Globalisation, social science and social policy

Social policy as a subject of academic study and research has given rise to a rich interdisciplinary field of study with a distinctive body of theory, concepts and methods that has underpinned timely, relevant and useful research with and for communities, social movement organisations, non-governmental organisations (NGOs) and governments. Traditionally, it strictly followed the tenets of **methodological nationalism** – the idea that domestic welfare institutions, policies and programmes of social action and their outcomes are the only meaningful subject of study and research, and that they are wholly shaped by social relations and interactions among domestic actors within national (or sub-national) spheres of **governance**. *Global* social policy challenges this methodological stance on the basis that it renders invisible the 'extra-national' and 'transnational' realms in which social policies are made, contested and implemented. GSP's **methodological transnationalism** aims to uncover the contours and textures of these extra-national and transnational realms – the institutions and actors, the relations between them, and the outcomes of their interactions (see **Box 1.1**).

### Box 1.1: Contrasting methodological approaches in social science and social policy

Methodological nationalism:
- Emphasises the institutions, actors and processes forging, sustaining and reconfiguring links and ties within countries.
- Focuses on the ways in which domestic politics, policy actors, policies and institutions influence national welfare states, welfare systems and social policies.

Methodological transnationalism:
- Emphasises the institutions, actors and processes forging, sustaining and reconfiguring links and ties cutting across countries.
- Focuses on the ways in which 'extra-national' global politics, policy actors, policies and institutions both influence and are influenced by national welfare states, welfare systems and social policies.

The conscious embrace of methodological transnationalism by GSP analysis opens up new ways of studying the social organisation of welfare and the processes by which welfare institutions are made and remade (see **Box 1.2**). GSP looks for:

- the direct and indirect impacts of transnational forces and relationships on countries' welfare systems and their outcomes;
- the ways in which states and other social actors vie for influence over the course of global social policy-making in cross-border spheres of governance;
- how the 'national' and 'transnational' realms are intermingled and co-constituted.

## Box 1.2: Global social policy

A GSP perspective challenges the idea that the social organisation of welfare is determined uniquely or primarily by local and national structures of power. It directs attention to modes of political organisation, social action and economic and cultural forces traversing countries and structurally linking welfare systems around the world. Broadly, GSP examines:

- How social policy issues are being perceived to be global in scope, cause and impact.
- Responses by state and non-state actors to global social policy issues.
- Structural social and economic changes affecting the social organisation and relations of welfare, such as:
  - cross-border flows of people, goods, services and ideas;
  - transnational forms of collective action, including multilateral and cross-border modes of governance.
- The impacts of these changes on systems of financing, regulation and provision of social welfare and on access to welfare services and human welfare outcomes around the world.

Processes of **globalisation** and the remaking of social relations on a global scale are central to GSP (see **Box 1.3**), although the ways in which they are doing so are diverse. Whatever one's 'take' on globalisation, there is broad agreement that it engenders far-reaching social and economic change while also requiring and/or enabling new sorts of responses to social issues. But this raises further questions: which social problems come to be defined as 'global' ones? What sorts of problems are they defined as being – and for whom? And what types of response ensue? (See **Box 1.4**.)

## Box 1.3: Globalisation

There is a great deal of controversy over the concept of globalisation and its onset, causes, effects and universal applicability. Its core idea is that the conditions of human existence are characterised by dense, extensive networks of links and ties routinely transcending national borders in ways that produce relations of interconnectedness and interdependence. These links and ties manifest in the form of:

- flows of capital, goods and services;
- the international integration of business activities and economies on global or world-regional scales;
- flows of images, ideas, information and values through media and communications;
- worldwide spread of ideologies such as consumerism, individualism and collectivism;
- international movements of people for leisure, work, medical treatment and personal safety;
- global political institutions, movements and action.

A principal consequence of globalisation is that events happening in one part of the world quickly produce effects in other parts of it, as seen in the global financial crisis (GFC) of 2007–09 and the COVID-19 pandemic of 2020–. Travel technologies enable the transmission of viruses, people and goods around the world in a matter of hours; communication technologies enable information to be circulated worldwide within seconds.

If modern technologies help shape a sense of the world as a single, shared place, culture and politics still matter. Whereas early studies of globalisation emphasised the convergence and 'flattening' of local and national cultures, social systems and welfare states, more emphasis is now placed on how these cultures and systems are 'remade' by global forces, with distinctive national features being retained despite convergent pressures.

The study of globalisation processes builds on significant traditions of thought that understand the world as a single global system. For example, the development of ecology as a science has seen ecological processes as planetary in scale, with changes in ecological conditions in one part of the planet affecting other parts of it. Here, the impact of human activity on ecological systems is also seen to have a planetary impact, in that toxic chemicals and pollution released in one locality are transported to and 'land' in other proximate and distant parts of the world. Similarly, climate change is an intrinsically global phenomenon, requiring a similarly scaled response to protect planetary health and the lives of all those who live on it.

## Box 1.4: Defining a global social policy problem

A question for students of GSP is, which social issues are defined as GSP ones? And how? George and Page (2004, p 2) argue that there are four criteria in the definition of a global social policy problem:

1. The cause of a problem should be found in global rather than national processes.
2. Such problems can easily spread across national borders.
3. The problem is increasingly difficult to resolve at national level.
4. International organisations can assist nation-states in dealing with the social problem at hand.

Processes of global social problem definition are complex, as is the formulation of responses through GSP. Some social problems are more global than others, and the content of GSP responses vary in their degree of 'globality'. This raises the prospect of comparative analysis in the study of GSP and the question of how GSP definition processes vary, depending on the issue and according to different constellations of factors.

The **global financial crisis** (GFC) of 2007–09 and the COVID-19 pandemic of 2020– are examples of how events in one part of the world rapidly reverberate to other parts of it, jeopardising jobs, incomes, health and the wellbeing of populations on a mass scale worldwide. In the GFC, massive economic shocks were transmitted rapidly around the world by a globalised financial system and globally integrated supply chains facilitated by extensive international trade and **foreign direct investment** (FDI). Similarly, the COVID-19 pandemic is an intrinsically global issue; like other highly infectious viruses, its transmission depends on close physical proximity and its spread is accelerated by high volume, high frequency transport links. The consequences of both types of event are far-reaching, touching every part of our lives. But even if we can agree that such global crises require global and not just national political responses, this raises questions about what sorts of global response are ethical, desirable and possible, which ones come to fruition in practice (or not) – and why – and whether they are effective. This is not just a question of whether the institutions and technologies are fit for purpose; it is as much about politics and the 'art' of making meaningful social change happen.

This is not to say that all social problems come to be defined as a matter for GSP, or that they are defined in the same sort of way, or that the nature of those responses is unchanging over time and/or among different parts of the world and populations. Indeed, GSP is dynamic; it is changeable, not fixed; differentiated, not **universal** in either form or impact. A key task of GSP scholarship is therefore to uncover these variations (between sectors, issues, parts of the world, populations and over time), and to explain the reasons for them.

A final point in this regard is that GSP is not irrevocably tied to forces of greater integration on a world scale ('globalisation'). Because GSP analysis examines the global dimensions of the social organisation of welfare, so with this is also included the possibility of **de**globalisations, or at least of uneven integration–disintegration processes. For example, if powerful states do not become members of **intergovernmental organisations** (IGOs), or withdraw from them, as the USA has done (under the Trump administration, from the Paris Climate Agreement, the World Health Organization [WHO] and the World Trade Organization [WTO]; under previous US administrations, from the International Labour Organization [ILO] and the United Nations Educational, Scientific and Cultural Organization [UNESCO]), and as the UK has from the European Union (EU), then global dynamics of social policy are reconfigured as 'new' actors and ideas emerge and global connections are restructured.

In sum, understandings of the contemporary world have moved away from a world made up of a multitude of bounded national social systems and towards an understanding of a global social system that links populations and places in different parts of the world and comprises various global and sub-global hierarchies and networks of border-spanning connections, interactions and effects. At the same time, this global system and the social policies instituted within it are changeable and structurally differentiated.

## Global social policy as a field of academic study and analysis

*From global social policy as a practice of elite global institutions and actors …*

The genealogy of GSP as an academic field conventionally starts in the mid–1990s with the publication of *Global social policy: International organisations and the making of social welfare* by Bob Deacon, Paul Stubbs and Michelle Hulse (Deacon et al, 1997). They defined GSP as:

> ... a practice of supranational actors [which] embodies global social redistribution, global social regulation, and global social provision and/or empowerment, and ... the ways in which supranational organisations shape national social policy. (Deacon et al, 1997, p 195)

Their core argument was that economic and political globalisation processes fundamentally shape the course of social policy. The restructuring of national welfare systems could only be fully understood, they argued, by reference to the pressures that global economic restructuring unleashed and the responses of **international organisations** (IOs). Several consequences of globalisation for welfare states and social policies were sketched out (see **Box 1.5**). These ranged from predictions of the demise of comprehensive welfare states where they exist and their stalled development where they don't, to how welfare systems were adapting and managed to remain (largely) resilient in the face of **neoliberalism**, to the possibilities that globalisation opened up new forms of social welfare financing, regulation and provision. For Deacon et al, a crucial part of any explanation of which paths were taken was the response of IOs. IGOs such as the World Bank, the International Monetary Fund (IMF), the United Nations (UN) 'social' agencies such as the ILO and the WHO, and international non-governmental organisations (INGOs) like Oxfam, Save the Children and so on are all meaningful social actors, addressing social policy questions as a matter of routine and intervening in political debates to shape welfare trajectories. Therefore, their policy discourses and programmes of social action had to be centre stage of analysis, rather than merely part of the background. Deacon et al's work had a strongly normative, political inflection to it, in the sense that not only were they trying to assess the extent to which GSP founded on social regulation, social redistribution and social rights could be said to *actually* exist, but also to delineate the kinds of reforms that *should* be instituted in order to realise such a GSP.

There is no doubt that this work was influential, even if the newness of global policy discourses about social policy and the extent of the shift of governance structures from national to global levels that Deacon et al claimed to have discovered was questionable. Notably, contemporary GSP studies is predated by a substantial body of theory and research by 'early pioneers' since (at least) the 1950s. For example, in the 1950s and 1960s Peter Townsend developed a global analysis of world poverty, combining the insights of global sociology, development studies and social policy. *The concept of poverty* set out an 'approach to development and stratification [to explain] how poverty arises, and is perpetuated, in low income and high income countries' (Townsend, 1970, p 30), and argued that '[a] wealthy society which deprives a poor country of resources may simultaneously deprive its own poor classes through maldistribution of those additional resources' (Townsend, 1970, p 42). The riches of those living in **high–income countries** are, Townsend argued, inextricably linked to the poverty of those living in **low-income countries**. He was, in essence, drawing attention to webs of interconnectedness and interdependency long before 'globalisation studies' took off in the 1990s. In addition, others argued that the shift in power away from the national level to the global level was overstated, and that Deacon et al's thesis was overgeneralised from the specific experience of one part of the world at one point in time, namely, Central and Eastern European countries following the end of the Cold War.

---

## Box 1.5: Some possible effects of globalisation on social policy and welfare states

- Creates new or additional social risks and opportunities for individuals, households, workers and communities.
- Sets welfare states in competition with each other. This is said to threaten comprehensive systems of public service provision where they exist, or to stall their future development where they do not. Among the anticipated effects are:
  - lowering of social and labour standards;
  - privatisation of public services;
  - creation of global health, education and welfare markets;
  - growing reliance on voluntary and informal provision.
- Raises the issues with which social policy is concerned to supranational and global institutions, agencies and forums.
- Brings new players into the making of social policy (for example, the Bretton Woods institutions; various UN agencies; development banks; and international commercial, voluntary and philanthropic organisations).
- Generates 'new' political coalitions within and between countries (regionally and globally) concerned with social policy reform.

Source: Yeates (2008), adapted from Deacon (2007)

---

Despite these objections, the lasting value of this work was to demonstrate how the battle over ideas and policy was being waged at the global level, within and between IGOs, as well as at the national level, and how national political and policy actors were faced with competing policy reform prescriptions in part defined by these IGOs. This work helped stimulate academic debates revolving around the extent to which GSP was implicated in trends in welfare convergence or welfare divergence, and whether national governments' dominant role in social policy formation had been displaced by the growing power of transnational actors (Yeates, 2001, 2014). It also energised the study of social policy, spurring a new generation of vibrant scholarship on how transnational social, economic and political processes – past and present – shape contemporary welfare development around the world in countries at all 'stages' of development. This, in turn, stimulated the 'globalisation' of concepts and, later, theories of social policy. Regarding concepts, they could either be 'stretched' to take greater account of transnational actors (as in the concept of the extended welfare mix; see **Table 1.1**) or entirely reformulated. Deacon et al put it this way:

> The classical concerns of social policy analysts with social needs and social citizenship rights becomes [sic] in a globalized context the quest for supranational citizenship. The classical concern with equality, rights and justice between individuals becomes the quest for justice between states. The dilemma about efficiency, effectiveness and choice becomes a discussion about how far to socially regulate free trade. The social policy preoccupations with altruism, reciprocity and the extent of social obligations are put to the test in the global context. To what extent are social obligations to the other transnational? (Deacon et al, 1997, p 195)

*Table 1.1: The extended welfare mix of social institutions and actors*

|  | **Domestic** | **Global** |
|---|---|---|
| State | National government, regional government, local authorities, town/city councils | IGOs, world-regional formations, international donors |
| Market | Domestic markets, local/national firms | Global markets, transnational corporations (TNCs) |
| Intermediate | National service NGOs, consultancy companies | INGOs (charitable and philanthropic bodies), international consultancy companies |
| Community | Local social movements, neighbourhood associations | Global social movements, diasporic communities |
| Family/household | Household survival strategies | Transnational household survival strategies, such as migration, remittances and care |

Source: Yeates (2007b)

*... To global social policy as a broader range of social policy dialogues involving a wider range of social actors and taking place across multiple locations and spheres of governance ...*

The last three decades have seen the maturation of the study of GSP (see **Box 1.5**). One aspect of this is the recognition that the range of social actors, locations and organisations involved in GSP formation, together with the transnational arenas in which GSP options and responses are debated and contested, is far broader than presented by Deacon et al (1997). Among the earliest contributors was Nicola Yeates (1999), who argued that a range of social dialogues among social actors about social policy take place outside the boardrooms and bureaux of elite IGOs as well as within them. The much wider realm of GSP formation that she pointed to included the activities of non-elites in global social politics and policy-making, notably social movements and NGOs operating in the numerous shadow congresses and social forums that accompany international governmental meetings. It also included citizen movements and NGO campaigns against (for example) local branches of **transnational corporations** (TNCs) alleged to be polluting the environment or harming the health and welfare of communities and workers' livelihoods. Even households' survival strategies of (for example) sending a member of the family to work overseas to send home **remittances** to supplement household income could be conceived as global social policy and/or as a social policy dialogue. The key point Yeates was making was that GSP formation takes place not just at the headquarters of the world's 'elite' and most visible IGOs, but across multiple levels and spheres of governance. This work (further developed in Yeates, 2001) also laid some of the foundations for a theory of GSP, in locating the emergence of GSP as a set of responses to regulate increased social and political conflict worldwide that accompanies contemporary globalisation processes.

*... To global social policy as co-determined and embedded*

Extending Yeates' focus on a broader range of sites of GSP and governance, Mitchell Orenstein broadened the definition of global social policies as 'those that are developed, diffused and implemented with the direct involvement of global policy actors and coalitions at or across the international, national or local levels of governance' (2005, p 177). This intervention highlighted that social policies enacted nationally and sub-nationally could be considered as 'global' to the extent that they are co-determined by global policy actors and are transnational in scope (2005, pp 177–8).

Hierarchy is implicit in GSP vocabularies of 'level' and 'tier' – with supranational entities placed at the top of the hierarchy and city authorities at the bottom, with power, authority and influence travelling 'downwards'. However, GSP scholars have come to emphasise how these different levels are parts of an overall system in which all parts affect each other, with influence 'travelling' multidirectionally. This opens up questions about: the ways in which, and extent to which, actors located in domestic arenas influence the formation of supranational policy; the 'embeddedness' of transnational policy actors in specific cultural/political territories; and how transnational policy actors operate at different 'levels' of and spaces within **global governance** – often concurrently (Stubbs, 2005; Yeates, 2007).

These works connect with literatures that reject conceptualisations of 'the global' as something 'out there', 'above' or beyond the nation–state, and emphasise the ways in which the global is 'in here', 'within' the nation–state and something that involves 'us'. This *embedded* notion of GSP points to the existence of transnational spaces within nation–states and the playing out of transnational processes within national territories as well as across them (Clarke, 2005). In this sense, welfare transnationalisms can be found in 'national' identities, social institutions, economic interactions and political processes *as well as* in the more visible border-spanning structures and 'high-level' forums and processes.

### The necessity of locating global social policy in time and place

The universalising claims that some saw in Deacon's approach to GSP rendered it vulnerable to criticisms of being decontextualised from time (history) and place (geography). The emphases on contemporary global institutions and present–day forms of GSP exaggerate breaks with the past and neglect older forms of global social welfare and GSP. For example, historians of welfare could reasonably point to how the social forces behind welfare state building and the social regulation of capitalism have long operated in a global economy characterised by extensive international trade and **migration**, TNCs and developed international monetary and exchange rate regimes (Hirst and Thompson, 1996). Taking account of this invites us to look beyond the Western 'global' welfare settlements embodied in the **Bretton Woods institutions** and the UN system after the Second World War. And while much recent commentary focuses on contemporary transnational political mobilisation in the anti–globalisation or 'alter-globalisation' movement, there are examples of political mobilisation on social policy issues dating back two centuries that were international and extended beyond Europe. The anti-slavery movement (1787–1807) is one such example; the Movement Against Congo Colonization (1890–1910) is another (Yeates, 2012). The history of the British welfare state is intricately bound up with its colonisation of the world's land mass and populations since the 16th century, and continues today in the postcolonial Commonwealth (Midgley and Piachaud, 2012; see also Schmitt, 2020). Not all of these transnational influences were colonial, however. Japan imported Western models of welfare in the 1870s (Goodman, 1992), while

Western thinking influenced the development of welfare in Taiwan and Korea (Goodman and Peng, 1996).

At the same time, GSP's changeable and differentiated structure is also seen in how it plays out across different countries and regions of the world. The experiences of, for example, African countries differ from those in East Asia, which differ again from those in North America, which contrast with those in South America. Many African countries, for example, have experienced the effects of global actors in very particular ways, variously (and often simultaneously) ignored by global corporations, exploited by them, and being subject to intense scrutiny and coercive policy prescriptions by **international financial institutions** (IFIs). Attentiveness to the uneven global political and economic geographies of GSP helps capture the spatially uneven outcomes of globalising processes, including the ways in which the relationship between people, state and territory in different parts of the world are being remade by global social policies. Keeping variation at the foreground of GSP analysis helps us, in turn, to understand how some countries are more embracing of neoliberalism than others, and how some countries have been able to forge social policy strategies that reject those prescribed by the Bretton Woods institutions, and how others still have even been a site of innovative social policy approaches that have been taken up and promoted by IGOs.

GSP is a maturing field of academic study and research that has already developed a rich body of research literature showing the power of global forces, institutions and actors in shaping welfare institutions worldwide. An ever-greater range of students and scholars worldwide from many disciplines is contributing to the development of GSP theories and concepts, and showing the diverse levels and spheres, territories and populations, and historical time periods across which GSP as a political practice of social actors is continually remade in different (and sometimes contradictory) ways. However, there remains much scope for further enriching knowledge and understanding of its changeable, differentiated and co-determined nature, and it is to the 'next generation' of GSP scholars that this book is addressed.

## Global social policy as a political practice

GSP is not just a field of academic study and research; it is a 'living' political practice of social actors. It comprises established institutions, commanding in some cases very substantial resources; diverse policy actors, ranging from governments to large international bureaucracies, to INGOs, to advocacy and campaign coalitions and global social movements seeking to represent diverse interests (business, labour, environment, health, and so on) in social policy initiatives; and tangible programmes of social provision and social action. The configuration of institutions, actors, ideas, policies and programmes that make up any GSP field varies. Whether by influencing domestic policy or policies emanating from spheres of cross-border governance, the 'real-life' worlds of 'high' and 'low' politics of policy all contribute to shaping how individual and collective welfare is governed, the broad direction and the specific content of social policy, the terms of social development and the social, cultural, economic and political conditions of human development.

Since the second edition of this book in 2014, several developments internationally and in global policy have shaped the GSP agenda. These include:

- A new global policy agenda for development. 'Agenda 2030' and the **Sustainable Development Goals** (SDGs) (2016–30) set out a comprehensive and universal global policy agenda that promises to leave no one behind, anywhere, reflects the vital role of social policy for **sustainable development**, and the interconnectedness of the social, economic, political and environmental dimensions of such development (UN, 2015).
- The ongoing 'greening' of social and political consciousness, including greater awareness of the ecological and environmental causes of global inequality and conflict, as well as of the human, non–human and planetary welfare and development impacts of climate change. These have propelled ongoing efforts to 'green' global policy at the UN and elsewhere, and have stimulated the concept of 'eco-social policy' (UNRISD, 2016, 2021).
- The ongoing impacts of the 2007–09 GFC and the **austerity** and welfare programmes that followed around the world. Global policy actors have been important in shaping policy responses to these (Dolphin and Chappell, 2010; Farnsworth and Irving, 2015; McBride et al, 2021).
- Major shifts in the geopolitical landscape that challenge **multilateralism** and global institutions as key forums for international social policy cooperation. These shifts include: the electoral rise of rightist **populism** and cognate forms of extremism internationally (Sandel, 2018); the electoral decline of leftist governments (especially in South America) (Manwaring and Kennedy, 2017; Gonzalez, 2019); and the worldwide impacts of African and Asian 'rising powers' (China's ascendancy as a policy actor in global governance is especially notable) (Kahler, 2013; Tan et al, 2013; Heldt and Mahrenbach, 2019).
- A reinvigorated international trade agenda in the form of new **bilateral** and transcontinental trade agreements, met by forms of engagement seeking to oppose them outright or to moderate them in the interests of public health and social welfare (von Bülow, 2009; Palmtag et al, 2020; Rone, 2020). Overlapping with, and potentially superseding this, have been increasingly conflictual trade relationships, and a shift in some key countries towards a more protectionist trade agenda (Baldwin and Evenett, 2009; Chaisse, 2017).
- The intensification of economic and political regionalisation processes (Fioramonti, 2013; Barbieri, 2019), with trade, health, migration and

development initiatives underway across Africa, South America and the Caribbean, and greater recognition of the role that regional blocs can play in realising the SDGs (Yeates, 2017).

- The COVID-19 pandemic of 2020, which triggered a whole-of-society shock to all countries worldwide, highlighting the threat to human health that unsustainable development poses, and exposing nationalism as an impediment to greater global social solidarity (Gostin et al, 2020). The gaping global inequalities in access to COVID-19 vaccines and the enduring weakness of many countries' health systems posed distinct challenges for global health governance and global health security (Gostin et al, 2020; Legge, 2020), among other things.

These 'new' and ongoing developments inform each of the chapters, and find concrete expression to different degrees. Chapter authors place different emphases in their approach to their topics in ways that reflect their personal intellectual and/or discipline-specific perspective. However, all chapters address the core tenets of GSP from the perspective of how these global imperatives and forces, governance structures and policy actors are (re)making GSP in practice.

## Outline of the chapters

Each chapter in this book surveys and illuminates the nature of contemporary GSP-making in relation to specific areas, issues, populations or sectors. Collectively, they illustrate the breadth and richness of GSP as a field of academic study and research and as a set of 'living' political ideas. Each discusses in tangible and illuminating ways the nature of social issues with which contemporary GSP is grappling, how global policy responses are, in turn, addressing them, and the challenges that lie ahead.

The book is divided into three main parts. Part One examines 'Institutions, actors and theories' and comprises five chapters. The main institutions of **global social governance** and the key actors in GSP are introduced first to provide a foundation on which later chapters build, and a lexicon that will familiarise readers with key terms and concepts in GSP. Sophie Mackinder, Chris Holden and Nicola Yeates (**Chapter 2**) introduce the actors and institutions that between them constitute global and regional social governance. Central to this governance is a multiplicity of IGOs, although **non-state actors** also play an important role. The different forms taken by IGOs relevant to GSP are examined, as are their overlapping mandates and different capacities to influence social policy and outcomes. Chris Holden (**Chapter 3**) focuses on global economic governance, trade and welfare. He discusses the changing nature of international trade agreements, the main forms that global economic governance takes, and the role of national welfare states within a liberalised world economy. Given recent shifts in the politics of trade, the chapter draws out 'behind the border' issues, such as regulatory cooperation and investor–state dispute settlement (ISDS), and relates them to GSP. Kevin Farnsworth and Robert O'Brien (**Chapter 4**) turn their attention to the role of business and labour actors in GSP, and why and how IGOs involve them in GSP-making. They discuss global initiatives to better regulate business globally and promote labour rights, and address the extent to which GSP can be understood as pro-business or pro-labour, and how this balance may be said to have shifted over time. With the key institutions and actors of GSP introduced, the remaining two chapters focus on GSP theory. Nicola Yeates and Chris Holden (**Chapter 5**) examine two different approaches to theorising GSP – on the one hand, 'globalising' theories of national welfare state development to take account of the different forms and circumstances of GSP, and on the other hand, 'welfarising' globalist social theories to incorporate the academic concerns of GSP scholars. Both approaches are reviewed and exemplars of each are briefly set out. The chapter also makes some suggestions for future work on theorising GSP. Finally, Theo Papaionnou (**Chapter 6**) discusses different schools of thought about how to 'globalise' social justice. Their differing normative claims are examined, as are how such claims can be operationalised to bring about meaningful pro-justice social change.

Part Two focuses on GSP issues and populations that cut across specific policy areas or domains, and comprises five chapters. Carolyn Snell (**Chapter 7**) considers climate change and environmental policy as a GSP issue of the first order. She uses the concept of **climate justice** to highlight how the harmful effects of climate change tend to be felt most by communities, countries and populations that have contributed the least to global environmental problems. Chris Holden (**Chapter 8**) focuses on global poverty and inequality. He considers the implications of global measures of poverty and inequality for the politics of GSP, the role of the World Bank in influencing knowledge and discourse about poverty, and the relevance of Agenda 2030 (SDGs) for the global politics of poverty and inequality. Nicola Yeates and Nicola Piper (**Chapter 9**) focus on GSP in relation to international migration. They emphasise how global migration governance is subject to gradual, yet intensified, institutionalisation, and how key developments in recent efforts to arrive at a global framework are marked by conflicting interests and politics. They also identify GSP issues raised by international migration and distinguish between GSP *for* migrants and GSP *by* migrants. Rianne Mahon (**Chapter 10**) discusses ways of thinking about where and how gender is embedded within GSP, and how it could better incorporate a gender-sensitive/equality lens. She focuses on the ILO's standard-setting work; women's social reproductive work via unpaid care and the broader **care economy**; and **sexual and reproductive health and rights** (SRHR). Finally, Ross Fergusson (**Chapter 11**) examines how young people have been incorporated into GSP. He shows the main focus of GSPs has been on education and employment, but also extends to crime and juvenile justice, and participation in development. The chapter brings a new example of global diffusion processes at work in social policy through discussion of the globalisation of the concept of 'not in education, employment or training' (NEET).

Part Three focuses on key GSP policy domains and is made up of four chapters. Jeremy Schmidt (**Chapter 12**) discusses where and how the interlinked policy areas of water, energy and food feature in GSP in practice. He traces the rise of the 'water–energy–food nexus' in global policy discourse, including its place in the operationalisation of the SDGs, and discusses what this means for social policy and social justice. Meri Koivusalo and Eeva Olilla (**Chapter 13**) consider the global policy agendas and programmes responding to an array of global health issues. They examine the multiple governmental and non-governmental actors involved in global health governance, as well as the ways in which international agreements can enhance or restrict the policy space for health. Susan Robertson and Roger Dale (**Chapter 14**) examine the key institutions, actors and policies in global education policy. They contrast different visions and models of education promoted by global actors, and how these are reframing education in policy and practice worldwide. The increasing interest of commercial businesses in education provision and the use of **public–private partnerships** (PPPs) in this sector is critically commented on, as are the ways in which education is promoted as an internationally tradable commodity. Last, but by no means least, Lutz Leisering (**Chapter 15**) reviews global **social security** policy around the world. He considers the experiences of countries, North and South, as well as the policies of the ILO, the World Bank and other IGOs in terms of their role in facilitating the 'spread' of particular models and pathways for income security around the world.

## Conclusion

The plethora of different initiatives and programmes, priorities and issues covered by the chapters of this book testify to burgeoning global policy activity and to the challenges that lie ahead. Fragmented systems of global governance, deeply entrenched global poverty, inequality and social injustice combine with a reluctance to meaningfully embrace a global shared responsibility for addressing critical social policy issues, the commercialisation and privatisation of public services, the philanthro-capitalisation of global social financing, the renewal and contestation of global trade and investment agreements, and an apparent preference in many areas of global policy-making for non-binding agreements and voluntary initiatives that fail to hold governments, corporations and others to account. However, recent history tells us that politics and ideas still matter, now, as much as ever. We see more universalistic models of health and **social protection** that disrupt the once seemingly inexorable tide of neoliberalism, while the global social harms caused by the GFC, the period of 'austerity' that followed it in many countries and the COVID-19 pandemic may serve as a spur for new ideas, policy innovations and movements for social justice.

Translating current promising initiatives into a robust and sustained commitment to shared global social responsibility for social development and human welfare will require substantial programmes of global social redistribution, regulation and rights (cf Deacon et al, 1997). As climate change and ecological degradation create widespread disruption, chaos and death, now, more than ever, there is an urgent need for sustained and vigorous collective action – globally, nationally and locally – to capitalise on opportunities to advance progressive and sustainable forms of action in support of human welfare and wider social development. In this, the need for a deeper and more sophisticated understanding of GSP in theory and in practice becomes ever more pressing by the day.

## Using this book

This book is written with non-specialist readers in mind, and for anyone looking for an accessible way into key approaches, debates and issues in GSP as a field of academic study and as a political practice of social actors. Several design features of the book help achieve this:

- Each chapter starts with a brief overview of its contents and ends with a summary of the key points covered.
- Each chapter makes good use of case study material from research, campaigns and policy, and incorporates illustrative and visual material drawn from around the world to aid the development of knowledge and understanding.
- Each chapter includes questions for discussion, follow-up activities and further resources to stimulate further thinking and discussion.
- At the end of each chapter, references are cited for ease of follow-up.
- A full list of abbreviations and acronyms used in this volume is located at the front of the book.
- A comprehensive glossary of the key terms used in the book is located at the back of the book. Glossary terms are highlighted in bold in each of the chapters the first time they are used.
- A comprehensive index helps easily locate items of particular interest. Some chapters in this edition of *Understanding global social policy* refer to materials published in *The global social policy reader* (Yeates and Holden, 2009). *The global social policy reader* comprises leading academic publications and key global policy documents. Together these provide comprehensive coverage of and a guide to key concepts, actors, institutions, initiatives and processes in the field.

## Summary

- The 'global turn' in social science has opened social policy analysis to the ways that transnational social processes, ties and links between people, places and institutions routinely cut across welfare states.
- GSP broadens and invigorates the study of social policy, bringing in a new range of concerns, issues and approaches to social policy and welfare provision.
- GSP analysts examine how global forces, governance structures and policy actors are implicated in the (re)making of social policy and its impact on human welfare around the world.
- GSP examines a wide range of transnational social policy actors and processes operating across a range of spheres, sites and scales.
- GSP-making is embedded in cultural and political contexts. It is historically specific. Time and place matter.
- GSP is not just an academic subject; it is a set of 'living' political ideas and practices. It is an ongoing (if incomplete) project of major social significance, and a major focus of collective social action and campaigning on a worldwide scale.

## Questions for discussion

- Are the effects of globalisation on welfare systems and policy-making always negative?
- What sorts of issues do GSP researchers examine?
- What does it mean to say that GSP is changeable, differentiated and co-determined?

## Further resources

GSP is a fast-moving field. The *Global Social Policy* 'Digest' section will help you keep track of latest developments. It is produced regularly and is available in each issue of the *Global Social Policy* journal. Palgrave's *The Global Dynamics of Social Policy* series publishes open access books on different aspects of global social policy, contemporarily and historically.

### References

Baldwin, R. and Evenett, S. (eds) (2009) *The collapse of global trade, murky protectionism, and the crisis: Recommendations for the G20*, London: Centre for Economic Policy Research (https://ycsg.yale.edu/sites/default/files/files/Murky_Protectionism.pdf).

Barbieri, G. (2019) 'Regionalism, globalism and complexity', *Third World Thematics*, 4(6), 424–41.

Chaisse, J. (2017) 'Rising protectionism threatens global trade: WTO law and litigation in Asia', *Asian Dispute Review*, 19(3), 112–18.

Clarke, J. (2005) 'Welfare states as nation states: Some conceptual reflections', *Social Policy and Society*, 4(4), 407–15.

Deacon, B. (2007) *Global social policy and governance*, London: SAGE Publications.

Deacon, B. with Hulse, M. and Stubbs, P. (1997) *Global social policy: International organisations and the future of welfare*, London: SAGE Publications.

Dolphin, T. and Chappell, L. (2010) *The effect of the global financial crisis on emerging and developing economies*, Institute for Public Policy Research (IPPR) Discussion Paper, London: IPPR (www.ippr.org/files/images/media/files/publication/2011/05/Financial%20crisis%20and%20developing%20economies%20Sep%202010_1798.pdf).

Farnsworth, K. and Irving, Z. (eds) (2015) *Social policy in times of austerity: Global economic crisis and the new politics of welfare*, Bristol: Bristol University Press.

Fioramonti, L. (ed) (2013) *Regionalism in a changing world: Comparative perspectives in the new global order*, London: Routledge.

George, V. and Page, R. (eds) (2004) *Global social problems*, Cambridge: Polity.

Goodman, R. (1992) 'Japan: Pupil turned teacher?', *Oxford Studies in Comparative Education*, 1, 155–73.

Goodman, R. and Peng, I. (1996) 'The East Asian welfare states: Peripatetic learning, adaptive change, and nation-building', in G. Esping-Andersen (ed) *Welfare states in transition: National adaptation in global economies*, London: SAGE Publications, 192–224.

Gonzalez, M. (2019) *The ebb of the pink tide: The decline of the left in Latin America*, London: Pluto Press.

Gostin, L.O., Moon, S. and Meier, B.M. (2020) 'Reimagining global health governance in the age of COVID-19', *American Journal of Public Health*, 110(11), 1615–19.

Heldt, E. and Mahrenbach, L. (2019) 'Rising powers in global economic governance: Mapping the flexibility–empowerment nexus', *Global Policy*, 10(1), 19–28.

Hirst, P. and Thompson, G. (1996) *Globalization in question: The international economy and the possibilities of governance*, Cambridge: Polity.

Kahler, M. (2013) 'Rising powers and global governance: Negotiating change in a resilient status quo', *International Affairs*, 89(3), 711–29.

Legge, D.G. (2020) 'COVID-19 response exposes deep flaws in global health governance', *Global Social Policy*, 20(3), 383–7.

Manwaring, R. and Kennedy, P. (eds) (2017) *Why the Left loses: The decline of the centre-left in comparative perspective*, Bristol: Policy Press.

McBride, S., Evans, B. and Plehwe, D. (2021) *The changing politics and policy of austerity*, Bristol: Bristol University Press.

Midgley, J. and Piachaud, D. (eds) (2012) *Colonialism and welfare: Social policy and the British imperial legacy*, Cheltenham: Edward Elgar.

Orenstein, M. (2005) 'The new pension reform as global policy', *Global Social Policy*, 5(2), 175–202.

Palmtag, T., Rommel, T. and Walter, S. (2020) 'International trade and public protest: Evidence from Russian regions', *International Studies Quarterly*, 64(4), 939–55.

Rone, J. (2020) *Contesting austerity and free trade in the EU: Protest diffusion in complex media and political arenas*, London: Routledge.

Sandel, M. (2018) 'Right-wing populism is rising as progressive politics fails – Is it too late to save democracy?', *New Statesman*, 21 May (www.newstatesman.com/2018/05/right-wing-populism-rising-progressive-politics-fails-it-too-late-save-democracy).

Schmitt, C. (ed) (2020) *From colonialism to international aid: External actors and social protection in the Global South*, Basingstoke: Palgrave.

Stubbs, P. (2005) 'Stretching concepts too far? Multi-level governance, policy transfer and the politics of scale in South East Europe', *Southeast European Politics*, VI(2), 66–87.

Tan, Y., Lee, K. and Pang, T. (2013) 'Global health governance and the rise of Asia', *Global Policy*, 3(3), 324–35.

Townsend, P. (1970) *The concept of poverty*, London: Heinemann.

UN (United Nations) (2015) *Transforming our world: The 2030 Agenda for Sustainable Development*, A/RES/70/1, New York: UN (https://sdgs.un.org/2030agenda).

UNRISD (UN Research Institute for Social Development) (2016) *Policy innovations for transformative change: Implementing the 2030 Agenda for Sustainable Development*, Geneva: UNRISD.

UNRISD (2021) *A new eco-social contract: Vital to deliver the 2030 Agenda for Sustainable Development*, UNRISD Issue Brief 11, Geneva: UNRISD (www.unrisd.org/80256B3C005BCCF9/(httpPublications)/2D51D21D694A94D4802586A1004D18FC?OpenDocument).

von Bülow, M. (2009) 'Networks of trade protest in the Americas: Toward a new labor internationalism?', *Latin American Politics and Society*, 51(2), 1–28.

Yeates, N. (1999) 'Social politics and policy in an era of globalisation', *Social Policy and Administration*, 33(4), 372–93.

Yeates, N. (2001) *Globalisation and social policy*, London: SAGE Publications.

Yeates, N. (2007) 'The global and supra-national dimensions of the welfare mix', in M. Powell (ed) *Understanding the mixed economy of welfare*, Bristol: Policy Press, 199–220.

Yeates, N. (ed) (2008) *Understanding global social policy*, Bristol: Policy Press.

Yeates, N. (2012) 'Globalisation and social policy', in J. Baldock, L. Mitton, N. Manning and S. Vickerstaff (eds) *Social policy* (4th edn), Oxford: Oxford University Press, 420–36.

Yeates, N. (ed) (2014) *Understanding global social policy* (2nd edn), Bristol: Policy Press.

Yeates, N. (2017) *Beyond the nation state: How can regional social policy contribute to achieving the Sustainable Development Goals?*, UNRISD Issue Brief No 5, Geneva: United Nations Research Institute for Social Development (www.unrisd.org/ib5).

Yeates, N. and Holden, C. (2009) *The global social policy reader*, Bristol: Policy Press.

# Part One
## Institutions, actors and theories

# 2

# Global and regional social governance

Sophie Mackinder, Chris Holden and Nicola Yeates

## Overview

This chapter introduces the concept of global social governance as incorporating a range of intergovernmental institutions and state and non-state actors. The focus is on those intergovernmental organisations that have the most relevance for global social policy. These take a variety of forms, have different capacities to influence social policy and have overlapping mandates, leading to a fragmented system of global social governance. The chapter introduces the intergovernmental organisations that are most important for global social policy, and illustrates the variety of ways that they are organised and their different impacts on social policy and social outcomes. It also discusses the importance of world-regional organisations and agreements for global social governance. It concludes that the future of global social governance is an uncertain one.

### Key concepts
Global social governance; world-regional social governance; intergovernmental organisations; complex multilateralism

## Introduction

This chapter provides an overview of the institutions and actors that constitute the **governance** of **global social policy** (GSP). This process is referred to as **global social governance**, and involves a complex web of public and private actors which pursue their agendas over a multiplicity of jurisdictions and countries. The first section introduces key concepts necessary for an understanding of the **intergovernmental organisations** (IGOs), structures and actors via which the processes of global social governance take place. The following section introduces key IGOs, and demonstrates how they are organised according to different principles and have blurred and overlapping mandates and differential degrees of power. The World Health Organization (WHO) and the World Bank are briefly compared to illustrate these differences. The chapter then turns to world-regional social governance, and considers the range of sub-global (world-regional) IGOs and the challenges they both face and present for global social governance. Finally, the chapter looks at the future of global social governance and reflects on contemporary challenges to GSP.

## Conceptualising global social governance

*Governance* is a tricky concept, with a variety of definitions. It can be distinguished from *government* in that it concerns various means of regulating or organising some activity or entity that may involve governments but that are not limited to them. Governance is sometimes thought of as referring to the environment in which governments act. Fidler (2005, p 162) provides a concise definition of governance as 'The process of governing, or of controlling, managing or regulating the affairs of some entity'. Note that this may include formal institutions that involve codified rules and norms as well as tacit or informal rules or norms. It may also include various types of political, economic or social actors and organisations – both state and non-state. As we will see, a multiplicity of institutions and actors is involved in the making of GSP, and they operate according to a range of rules and norms.

Since there is no world government, the concept of **global governance** is central to understanding the nature of GSP. We can make a distinction between *global* governance and what is strictly speaking *international* governance, although some authors use these terms interchangeably. Fidler (2005, p 162) defines *international governance* as 'The process of governing the relations between states that involves only the states as legitimate actors'. Although states, via their governments, may engage in **bilateral** relationships, we are most concerned with their **multilateral** relationships (namely those that involve many states). Multilateral relationships have been institutionalised to a large extent via IGOs, most of which were created towards the end of the Second World War. IGOs can be thought of as both *institutions*, in that they involve sets of formal rules through which governments relate to each other, and as *actors* in their own right, since they are also organisations that have some level of autonomy from the governments that created them. IGOs are organised in a variety of ways, but what most have in common is that cooperation between *national states* via their governments is at their heart.

In contrast to international governance, we can define *global governance* as, 'Governance among states (including intergovernmental organisations) *and* non-state actors' (Fidler, 2005, p 161), with the latter including **international non-governmental organisations** (INGOs), **transnational corporations**

(TNCs) and other entities. It is this mix of states, IGOs, **civil society** and private actors, engaged in complex processes of influencing, decision-making and administration, that we refer to as global governance. The social policy aspects of this, global *social* governance, comprise the governance mechanisms through which GSP is produced, contested and implemented.

The role and influence of **non-state actors** varies. There are several avenues of involvement through the formal mechanisms of global governance that are managed through the IGOs; for example, IGOs increasingly encourage corporations to become involved in the development and implementation of GSPs through multistakeholder partnerships (see **Chapter 11**, this volume), most commonly **public–private partnerships** (PPPs) (see **Chapters 11, 13 and 14**, this volume). INGOs are also sometimes afforded observer status at international negotiations that are overseen by IGOs, and they often work with IGOs and states to deliver social policies, particularly in developing countries. Non-state actors also develop their own mechanisms of global governance through the use of private regulation. This occurs when TNCs, keen to avoid formal, mandated oversight of their activities by states or IGOS, cooperate with their competitors to develop their own voluntary rules and regulations to regulate an industry. In addition to these corporate codes of conduct, international codes of practice set out rules and norms governing the actions of private actors. Yeates and Pillinger (2019) draw attention to the importance of such codes in respect of international health workforce recruitment. O'Brien et al (2000) characterise the resulting form of global governance as **complex multilateralism**. This conveys how the role of states remains central, especially via IGOs, but the formal avenues of cooperation through this multilateral system are complemented by complex modes of interaction with (and among) non-state actors.

While IGOs at the global level are important, governance mechanisms are multitiered, and operate across different levels or scales. This is encapsulated within the concept of **multilevel governance** (see **Box 2.1**). Five 'layers' of political and administrative decision-making can be identified:

- *Global*, comprising the complex multilateral system.
- *World-regional*, whereby states cooperate in geographical areas, such as the European Union (EU).
- *National*, managed by governments.
- *Sub-national*, such as the devolved governments in the UK, or the federal system adopted by several countries.
- *Local*, comprising small districts overseen by local governments or councils.

## Box 2.1: Multilevel governance

This concept originally emerged within studies of the EU, where supranational institutions were built that stand 'above' EU member states and operate quasi-independently of them. Importantly, scholars noted that sub-national governments within member states were able to form relationships with and influence EU-level institutions, without necessarily being directly represented by their national governments (Hooghe and Marks, 2003). However, the concept has since been extended beyond the EU to incorporate the ways that global or international institutions can be multitiered in a number of ways. For example, an additional 'layer' of governance now exists between EU member states and global governance structures, wherein the European Commission (EC) often represents EU states within IGOs and in multilateral negotiations on trade, labour and health.

While these different 'levels' of governance may appear to be clearly delineated, the 'competences' of the different layers can overlap. With so many arenas of authority, it is not always clear who has the ultimate decision–making authority or responsibility for different areas of policy. Consequently, the boundaries between decision–making bodies become blurred. Multilevel governance is also not as hierarchical as the clean delineation of 'levels' suggests. Sub-national bodies can interact and further their own interests through taking their claims directly to world-regional and global-level institutions. Different territories may be incorporated into geographically overlapping governance structures. For example, South Africa is at once a member of the Southern African Development Community (SADC), the African Union (AU), the United Nations (UN) and the World Trade Organization (WTO), as well as international networks such as the BRICS group of 'emerging economies' (Brazil, Russia, India, China and South Africa). This shows that national governments see no contradiction between national, world-regional and global development strategies. Global governance is therefore in practice a complex structure of governance arrangements, comprising multiple institutions and actors, and multiple and interacting levels of decision–making.

We can see, therefore, that the concept of global governance goes beyond the idea of simple interactions between states within IGOs. IGOs are nevertheless particularly important to the global governance system. The following section looks in more detail at their roles and forms of organisation.

## Introduction to intergovernmental organisations

Most IGOs have their origins in the political settlement hammered out by the victorious powers at the end of the Second World War. In 1944, representatives from 44 allied states met in **Bretton Woods**, New Hampshire, at the UN Monetary and Financial Conference (informally known as the Bretton Woods Conference). The aim of this conference was to decide on a series of rules for a new international monetary system; the International Monetary Fund (IMF) and the World Bank were the result. Later the same year, delegates from China, the Soviet Union, the USA and the UK met in a private mansion in Washington DC named Dumbarton Oaks, to develop more ideas regarding a wider system of international organisations that would facilitate global peace and prosperity. These were the foundations of the UN, and were ratified in 1945 when representatives of 50 countries met in San Francisco at the UN Conference on International Organization. From this was born the UN system, the 'umbrella' system for the majority of IGOs. Most IGOs operate as 'specialised agencies' within the UN system. From the outset, the institutions of global economic governance (see **Chapter 3**, this volume), such as the IMF and the World Bank, were kept separate from those of global social governance. This separation has had far-reaching consequences for GSP and the extent to which global social and economic justice can be attained.

**Table 2.1** demonstrates that the majority of these institutions appear to have clear single-issue mandates. The WHO, for example, is concerned with global health; the WTO oversees global trade; the International Labour Organization (ILO) oversees labour and **social protection**. In reality, however, we find that there are overlapping mandates. As the boundaries between IGOs' mandates are blurred, there arises from this a rationale for inter-IGO cooperation, but also the potential for a degree of competition among IGOs, as they attempt to further their own agendas.

IGOs differ from each other in a variety of ways: in their forms of organisation, in their missions, and in the amount of resources they receive (which come mainly from **member states**). The different ways that IGOs are structured internally can affect how they make policy, which, in turn, can affect the content of the resulting policy. The ILO's tripartite structure, for example, can result in policies that might not be adopted by other IGOs, due to the presence of workers' representatives. IGOs' varying organisational structures can also affect how much power they afford to particular states within them, depending on the differing economic size of states and the way power was institutionalised within the particular organisation at the time the IGO was created (see **Chapter 5**, this volume). While some IGOs offer equal voting power to each country (one country, one vote), for example, others organise voting power based on the size of member states' economies. The financial contributions that states make to IGOs through different funding mechanisms can contribute to power differentials. For example, the USA wields extensive power over the World Bank through its dominant role as the biggest contributor of funds.

*Table 2.1: Key intergovernmental organisations in global social policy making*

| Intergovernmental organisation | Purpose, powers and influence on social policy |
|---|---|
| World Bank | Established in 1944 at the Bretton Woods Conference. Originally designed to support the reconstruction of European countries after the Second World War, it now plays a pivotal role in supporting development and alleviating extreme poverty in low-income countries. It influences national social policy through conditions attached to loans that it extends to governments |
| International Monetary Fund (IMF) | Established alongside the World Bank in 1944, and similarly structured. It was set up to ensure currency stability in the aftermath of the Second World War, but is now focused more generally on ensuring the stability of the world economy. Similar to the World Bank, voting power within the IMF is skewed towards rich economies, as votes are allocated to countries based on the size of their economies. Like the World Bank, it influences national social policy via loan conditionality |
| World Trade Organization (WTO) | Formed in 1995, the WTO superseded the General Agreement on Tariffs and Trade (GATT, founded in the post-Second World War period). Its mandate concerns the regulation of trade in goods and services and of intellectual property. It does this by providing a forum through which trade agreements are negotiated. It operates via 'hard law', in that it possesses a dispute settlement system, and its agreements can be enforced through trade sanctions. Its agreements can influence national social policy in diverse and controversial ways |
| International Labour Organization (ILO) | The ILO was created in 1919. It is now a UN agency that seeks to promote social and economic justice through international labour standards. Uniquely for an IGO, it has a 'tripartite' structure involving national governments, business representatives and trade union representatives. It operates primarily via 'soft law', that is, its power lies in norm-setting |
| World Health Organization (WHO) | Created in 1948, its mission is 'The attainment by all peoples of the highest possible level of health'. It operates primarily on the basis of 'soft law', but oversees two binding international treaties (which nevertheless lack a means of enforcement): the International Health Regulations and the Framework Convention on Tobacco Control |
| United Nations Educational, Scientific and Cultural Organization (UNESCO) | UNESCO, founded in 1945, is one of the smallest (and least-funded) IGOs within the UN group. Its mandate is to contribute to 'the building of peace, the eradication of poverty, sustainable development and cultural dialogue through education, the sciences, culture, communication and information'. It relies principally on discursive and normative influence and state cooperation |

(continued)

*Table 2.1: Key intergovernmental organisations in global social policy making (continued)*

| Intergovernmental organisation | Purpose, powers and influence on social policy |
|---|---|
| United Nations Children's Fund (UNICEF) | UNICEF was founded in 1946, then called the International Children's Emergency Fund (ICEF), to help children and their mothers in the aftermath of the Second World War. In 1950 its mandate was extended to address the long-term needs of children and women. Its mandate is to 'advocate for the protection of children's rights, to help meet their basic needs and to expand their opportunities to reach their full potential'. It works with governments to develop community-level programmes that support the health and well-being of children |
| Organisation for Economic Co-operation and Development (OECD) | The OECD, founded in 1961, is a research and norm-influencing organisation that comprises 37 mainly high-income countries. Its mission is to 'foster prosperity, equality, opportunity and well-being for all', by acting as a forum for the most 'developed' countries to find solutions to economic and social problems. It is not formally part of the UN system |

IGOs' powers of enforcement are a key issue for GSP – there is a wide variety in the ability of different IGOs to enforce their policies (see **Box 2.2**). On the one hand, there are organisations such as the WTO that operate on the basis of **hard law**, whereby they are the arbiters of legally binding agreements to which means of enforcement are attached. The WTO's **dispute settlement mechanism**, for example, can authorise a state party to impose trade sanctions on another party that refuses to implement a ruling (see **Chapter 3**, this volume). At the other end of the spectrum are IGOs that operate primarily through **soft law**, such as the ILO or the WHO. The ILO, for example, can adopt two kinds of legal instruments: **recommendations** and **conventions**. While recommendations are non–binding guidelines, conventions are binding on all ILO members. The ILO, however, has no effective means of enforcement, even for conventions. This means that a state can, in practice, ratify a convention but fail to properly implement it. Soft law organisations are not impotent, however – they have influence in the form of **normative power** (Manners, 2009). This means that their legal instruments are validated through the fact that they have been negotiated and discussed within a legitimate and accountable forum, among relevant actors. The global norms that are generated through these legal instruments embody shared values and priorities and can be important foci around which supportive governments and civil society actors can organise. The overarching normative framework for global social governance is currently provided by the **Sustainable Development Goals** (SDGs) (see **Chapter 8**, this volume).

## Box 2.2: Forms of 'policy power' in intergovernmental organisations

We can differentiate IGOs partly on the basis of how, and to what extent, they exert power over the policies of national governments (and sometimes other actors).

*'Hard law' power* involves:
- legally binding international treaties;
- an enforcement mechanism, such as a dispute settlement mechanism.

Sources of power: law; sanctions.

*'Soft law' power* involves:
- recommendations or guidelines;
- norm generation;
- ideational influence.

Sources of power: expertise; moral authority.

*Conditionality power* involves:
- the attachment of conditions to loans or grants.

Sources of power: money.

Hard law and **conditionality** power tend to be located in 'economic' IGOs, while soft law power tends to be located in 'social' IGOs. However, these distinctions do not always map neatly onto specific organisations. For example, while the ILO and WHO rely much more on soft law than the WTO, they both oversee some legally binding international treaties, although these lack clear enforcement mechanisms. The WTO, on the other hand, oversees legally binding international treaties *and* a dispute settlement mechanism that can authorise member states to impose sanctions on other member states. Yet even the WTO can have difficulty imposing its will on powerful states, as demonstrated by the undermining of the WTO's processes by the USA under President Trump. The World Bank can exert strong influence on the policies of states that are recipients of its loans, but it also uses the expertise of its staff to engage in norm generation and ideational influence.

The distinction between hard law and soft law is important because the former tends to be the preserve of economic organisations, such as the WTO, while the latter is more prevalent in organisations with a more direct focus on social policy, such as the WHO and the ILO. The consequence of this is that there are not only imbalances in terms of the power that IGOs possess within countries, but also between the IGOs themselves. Since IGOs' mandates significantly overlap, this means that 'prosocial' policies and principles can sometimes be overruled by hard laws regarding the economy. Furthermore, as economic and social issues are so closely related, the hard law IGOs, principally the WTO, often encroach on the realm of social policy in order to further the interests of global trade and business.

In addition to the distinction between hard and soft law, a third mechanism can be identified that some IGOs can use to influence policy – conditionality. The World Bank and the IMF, for example, can extend loans to countries, and the loans can come with stringent conditions. **Low-income countries**, and more generally, countries that are experiencing economic crises, therefore often have little choice but to accept a high degree of IGO influence over their economic and social policies.

The fact that the mandates of the IGOs overlap so significantly also gives rise to the possibility of **venue shopping** and **venue shifting** (Baumgartner and Jones, 1993). *Venue shopping* refers to the activities of policy actors (such as governments, corporations and non-governmental organisations [NGOs]) in selecting the most appropriate and beneficial forum for them to pursue their policy ideas and goals. Closely related is *venue shifting*, where policy actors can move a given discussion from one forum to another where a decision is more likely to reflect their interests. The multiple and overlapping mandates of IGOs, therefore, not only blur the line between global policy issues, but also provide strategic opportunities for powerful global actors to pursue their goals and interests.

The formal system of global governance institutions is therefore a fragmented one, through which myriad struggles and contests are played out between multiple policy actors seeking to further their own agendas. The following section looks briefly at two IGOs in more detail – the WHO and the World Bank – to examine the issues highlighted in this section in more detail.

## Comparing intergovernmental organisations: the World Health Organization and the World Bank

In this section we will briefly look at two IGOs to illustrate in more detail the different ways that IGOs are organised and the differential influence they have in terms of enforcement power. The two cases illustrated here, the WHO and the World Bank, are examples of soft law and conditionality power (further discussion of a 'hard law' organisation, the WTO, is available in **Chapter 3**, while further analysis of the WHO and global health governance can be found in **Chapter 13**, both this volume).

The WHO's constitution defines it as 'the directing and coordinating authority on international health work'. It is governed by the World Health Assembly (WHA), which meets annually and comprises all 194 **member states**. The WHO has a 'one country, one vote' system. This is not uncontroversial, as larger states with bigger populations have less voting power per capita of population than small states. However, as in most other IGOs, a vote very rarely takes place. Instead, decisions are made by *consensus*. This means that prior to a decision being made, a long period of negotiation takes place whereby member states can develop a solution to which they are all able to agree. This may not produce the 'best option' by other parameters, but it is generally the solution that is the most acceptable politically. The WHA appoints a Director General and an Executive Board every five years. Unusually for an IGO, the Executive Board does not consist of country representatives. Instead, the 34 individuals that comprise the Executive Board are *technically qualified individuals* – experts in medicine and public health.

The WHO has two mechanisms of funding: Regular Budgetary Funds (RBFs) and Extra Budgetary Funds (EBFs) (Lee, 2008). In theory, RBFs are the principal mode of finance and the source of the majority of its finances. They entail assessed contributions from member states, based on each state's ability to pay according to **gross national product** (GNP) and population. However, large contributors such as the USA have increasingly frozen their payments, or paid them late. The WHO has consequently had to rely more on EBFs, which are discretionary funds, whereby states donate money. States favour this method, as they can have control over how the money is spent. The shift in funding mechanism is significant: RBFs comprised 62 per cent of the WHO's budget in 1970–71, whereas in 2019 they comprised only 19 per cent (WHO, 2020). The WHO has also increasingly turned to non-state funders – while the biggest contributor to the WHO in 2019 was the USA (contributing roughly 15 per cent of the WHO's total budget, with less than a third from RBFs), the second largest contributor was the Bill & Melinda Gates Foundation (BMGF) (approximately 9.8 per cent of the total budget) (WEF, 2020).

One important role of the WHO is to oversee the International Health Regulations (IHR), which are a set of legally binding international laws that seek to prevent the global spread of **communicable diseases**. This enables the WHO to declare a Public Health Emergency of International Concern and coordinate responses, as in the case of the COVID-19 pandemic that began in 2020. However, the relatively constrained influence that the WHO has over national governments was demonstrated during the pandemic, when it was caught up in geopolitical tensions between China and the USA. On the one hand, it had to engage in diplomacy to persuade the Chinese government to provide it with the information it needed about the virus and its spread, while on the other hand, US President Trump withdrew from the organisation, accusing it of being too 'soft' on China.

Despite being the lead IGO for matters of global health, the restricted resources and mandate of the WHO have allowed the World Bank, with its greater resources, to exert significant influence in the global health arena since the 1980s. The World Bank is one of the most significant IGOs in terms of GSP. It is made up of five principal component bodies, two of which are particularly pertinent to social policy: the International Bank for Reconstruction and Development (IBRD) and the International Development Association (IDA).[1] The IBRD was the original component of the World Bank, which was created in 1944 after the Bretton Woods Conference. Its mission in these early years of the post–war period was the reconstruction of European countries impacted by the conflict. In 1960 the IDA was created, to complement the IBRD's existing focus on **middle–income countries** with an approach that targeted low-income countries. Throughout the 1960s and 1970s the World Bank situated itself as the principal international development bank. Today, its mission is encapsulated by its twin goals of 'ending extreme poverty' and 'promoting shared prosperity' (see **Chapter 8**, this volume).

The World Bank's Board of Governors is made up of its 189 member states, but this body delegates many decisions to 25 Executive Directors. Voting power, however, is not distributed equally. Unlike the WHO, with its 'one country, one vote' system, the Bank assigns voting power based on the *number of shares* each country holds within it. This means that voting power is heavily weighted towards **high–income countries** and towards those countries that created the institution. This is seen particularly acutely in the case of the USA, which holds over 15 per cent of the voting power. As the most important votes require an 85 per cent majority, this means that the USA has veto power over significant decisions, even if all other member states are in agreement.

The World Bank's broad policy mandate and financial resources create significant overlaps with the mandates of other IGOs, including the WHO. Comparing the WHO and the World Bank, we can see that the Bank's ability to shape the economic policies of loan recipients allows it to also influence social policy, including health policy, by imposing conditions on how recipient governments spend their money. The WHO, by contrast, relies more on its expertise, its normative power and its ability to persuade governments to act in the interests of global health.

The comparison illustrates some of the differences between 'economic' IGOs such as the World Bank and those IGOs like the WHO that have more explicitly social mandates, but it also illustrates the extent to which IGOs' remits intersect in practice. Health policy, for example, clearly falls under the mandate of the WHO, but the funding and delivery of health services is also a development issue, and therefore of concern to the World Bank. Health is also in part a nutritional issue, and therefore of concern to the Food and Agriculture Organization (FAO). Health policy might also be seen as a labour issue, for example where it concerns health worker **migration**, and therefore a concern of the ILO (Yeates and Pillinger, 2019). While there may be some competition between IGOs, to some extent policy overlaps are simply the result of IGOs attempting to fulfil their mandates, which can never be completely circumscribed.

While global-level IGOs like the WHO and the World Bank are central to global social governance, **world–regional organisations** and agreements are also of importance. We turn our attention to these next.

## World-regional social governance and policy

The complexity of multilevel governance in today's world draws our attention to the significance of regional integration projects for GSP. Such projects have long existed in Africa, South America and East Asia, but they have become more numerous over the last 30–40 years as international integration on a regional scale has become an important facet of state and non-state actors' **globalisation** strategies (Yeates, 2019). In some cases, substantial political projects of world–region building have spurred the development of very complex sub–global governance systems, with common policies on a range of fronts backed by enforceable laws and, in some cases, finance. The best-known example of such region building is the EU with its Single Market project, pooled sovereignty on matters such as trade, currency and migration, and common foreign and development policies. However, all continents have some sort of world–regional governance system to accompany countries' regionalisation strategies. The EU is the only world–regional group acting as a single entity in global governance, with the authority to negotiate binding international agreements on behalf of all its member states.

Many governments and NGOs in the **Global South** are confronting the relationship between trade and social (for example, labour, health) standards, and asking how to maintain levels of taxation in the face of international competition to attract internationally mobile capital. In this context, there are several potential advantages for developing countries of building a social dimension to regional groupings: they afford a degree of protection from global market forces that may otherwise erode national social entitlements and amplify the influence of such grouped countries, especially small countries, in the global economic and social policies of the UN, the World Bank and other global forums (Yeates and Deacon, 2010; Yeates, 2014, 2019).

Developed systems of regional social governance can make significant contributions to more socially equitable development through:

- cross-border forms of social redistribution (for example, funds to target economically depressed localities); pooling systems, resources and capacity to make better (or specialised) social provision that would not otherwise have been possible (for example, health specialisation); and tackling significant disease outbreaks or pandemics, or food shortage issues;
- regional social and labour regulations, for example, regional health and safety regulations to prevent the competitive lowering of social standards, or forms of cooperation that enable, for example, mutual recognition of qualifications and experience or portability of **social security** rights;
- regional social rights, for example, legal rights and other mechanisms giving citizens of member countries a formal means of challenging their governments and means of redress (Deacon et al, 2010).

Compared with economic policy, social policy has not been a major area for the development of common region-wide policies. Even in the EU, 'positive' forms of social policy integration, which aim at creating common standards or policies, are outweighed by 'negative' forms of social policy integration, which aim at the removal of barriers to competition and the Single Market, including in labour markets. Also, social policy is still primarily a national matter. Nevertheless, regional groupings are increasingly engaged with a wide range of social policy issues across many different sectors, and have developed mandates and plans of action and initiatives to realise a range of social policy goals (Yeates, 2019). **Table 2.2** provides examples from a range of social sectors, showing the variety of forms that regional social policy takes.

World-regional forms of social governance and policy are becoming more prominent in GSP for a variety of reasons. One is that regionalisation processes, regional structures and regional actors are explicitly recognised as important for realising social policy and related SDGs (see **Box 2.3**). Many regional groupings have been encouraged to develop plans or 'roadmaps' for realising SDGs in their specific context (Yeates, 2017b). Indeed, one benefit of regional-level social policy is that, compared with more extensively multilateral groups and organisations, responses can be attuned to the context-specific needs and circumstances of the members. This, together with being able to negotiate agreements on, for example, social standards more quickly among the smaller number of members, means that, in theory, regional agreements can be concluded more rapidly (Yeates and Deacon, 2010). For poorer developing countries, regional groupings provide a prospect of being able to work through 'local' multilateral organisations and of influencing the content of wider multilateral initiatives to work better in their favour (Yeates and Deacon, 2010; Yeates, 2017a, 2017b).

Some in the Global South (Keet and Bello, 2004; Keet, 2007) have argued that it may be better to concentrate efforts on empowering world-regional governance systems than on reforming the existing institutions of global social governance. They argue that reforming and strengthening institutions that operate in the interests of the **Global North** will do little for developing countries, but reforming and strengthening Southern regionalisms will create more effective countervailing sources of power that can outflank the North and promote more socially equitable outcomes (Yeates and Deacon, 2010). This means that social policy reform initiatives might be better directed at strengthening regional groupings of countries that have a partly Southern protectionist purpose and that can counterbalance the dominant power of the Bretton Woods institutions in different contexts. From this perspective, the focus for global social governance reform should perhaps be to build several world-regional social policies of comprehensive redistribution, regulation and rights – a sort of world federation of regions, each with competence in their own locations (Deacon, 2014).

*Table 2.2: World-regional social policy instruments and examples from five continents*

| 1. Instrument | 2. Functions to … | 3. Instances |
|---|---|---|
| Regional forum | Share information for mutual education, analysis and debate; promote shared analyses and create epistemic communities and networks, that can inform policy debate and provide a platform for collaboration | CARICOM: capacity building and communicable diseases<br><br>PIF: regional compact (eg, peer review mechanisms for country development plans)<br><br>SAARC: cross-border information exchange |
| Social standard setting | Define international social standards and common frameworks for social policy (eg, human rights charters, labour, social protection and health conventions) | SAARC Social charter<br><br>UNASUR: Constitutional Treaty enshrines common normative framework<br><br>ASEAN – charter: regional framework on people trafficking |
| Resource mobilisation and allocation | Provide resources supporting policy development and provision (eg, stimulus finance, technical assistance, policy advice and expertise) | CAN: Social Humanitarian Fund<br><br>ALBA: anti-poverty projects, trading schemes<br><br>SAARC, ASEAN: food security schemes<br><br>ECOWAS: regional health organisation |
| Regulation | Provide or reform regulatory instruments that affect entitlements and access to social provision | ECOWAS, EU: regional court of justice adjudicating on labour rights<br><br>SADC, CARICOM, ECOWAS, SAARC, EU: removal of work visa requirements for migrant workers from member states<br><br>MERCOSUR, CAN, ASEAN, ANZCERTA, EU: mutual recognition agreements in education<br><br>MERCOSUR, CARICOM, ANZCERTA, SADC, EU: social security portability<br><br>ECOWAS, SADC, EAC: regulation of pharmaceutical products |

Note: ALBA = Bolivarian Alliance for the Peoples of Our America; ANZCERTA = Australia–New Zealand Closer Economic Relations Trade Agreement; ASEAN = Association of Southeast Asian Nations; CAN = Andean Community; CARICOM = Caribbean Community; ECOWAS = Economic Community of West African States; EU = European Union; MERCOSUR = Southern Cone Common Market; PIF = Pacific Islands Forum; SAARC = South Asian Association for Regional Cooperation; SADC = Southern African Development Community; UNASUR = Union of South American Nations.

Source: Yeates (2017a), updated using data from Yeates and Surender (2021)

---

## Box 2.3: Regional dimensions of the Sustainable Development Goals (SDGs)

*SDG 17* identifies regional integration frameworks as key to the implementation of the 2030 Agenda. This attaches great importance to 'the regional and sub-regional dimensions, regional economic integration and interconnectivity in sustainable development'. It states that 'Regional and sub-regional frameworks can facilitate the effective translation of sustainable development policies into concrete action at the national level'. Similar recognition of regional frameworks exists in relation to global development financing.

Source: Yeates (2017b)

---

However, critics insist that regionalism is no safe haven from **neoliberal** forms of globalisation and its socially liberal varieties (Yeates, 2014). Many regional groups have instituted regional **free trade** agreements that give unprecedented rights to the free movement of capital plus some labour migration rights necessary for the creation of regional markets in, for example, the education, social and health care and pharmaceutical sectors (Yeates, 2019). The African Continental Free Trade Area (ACFTA) is the most recent example of such market-making initiatives at the time of writing. Launched in 2018, the ACFTA contains no social clause, social policy agenda or other 'positive' forms of integration. Indeed, it promotes the goal of economic integration and attendant degrees of freedom mainly for cross-border capital (Yeates and Surender, 2021). The issue with such free trade areas is that, without robust forms of regional social policy, national social standards will be lowered by regional market-building efforts that involve 'negative' social policy integration. Furthermore, the track records of actually instantiated social policy by these regional institutions have tended to be at best social-liberal in nature, with minimal constraints on regional markets. In some cases, they have promoted the development of regional welfare markets. None (so far) have taken the more substantive social democratic (or democratic socialist) form that could provide more effective protection of human rights from the socially adverse effects of economic globalisation (Yeates, 2014).

## The future of global social governance

Bob Deacon identified three aspects of global social governance: global redistribution, global regulation and global rights (Deacon et al, 1997; Deacon, 2006, 2007). *Global redistribution* refers to transnational resource transfers; *global regulation* involves mechanisms that (at their strongest) impose mandatory constraints on the actions of actors or that (somewhat more weakly) provide guidelines for their behaviour, so that these actors are more accountable for the social consequences of their activities; and *global rights* involve mechanisms by which social rights are prescribed and upheld across jurisdictions. The achievement of GSP in these three areas that can substantially improve wellbeing around the world is, of course, subject to the constraints of the global governance mechanisms discussed above (see **Box 2.4**). An important aspect of GSP scholarship and political practice has therefore been the articulation of various proposals for global social governance *reform*. Some of these proposals are discussed in Section 5 of *The global social policy reader* (Yeates and Holden, 2009), and many more have been put forward in response to the **global financial crisis** (GFC) of 2007–09, the shift towards nationalistic **populism** in 2016 (see, for example, Holden, 2017), and the COVID-19 pandemic that began in 2020.

## Box 2.4: Progress in global social governance – redistribution, regulation and rights

In the second edition of this volume, Deacon (2014) revisited the '3 Rs' to examine progress in global social governance. He argued that the world was 'stumbling towards' articulating a GSP based on these 3 Rs. Reviewing them again, we can conclude that the world continues to 'stumble', and may even be closer to actually falling.

In terms of global redistribution, Deacon noted that one of the main mechanisms that has emerged is the use of global funds, such as the Global Fund to Fight Aids, Tuberculosis and Malaria, and such funds continue to play a crucial role today, particularly after the COVID-19 pandemic. Despite this, vaccines have been available to high-income countries much more readily than low-income countries. There is also the continued transfer of income from rich countries to poorer ones through development aid channelled via both bilateral and multilateral routes. The OECD continues to try to find international consensus on the taxation of TNCs, including by the setting of a global minimum corporate tax rate, with some success. There are also increasingly practical calls for the raising of new funds via the supranational taxation of airline travel and financial transactions.

Global regulation demonstrates little progress, driven as it is through soft law. For example, the UN's **Global Compact** continues to ask TNCs to adhere to a social compact, and the ILO continues to exhort governments to enforce minimum **labour standards**. However, self-regulation by TNCs is rife, and trade laws such as the WTO's Agreement on Trade-Related Aspects of Intellectual Property Rights (TRIPS) force governments to regulate in the interests of large corporations. Little progress has been made in tying social and labour standards to trade agreements.

In terms of global social rights, the Universal Declaration on Human Rights and the International Covenant on Social, Cultural and Human Rights remain as a 'a clear expression of a universally agreed set of social entitlements to be aspired to' (Deacon, 2014, p 65). Added to this, the ILO's Social Protection Floor (SPF) Recommendation now calls on governments to ensure a set of minimum social protection guarantees, and the SDGs provide a set of norms for the global community to work towards that are more comprehensive than those of the **Millennium Development Goals** (MDGs). As discussed above, however, these latter forms of 'soft law' lack enforcement mechanisms.

The impact of global crises on global social governance can be both extremely challenging and ultimately positive. The stagnation of living standards and continued growth of inequality in many countries following the GFC gave rise to challenges from both the left and the right. On the one hand, the Occupy Wall Street movement in the USA and similar movements in other countries challenged the power of the global financial industry and TNCs, but on the other, right–wing populism gained a foothold in some countries, resulting in the decision of the UK to leave the EU and the election of Donald Trump as US President in 2016. Right-wing **populist** governments, particularly that of Trump, challenged the existing global governance architecture, with the USA pulling out of the UN's Paris Climate Agreement and the WHO, and undermining the WTO by launching a trade war with China, although much of the damage was subsequently reversed by US President Biden. The nationalist backlash against existing forms of global governance also sparked its own response, with a growing discourse about the necessity of a more inclusive globalisation, including from within institutions such as the IMF that are often associated with neoliberal policy prescriptions. Nevertheless, the global response to the COVID–19 pandemic revealed a dysfunctional level of 'vaccine nationalism'.

These developments and processes mean that the current period for global social governance is a highly uncertain one. Tensions within countries and geopolitical tensions between major powers, such as the USA and China, mean that global social governance could develop along a number of different trajectories. Possibilities include a shift to a more nationalistic world in which existing global governance institutions are undermined by forms of **deglobalisation**, the consolidation of and/or retreat into regional blocs, and (more positively) a move towards significant 'prosocial' reform of IGOs as the world recovers from the global crisis of COVID-19. The outcomes will depend on the actions of a wide range of actors that have a bearing on global social governance, including national governments, decision-makers and experts within IGOs, and national and transnational political and social movements.

## Conclusion

This chapter has demonstrated that global social governance is best understood as a fragmented system, within which policy mandates overlap and where a variety of actors compete for influence. IGOs are at the heart of this system, but they are organised in different ways, have different missions and have varied ability to influence social outcomes. IGOs whose missions are primarily economic, such as the World Bank, the IMF and the WTO, are among those that have the most influence on social policy and social outcomes, via either loan conditionality or hard law. IGOs that are most focused on social policy, such as the WHO and ILO, often have to rely on the power of norm-setting and consensus-building to achieve their goals. However, global social governance also involves non-state actors, including both TNCs and INGOs, which can be highly influential. The future of global social governance is highly uncertain, in part due to the actions of powerful national states.

### Note
[1]  The other arms of the World Bank are the International Finance Corporation (IFC), the Multilateral Investment Guarantee Agency and the International Centre for Settlement of Investment Disputes.

## Summary

- Global social governance involves a range of state and non-state actors.
- IGOs are at the heart of global social governance, but non-state actors such as TNCs and INGOs can also be highly influential.
- IGOs differ in their missions, the ways they are organised and the amount of power and resources they can use to influence social outcomes.
- The overall system of global social governance is fragmented, with overlapping mandates and even competition between different IGOs.
- Global social governance takes place at a number of levels and scales, with world-regional organisations playing an increasingly important role.

## Questions for discussion

- How is *global social governance* different from *international social governance*?
- Why do some IGOs have more influence over global and national social policies than others?
- What are the most significant contemporary challenges to global social governance?

## Follow-up activities

- Choose one of the IGOs listed in **Table 2.1** and consider the following questions (make use of the organisation's website to help you):
  - How is it organised?
  - What changes would you recommend to the way it is organised and why?
  - What key changes to the policies of the organisation would you make in areas relevant to social policy, and why?
  - What changes would you make to the way the organisation works with other IGOs, and why?
- Search the UN website (www.un.org) to see what IGOs (namely 'specialised agencies'), programmes and funds are part of its overall system, but which are not listed in **Table 2.1**. What relevance does each of them have for social policy?
- Search for examples of developing country perspectives on GSP issues on websites such as that of the Transnational Institute (www.tni.org) and Focus on the Global South (https://focusweb.org).

## Further resources

*The global social policy reader* (Yeates and Holden, 2009) collates useful readings, particularly Sections 3 and 5. Deacon (2007), although a little dated now, provides an overview of global social governance, while Deacon (2013) provides a fascinating study of how GSP was made in one organisation. The Routledge *Global Institutions* and the Edward Elgar *Global Governance* series cover relevant IGOs in greater depth. The open access edited collection *International organizations in global social governance* (Martens et al, 2021) is a useful collection of research chapters on the 'institutional architecture' of global and regional governance across different topics and issues.

## References

Baumgartner, F. and Jones, B. (1993) *Agendas and instability in American politics*, Chicago, IL: University of Chicago Press.

Deacon, B. (2006) 'Global social policy reform', in P. Utting (ed) *Reclaiming development agendas: Knowledge, power and international policy making*, Basingstoke: Palgrave.

Deacon, B. (2007) *Global social policy and governance*, London: SAGE Publications.

Deacon, B. (2013) *Global social policy in the making: The foundations of the social protection floor*, Bristol: Policy Press.

Deacon, B. (2014) 'Global and regional social governance', in N. Yeates (ed) *Understanding global social policy* (2nd edn), Bristol: Policy Press, 53–76.

Deacon, B. with Hulse, M. and Stubbs, P. (1997) *Global social policy: International organisations and the future of welfare*, London: SAGE Publications.

Deacon, B., Macovei, M., van Langenhove, L. and Yeates, N. (eds) (2010) *World-regional social policy and global governance: New research and policy agendas in Africa, Asia, Europe and Latin America*, London: Routledge.

Fidler, D. (2005) 'Health, globalisation and governance: An introduction to public health's "new world order"', in K. Lee and J. Collin (eds) *Global change and health*, Maidenhead: Open University Press, 161–77.

Holden, C. (2017) 'Confronting Brexit and Trump: Towards a socially progressive globalisation', in J. Hudson, C. Needham and E. Heins (eds) *Social policy review 29*, Bristol: Policy Press.

Hooghe, L. and Marks, G. (2003) 'Unravelling the central state, but how? Types of multi-level governance', *American Political Science Review*, 97(2), 233–43.

Keet, D. (2007) 'Alternative regional strategies in Africa', *Global Social Policy*, 7(3), 262–5.

Keet, D. and Bello, W. (2004) *Linking alternative regionalisms for equitable and sustainable development*, Amsterdam: Transnational Institute.

Lee, K. (2008) *The World Health Organization*, London: Routledge.

Manners, I. (2009) *The concept of normative power in world politics*. DIIS Brief (https://pure.diis.dk/ws/files/68745/B09_maj_Concept_Normative_Power_World_Politics.pdf).

Martens, K., Niemann, D. and Kaasch, A. (eds) (2021) *International organizations in global social governance*, London: Palgrave Macmillan.

O'Brien, R., Goetz, A.M., Scholte, J.A. and Williams, M. (2000) *Contesting global governance: Multilateral economic institutions and global social movements*, Cambridge: Cambridge University Press.

WEF (World Economic Forum) (2020) *How is the World Health Organization funded?* (www.weforum.org/agenda/2020/04/who-funds-world-health-organization-un-coronavirus-pandemic-covid-trump).

WHO (World Health Organization) (2020) *Audited financial statements for the year ended 31st December 2019*, Geneva: World Health Organization.

Yeates, N. (2014) *Global poverty reduction: What can regional organisations do?*, Poverty Reduction and Regional Integration (PRARI) Policy Brief No 3, Milton Keynes: The Open University.

Yeates, N. (2017a) *Southern regionalisms, global agendas: Innovating inclusive access to health, medicines and social protection in a context of social inequity*, PRARI Policy Brief No 8, Milton Keynes: The Open University.

Yeates, N. (2017b) *Beyond the nation state: How can regional social policy contribute to achieving the Sustainable Development Goals?*, UNRISD Issue Brief No 5, Geneva: United Nations Research Institute for Social Development (www.unrisd.org/ib5).

Yeates, N. (2019) 'World-regional social governance, policy and development', in J. Midgley, R. Surender and L. Alfers (eds) *Handbook of social policy and development*, Cheltenham: Edward Elgar, 224–45.

Yeates, N. and Deacon, B. (2010) 'Globalisation, regionalism and social policy', in B. Deacon, L. van Langenhove, M. Macovei and N. Yeates (eds) *World-regional social policy and global governance: New research and policy agendas in Africa, Asia, Europe and Latin America*, London: Routledge, 27–39.

Yeates, N. and Holden, C. (eds) (2009) *The global social policy reader*, Bristol: Policy Press.

Yeates, N. and Pillinger, J. (2019) *International health worker migration and recruitment: Global governance, politics and policy*, London: Routledge.

Yeates, N. and Surender, R. (2021) 'Southern social world-regionalisms: The place of health in nine African regional economic communities', *Global Social Policy*, 21(2), 191–214.

# 3

# International trade, global economic governance and welfare

## Chris Holden

### Overview

International trade is a core element of economic globalisation, and its regulation in the interests of social welfare is a central concern of global social policy. This chapter introduces the global trade system and its institutions, and examines a number of key perspectives and debates about the relationship between international trade and welfare. While many economists favour 'free' trade, in practice, international trade has been characterised by bargaining between states of varying degrees of power. Despite fears of a 'race to the bottom' in welfare provision engendered by economic competition, welfare states provide a key mechanism by which the risks and gains from trade can be more evenly distributed and inequalities reduced.

### Key concepts

Global economic governance; trade negotiations; protectionism; liberalisation; global standards

## Introduction

Trade has always been an important form of economic relationship between people of different communities and countries. International trade in the period after the Second World War laid the basis for the kind of international economic integration we now associate with **globalisation**. This chapter reviews how the international trading system and its **governance** has developed in the post-war period, what forms trade policy-making takes, and how trade relates to the welfare state and 'welfare' more generally. It begins with a discussion of the different ways that economists and social policy analysts think about welfare, and why trade is important for social policy. It then explains how the trading system has developed in the post–war period, before looking in detail at trade policy-making processes and institutions as core parts of global economic governance. The role of the World Trade Organization (WTO) and the centrality of bargaining between states is explained. The final section examines in detail the social policy implications of international trade, focusing on the relationship between the welfare state and trade.

## Economics, trade and welfare

The development of capitalism as an economic system has been intimately entwined with the development of national states. States have played a crucial role in facilitating the development of capitalism through providing a system of law and contract that guarantees the rights of property owners and sets a framework within which exchange can take place, as well as legitimising and regulating a common currency. Of course, trade across the borders created by these states has taken place as long as those borders have been in place, but the existence of national institutions, governments and currencies has meant that such trade is necessarily *inter*national, that is, it takes place between countries as well as between specific individuals or firms. Governments have therefore usually tried to regulate this international trade to some extent, from the mercantilism of early capitalism (when the goal was seen as making the nation rich by accumulating as large a trade surplus as possible), to the trade barriers (and negotiations aimed at reducing them) still prevalent today. However, ever since the 19th century, the most orthodox economists have operated on the premise that **free trade** has the potential to make everyone better off, and that the protection of domestic industries against foreign competition (often referred to as **protectionism**) is therefore to be discouraged (see **Box 3.1**).

This commitment to free trade is based on the concept of **comparative advantage**, which says that all countries will gain if every country specialises in those industries in which it is most efficient (or least inefficient). If every country specialises in this way and then trades with others to import the things in which those other countries have a comparative advantage, this should lead to the optimum use of the world's resources. Although trade theory has subsequently been modified significantly, including through the development of the concept of competitive advantage (which recognises that the competitive position of specific industries in different countries is affected by historical, cultural and even political factors, as well as purely economic ones), this basic premise still informs the thinking of many economists. Although economists often speak of free trade maximising the economic 'welfare' of societies, what they are usually referring to is economic growth, usually measured in relation to **gross domestic product** (GDP), rather than the broader and deeper concepts of welfare favoured by social policy analysts.

## Box 3.1: Trade protection

Trade 'protection' entails the use of certain mechanisms such as **tariffs** and **quotas** in order to protect the interests of owners and workers in domestic industries from foreign competition. Tariffs are taxes that are levied on goods entering a country. Since the cost of these is usually passed on to consumers, the foreign goods end up being more expensive than would otherwise be the case. Quotas are restrictions on the amount of a given category of foreign goods that is permitted to be imported, thus limiting competition with domestically produced goods of the same type. More recently, various forms of government intervention in the domestic economy, such as subsidies and regulatory mechanisms, have been identified as sometimes offering 'unfair' advantages to domestic firms. Including such domestic regulations in trade agreements has proved particularly controversial, as it may limit the 'policy space' that governments have to implement policies to protect or improve the health and wellbeing of their citizens.

Many economists therefore expect free trade to lead to greater efficiency and therefore higher average incomes than protection. While this is clearly an important goal, from the point of view of social policy analysts, there are two potential problems with this approach. The first is that, although free trade may lead to average incomes rising over time, this tells us nothing about the actual distribution of those incomes. Social policy is centrally concerned with questions of income and wealth distribution, and government intervention may be required to bring about more equal outcomes. The second, related, problem is that there are both 'winners' and 'losers' from the play of market forces. While the benefits of a more open trade policy may be distributed quite widely across society (via cheaper or better quality products, for example), the 'losers' are sometimes highly concentrated and visible. What happens to these people is also the remit of social policy. Given that the losers from economic globalisation may not just vary between economic sectors within a country but also between countries, affecting millions of people in both rich and poor countries, international trade is a key issue for **global social policy** (GSP).

These problems have been brought into particularly sharp relief because, in common with many areas of economic and social policy, the free trade agenda at the global level was driven by a strongly **neoliberal** ideology from the 1980s onwards. In the global arena, the neoliberal approach assumes that **liberalisation** of trade and a minimisation of the regulatory functions of the state will usually have net positive consequences, regardless of the short- or long-term social costs.

In contrast to this 'free trade' approach, proponents of **fair trade** focus on the inequalities and exploitative relationships that are often produced by the trading system, arguing that trade should take whatever form most benefits the poorest and least–developed countries. Fair trade initiatives sometimes take the form of consumer campaigns, whereby consumers are encouraged to buy goods from accredited suppliers that have ensured adequate working conditions and pay rates for workers, or to boycott companies that have been identified as engaging in particularly exploitative practices. Supporters of fair trade and 'trade justice' also run political campaigns aimed at exposing the way the global economic and political system seems to be stacked in favour of the richest and most powerful countries, and point to the ways in which trade relationships in practice often fall short of free trade ideology, so that poorer countries are expected to open up their markets while richer countries maintain degrees of protectionism over theirs.

A different response to free trade was evident in the actions of Donald Trump after he assumed the US presidency. He took advantage of increasing political polarisation in the USA, which followed from the loss of manufacturing jobs as a result of greater trade with China from the 1990s onwards (Autor et al, 2016). According to one estimate, total US job losses from rising Chinese import competition between 1999 and 2011 were in the range of 2–2.4 million (Acemoglu et al, 2016). China's trade surplus has been highly correlated with the USA's trade deficit; China's average current account surplus rose from 1.7 per cent of GDP in the 1990s to 4.8 per cent in the 2000s, while the USA's average current account deficit rose from 1.6 per cent of GDP in the 1990s to 4.4 per cent in the 2000s (Autor, Dorn and Hanson, 2016, p 214). Taking an economically nationalist approach, Trump moved aggressively against China (and some other countries), imposing extensive new tariffs on imports from there. Trump also pressed the Chinese government on the long–held grievances of some US corporations, including the alleged coercive transfer of intellectual property, and what US corporations regarded as unfair competition from subsidised Chinese state–owned enterprises (SOEs). The resulting 'trade war' proved to be highly disruptive for the global trading system. Yet, as we shall see in the next section, the reality of the modern world trading system has always deviated significantly from neoliberal prescriptions, and has often been characterised by extensive protection and bargaining between states.

## The development of the international trading system

The world economy has only rarely been characterised by anything close to free trade. The development of international trade between emerging capitalist economies first took the form of 'mercantilism', whereby governments tried to get rich by exporting more goods than they imported. However, in keeping with the free trade views of the classical economists, in which foreign exchange reserves are regarded as merely a means to pay for imports, the second half of the 19th century was characterised by a more 'hands–off' or 'laissez–faire' approach. Yet by the end of the century, protectionism had begun to increase again. In the period between the two world wars of the 20th century, governments resorted to protectionist policies against each other in a cycle that both responded to and deepened the economic depression of that time. The political and economic settlement that followed the Second World War, which led to the creation of a new system of global economic governance, was thus based partly on the recognition that protectionism in the interwar period had damaged growth for all countries, and partly on the need to bind the capitalist economies of the West together in the face of economic and military competition from the expanded Soviet bloc. In Western Europe, the desire to avoid another European war and cohere the capitalist countries against the perceived threat from the East led to the creation of the European Economic Community (EEC) in 1957 (which formed the basis for what we now call the European Union [EU]).

The post-war settlement led to the creation of new institutions of global economic governance. In the financial sphere, the International Monetary Fund (IMF) and the World Bank were created (see **Chapter 2**, this volume). However, the allied countries were unable to agree on the creation of an international trade organisation until the WTO was set up in 1995. The WTO is based on the system of negotiated trade agreements that formed the basis for the lowering of trade barriers up until that time, known as the General Agreement on Tariffs and Trade (GATT). The GATT and other subsequent trade agreements, such as the General Agreement on Trade in Services (GATS) (see **Box 3.2**), are now administered through the WTO. The GATT and other agreements work on the basis of 'negotiating rounds', that is, a series of protracted negotiations between governments, the aim of which is to progressively lower trade barriers between countries. These rounds are based on 'reciprocity', that is, a quid pro quo process in which governments agree to concessions to each other that lead to an incremental reduction in protection.

Since the WTO has 164 **member states** and the aim is a general reduction in protection, agreements are facilitated by the principle of 'non-discrimination', which has two components – the 'most favoured nation' (MFN) rule and the 'national treatment' rule (Hoekman and Kostecki, 2001, p 29). The MFN rule requires that a product made in one member country be treated no less favourably than a like good made in any other country. Thus, by immediately treating all member nations in the same manner as the country afforded best treatment relating to a specific product, the gains of tariff reduction are generalised to all member countries. The national treatment rule requires that foreign goods, once they have passed customs, be treated no less favourably than like or directly competitive goods produced domestically in terms of internal taxes or regulations.

On this basis, barriers to trade in goods were significantly lowered as the result of a series of negotiating rounds, each of which usually took years to accomplish. The last successful round of **multilateral** negotiations, the Uruguay round, was held between 1986 and 1993. The most significant outcomes of the Uruguay round were the agreement to create the WTO and the agreement of a number of further treaties in addition to the GATT, the most important of which are the GATS and the Agreement on Trade-Related Aspects of Intellectual Property Rights (TRIPS). These agreements substantially expanded the scope of trade negotiations so that they now cover services as well as manufactured goods, and incorporate issues relating to intellectual property rights, investment and domestic regulation as well as tariffs and quotas. Both the GATS and the TRIPS have important implications for social policy, particularly for healthcare and education (see **Chapters 13 and 14**, this volume). The GATS is summarised in **Box 3.2**.

---

### Box 3.2: The General Agreement on Trade in Services (GATS) and trade in welfare services

The WTO's GATS identifies four modes of supply for services, all of which apply to welfare services:

- Mode 1: *Cross-border trade* takes place where services are traded across borders without the need for the movement of people. Advances in communications technologies have led to a significant increase in this form of trade. The internet enables providers of diagnostic health services or education services, for example, to reside in one country while the consumers reside in another.
- Mode 2: *Consumption abroad* refers to the movement of the consumer of a service to another country where the service is provided, such as when patients travel abroad to have an operation in another country or students travel abroad to study.
- Mode 3: *Commercial presence* involves **foreign direct investment** (FDI) in the establishment of business outlets such as hospitals, schools or universities.
- Mode 4: *Movement of natural persons* refers to the movement abroad of practitioners such as healthcare workers or teachers. It may arise from labour demand and supply imbalances between countries, or from the search by practitioners for better wages or working conditions.

Some aspects of the GATS have been highly controversial because of concerns that the agreement may facilitate privatisation of health or other welfare services, or limit the freedom of governments to appropriately regulate those services (see Yeates, 2005; Holden, 2014).

---

One of the key outcomes of this process of trade liberalisation in the post-war period has been a substantial growth in trade as a proportion of world output.

Thus, for most countries, and for the world economy as a whole, trade has grown at a faster rate than GDP. This means that trade has been one of the most important engines of the increasing integration of national economies, or what has come to be known as 'economic globalisation'. However, it is difficult to entirely separate trade from other aspects of economic integration. Economic globalisation is typically thought of as also encompassing two other key aspects: foreign direct investment (FDI) and the globalisation of financial markets. Financial globalisation resulted in part from liberalising reforms to the banking system implemented by Margaret Thatcher in the UK and Ronald Reagan in the USA in the 1980s, as well as the abandonment by most governments of attempts to control capital flows into and out of their countries.

From the 1980s, FDI grew at an even faster rate than trade. This has led to the growing importance of **transnational corporations** (TNCs), which invest in multiple countries rather than simply producing their goods at home and exporting them to other countries. So dominant have TNCs become in the world economy that intra-firm trade (trade between different national branches of the same TNC) came to account for up to a third of total world trade (Lanz and Miroudot, 2011, p 12). This intra-firm trade has important implications for social policy and power in the world economy, since it allows firms to, for example, minimise the taxes they pay to governments by manipulating the prices of goods traded within the firm so that they can declare their profits where taxes are lowest. It has also been a significant factor in the movement of certain kinds of employment from **high-income countries** to **low-** and **middle-income countries**.

## Global institutions and policy processes

The creation of the WTO formalised and extended the structure of the global trading system that had been developed over a period of 50 years (Hoekman and Kostecki, 2001, pp 49–53). The WTO, the IMF and the World Bank together constitute the most important institutions of global economic governance. The WTO now has 164 member states, with a number of others engaged in accession negotiations. It facilitates the implementation and operation of the multilateral trade agreements, provides a forum for government negotiations, administers a **dispute settlement mechanism**, provides surveillance of national and regional trade policies and cooperates with the World Bank and the IMF with a view to achieving greater coherence in global economic policy-making. It is headed by a Ministerial Conference of all member states that meets at least once every two years, but between these meetings it is run by a General Council of officials that meets about 12 times a year. Three subsidiary councils deal with trade in goods, trade in services and intellectual property rights, and it has a number of other committees and working parties.

Although the trading system remains one characterised principally by bargaining between states, the primary function of the WTO is to facilitate the creation of a *rules-based* international trading system. The organisation's reliance on its member states means that its secretariat is relatively small, with only 625 regular staff (WTO, 2020). However, the secretariat stands at the centre of a much larger network of people who work on trade matters in its member governments' trade and other ministries, central banks, and so on (Hoekman and Kostecki, 2001, pp 54–5). Developing countries therefore find themselves at a particular disadvantage when it comes to participating fully in WTO activities, since although they have formal equality with rich countries, they often do not have the resources to devote to these matters that developed countries do. Many developing countries do not have officials based permanently at the WTO in Geneva, and when they do, they might have only one or two people to cover all the activities of the WTO as well as the other **intergovernmental organisations** (IGOs) based in Geneva (Hoekman and Kostecki, 2001, pp 54, 396).

Trade negotiations take the form of bargaining between formally independent and equal states, based on the principle of 'one country, one vote', yet it is clear that the economic, political and military power of these states varies considerably, and that this disparity is a key factor in influencing the outcomes of trade negotiations. The WTO attempts to work by 'consensus', but consensus in negotiating rounds is often arrived at in informal meetings in the so-called 'Green Room', which are dominated by the USA and the EU (Jones, 2009). Developed countries also have access to a far higher level of technical advice in what are highly complicated negotiations, and sometimes bring various forms of informal pressure to bear on developing countries (Jawara et al, 2004). This differential power often translates into differential outcomes from the negotiations, and it was to deal with the perception that previous trade rounds had served the interests of developed countries more than developing ones that a new 'development round' was launched in Doha in 2001. However, the Doha round failed to reach a resolution on the most important issues and was abandoned after many years of negotiation, with very little having been achieved.

World-regional trade agreements and formations, such as the EU and the USA–Mexico–Canada Agreement (USMCA) (previously the North American Free Trade Agreement, or NAFTA), have taken on renewed significance since the stalling of the Doha round. The EU is the most developed regional initiative of this type; starting as a customs union (in which members eliminate all trade restrictions against each other and adopt a common external tariff), its goal is now full economic union (in which labour and capital as well as goods and services are free to move and there is a common monetary policy with a single currency for most members), and it has its own **supranational political institutions** in the form of the European Commission (EC) and European Parliament (EP) and a supranational legal institution in the form of the European Court of Justice

(ECJ). Most other regions of the world also have some form of regional trade agreement, some of which are developing social policies, but none of them is as advanced as the EU, which also aims at a degree of harmonisation of social policies (see **Chapter 2**, this volume).

The difficulties in concluding the Doha round also led to more **bilateralism** on the part of the USA and the EU, as well as more negotiations between and across regional formations, leading to a much more complex picture of overlapping agreements. While these new agreements have sometimes included social provisions, such as minimum **labour standards**, they have often provided an opportunity for high-income countries to conclude agreements with low- or middle-income countries that go beyond what is contained in WTO agreements (Yeates et al, 2009). These have included more stringent intellectual property protection, such as so-called 'TRIPS-plus' provisions (see **Chapter 13**, this volume), and investment protection for TNCs. Bilateral negotiations tend to shift the balance of power even more in favour of the high-income countries than multilateral ones carried out through the WTO, since they preclude the alliances that can be formed within the latter (Yeates et al, 2009). The proliferation of bilateral treaties also leads to a far more complex and messy system of trade governance, to some extent undermining the multilateral system of rules the WTO has attempted to establish (Yeates et al, 2009; Adlung, 2010).

The problems of bilateralism can be seen in global investment governance, where bilateral investment treaties (BITs) dominate. These involve governments agreeing to a range of obligations such as 'fair and equitable treatment' and national treatment for foreign companies investing within their borders. Such provisions in BITs and other treaties represent a shift towards investment obligations, rather than simply those concerning trade, and tend to be organised in overlapping hub and spoke systems around particular high-income countries. They often shift power in favour of TNCs by allowing them to initiate disputes directly with governments via investor–state dispute settlement (ISDS) mechanisms, something not possible in the WTO where only governments can initiate disputes. ISDS provisions often involve an obligation for governments to compensate companies that are deemed to have had their property expropriated in some way, and consequently may make it harder for governments to reverse past policies of privatisation or to expand the public sector (Adlung, 2010, p 237). Hawkins and Holden (2016) argue that the overlapping 'spaghetti bowl' of BITs and other agreements increases the power of TNCs, by providing them with the opportunity to **venue shop**, that is, to find the best treaty for their particular purposes when attempting to resist government regulation. The policy area of tobacco control provides a good example of how TNCs have used multiple trade and investment agreements to try to block effective government health policies (Hawkins et al, 2019). **Box 3.3** summarises disputes that have been initiated by transnational tobacco companies.

## Box 3.3: Tobacco control and trade and investment agreements

Transnational tobacco companies (TTCs) have initiated trade and investment disputes with governments, or lobbied other governments to do so on their behalf, on a number of occasions.

- In 1990, the US government initiated a GATT dispute with Thailand following lobbying by US TTCs, in an attempt to force the removal of Thailand's ban on imports of foreign cigarettes and overturn a ban on tobacco advertising. The GATT panel ruled that Thailand must lift its import ban, but that it could keep advertising restrictions as long as these were applied in a non-discriminatory way. TTCs were thus allowed to enter the Thai market and then engaged in aggressive marketing practices in order to increase sales of their cigarettes.
- In 2010, Indonesia initiated a WTO dispute against the USA, arguing that the USA's newly imposed ban on flavoured cigarettes discriminated against Indonesian clove cigarettes because it exempted US-manufactured menthol cigarettes. The WTO ruled against the USA, requiring the country to change its law, although the USA later came to an agreement with Indonesia.
- In 2010, the TTC Philip Morris initiated a dispute with the government of Uruguay under the terms of the Switzerland–Uruguay BIT, arguing that its intellectual property rights had been violated. Philip Morris claimed that Uruguay's increase of the size of health warnings on cigarette packs, to 80 per cent of the total size of the pack, unnecessarily restricted the use of its trademarks. Phillip Morris lost the case, but not before tying up the Uruguayan government in expensive litigation for many years.
- In 2011, Philip Morris initiated a dispute with the Australian government under the terms of the Australia–Hong Kong BIT, arguing that Australia's introduction of plain packaging legislation for cigarettes violated the company's intellectual property rights by restricting the use of its trademarks. Philip Morris lost the case because it had moved ownership of its Australian subsidiary to Hong Kong, to take advantage of the BIT, only *after* the Australian government had announced its policy.
- In 2012, the Ukraine, Honduras, the Dominican Republic, Cuba and Indonesia all initiated a WTO dispute against Australia, arguing that its introduction of plain packaging legislation for cigarettes violated tobacco companies' intellectual property rights under the TRIPS agreement. TTCs paid the legal costs of three of the governments that initiated the dispute. The WTO panel found in favour of Australia.

See WHO (2012) for a more detailed examination of the impact of trade and investment agreements on tobacco control.

The failure of the WTO's Doha round also led the USA to pursue new 'mega-regional' trade agreements, in the form of the Transatlantic Trade and Investment Partnership (TTIP) with the EU and the Trans-Pacific Partnership (TPP) with 11 other Pacific Rim countries. These agreements were notable for their inclusion of 'behind the border' provisions, including, in addition to ISDS provisions, provisions relating to 'regulatory cooperation' or 'regulatory coherence'. Such provisions aim at harmonising the domestic regulatory regimes of the countries involved, in order to create a 'level playing field' on which economic competition by companies can take place. However, they allow for corporate influence on the process of creating new regulations, and risk a downward harmonisation of regulatory standards to a level that may not adequately protect human health, labour conditions or the environment (Holden and Hawkins, 2020).

The election of Donald Trump in 2016 brought an abrupt shift in US trade policy. The USA abandoned the TTIP and the TPP in favour of an aggressively unilateral trade policy. Meanwhile, the other 11 countries in the TPP forged ahead with their own version of the agreement, now called the Comprehensive and Progressive Agreement for Trans-Pacific Partnership (CPTPP). While Trump abandoned the TPP, he renegotiated the NAFTA agreement between the USA, Mexico and Canada, resulting in a new version of the agreement, the USMCA, which contained regulatory coherence provisions that were even more stringent than those of the CPTPP (Labonte et al, 2019). Trump's unilateralism fundamentally destabilised the global trade regime overseen by the WTO, leaving much uncertainty about the form that global trade relations will take in the forthcoming period.

The trade and investment agreements discussed above are not without opposition. **Civil society** organisations (CSOs) and social movements have long made key interventions in the political process surrounding global trade and investment talks (O'Brien et al, 2000). CSOs have vigorously campaigned on a national and transnational basis against the perceived negative effects of WTO and other agreements, including the health issues related to TRIPS and GATS, the potential threat to public policies posed by ISDS provisions in the TTIP and other agreements, and the wider issues of development and inequality related to trade more generally. CSOs form an important **transnational advocacy coalition** seeking to promote fairer terms of international trade, and, to the extent that they have been able to shape the process, they are to be regarded as key players in global economic governance.

## The welfare state and trade

The relationship between the welfare state and international trade (and the global economy more widely) is not a straightforward one. It has often been argued that economic globalisation undermines the welfare state, since the competition it creates between countries leads to a '**race to the bottom**' in welfare provision, as governments pare back the costs imposed on businesses to the minimum. Trade openness is seen as one element in this process, since if labour and other production costs are cheaper elsewhere, businesses will choose to locate in those areas and export their goods from there. The relatively well-paid workers of advanced nations may then experience both downward pressure on their wages and unemployment as whole sectors of business become uncompetitive. While this may present an opportunity for developing countries to grow their own businesses, these are often (initially at least) confined to particular, low-skilled, sectors of the economy. Where production does shift to developing countries, the owners are often TNCs based in the developed countries that take advantage of lower wages and poorer working conditions while retaining control over technical knowledge and capital. Those developing countries that have moved from predominantly low-skilled production to more skilled capital-intensive production, such as in East Asia, have often done so by using selective trade barriers alongside an aggressive export-oriented industrial policy.

Furthermore, given South–South competition, developing country governments may feel that they need to continue to suppress wages and other conditions for their own workers, with the result that trade openness not only damages jobs in the advanced economies, but also legitimises poor working conditions and even child labour in developing countries. One response to this is for **trade unions** and others in the advanced countries to try to tie labour standards to trade agreements, so that developing countries competing with advanced countries are forced to agree to certain minimum standards. Indeed, attempts have been made to try to pursue such labour standards agreements through the WTO itself. These have failed for various reasons, including the perception by developing country governments that this is a form of 'back door' protectionism by rich countries (see also **Chapter 4**, this volume).

There is, in fact, a range of factors in addition to trade (and other aspects of economic globalisation) that have been identified as contributing to unemployment in the advanced capitalist countries, the foremost of which is technological advancement. Both technological advances and greater trade openness can impact deleteriously on low-skilled, low-waged workers. This has led to the widespread realisation on the part of governments in these countries that they cannot compete in the world economy on the basis of low wages, but only on the basis of high skills. A highly skilled workforce is likely to attract investment in industries that pay high wages, thus maintaining prosperity. Education and training have thus become a central plank of social policy in many high-income countries, although the high level of mobility of both data and people facilitated by technological development means that even highly skilled people will be competing in a global labour market.

However, the relationship between trade openness and the welfare state, and human welfare more generally, is by no means a straightforward or obvious one.

While increased trade often leads to the displacement of particular industries and groups of workers, its effect on overall growth can be a positive one. Jobs may not be so much destroyed, as moved from one sector of the economy to another, while the result for consumers is often that the goods and services they buy are cheaper than they otherwise would be. This may seem like scant consolation for those whose lives are disrupted, and it is often the case that those who lose out have difficulty in finding jobs elsewhere because, for example, their skills are redundant. Workers in high-income countries who are trade-displaced may, in subsequent years, earn less than their peers, experience greater job 'churn', and be more likely to be unemployed and to claim welfare (including disability-related) benefits (Autor, Dorn and Hanson, 2016, pp 232–4). It is commonly accepted that while the gains from more open trade are widely diffused, the costs can sometimes be very concentrated, making it a difficult and highly contested political issue. Yet the consequences of protectionism may be that citizens pay to maintain inefficient producers.

The role of the welfare state in all this is crucial. Welfare states have played a key role in capitalist economies ever since they were created in *facilitating* economic change. It is in the nature of capitalist economies, even conceived of as isolated national entities (which they have rarely ever been), that readjustments constantly take place between and within businesses and industrial sectors. These adjustments are usually the outcome of the play of market forces rather than the decisions of governments. The welfare state has played a key role in allowing these adjustments to take place without the disastrous impact on workers that they would otherwise have. While unemployment benefits and other forms of income maintenance have provided an income for workers that substitutes for their wages while they are unemployed, education, retraining and job search services have facilitated their return to work. A number of authors have argued that welfare states have played the same role for workers within the world economy, providing protection from the potential impact of more openness to international trade.

An early example of this work is that by Cameron (1978), which showed that the size of the public sector tends to be positively correlated with a country's openness to trade. A number of smaller European countries in particular have had both greater exposure to the world economy, as a result of the limited size of their domestic economies, and more extensive welfare states. Welfare benefits, active labour market policies and public sector employment have all, therefore, compensated workers to some extent for losses from international competition and provided a form of 'insurance' against their greater vulnerability to external economic shocks (see Katzenstein, 1985; Rodrik, 1997, 1998; Garrett, 1998).

Rieger and Leibfried (2003) draw an explicit inverse link between trade protection and the welfare state, arguing that the welfare state has facilitated open trade by substituting for protectionism. The USA, for example, historically relied on protectionism as a means of shielding certain industries (and therefore workers) from foreign competition, but has a much less developed welfare state than most other economically advanced countries. Given the weaker welfare state in the USA, some state benefits have even been tied explicitly to trade. Trade Adjustment Assistance (TAA) was introduced by President Kennedy in 1962 to build support for tariff cuts, and was expanded as part of the NAFTA in 1993 and again in 2002, when President Bush asked Congress for special negotiating authority on trade (*The Economist*, 2007). TAA provides extended unemployment benefits for up to 18 months for eligible workers, as well as other allowances.

Nevertheless, there are problems with targeting benefits specifically at those displaced by international trade. Given that the (positive and negative) effects of trade are often diffuse, it is not always easy to identify who has been affected, or whether trade is the cause of any particular outcome. The USA targets benefits in this way because its welfare state is less developed than those in Europe, and because its political system encourages bargaining on policy choices in order to get specific measures, such as trade liberalisation, passed. Even in the USA, other welfare benefits are of more importance for trade-displaced workers in practice than TAA (Autor, Dorn and Hanson, 2016, pp 230–1). European welfare states have tended to be more extensive and less based on targeting than in the USA. This more institutionalised and comprehensive form of welfare support makes more sense in a (global) market economy where the gains from growth are diffuse and, even though the losses may be more concentrated, the risks are shared.

Such arguments demonstrate the key role that the welfare state has played in allowing capitalist economies to operate effectively, while shielding workers from the worst risks of markets and redistributing the gains from growth. They provide a sound justification for the maintenance and strengthening of welfare states within the context of the current world economy, and a corrective to claims that welfare states are incompatible with globalised markets and must 'inevitably' wither away in the face of global economic forces. Indeed, both the **global financial crisis** (GFC) of 2007–09 and the global COVID-19 pandemic that began in 2020 demonstrated just how unstable the world economy can be. However, while the developed countries with welfare states can largely withstand these pressures, what of developing countries where welfare states have not yet been built, but where the desire and potential for economic growth are great? These countries often have a clear comparative advantage in low-skilled, low-waged, labour-intensive production. Such issues, and the potential for a competitive 'race to the bottom' in labour standards, indicate the importance of global social policies that can set a 'floor' below which labour and other social standards cannot fall. However, developing country governments have often resisted agreements on labour standards, such as the insertion of a social clause into WTO or other trade agreements, fearing that they might lose one of their few advantages.

Developments in China and elsewhere indicate that welfare provision tends to grow as economies grow. Welfare development in some East Asian countries actually sped up *after* the financial crisis of 1997, indicating once again the role that welfare states can play in both protecting people from the worst effects of economic crises and facilitating economic adjustment. Yet reasons of cost, the influence of the IMF and the World Bank, and the desire for economic growth among governments may all militate against more than minimal welfare development in the poorest countries with the worst labour conditions. For governments in the developed countries, the more their competitors in developing countries seem to undercut their own working conditions and welfare provisions, the more they may feel the pressure to scale these back.

Mishra (1999) has suggested one way of addressing this. This would involve the agreement at international level of social standards that are related to the level of economic development of each country, so that those with the most developed economies would have the most developed welfare states. According to Mishra (1999, p 119), this link with economic development 'would provide an automatic "social escalator", in that as societies develop economically, their social standard of living rises in tandem', making for 'an upward harmonization in social standards'. Echoing the emphasis the WTO places on a rules–based global economy, Mishra (1999, p 122) concludes that these social standards 'must not be allowed to become a part of the competitive game but must form a part of the *rules* of the game' (original emphasis). Allied with greater global redistribution to help fund welfare provision in developing countries, an agreement on this basis could properly integrate social concerns into the almost exclusively economic (and neoliberal) concerns of the WTO as it is currently constituted. This would not only provide a multilateral basis for extending the welfare achievements of the advanced capitalist countries to developing countries, but would also in itself help to overcome the suspicion of and resistance to international trade present in both developed and developing countries, by recognising the social costs of economic adjustment and allowing for the social redistribution of the gains from economic growth (both nationally and globally). However, such a system would have to set a 'floor' of minimum standards below which no country could fall, in order to ensure the universality of basic human and social rights. The International Labour Organization's (ILO) core labour standards currently establish global minimum labour rights (see **Chapter 4**, this volume), and its Social Protection Floor (SPF) initiative is an important step forward in terms of global agreement on minimum welfare provision (see **Chapter 15**, this volume), but neither of these has the enforcement capacity of WTO agreements.

These issues indicate the importance not only of national welfare states, but also of global social policies in responding to the challenges of a globalised economy. The roles of international trade and other forms of economic globalisation in facilitating economic growth are central to debates about global poverty reduction and the achievement of other global social goals (as we will see in **Chapter 8**, this volume). Economic globalisation and its governance are thus at the heart of GSP.

## Conclusion

International trade has played a key role in the development of economic globalisation, laying the basis for the economic integration that also includes extensive FDI and global financial flows. Yet we have seen that trade has rarely been genuinely 'free', and that governments use various forms of economic protection to pursue domestic political, social and economic goals. While international trade and economic globalisation more generally may exert pressure on them, welfare states have played a crucial role in allowing market economies to adjust. Strong welfare states that provide high levels of **social protection** and **universal** access to health and education services have the potential to coexist with international trade in a way that allows economies to grow, while sharing both the risks and the gains of trade in a fairer way. International trade provides a means by which, in the right circumstances, developing economies can grow, but the outcomes, both domestically and globally, can involve large inequalities. There is an extremely strong case, therefore, for trade negotiations to be conducted in a way that genuinely serves the needs of the poorest and least-developed countries and their populations. A comprehensive multilateral agreement could also lay the basis for the development of social protection floors in all countries that would match the development of their economies in appropriate ways, avoiding any 'race to the bottom' in welfare provision and labour conditions.

### Summary

- Many economists support free trade as leading to an increase in average incomes, while social policy analysts are also concerned with the inequality of outcomes and the distribution of risks between 'winners' and 'losers'.
- The modern world trading system is overseen by the WTO, whose job is to facilitate a rules-based system as a core part of global economic governance. However, increasing numbers of regional and bilateral agreements threaten to undermine the WTO's multilateral system.
- Welfare states play a crucial role in allowing economic adjustment to take place in capitalist economies, but a global economy also needs global social policies. Multilateral agreement could provide the basis for social welfare provision to be written into the 'rules' governing trade at the global level.

## Questions for discussion

- Why does genuinely 'free' trade very rarely exist?
- Why do economic considerations seem to dominate over social ones in organisations like the WTO?
- Why might the welfare state be seen as complementary to international trade rather than antagonistic to it?

## Follow-up activities

- Take the interactive training modules on the WTO website at: www.wto.org/english/res_e/d_learn_e/d_learn_e.htm
- Using the websites listed below, compare the different ways that trade issues are presented by the WTO and the Trade Justice Movement (TJM). What kinds of issues concern the TJM?

## Further resources

O'Brien and Williams (2013) and Andersson (2020) provide good detailed introductions to the global economy, including trade issues. Yeates (2001) and Mishra (1999) provide good introductions to social policy and globalisation that complement this volume, and pay particular attention to trade issues. Smith et al (2009) analyse trends in health services trade as an example of how welfare services can be traded across borders, while Adlung (2010) examines the implications of the GATS for healthcare and health insurance services from a WTO perspective. For a discussion of how the GATS relates to **social security**, see Yeates (2005). Holden and Hawkins (2020) provide a detailed analysis of the implications of various trade agreements for health policy, while Hawkins and Holden (2016) analyse the specific implications of ISDS. Fergusson and Yeates (2021) provide an excellent in-depth analysis of how young people's welfare and jobs are impacted by the dynamics of global trade.

World Trade Organization: www.wto.org
United Nations Conference on Trade and Development: https://unctad.org
Trade Justice Movement: www.tjm.org.uk

## References

Acemoglu, D., Autor, D., Dorn, D., Hanson, G.H. and Price, B. (2016) 'Import competition and the great US employment saga of the 2000s', *Journal of Labor Economics*, 34(1–2), S141–98.

Adlung, R. (2010) 'Trade in healthcare and health insurance services: WTO/GATS as a supporting actor(?)', *Intereconomics*, 45(4), 227–38.

Andersson, E. (2020) *Reconstructing the global political economy: An analytical guide*, Bristol: Bristol University Press.

Autor, D.H., Dorn, D. and Hanson, G.H. (2016) 'The China shock: Learning from labor-market adjustment to large changes in trade', *Annual Review of Economics*, 8, 205–40.

Autor, D.H., Dorn, D., Hanson, G. and Majlesi, K. (2016) *Importing political polarization? The electoral consequences of rising trade exposure*, Working Paper 22637, Cambridge: National Bureau of Economic Research.

Cameron, D.R. (1978) 'The expansion of the public economy: A comparative analysis', *American Political Science Review*, 72(4), 1243–61.

*Economist, The* (2007) 'In the shadow of prosperity', Briefing: Trade's victims, 20 January.

Fergusson, R. and Yeates, N. (2021) *Global youth unemployment: History, governance and policy*, Cheltenham: Edward Elgar.

Garrett, G. (1998) *Partisan politics in the global economy*, Cambridge: Cambridge University Press.

Hawkins, B. and Holden, C. (2016) 'A corporate veto on health policy? Global constitutionalism and investor–state dispute settlement', *Journal of Health Politics, Policy and Law*, 41(5), 969–95.

Hawkins, B., Holden, C. and Mackinder, S. (2019) 'A multi-level, multi-jurisdictional strategy: Transnational tobacco companies' attempts to obstruct tobacco packaging restrictions', *Global Public Health*, 14(4), 570–83.

Hoekman, B.M. and Kostecki, M.M. (2001) *The political economy of the world trading system: The WTO and beyond*, Oxford: Oxford University Press.

Holden, C. (2014) 'International trade and welfare', in N. Yeates (ed) *Understanding global social policy* (2nd edn), Bristol: Policy Press, 105–28.

Holden, C. and Hawkins, B. (2020) 'Trade and investment agreements and the global politics of health', in C. McInnes, K. Lee and J. Youde (eds) *The Oxford handbook of global health politics*, Oxford: Oxford University Press, 427–44.

Jawara, F., Kwa, A. and Sharma, S. (2004) *Behind the scenes at the WTO: The real world of international trade negotiations/lessons of Cancun*, London: Zed Books.

Jones, K. (2009) 'Green room politics and the WTO's crisis of representation', *Progress in Development Studies*, 9(4), 349–57.

Katzenstein, P.J. (1985) *Small states in world markets*, Ithaca, NY: Cornell University Press.

Labonte, R., Crosbie, E., Gleeson, D. and McNamara, C. (2019) 'USMCA (NAFTA 2.0): Tightening the constraints on the right to regulate for public health', *Globalization and Health*, 15(35), 1–15.

Lanz, R. and Miroudot, S. (2011) *Intra-firm trade: Patterns, determinants and policy implications*, OECD Trade Policy Papers, no 114, Paris: OECD Publishing (http://dx.doi.org/10.1787/5kg9p39lrwnn-en).

Mishra, R. (1999) *Globalization and the welfare state*, Cheltenham: Edward Elgar.

O'Brien, R. and Williams, M. (2013) *Global political economy: Evolution and dynamics*, New York: Palgrave.

O'Brien, R., Goetz, A.M., Scholte, J.A. and Williams, M. (2000) *Contesting global governance: Multilateral economic institutions and global social movements*, Cambridge: Cambridge University Press.

Rieger, E. and Leibfried, S. (2003) *Limits to globalization*, Cambridge: Polity Press.

Rodrik, D. (1997) *Has globalization gone too far?*, Washington, DC: Institute for International Economics.

Rodrik, D. (1998) 'Why do more open economies have larger governments?', *Journal of Political Economy*, 106, 997–1932.

Smith, R., Chanda, R. and Tangcharoensathien, V. (2009) 'Trade in health-related services', *The Lancet*, 373(9663), 593–601.

WHO (World Health Organization) (2012) *Confronting the tobacco epidemic in a new era of trade and investment liberalization*, Geneva: WHO.

WTO (World Trade Organization) (2020) *Overview of the WTO Secretariat* (www.wto.org/english/thewto_e/secre_e/intro_e.htm).

Yeates, N. (2001) *Globalization and social policy*, London: SAGE Publications.

Yeates, N. (2005) 'The General Agreement on Trade in Services: What's in it for social security?', *International Social Security Review*, 58(1), 3–22.

Yeates, N., Macovei, M. and van Langenhove, L. (2009) 'The evolving context of world regional social policy', in B. Deacon, M.C. Macovei, L. van Langenhove and N. Yeates (eds) *World-regional social policy and global governance: New research and policy agendas in Africa, Asia, Europe and Latin America*, London: Routledge, 191–212.

# 4

# Business, labour and global social policy

## Kevin Farnsworth and Robert O'Brien

### Overview

Business and labour organisations are key players in global social policy. Business interests tend to advocate for policies that help to boost production, sales and, ultimately, profits. Labour organisations seek more extensive social policies and resist business efforts to deregulate social and economic protection. Although precise arrangements vary around the world, business organisations have the advantage in this contest for influence, and many intergovernmental organisations adopt market-friendly social policy approaches. Labour organisations, in contrast, have often been on the defensive, trying to limit or derail neoliberal social policy initiatives. For their part, intergovernmental organisations have developed relationships with business and labour organisations both because they see them as a source of policy ideas and because they are potential political allies.

### Key concepts

Business associations; trade unions; structural power; labour standards; self-regulation; market-friendly social policy

## Introduction

Business and labour groups are better organised and exert greater influence at the international level than ever before. Cooperation and organisation beyond borders has increased, as has international lobbying. Some business and labour organisations operate independently and on the periphery of **intergovernmental organisations** (IGOs), trying to influence them from the outside. Others are institutionally embedded within the decision- and policy-making structures of IGOs. As the number and importance of IGOs has grown, so too have the number of formal and informal opportunities for engagement in global policy processes. Although business and labour organisations can find common ground between them on certain issues, they often pursue policies that are at odds with each other, especially when it comes to questions of economic and social regulation. This chapter examines all of these issues. The first section provides an overview of how major business and labour actors exercise power, and how they are represented in **global social policy** (GSP). The second section outlines the competing perspectives business and labour have on social policy. The third section examines some important global issues relevant to labour and business interests, including **labour standards**, corporate regulation and international taxation. The fourth section examines **global governance** and the responses of IGOs to business and labour positions.

## Business and labour power and representation

As global frameworks and agreements on trade, regulations and social policies have become more important and, in some instances, more binding, so business and labour organisations have sought to shift their spheres of influence to the global and world-regional levels in addition to the national level to defend their interests. The policy playing field is far from level, however, and it is skewed even before non-state actors become involved. Not only do the most powerful economic nations (read most liberal economies) exert greater power at the international level, the most powerful representatives of nation-states in international policy-making also tend to be finance ministers and central bank governors, who also happen to reflect the concerns of the business community (Stiglitz, 2002, p 19). Power is structural in this case because business interests do not have to engage with policy in order to shape it.

This second area of power inequality exists between business and labour. Numerous theoretical perspectives, from pluralist politics to Marxist analysis, have noted the advantage that business organisations have over labour in influencing national and international politics. Pluralists view national politics as a competition between interest groups, but they have also highlighted how business has an advantage over other interest groups because governments rely on business investment for a healthy economy. This advantage has grown as governments increasingly rely on foreign investment to generate growth and employment. Business exercises both structural power because of its control over investment and agency power because of its privileged access to decision-makers. In contrast, labour lacks structural power but is able to engage in protest (see **Box 4.1**).

In addition to influencing global social policy through their national states, business and labour groups engage directly with IGOs. Within each IGO there are formal and informal mechanisms through which external organisations engage with it. Some provide formal mechanisms for business and labour interest representation. Those of the International Labour Organization (ILO) and the

## Box 4.1: Business and labour power – structure, agency and protest

Structural power as it relates to the power of business stems from control over present and future economic investment. Investment decisions have long-lasting and far-reaching consequences for governments and citizens, directly influencing future tax revenues, growth, employment and consumption. Governments and citizens depend on sustained business investment, but they have little or no control over it. The only thing they can do is induce investment through policies that either encourage investment or at least do not undermine it.

Agency perspectives stress the importance of direct political engagement to an understanding of business power. Businesspeople may become politically active and seek election; others may be nominated to public decision-making bodies. Business organisations also use media and other resources to win popular support and make direct representation to policy-makers and decision-makers through their lobbying activities. Businesses may employ politicians as consultants or appoint them to their executive boards.

Labour groups are unable to exercise the structural power of business and often lack direct access to decision-makers, unless a left-wing government is in power. This causes them to rely on the power of protest and disruption. By mobilising their members and the public, labour groups can shut down production, block the circulation of goods, or impose economic and political costs on business and government decision-makers through strikes, boycotts of products or public demonstrations. These tactics require considerable effort and are often limited in their success, but they remain an essential tool for labour actors.

European Union (EU), for example, are based on tripartite **governance** that brings together government, labour and business interests (see **Box 4.2**). The Organisation for Economic Co-operation and Development (OECD) has advisory bodies for business (Business and Industry Advisory Committee, BIAC) and labour (Trade Union Advisory Committee, TUAC). Even those IGOs that do not formally integrate business and labour into their organisations still reach out and actively engage business and labour interests. The International Chambers of Commerce (ICC) have established firm links with the United Nations (UN), and the European Round Table of Industrialists (ERT) and BusinessEurope, a generic business organisation, have become integrated into EU decision-making structures.

## Box 4.2: Tripartite governance at the International Labour Organization

The ILO was created in 1919 following the First World War to advance labour rights and thereby reduce the attractiveness of communism to workers. Today its role is to foster social dialogue between governments, business and labour. It sets labour standards, develops labour policies and devises programmes to advance fair working conditions (ILO, 2020). The ILO is unique among the major IGOs in providing formal representation for business and labour in its governing structures.

It has three main components:

- The governing body of the ILO meets three times a year and makes decisions about ILO policy, programmes and budget. It has a tripartite structure that includes representatives from governments, business and labour. It includes 56 representatives from different governments, 33 representatives from employer organisations and 33 from workers' organisations.
- The International Labour Conference (ILC) sets labour standards and the broad policies of the ILO. Often called the 'international parliament of labour', it meets annually in Geneva. Each state is represented by a delegation composed of two government delegates, an employer delegate, a worker delegate and their respective advisers.
- The International Labour Office is the secretariat of the ILO. It is led by a Director-General. Based in Geneva, it employs 2,700 officials from 150 countries. It has 40 field offices around the world, which employ 900 people working on technical programmes and projects.

Such engagement is designed partly to assist with policy development and is a way for IGOs to increase their own voice and legitimacy, relative to national governments. These processes have certainly helped to strengthen the voice of both business and labour organisations. The key point here is that IGOs have processes in place to bring external organisations in, and sometimes go out of their way to do so, although some organisations are more likely to receive such invitations than others. At the same time, some organisations are sidelined by some IGOs. Labour's relationship with the World Bank, for example, has been more difficult, in part because organised labour (via **trade unions** and workers' groups) is relatively weak in many developing countries. At times the World Bank has seen organised labour in those countries as a small unrepresentative elite of developing country workers, and has tended to sideline them in development policy (O'Brien, 2014). The International Monetary Fund (IMF) has relatively few contacts with organised labour unless it chooses to consult with workers in working through the terms of any financial rescues and interventions. At the same time, both organisations have expanded their engagement with business in order to ensure that nation-states open up trade and investment opportunities to **transnational corporations** (TNCs). The World Bank's extensive work on 'Doing Business' is one illustration of this (see www.doingbusiness.org).

To ensure their voice is amplified where decisions are being made, and to capitalise on the opportunities offered to them, business and labour groups have formed organisations to represent their interests on the international stage (see **Table 4.1**). As noted, some are formally tied to, and embedded within, specific IGOs while others operate more independently. Most have close links to nationally based employer organisations and trade unions. Some have global reach, such as the ICC or the International Trade Union Confederation (ITUC). Business and labour have also established world regional-level organisations such as the ERT or the European Trade Union Confederation (ETUC). The EU is an important target for these groups because of its influence on national policy. Particular sections of business or labour also have their own organisations to represent their sector since they may have interests different from business or labour as a whole. For example, small and medium-sized enterprises (SMEs) in Europe have their own organisation – the European Association of Craft, Small and Medium-Sized Enterprises (SMEunited, formerly UEAPME) – to represent their interests separate from big business. Workers in various industries have formed **global union federations** (GUFs) to advance the particular interests of workers in their sector, such as public service, manufacturing or service workers. The list of organisations in **Table 4.1** shows both the complexity of having to organise on different levels and the possibility that within the broad categories of business and labour there can be conflicting interests and policy positions.

## Competing interests and competing perspectives on welfare

It is useful to examine more directly the opinions of key business and labour organisations in relation to global social policies. This section considers the 'general' opinions of global business and labour associations on welfare, drawn from analysis of inputs into international policy forums over a 40-year period. It examines in particular two key international labour and business voices: the TUAC and the BIAC. The organisations covered here ostensibly reflect the opinions of their constituencies – essentially the largest and most important employer and trade union associations within **member states** – but, since they operate at the international level, they are unlikely to be bogged down by national political concerns. In this way they also provide a good proxy for broad class interests.

It is important to acknowledge from the outset that the views of international business and labour organisations, in common with national organisations,

*Table 4.1: Business and labour associations*

| Group | Membership | Engagement |
|---|---|---|
| International Chambers of Commerce (ICC) | Drawn from various trade organisations and companies from all sectors in over 130 countries throughout the world | Has direct access to the most important political and economic institutions, including the OECD, the World Bank, the IMF and the UN, where it promotes 'open international trade and investment … and the market economy'. Has a particularly close relationship with the UN |
| European Round Table of Industrialists (ERT) | Represents chief executive officers (CEOs) from around 45 leading EU companies. Membership is by invitation, and only the most powerful and largest corporations are allowed to join. As a result, it commands a huge amount of attention from Europe's policy-makers | Consulted regularly by institutions within the EU. It often coordinates its lobbying efforts with BusinessEurope |
| Union of Industrialists and Confederation of Employers (formerly UNICE, now BusinessEurope) | Membership consists of 33 employer federations from 25 European countries | The official voice of industry in the EU and partner in the EU's Social Dialogue. It commonly attempts to influence policy at the EU level, but also acts to provide a steer to national employers' federations within member states. Often coordinates its efforts with the ERT |
| European Association of Craft, Small and Medium-Sized Enterprises (SMEunited, formally UEAPME) | Represents the interests of small and medium-sized employers within the EU. It has a relatively small membership that is drawn from SME trade associations from each of the EU member states | Lobbies on a range of issues that directly impact on SMEs within the EU. Sits alongside BusinessEurope within the EU's Social Dialogue |
| International Trade Union Confederation (ITUC) | Represents over 200 million trade unionists from 163 countries. Members are national or regional union federations | Campaigns on a wide range of workers' issues. Engages with the ILO, the World Bank, the IMF and other IGOs |
| Global union federations (GUFs) | Represent national trade unions in particular sectors (education, transport, manufacturing, mining, etc) | Engages with IGOs and TNCs to advance workers' rights and improve working conditions |
| European Trade Union Confederation (ETUC) | Represents 45 million trade unionists from 35 European countries | Advocates for a 'social Europe' in its engagement with EU decision-making bodies |

change over time, reacting to prevailing discourse and political economy as well as to each other. Thus, the views of the TUAC and the BIAC have changed somewhat over the past four decades. Early discussions of the role, purpose and desirability of social policies from the early 1980s tended to follow broad and simplified class interests – the TUAC favoured comprehensive and **universal** welfare benefits; the BIAC opposed them. This is clear from the submissions to a key meeting that was organised by the OECD in the early 1980s to formulate a blueprint for welfare states emerging after the turmoil of the 1970s, when the BIAC (1981, p 83) stated that 'social policy must be shaped in such a way that it is compatible with the long-term possibilities of the economy', that 'high social benefits can only be financed by a corresponding high level of economic performance' and that 'policy makers desiring to guarantee higher social benefits must also create or improve the conditions for sufficient, non-inflationary economic growth'.

The era of **globalisation**, and criticisms levelled against the growth in inequality it had fostered by the mid-1990s, encouraged the BIAC to make more positive noises regarding **social protection**, in particular where individuals are victims of structural economic changes. By 1997, the BIAC was acknowledging that 'there will always be people who experience difficulties in adjusting to change despite their personal willingness to adapt' (BIAC, 1997, p 5), albeit with the implication that those who are unwilling to 'adapt' are undeserving of state assistance. For those who did qualify, state assistance should be provided to facilitate 're-integration to the labour market' through measures such as 'temporary income support combined with re-training and re-location assistance' (BIAC, 1997, p 5). But the BIAC has also warned of the dangers. In many welfare states, it argued, a 'dependency culture has been created with unemployment benefits being so high that active job-seeking is discouraged' (BIAC, 1998, para 7). State benefits should, the BIAC argued, be low and based on rules and regulations to ensure that they incentivise claimants to 'enter the labour market where their skills are most applicable' (BIAC, 1998, para 7). Thus, welfare programmes should be 'employment-oriented' and 'support work rather than inactivity' and promote 'individual responsibility' (BIAC, 1998, para 7).

Such perspectives fitted well the **neoliberal** assumption about the efficacies and efficiencies of small government and free economies, but they have been challenged by a number of seismic events over the past three decades. Globalisation presented its own challenges throughout the period, but the **global financial crisis** (GFC) of 2007–09, the following Great Recession from 2009 and the global COVID-19 pandemic from 2020 have all tested the idea that small welfare states are most compatible with global capitalism. As a result, global business has come to accept, albeit grudgingly at times, that social policies are useful and even necessary. By 2009, in the face of global economic crisis, the BIAC was stating at the highest level of the OECD that:

> Public services, including health, education, child care services, transportation and housing infrastructure, are important elements of an effective social safety net, as well as important contributors to ensuring that people have the best chances to find and remain in employment. (BIAC, 2009)

At the same time that the GFC focused the minds of business on the importance of social policies in managing economic crises, it did little to change the overriding business agenda. The BIAC told the 2010 OECD Social Policy Ministerial meeting that:

> ... social policies must support private sector growth and employment creation, and work to effectively support the benefits of labour market flexibility ... and ensure that social benefit systems provide the incentive to work. (BIAC, 2009)

This focus on work incentives echoes a long-standing demand of the BIAC from the 1980s, although it has been highlighted less and less since the GFC, and was not raised as a key concern at all between 2010 and 2019. What has remained as a constant is that the key function of social policy is to promote economic growth. In evidence presented to the 2018 ministerial meeting on employment and social protection, the BIAC urged the OECD and governments to promote social protection systems that would provide wider forms of coverage for a wider range of work, including the self-employed. The BIAC (2018, p 3) argued that 'all types of contracts should be possible', which, in some nations, would require the deregulation of labour markets. But here there is recognition that this might be facilitated through changes in social provision, so that 'all should have access to social protection' (BIAC, 2018, p 3).

This difference in approach has continued in the wake of the COVID-19 pandemic. In 2020, the BIAC defended social protection on the grounds that it helps to create 'resilience' and enables individuals to 'prepare for future labour market disruptions' (BIAC, 2020). The details are vague, but this acceptance of the positive role of 'active' social protection, as opposed to using tighter rules and regulations in welfare provision to encourage individuals back into work, appears to be a change in emphasis.

Speaking for organised labour, the TUAC has consistently defended progressive social policies to create more efficient and equitable economies. **Social security** is especially important to balance the operation of flexible and casualised employment markets. Thus, the TUAC has engaged in arguments that connect social policies with economic growth, but it has tended to reach very different conclusions to the BIAC. Even before the GFC, it defended social protection on the grounds that it prevents nations from having to compete on the basis of lower wages and regulations (TUAC, 2007). It also responded to the business lobby and the neoliberal consensus by pointing out the lack of international and comparative evidence to suggest that social protection is economically harmful. The TUAC stated that:

> … there is no negative international relationship between employment rates and the main welfare state indicators, such as the share of transfers in GDP or the statutory generosity of unemployment benefits. (TUAC, 2007)

Growing economic inequality leading up to, and in the wake of, the GFC, has been a shared concern of the BIAC and the TUAC, albeit for different reasons. What has contributed to growing inequality for the TUAC is **austerity** and labour market changes (TUAC, 2011). For the BIAC, it is a lack of state investment in **human capital** as well as public and social policies that can respond to labour market needs (BIAC, 2012, 2016). The BIAC also varies in its approach to economic inequality. For it, inequality is a concern because:

> Business relies on an expanding pool of talent, customers and consumers. To the extent that income inequality reflects the exclusion or marginalization of certain groups from economic life, it limits the size and purchasing power of the consumer base and stifles business growth. (BIAC, 2016)

The solution being offered by the BIAC by 2016, in the aftermath of austerity, was investment in social policies. The support for social provision may be ambivalent, but this is a turnaround for the BIAC, which has been more hostile to collectivised welfare in the past:

> The achievement of sustainable and inclusive growth requires pro-growth policies … [which] include comprehensive policies relating to health care systems, housing, early childhood to tertiary education and public services. Minimum wages may be helpful in reducing poverty in the short term, but they do not address issues of rising inequality or long-term employability. (BIAC, 2016)

In the wake of austerity, growing inequality and unemployment, the TUAC and the BIAC have voiced similar concerns regarding the positive role of social policies in managing and alleviating the impact of precarity, flexible job markets and the rise of 'self-employment'. The TUAC argued:

> Workers on temporary contracts all too often have difficulties in having adequate access to social protection. Self-employed workers

tend to have less social protection coverage. In many countries the self-employed are for example not covered by mandatory work accident insurance and are thus exposed to the risk of a work–related accident and its consequences. It also means that there is no level playing field in terms of competition with firms and workers that do pay for social insurance. Firms are thus provided with the incentive to shift work onto employees that have the least protection, thus undermining the capacity of social security systems to raise revenue and to pool risks. (TUAC, 2018)

Note here the argument that the lack of state provision ultimately undermines everyone – employees, employers and the state – by reducing tax revenues.

Labour organisations respond to business social policy proposals, but they also bring their own set of issues to the table. Labour organisations often advocate for action on issues outside the traditional social policy realm that have an impact on whether states are able to implement strong social policies. Three of the most important are labour standards, business regulation and tax abuse.

## Labour standards, corporate regulation and taxation

The most important issue for labour organisations is the observance of core labour standards. These are enabling rights that allow workers to pursue other rights (see **Box 4.3**). For example, the right to form a union allows workers to organise and articulate their views. Labour organisations view core labour standards as important for two reasons. First, respecting core labour standards improves the living conditions of workers because it gives them the power to negotiate and protect fair working conditions. Second, basic rights such as freedom of association, collective bargaining and elimination of forced labour are required if labour organisations are to build sufficient political strength to defend their interests and advance broadly based social policies. The trade union movement has engaged with a wide range of IGOs in its campaign to bolster adherence to core labour standards. The campaign has included targeting the World Trade Organization (WTO) and regional trade agreements, pressuring **international financial institutions** (IFIs) such as the World Bank and regional development banks, and monitoring **bilateral** aid policies (Bakvis and McCoy, 2008).

A key element of supporting core labour standards is some form of regulation of business practices and cross–border activities. Labour organisations have advocated mechanisms to curb business abuses. They have lobbied (unsuccessfully) for the WTO to use its power to penalise states for abusing labour standards. Labour organisations take advantage of their ability to bring complaints to the attention of a TNC's 'home state' via the *OECD guidelines for multinational enterprises*. They have

## Box 4.3: Core labour standards

Core labour standards are set out in the 1998 ILO Declaration of Fundamental Principles and Rights at Work. The Declaration brings together seven crucial ILO conventions (20, 87, 98, 100, 105, 111, 138), which provide for:

1. Freedom of association and the effective recognition of the right to collective bargaining.
2. Elimination of all forms of forced or compulsory labour.
3. Effective abolition of child labour.
4. Elimination of discrimination in respect of employment and occupation.

participated in UN initiatives such as the **Global Compact**, which is a voluntary corporate sustainability initiative designed to encourage businesses to follow best practices in the areas of human rights, labour, environment and anti-corruption (see **Table 4.2**). The machinery of the ILO is used to shame companies and states into respecting labour standards. Finally, labour organisations have tried to use market pressure through boycotts and demonstrations to highlight the worst corporate abuses, in the hope that corporations change behaviour when faced with some economic cost for their actions.

Businesses' response to labour's push for greater regulation is to advocate for self-regulation where corporations set and monitor their own rules. This can take place through the actions of either an individual corporation or **business associations** in a particular sector. Businesses argue that **corporate social responsibility** (CSR) is the solution to **civil society's** concerns about business behaviour. CSR policies have been put into practice by many firms, including many of those caught in sweatshop scandals.

Although there are literally hundreds of corporate codes of conduct in existence, doubt has been expressed about whether this will resolve the labour standards issue. Numerous studies have documented the serious weaknesses of these private regulatory approaches, and it is apparent that they do not serve as an effective substitute for traditional labour regulation (Christian Aid, 2004; Rowe, 2005). Self- and voluntary regulation of labour standards is not successful in national markets, and is even less likely to succeed transnationally. This is because of the physical and informational distance between where production is taking place and the consumers who might pressure companies to take action. An extreme example of the divergence between intentions stated in codes of conduct and alleged practices on the ground is provided in **Box 4.4**.

*Table 4.2: OECD guidelines for multinational enterprises and the UN Global Compact*

| OECD guidelines | UN Global Compact |
| --- | --- |
| The common aim of the governments adhering to the guidelines is to encourage the positive contributions that multinational enterprises can make to economic, environmental and social progress and to minimise the difficulties to which their various operations may give rise. | **Human rights** Principle 1: Businesses should support and respect the protection of internationally proclaimed human rights |
| Two key principles underpin the guidelines: they are voluntary but apply worldwide. | Principle 2: Businesses should make sure they are not complicit in human rights abuses |
| The guidelines: <ul><li>call on enterprises to take full account of established policies in the countries in which they operate;</li><li>recommend disclosure on all matters regarding the enterprise such as its performance and ownership, and encourage communication in areas where reporting standards are still emerging, such as social, environmental and risk reporting</li><li>rule out child and forced labour and discrimination, and encourage employee representation and constructive negotiations;</li><li>encourage enterprises to raise their performance in protecting the environment;</li><li>stress the importance of combating bribery;</li><li>recommend that enterprises, when dealing with consumers, act in accordance with fair business, marketing and advertising practices, respect consumer privacy, and take all reasonable steps to ensure the safety and quality of goods or services provided;</li><li>promote the diffusion by multinational enterprises of the fruits of research and development activities among countries where they operate, thereby contributing to the innovative capacities of host countries;</li><li>emphasise the importance of an open and competitive business climate;</li><li>call on enterprises to respect both the letter and spirit of tax laws to cooperate with tax authorities.</li></ul> | **Labour** Principle 3: Businesses should uphold the freedom of association and the effective recognition of the right to collective bargaining Principle 4: The elimination of all forms of forced and compulsory labour Principle 5: The effective abolition of child labour Principle 6: The elimination of discrimination in respect of employment and occupation **Environment** Principle 7: Businesses should support a precautionary approach to environmental challenges Principle 8: Undertake initiatives to promote greater environmental responsibility Principle 9: Encourage the development and diffusion of environmentally friendly technologies **Anti-corruption** Principle 10: Businesses should work against corruption in all its forms, including extortion and bribery |

Source: OECD (2011) and UN Global Compact (nd)

## Box 4.4: Codes versus practice

Statement from the Code of Conduct of Chiquita (famous for selling bananas):

> Chiquita believes in doing business with suppliers and other business partners who demonstrate high standards of ethical business conduct. Our ultimate goal is to direct all of our business to suppliers that demonstrate their compliance with the social responsibilities included in our Code of Conduct and that operate in an ethical and lawful manner. (Chiquita, 2000)

Complaint filed by lawyers suing Chiquita for alleged activities in Colombia:

> This case arises as a result of the actions of ... "Chiquita" ... in funding, arming, and otherwise supporting terrorist organizations in Colombia, in order to maintain its profitable control of Colombia's banana-growing regions. Plaintiffs are family members of trade unionists, banana workers, political organizers, social activists, and others targeted and killed by terrorists, notably the paramilitary organization ... AUC [United Self-Defense Forces of Colombia] ... during the 1990s through 2004. In order to operate its banana production in an environment free of labor opposition and social disturbances, Chiquita funded, armed, and otherwise supported the AUC and other terrorist groups during this period. The deaths of Plaintiffs' relatives were a direct, foreseeable, and intended result of Chiquita's illegal and tortious actions. (US District Court, 2007; see also IR Advocates, nd)

A third issue of great concern to labour is tax abuse (Bernards et al, 2016). Tax abuse occurs when wealthy corporations or individuals exploit the international tax system to avoid paying taxes to national governments. Corporations can avoid tax through transfer pricing, which allows them to declare their profits in low tax jurisdictions by exploiting tax loopholes and by disguising profits and wealth by sheltering them in tax havens. The amount of funds diverted from state treasuries is immense (see **Box 4.5**). This has significant implications for social policy. States starved of tax revenue are unable to fund development or comprehensive welfare systems. Taxes on corporations and individuals pay for schools, hospitals, unemployment insurance, pensions and many other social policies. The ITUC sees a clear relationship between fighting tax abuse and fostering social programmes and equity:

> The fight against financial opacity, fraud and tax evasion must be determined and effective. This will mean combating money

laundering, tax optimisation and tax havens, practices which stand in the way of fair development and the reduction of inequality. (ITUC, 2014a, p 5)

---

### Box 4.5: Scale of the tax avoidance problem

- US$400 billion of tax revenue lost by OECD members.
- US$200 billion of tax revenue lost by developing countries.
- Developing countries lose between 6–13 per cent of their possible tax revenues.
- US tax loss due to corporations shifting profits rose from US$12 billion in 1994 to US$130 billion in 2012.
- US$21–32 trillion of private wealth sheltered beyond national jurisdictions.

Source: Tax Justice Network (2017)

---

The reality at the global level is not simply reducible to the idea that business is opposed to social policy while labour is supportive, but there are clear core interests here that push in different directions. Some degree of consensus appears to have developed at the centre, with business having shifted its view towards a more positive perspective on social policy since the GFC of 2007–09, but it is not clear whether this will continue. Perhaps the reality has set in that thriving businesses have always needed big government, and continue to do so (Farnsworth, 2012). It is the battles over the functions of the welfare state (whether they are needed in 'ordinary times'), the provision of services (whether they should be provided exclusively by the state) and who pays for them (whether through progressive taxation including corporation taxes) that most clearly divide the two.

## Global governance and social welfare

A large number of actors are involved in shaping global social policies (see **Chapter 2**, this volume). The power and influence of those actors, especially **non–state actors**, varies by policy area, by IGO, and over time (Hacker and Pierson, 2002). At the global level, policy discourse suggests that ideas and actors both matter (Kuhnle, 2005; Béland, 2010). Together these have shaped policy designs, which, in turn, have had an impact on the fortunes of businesses, workers and citizens nationally and globally.

In response to global business opinion and lobbying, the dominance of neoliberal ideas and the challenges presented by globalisation, IGOs have, since the late

1970s, tended to promote ideas and approaches to social policies that place the economy and business interests at the fore. This is clear if we examine welfare discourse within major IGOs such as the EU, the OECD, the IMF and the World Bank (the WTO is examined in detail in **Chapter 3**).

Within the EU, emphasis has been placed on competitiveness and corporate-centred policies since the 1990s. The 1997 Amsterdam European Council summit urged 'more attention be given to improving European competitiveness as a prerequisite for growth and employment' through the development of a 'skilled and adaptable workforce responsive to economic change'. It went on to recommend 'a reduction in the overall tax burden' and 'training and lifelong learning in order to increase employability' (Balanya et al, 2003, pp 64–5). The Lisbon Agenda from 2000 until 2010 sought to push member states towards making improvements to education and training provision, cutting regulations and red tape on corporations, increasing work incentives, cutting non-wage labour costs and completing the internal market in services, with the aim of making Europe 'the most competitive and dynamic knowledge-based economy in the world' by 2010 (EC, 2003, 2004). Europe 2020, which replaced the Lisbon Treaty, did make more positive noises about the value of the welfare state, emphasising 'smart, sustainable and inclusive growth', but EU responses to the 2007–09 global financial crisis (GFC) presented a much harder, antisocial policy line. The approach of the European Commission (EC) and the European Central Bank (ECB) to austerity was more draconian and more economically libertarian in its approach than the USA and even the IMF. The sanctions, **conditionality** and controls imposed on Greece and Ireland in exchange for financial assistance resembled IMF conditionality at its harshest. It also resulted in huge cuts to social policies and a reversal in the fortunes of the welfare state in both countries (Farnsworth and Irving, 2012).

What underpins the social policies of the OECD is an ongoing tension between **neoliberalism** and other models of welfare. As already noted, business, in the form of BIAC, has been more than capable of seeing the positives in social policies. This is an indication of the fact that business interests recognise, at some level, the importance of state provision, even where dominant discourse suggests the opposite.

Despite frequently pointing to (economic) inequality as a problem, official OECD reports in fact seldom present a clear defence of comprehensive, redistributive social democratic welfare systems. One obvious reason for this is that very few OECD nations have comprehensive and redistributive welfare states. Thus, the OECD has tended to blame growing inequality on 'traditional' social policies. 'Active' social policies have tended to be supported more enthusiastically, on the basis that they can 'change the conditions in which individuals develop, rather than limiting themselves to ameliorating the distress these conditions cause' (Farnsworth and Irving, 2012). State education and training play an important role here, of course.

The OECD has similarly hedged its bets on the question of the funding of social policies. Despite acknowledging the growing problem of inequality in 2018, the ministerial report does not mention redistribution or even taxation. In contrast, the earlier report, *Extending opportunities* (OECD, 2005), stated that redistributive taxation is untenable so that only redistribution across the life course was feasible in future.

By and large, OECD comments echo the views of global business. Generally, the economic takes precedence over the social. Social policies are viewed as being important to people, but their functioning in terms of the needs of business and employment are prioritised. Social policies should contribute to economic growth by creating greater flexibility within employment markets, and assisting those who are not yet, or are no longer, needed by employers.

The IMF similarly tends to prioritise the economic over the social, both in terms of its policy prescriptions and discourse. While the IMF has been forced to adapt since the 1990s in the face of opposition to its policy prescriptions and its reduced relevance – many countries broke ties with the IMF during the 1990s and 2000s, and the organisation began to appear less relevant and more anachronistic over this period (Masson, 2007) – the 2007–09 financial crisis revived its fortunes and gave it new relevance.

The economic libertarian position of the IMF, established and promoted over the period of neoliberal globalisation, is deeply embedded within the institution, such that the IMF has reinforced the structural power of businesses by pressuring countries to create conditions that are most conducive to private sector investment. The mechanism of ensuring this is the application of lending conditionalities to debtor nations, but the IMF has also played a key role in establishing neoliberal hegemony to other organisations and nations through its country reports and policy papers. The constant ideas, rehearsed, replicated and reinforced by senior members of the organisation, prioritise fiscal stability, fiscal responsibility and balanced budgets over social justice. Even when social policies are promoted, the tendency is to reduce them to their economic function. The IMF cautioned against austerity when it risked undermining some of the largest economies in Northern Europe in the 2010s, but supported it as a price worth paying when it came to smaller EU economies, especially the Southern European countries of Greece, Spain and Italy. This chimes with the critique of IMF and World Bank discourse offered by Robert Wade, a former staffer at the World Bank, who argued that the World Bank and the IMF are divided between their 'economic' and 'social' wings, both of which put forward policy proposals. Ultimately, however, according to Wade, it is the economic wing that dominates and wins out (Wade, 2002).

Whereas IGOs are generally open to business prescriptions for social policy, labour organisations often struggle to have their positions accepted. Two aspects of IGO activity are particularly problematic for labour. The first aspect is international policies advocating labour market deregulation and privatisation. The World

Bank and the IMF have a long history of seeing the deregulation of the labour market as a recipe for economic development and growth (O'Brien, 2014). The justification for labour market deregulation is that 'rigid' labour markets make it difficult for businesses to adjust to economic conditions, and workers are prevented from moving to available jobs. Deregulation can involve eliminating centralised bargaining (where an industry-wide agreement is made with major unions), making it harder for unions to organise and strike, extending the working age, encouraging casual employment relationships, and reducing welfare benefits to encourage people to take lower paying employment. Many of these policies are supported by business associations, since it makes it easier to hire and fire workers. For their part, labour organisations argue that labour market deregulation leads to greater inequality, since workers are forced into insecure and low-paid employment (ITUC, 2014b). This, in turn, causes greater economic instability and lower growth.

The second aspect is the tendency for IGOs to attack labour and welfare policies during times of economic and financial crisis. States that are unable to service debt payments or find themselves in a financial crisis often have to seek loans from international institutions to stabilise their economies. When these loans are granted they come with conditionalities or requirements for economic restructuring. Often termed **structural adjustment programmes** (SAPs), the requirements demand governments reduce welfare spending and deregulate labour markets to increase economic growth. IGOs also often urge countries to adopt budget-reducing austerity measures in the mistaken belief that these will return countries to economic growth. Commenting on several decades of IMF-sponsored structural adjustment and austerity policies, the ITUC has highlighted the negative social impacts of a series of IMF policies, including:

> ... pension, social security and safety net reforms consisting of more restrictive or reduced benefits; capping public-sector wage bills; labour flexibilisation reforms; reduced consumer subsidies; increased regressive consumption taxes such as VATs; privatising public services and expanding Public–Private Partnerships; and healthcare reforms aimed at reducing expenditures. (ITUC, 2020, p 38)

Business organisations have enjoyed some success in having IGOs adopt a market-friendly approach to social policy, while labour organisations have been on the defensive, trying to protect basic rights for workers and universal approaches to social policy.

## Conclusion

Business and labour organisations have been active nationally and globally, working to influence the content of GSP. Business organisations have had the advantage in this contest for influence, and many IGOs have adopted market-friendly social policy approaches. Labour organisations have often been on the defensive, trying to limit or derail neoliberal social policy initiatives. For their part, IGOs have developed relationships with business and labour organisations, both because they see them as a source of policy ideas, and because they are potential political allies.

In the wake of the economic and health dislocations caused by COVID-19, business and labour organisations can be expected to increase their efforts to influence IGOs as they devise social policy responses to the pandemic and its aftermath.

## Summary

- Business and labour organisations are actively engaged in trying to shape GSPs.
- Business organisations have an advantage over labour in influencing GSPs because they exercise both structural and agency forms of power.
- IGOs engage with business and labour as a source of policy ideas, to increase IGO legitimacy and to smooth policy implementation.
- IGOs such as the EU, the OECD, the IMF and the World Bank have adopted 'business-friendly' social policy prescriptions, such as stressing the role of private corporations in social policy and labour market deregulation.
- Labour organisations continue to advocate for more social democratic social policy arrangements than those favoured by business.

## Questions for discussion

- Why do business organisations seem to have more influence over GSPs than labour organisations?
- What are the competing visions for GSP advanced by business and labour?
- How have IGOs responded to business and labour social policy proposals?

## Follow-up activities

- Examine the news stories from the LabourStart website (www.labourstart.org). Did you realise that all this activity was taking place? How many of these stories are covered by the news sources you read? How might the issues covered at LabourStart intersect with GSP discussions?
- Visit the Fairtrade website (www.fairtrade.net) to get a sense of the extent and scope of fairtrade practices. Have you ever bought any fairtrade products? What are the benefits and shortcomings of such products? How do they improve working conditions?

- Research an alleged corporate harm (for example, the Bhopal [India] disaster of 1984, or the Rana Plaza [Bangladesh] factory collapse in 2016). Examine the allegations made against the corporations involved and how they have responded to them. Now look at campaign groups' responses to these and whether they have been successful in holding the corporations to account.

## Further resources

A wide range of labour issues is addressed in the open access online publication *Global Labour Journal* (https://mulpress.mcmaster.ca/globallabour). The chapter by Römer et al (2021) on international organisations and global labour standards provides a reasonable overview of global policy on working conditions. The formal texts of international agreements relating to the issues in this chapter are available on IGOs' websites: UN Global Compact (www.unglobalcompact.org) and the *OECD guidelines for multinational enterprises* (2011). See also the ITUC's website (www.ituc-csi.org).

## References

Bakvis, P. and McCoy, M. (2008) *Core labour standards and international organizations: What inroads has labour made?*, Friedrich Ebert Stiftung Briefing Papers, No 6 (https://library.fes.de/pdf-files/iez/05431.pdf).

Balanya, B., Doherty, A., Hoedeman, O., Ma'Anit, A. and Wesselius, E. (2003) *Europe Inc: Regional and global restructuring and the rise of corporate power* (2nd edn), London: Macmillan.

Béland, D. (2010) 'The idea of power and the role of ideas', *Political Studies Review*, 8(2), 145–54.

Bernards, N., O'Brien, R. and Zhang, F. (2016) 'Labour and tax justice' in A. Beiler and R. O'Brien (eds) *Developing alternatives to neo-liberalism: Tax justice, fair trade, democracy-driven public sector transformation and eco-socialism*, South Africa: Rosa Luxemburg Foundation, 19–30.

BIAC (Business and Industry Advisory Committee to the OECD) (1981) 'A view from the entrepreneurs', in OECD, *The Welfare state in crisis*, Paris: Organisation for Economic Co-operation and Development (OECD).

BIAC (1997) *Addressing the social impact of globalisation: Promoting the benefits of change. Submission to the OECD Liaison Committee with International Non-Governmental Organisations*, Paris: BIAC.

BIAC (1998) *Statement to the meeting of the Employment, Labour and Social Affairs Committee at ministerial level on social policy*, Paris: BIAC.

BIAC (2009) *Business statement to the G8 Social Summit*, Rome, Italy, 29 March, Paris: BIAC.

BIAC (2012) 'Business statement', G20 Labour Ministers' meeting, 17 May, Paris: BIAC.

BIAC (2016) 'Building more resilient and inclusive labour markets', Meeting of the Employment and Social Affairs Committee at the Ministerial Level, 15 January, Paris: BIAC.

BIAC (2018) *The new OECD jobs strategy: Guidance for a successful digital transformation of work. Business at OECD statement on the occasion of the launch of the new OECD jobs strategy*, Paris: BIAC.

BIAC (2020) *Leveraging investment for more resilient health care systems*, Paris: BIAC.

Chiquita (2000) *Code of conduct: Living by our core values* (www.sec.gov/Archives/edgar/data/101063/000119312504038903/dex14.htm).

Christian Aid (2004) *Behind the mask: The real face of corporate social responsibility*, London: Christian Aid.

EC (European Commission) (2003) *Jobs, jobs, jobs: Creating more employment in Europe*, Brussels: EC.

EC (2004) *Facing the challenge: The Lisbon strategy for growth and employment*, Brussels: EC.

Farnsworth, K. (2012) *Social versus corporate welfare: Competing needs and interests within the welfare state*, London: Palgrave.

Farnsworth, K. and Irving, Z. (2012) 'Varieties of crisis, varieties of austerity: Social policy in challenging times', *Journal of Poverty and Social Justice*, 20(2), 133–47.

Hacker, J.S. and Pierson, P. (2002) 'Business power and social policy: Employers and the formation of the American welfare state', *Politics and Society*, 30(2), 277–325.

ILO (International Labour Organization) (2020) 'How the ILO works' (www.ilo.org/global/about-the-ilo/how-the-ilo-works/lang--en/index.htm).

IR (International Rights) Advocates (no date) *Does v Chiquita Brands International et al* (www.iradvocates.org/case/latin-america-colombia/does-v-chiquita-brands-international-et-al).

ITUC (International Trade Union Confederation) (2014a) *Building workers' power: Conference statement*, 3rd World Congress, Berlin (www.ituc-csi.org/IMG/pdf/ituc-3co_e_5-congressstatement-en-210x297-140630.pdf).

ITUC (2014b) *Labour market deregulation measures in IMF loan conditionality and policy advice for European countries* (www.ituc-csi.org/ituc-background-paper-labour).

ITUC (2020) *The IMF's renewed supply side push: Four decades of structural adjustment and austerity conditionality*, Washington, DC: ITUC (www.ituc-csi.org/imf-renewed-supply-side-push).

Kuhnle, S. (2005) 'Global social policy forum: Global ideas matter, local power decides? Guest Editor's Introduction', *Global Social Policy*, 5(1), 5–7.

Masson, P.R. (2007) *The IMF: Victim of its own success or institutional failure?*, York, CA: The Centre for International Governance Innovation.

O'Brien, R. (2014) 'Antagonism and accommodation: The labour–IMF/World Bank relationship', in A. Kaasch and P. Stubbs (eds) *Transformations in global and regional social policies,* Basingstoke: Palgrave Macmillan, 153–74.

OECD (Organisation for Economic Co-operation and Development) (2005) *Extending opportunities: How active social policy can benefit us all*, Paris: OECD.

OECD (2011) *OECD guidelines for multinational enterprises*, Paris: OECD Publishing (http://dx.doi.org/10.1787/9789264115415–en).

Römer, F., Henninger, J. and Thuy Dung Le (2021) 'International organizations and global labor standards', in K. Martens, D. Niemann and A. Kaasch (eds) *International organizations in global social governance*, Cham, Switzerland: Palgrave Macmillan, 57–82.

Rowe, J.K. (2005) 'Corporate social responsibility as a business strategy', in R. Lipschutz and J.K. Rowe (eds) *Globalization, governmentality and global politics: Regulation for the rest of us?*, London: Routledge, 122–60.

Stiglitz, J. (2002) *Globalization and its discontents*, London: Norton House.

Tax Justice Network (2017) *Tax avoidance and evasion – The scale of the problem*, Briefing Paper (http://taxjustice.wpengine.com/wp-content/uploads/2017/11/Tax-dodging-the-scale-of-the-problem-TJN-Briefing.pdf).

TUAC (Trade Union Advisory Committee to the OECD) (2007) *Towards a fair globalisation: Trade union statement to the G-8 Summit*, Paris: TUAC.

TUAC (2011) 'The OECD in the wake of the Great Recession', TUAC Statement to the OECD Ministerial Council and OECD 50th Anniversary Forum, 25–26 May, Paris: TUAC.

TUAC (2018) 'The future of social protection in a changing world of work', Social Policy Ministerial Meeting, 15 May, Paris: TUAC.

UN (United Nations) Global Compact (no date) *The ten principles of the UN Global Compact* (www.unglobalcompact.org/what-is-gc/mission/principles).

US District Court (2007) *Class action complaint for damages*, 19 July, United States District Court, District of New Jersey (www.courtlistener.com/docket/4309237/1/john-doe-1-v-chiquita-brands-international-inc).

Wade, R.H. (2002) 'US hegemony and the World Bank: The fight over people and ideas', *Review of International Political Economy*, 9(2), 215–43.

# 5

# Theorising global social policy

Nicola Yeates and Chris Holden

## Overview

Global social policy demands new theories to account for its development and the different forms it takes. This chapter reviews different ways of theorising global social policy. It distinguishes between social theories concerned with the *impacts* of global social policies on welfare outcomes and social theories concerned with *why* global social policy takes the forms that it does. We focus on the latter. First, we consider the possibility of globalising theories of national welfare state development. Second, we consider the opportunities to 'welfarise' globalist social theories that were not originally devised with the concerns of global social policy in mind. The chapter argues that a single social theory of global social policy is neither desirable nor possible, but that better integration of social theory into global social policy studies is attainable. It concludes by briefly considering possible future lines of direction for thinking theoretically about global social policy.

## Key concepts

Global social policy theory; industrialisation; class struggle; political mobilisation; institutionalism; international organisation; diffusion theory; World Society theory; World Systems theory; exploitation theory; organisation theory

## Introduction

A foundational idea in **global social policy** (GSP) is that the enactment of social policy transcends the nation–state. That is, social policies are formulated in many extra-national sites, spaces and forums that are outside the sole control of national governments and other domestic actors (see **Chapters 1 and 2**, this volume). If the forms that GSPs take and the conditions under which they develop are distinct from those of national welfare states and social policies, what does this mean for the ways in which we theorise GSP? Few would argue that theories of national social policy development are *directly* applicable to GSP, but the real questions are whether existing theories can be repurposed for GSP, or whether entirely new theories need to be devised. If the latter, from which bodies of scholarly thought might we seek inspiration for developing GSP theory?

What role does theory play in GSP studies? One part of the answer is that theory helps make sense of complexity. Theory systematically – that is, *according to a logic* – prioritises and orders the many different elements involved in the production, distribution and outcomes of individual and collective welfare and the relationships between them. Different theories vary in their priorities for what they aim to explain, and accordingly emphasise different elements. For example, a theory about the origins of GSP might focus on broad social, economic or political conditions, whereas a theory about how GSP is implemented might focus on institutional design. No single theory can explain all aspects of GSP. Also, theories arise from different sociopolitical projects. For example, theories connected with equality or liberationist movements seeking total social or political transformation develop along different lines than theories focused on more efficient **governance** of the existing world order.

To help clarify these points, we adapt O'Brien and Penna's (1998) distinction between *theories of social welfare* and *social theories of welfare*, as follows:

- *Theories of global social welfare/policy* systematise knowledge about the actual impacts of GSP on individual and collective welfare outcomes worldwide.
- *Social theories of GSP* systematise knowledge about why GSP takes the forms that it does.

Such theories of how GSP actually 'is' are different from *normative theories of GSP* (although normative theories may build on theories of global social welfare/policy):

- *Normative theories* address the question of what *ought* to be done (as opposed to what is actually done). They feature strongly in GSP-making in practice, to make it more effective, rational, socially just, humanitarian, and so on.

Theories of global social welfare/policy constitute the 'bread and butter' of GSP as a field of social research and as a political practice. They mobilise research findings and formulate knowledge claims about the impacts of actual GSPs on individual and collective welfare. Such theories feature across the book. **Chapter 6** focuses specifically on normative theories concerning **global social justice**. We do not dwell further on either of these types of theory in this chapter; instead, we focus on social theories of GSP that aim to explain the forms that GSP takes and why. We start by looking at how social theories of national welfare state development may be 'scaled up' or 'globalised' to explain GSP.

# Globalising theories of national welfare state development

Holden (2018) discussed three main types of social theories of welfare state development – theories of economic development, industrialisation and urbanisation; theories of class struggle and political mobilisation; and theories of the effects of differing political institutions – in terms of how they may be applied to GSP. We summarise some main elements of that discussion and introduce additional elements.

## *Economic development and capitalism*

Early welfare state theory explained the welfare state in functionalist terms, arguing that the welfare state is essentially the outcome of the 'needs' of industrial society (Wilensky, 1975; Flora and Alber, 1984). The increasing specialisation and division of labour associated with economic growth and industrialisation, coupled with urbanisation and increasing labour mobility, undermined the security functions of the family and generated new social problems. Social policies and welfare provision were a response to these problems, and states variously controlled, supplemented or substituted for the open market.

Some Marxist approaches share the functionalist emphasis of the industrialisation thesis, pointing to the role of the welfare state in meeting the accumulation needs of advanced capitalism by, for example, ensuring a healthy, educated labour force, although some writers in this tradition have also emphasised that the welfare state legitimises capitalism by meeting certain needs of the working class within it (Gough, 1979; Offe, 1984). Muller and Neususs (1978) argued that the English Factory Acts were necessary because unrestrained use of female and child labour, long working hours and dangerous working conditions could destroy the ability of the labour force to reproduce itself. Feminist political economists have argued that state interventions like the Factory Acts were also important in maintaining gender norms. By placing limitations on the work of women and children, the Acts simultaneously reinforced gender norms and facilitated the reproduction of the workforce (Moos, 2021).

On first consideration, the industrialisation thesis has little to tell us about GSP, since it suggests that welfare states will develop only where there is industrialisation, and industrialised countries are a minority in the world. Nevertheless, greater economic integration among countries, especially, but not exclusively, industrial ones, may have implications for welfare provision. For example, greater labour mobility *between* countries has stimulated the development of reciprocal **social security** agreements and portable social rights for the purposes of taxation and medical treatment. At the same time, inter–country competition to retain or attract investment (and jobs) from mobile capital seeking to lower production costs may result in lower social standards and reduced welfare provision.

We might therefore ask whether there is something about capitalism in its globalising phase that suggests a *need* for GSP. There is certainly some evidence for this. For example, the establishment of international **labour standards** in the early 20th century was widely supported by social liberals as well as by workers' representatives, on the basis that this would provide an international mechanism for ensuring a 'level playing field' for all countries, thereby preventing competitive social devaluation. The International Labour Organization (ILO) was established as the **intergovernmental organisation** (IGO) to broker international dialogue in relation to this question of global social standards.

We also find 'positive' forms of social policy integration instituted at world-regional level to accompany the establishment of regional markets (for example, the European Union's [EU] Single Market). Many region-building projects have instituted common social standards and other social programmes to deter member governments from pursuing competitive social devaluation and facilitate institutional cooperation on other social policy matters. However, 'negative' forms of regional social policy integration, which relate strictly to the removal of barriers to labour mobility and other forms of integration, have tended to prevail (Yeates, 2019; see also **Chapter 2**, this volume). This could be seen as consistent with the industrialisation thesis, first, because transnational forms of governance and regulation express how institutional capacity evolves with capitalism (Wilensky, 1975), and second, because the limited forms of 'positive' social policy express the minimal state intervention needed to make global markets function effectively.

Overall, Holden (2018) argues that theories of economic development provide *some* explanation for the emergence of forms of GSP aimed at ensuring social stability, **social reproduction** and the incorporation of developing countries into the world market. However, such theories do little more than tell us whether the preconditions exist for the further development of GSP. They cannot explain the emergence of GSPs that are not a function of the 'needs' of the global economy or capitalism. Nor can they easily explain social and political relationships among states and other social actors, including their capacity for building global alliances, which (arguably) determine whether such developments take place, when they happen and the forms they take.

### Class struggle and political mobilisation

In 'modernisation' theory, mass democracy is a key factor in the development of welfare states because it allows working-class demands to be heard (Flora and Alber, 1984). For T.H. Marshall (1950), the emergence of social rights was the culmination of the development of citizenship. Marxist theories often argue that welfare states developed partly to head off revolution or instability caused by mass revolt. Many theories emphasise the importance of political parties (particularly leftist ones) and organised labour movements to the creation of national welfare states. Korpi's (1983) 'power resources' model is one example. Esping-Andersen (1990, p 111) built on this approach to argue that it is not simply the overall level of welfare expenditure that is influenced by the relative power of left and other parties, but the *type* of welfare state that is created.

Economic **globalisation** has often been considered to have led to welfare state retrenchment and declining social standards because it sets in motion international competition. A more sophisticated approach, however, recognises the role of politics and the balance of power, globally, regionally and nationally, as major factors shaping the pace, timing and effects of national welfare retrenchment and GSP development or the lack thereof (Yeates, 2002). However, globalist platforms have not generally been adopted by left parties or mass movements, although there are numerous examples of **trade unions** organising effectively on a transnational basis (Yeates, 2002, p 78). While there have been significant moves towards transnational organisation by both labour and business interests, globalisation has shored up the power of capital by enabling it to be more mobile internationally (see **Chapter 4**, this volume).

Agrarian interests were important in influencing many welfare settlements at the national level (Esping-Andersen, 1990; Pierson, 2006). Alliances between agrarian interests and those of workers or social democratic movements are more likely to give rise to more progressive outcomes than agrarian alliances based on nationalism or with more middle-class interests. This would seem to be particularly important to the development of GSP, given the largely agrarian nature of many developing economies. Yet, while there may be some scope for transnational alliances of farmers, possibly together with workers, such alliances may be difficult to form given the different interests of farmers in **high**- and **low-income countries** within the world trade system.

The global movement against **neoliberal** capitalism contains a wide spectrum of groups and opinions, from **protectionist** unions and small farmers in the developed countries to guerrilla groups and landless labourers in the developing countries. This diversity enables the movement to construct coherent coalitions primarily when conducting focused single-issue campaigns rather than politically broader ones (Yeates, 2002, p 82). The World Social Forum (WSF) process (created in 2001) functions more as a space within which ideas and tactics can be exchanged and developed rather than as a single movement with a common programme. In effect, the global anti-capitalist or anti-globalisation movement influences the course of GSP primarily by campaigning *against* what it finds unacceptable in the agendas of the World Bank, the International Monetary Fund (IMF) and the World Trade Organization (WTO) (Patomaki and Teivainen, 2004), and by challenging their legitimacy, rather than by promoting a common global vision.

However, because IGOs have acted as a conduit for reform demands, much as national parliaments often did in the period of initial welfare state development, and because they are now more closely monitored and visible to wider publics, they arguably need to respond to challenges to their legitimacy. Such pressures may therefore incentivise them to foster collaborative relations with relevant **civil society** groups and **international non-governmental organisations** (INGOs) and to develop stronger GSPs.

Theories of class struggle and political mobilisation highlight the role of social and political forces in GSP and the wide range of social actors involved. They can help explain the timing and nature of GSPs. However, such theories tell us little about the political institutions that structure the possibilities for global alliances in favour of stronger GSPs. In order to understand more fully the forms that GSPs take and the scope for their further development, we therefore need to consider political institutions more closely.

### Political institutions

Some writers have emphasised the role of political institutions in the development of the welfare state (Flora and Alber, 1984; Huber et al, 1993; Bonoli, 2001). Institutionalists point to the importance of both temporal aspects of institutional development, such as sequencing and **path dependency** (Pierson, 2004), and to the effects of different institutional configurations on policy outcomes (Bonoli, 2001). Bonoli (2001) outlines how political constitutions that concentrate power with the executive branch of government have generally been found to be associated with big welfare states, whereas more fragmented political systems, which include a greater number of **veto points**, have tended to produce smaller welfare states. Fragmented systems, such as in the USA, provide opportunities for anti-welfarist groups to block the adoption of comprehensive social policy programmes of public provision. Libertarian groups have taken advantage of these to oppose progressive welfare reforms.

The development of GSP is at least as dependent on international and global political processes as it is on those occurring within individual countries. GSP actors, however, are not necessarily institutionalised in any narrow, constitutional sense (although see Hawkins and Holden, 2016, for a discussion of how some aspects of trade and investment law can be seen as a form of **global constitutionalism**). There is no global equivalent to (liberal) parliamentary democracy. Instead, multiple GSP actors are engaged in dynamic relationships with each other, as often working outside the bureaux and boardrooms of IGOs as inside them (Yeates, 1999).

The United Nations (UN) system provides the closest thing to a structured, hierarchical system of global political institutions, with citizen representation via governments that regularly meet collectively in its General Assembly.

Otherwise, the UN encompasses a wide range of IGOs with markedly different mandates, resources and modes of operation (see **Chapter 2**, this volume). These organisations have a degree of autonomy within their specific areas of responsibility, but outcomes usually lie with governments and the bargains they may strike between them. In any case, capacity to utilise different means of influence (for example, by exercising proposal rights and veto points) is likely to reflect differences in wealth and power between governments. Fragmentation and competition between IGOs within the UN may exert a brake on the further development of GSPs, in a manner that is consistent with the thesis outlined by Bonoli and others in relation to national social policies and political constitutions.

The IMF provides a useful example of the importance of both a focus on path dependency in the historical development of institutions and of veto power, both of which privilege the USA. Many important IMF decisions require the support of 85 per cent of votes on its Executive Board. Due to the weighting of votes, initially established in 1944, the USA therefore has an effective veto. Decisions over which the USA can exercise its veto include measures to increase the number of Executive Directors and to adjust voting quotas. The USA can therefore veto measures to give developing countries more influence in the IMF and steer it in a more egalitarian direction (see also **Chapter 2**, this volume, where this point is discussed in relation to the World Bank).

Nevertheless, since the **global financial crisis** (GFC) of 2007–09, there have been signs that major global institutions have shifted their position on important social policy issues. While these shifts indicate the importance that ideas can have in GSP, they also demonstrate the continuing importance of broader economic forces and of political mobilisation in shaping GSP; the extreme growth of inequality is now seen as dysfunctional for the global economy, and may itself be seen as a cause of political discontent, manifested in the rise of both right-wing populists (Holden, 2017) and left-wing movements. However, the implementation of new social policy ideas in tangible GSPs will remain subject to the institutional constraints discussed above.

Theories of political institutions highlight the wider institutional landscape that is missed by the previous two approaches, but they do not tell us very much about the varied range of social actors involved in GSP-making and *how* they navigate this institutional landscape. Combining these three approaches to national welfare state development and applying them to GSP may help provide a more rounded explanation of the drivers and forms of GSP. However, there are some further difficulties in applying these theories to GSP. Notably, theories of national welfare state development were created primarily to understand how welfare states in high-income countries came about, whereas GSP is also concerned with low- and **middle-income countries** as well as with transnational processes that impact on welfare in a world without a centralised government or state.

## 'Welfarising' globalist social theories

Theories of national welfare state development are a good place to start thinking about the nature of GSP, but doing so leads us to realise how far GSP as a political practice is structurally different from national social policy. Globalist social theories, on the other hand, were developed to understand global processes, but they were not developed with welfare in mind. In what follows, we briefly consider what insights welfarising three types of global social theory – theories of organisational behaviour, theories of diffusion and theories of domination and exploitation – may afford for GSP.

### *Theories of organisational behaviour*

Social theories addressing how formal organisations work – their origins, structure, performance, survival and their relationships to their wider environments – are clearly of potential relevance to GSP. In principle, organisation theory can provide insights into the institutional and other characteristics of IGOs, their behaviours and interactions with other IGOs and other social actors, the effects of their wider environment(s) on IGOs, and the influence and impacts of IGOs. Relations of power, interdependence and (mutual) influence among them and how these relations change over time are all important areas of interest (see Niemann et al, 2021). From a constructivist perspective, the theoretical challenge is to explain why some IGOs are 'more meaningful' than others and to discern the conditions for IGOs' success, failure, rise and decline (see **Box 5.1**).

### Box 5.1: Realist and constructivist approaches to intergovernmental organisations

The 'realist' tradition within the academic discipline of International Relations has long regarded IGOs as 'insufficiently interesting' (Reinalda, 2009) because the main locus of power and authority in global politics is seen to reside in nation-states. In this view, IGOs are no more than the institutionalisation of relations among sovereign states – organisational forums and mechanisms that governments can use to dialogue with each other using an agreed method of communication (including provision for managing disagreements). IGOs facilitate this dialogue and execute the wishes of governments, but they do not have much independent agency from them.

The 'constructivist' tradition sees IGOs as meaningful actors in their own right (as opposed to agents of national governments). Constructivists point to how IGOs are sources of significant ideas, expertise and authority, and how they shape the behaviour of state and non-state actors. IGOs play significant roles in managing international relations, facilitating exchanges, adjudicating in dispute settlement, generating ideas, disseminating norms and enforcing them (Reinalda, 2009). They play a key role in forming global public policies and the instruments and programmes that enact them (Barnett and Finnemore, 1999, 2004).

Theories of organisations chime with institutionalist theories that see differing political institutions as significant in explaining social policy development, as well as with theories of political mobilisation insofar as formal organisations are social policy actors in their own right (as opposed to convenors of other transnational actors) embedded in wider policy and social movement networks.

For institutionalists, organisational characteristics and behaviours are of vital importance. It matters greatly, for example, whether, in the lexicon of organisational theory, an IGO's institutional 'birth characteristics' are such that its mandate and governance structure bind it to certain social policy perspectives and shore up the power of particular social actors. It matters immensely whether such characteristics enable an IGO to be agile in the face of a hostile political environment that threatens its resource or power base, or to mark out a stake in new social policy fields not originally within its scope. These 'inner–organisational' characteristics resonate with institutionalist theories of social policy change, in particular with theories of path dependency, since they help explain the long-term effects of original design features of IGOs, the difficulty or ease with which they can flex their agenda or position to survive or gain ground, and the future survival chances of the organisation – and thus its capacity to remain influential, under changing conditions (Kaasch et al, 2019).

Some neo–institutionalists suggest that an organisation's success is not only attributable to how rationally it acts (for example, how efficiently it uses its resources), but also to *how it interacts* with other organisations and its wider societal environment. Thus, an IGO may be formally mandated to make social policies, but its success as a knowledge actor and norms–shaper depends on being accepted as legitimate and how it relates to widely accepted norms and values (Kaasch et al, 2019). Such actors may include other IGOs, but the relevant universe of actors typically extends beyond them. We might conclude that if IGOs' social policies are seen to chime with widely shared norms and values prevailing at a given time, they are likely to be recognised as having valid contributions to make. An implication of this may be that IGOs need to follow meta sociocultural or political 'scripts' to be successful. This may lead, in turn, to greater standardisation, homogenisation or convergence. Sociologists term this process 'institutional isomorphism' (DiMaggio and Powell, 1983). GSP scholars might accordingly examine what sorts of isomorphic mechanisms – imitation, persuasion, coercion, or the effects of working under similar constraints – result in greater convergence (or not) among IGOs' social policy interventions.

Organisational theory tells us that *how* an IGO interacts with other actors and its environment(s) is important to becoming and remaining a meaningful actor, but what drives such interactions? Resources are a fairly obvious example (Brosig, 2011) but they come in various forms: funding, access to expertise, credibility and power. For GSP studies, a key question relating to social policy-focused IGOs is what sorts of resources are deemed most 'tradable'? The ILO and the World Health Organization (WHO), for example, are both relatively funding-poor but expertise-rich, and convey a high degree of moral authority, so they might wish to 'trade' with organisations with complementary resources. At the same time, the resources that IGOs 'trade' with others risk undermining their autonomy and/or legitimacy (Kaasch et al, 2019).

Theories of formal organisations can help explain aspects of GSP insofar as they explain the conditions under which different IGOs become and remain meaningful actors – the contexts, sources of legitimacy and mechanisms (Kaasch et al, 2019). Such theories may help surface new insights into how IGOs navigate multiple sites, structures and levels of **global social governance** and the 'inner' and 'outer' organisational relations mediating inter-IGO coordination. Some see improvements in IGOs' navigational capacities as a condition for more coherent and robust GSPs to develop and prosper.

### Theories of worldwide cultural and policy diffusion

A second set of global social theories emphasises **cultural diffusion** and **policy diffusion** on a worldwide scale. World Society theory is the pre-eminent example of an explicitly global 'take' on cultural diffusion. It 'emphasizes the importance of global institutions and culture in shaping the structure and behavior of individuals, organizations, and nation-states around the world' (McNeely, 2012). World Society theory (also known as World Polity theory, global neo-institutionalism and the Stanford school of global analysis [Boli et al, 2010]) was developed by, and remains most associated with, sociologist John W. Meyer (Meyer et al, 1997; Krücken and Drori, 2009).

World Society theory is less focused on IGOs per se than on how 'whole arrangements of organisations and roles and relations, structurally' (Meyer, 2009, p 41) come to exist. In particular, it seeks to explain the emergence and dominance of the nation-state model founded on 'global models of nationally organized progress and justice' (Meyer et al, 1997, p 174), and the organisation of the world into 'formally equal, autonomous, and expansive nation-state actors' (Meyer et al, 1997, p 174). The theoretical challenge is to explain the spread of nation-states with standard identities and structural forms in the absence of centralised systems to enforce such structures and in the presence of diverse local cultural, functional or power processes worldwide (Meyer et al, 1997, p 173). How is it that nation–states are 'more isomorphic than most theories would predict' (Meyer et al, 1997, p 174)? For World Society theorists, the answer lies in worldwide cultural and associational processes founded on universalistic definitions of justice and progress (of individualism, **universalism**, rationality, social equality, and so on).

World Society theory 'speaks' to institutionalist accounts of GSP seeking to understand how certain ideas and models become the norm. Take the example of human rights – governments instituted expansive concepts of universal and indivisible human rights, comprising social, economic, civil and political rights, in various UN treaties after the Second World War. These concepts were then incorporated into national social policies. These diffusion processes were an outcome of the prior diffusion of global cultural constructions of individualism and the acceptance that all human beings have legitimate entitlements to rights of association, decent work, appropriate education, affordable healthcare, comprehensive social security, protection from abuse, and so on. But they were also a further spur to it, and consolidated the domination of certain structural features of 'modern' nation–states (Koo and Ramirez, 2009).

A second example is education. The expansion of mass primary, secondary, tertiary and life–long education links many more people directly to 'universalistic and rationalized cultural rules' (Meyer, 2010, p 9), both entitling and obligating them to incorporate highly valued cultural attributes and values of liberal individualism (Meyer et al, 1992; Schofer and Meyer, 2005). From this perspective, education is a major social institution for socialising people into world society. Educational and knowledge–producing IGOs such as UNESCO, the OECD, the World Bank and others are channels through which such cultural constructs are re–created, reproduced and further diffused (Chabbott, 2003; Jakobi, 2009; see also **Chapter 14**, this volume).

World Society theory offers a radically different 'take' on social theories of welfare state development in that *national* welfare states and social policies are conceptualised as the outcome of *global* social processes. The worldwide spread of certain sorts of social policies involves a range of social actors (nation–states, professions, IGOs) and diffusion processes that unfold transnationally and on a worldwide scale, even if they 'touch down' in national contexts in different ways. The implication of this for GSP is profound; it means that *national* education, health, social security systems and so on can be considered first and foremost the result of *global* diffusion processes. Also, what matters theoretically is *which* cultural precepts come to dominate by virtue of being 'imagined' as universal, *which* social actors are recognised and which are not, and by *which* social processes.

As a theory of global diffusion, World Society theory does not deny differences in the specifics of how countries organise (fund, regulate, provide) their welfare states, but its main concern is isomorphic tendencies that produce degrees of standardisation, homogenisation and convergence. It also suggests an expansive definition of GSPs as encompassing national welfare states in addition to the social policies of global bureaucracies and **non–state actors**. *How GSP is constructed* is at the forefront of World Society theory – how certain actors come to be validated as legitimate partners and how certain social issues are taken up as matters of world–societal importance by global policy actors (Tag, 2013).

In terms of future development of World Society theory in GSP, Meyer's interest in education has been a key point of engagement with GSP, but there remains ample scope to investigate whether the strong degrees of homogenisation and diffusion in education occur in other sectors (see Tag, 2013, for an initial application to early childhood as a GSP issue). Such research would help test and develop Meyer's observation that 'the growing list of perceived "social problems" in the world indicates not the weakness of world–cultural institutions but their strength' (Meyer et al, 1997, p 175). Also, the processes by which certain social policy issues become seen as of world–societal significance and as matters for GSPs to redress, while others do not, is of interest.

Political science and public policy studies focusing on the international 'movement' of ideas and practices also use the concepts of diffusion, **policy transfer** and **lesson drawing** to explain why some policy ideas or models are taken up by other countries and identify the key transferring actors and mechanisms involved (Rose, 1991; Dolowitz and Marsh, 2000; Hulme, 2005). Although the initial focus of this work was on high–income countries, its usefulness for explaining policy change (or continuity) in a **multilevel governance** framework has come to the fore (Hawkins et al, 2020), as has its potential to offer insights into the complex dynamics of the global policy community, and the rise of generic agendas in education and social welfare (Hulme, 2005, p 418). Stone (2004) led the way in arguing for the integration of non–state transnational actors, networks and market mechanisms into policy transfer theory, while Haas (1990) identified the significance of transnational knowledge networks and the importance of **epistemic communities** of knowledge–based experts in diffusion processes.

The concepts of travelling and embedded policy have also become significant in global policy sociology. Such approaches have been used in GSP studies to elaborate how social policy ideas and discourses are formulated, communicated and circulated among communities of transnational and national actors. For example, Orenstein (2008) showed the existence of epistemic communities supportive of pension privatisation and how these ideas 'travelled' through global and national institutions (IGOs, policy networks, international partnerships). Many GSP studies, however, overly focus on unidirectional diffusion or travel processes resulting from interventions by IGOs and their impact on country–level social policy (Deacon et al, 1997; Deacon, 2007). Yeates (2007) argued that a productive approach is to see such global policy processes as multidirectional, involving interactions among multiple actors within multilevel governance systems in which all parts interact with each other.

## Theories of global domination and exploitation

A third set of global social theories seeks to explain structures, relations and behaviours of social actors in the global order in terms of inequality and power. World Systems theory exemplifies one such approach. Globalisation is, in this view, the 'becoming of the world–system' that has been continuously developing over thousands of years. World Systems theory is most associated with the work of Immanuel Wallerstein (1974, 2004). Wallerstein aimed to integrate the study of society, economy and polity in a globalist analysis capable of explaining the existence of transnational social or economic structures and dynamics that condition development in *all* parts of the world as well as the persistence of global social relations of inequality and underdevelopment. He traced the long–term rise of the capitalist world economy and its associated organisation of the world into core, semi–periphery and periphery zones (Chirot and Hall, 1982; Chase–Dunn and Grimes, 1995; Chase–Dunn and Hall, 1997). Unlike (most) other global social theories, World Systems theory emphasises zones and the interconnections between them, not inter–state relations among countries. World Systems theory is not a theory of capitalism per se; the world–system is the canvas on which capitalism paints.

Relations of domination and exploitation are seen in how, historically, certain countries gained control of much of the world economy, and how this global power is reflected in the dominant economic and political position of the core zone countries that sustain the under- or mal-development and exploitation of other core zone countries. For example, the socioeconomic structures and robust public institutions of core zone states enable them not only to manage internal affairs but also to influence other states, IGOs and institutions in ways that maintain their dominant position in the world. Periphery states have lesser capacities to significantly influence the world around them or build the socioeconomic infrastructures needed for development. This is not to say that the country composition of the zones cannot or does not change – mobility is possible within this hierarchical system. For example, over the last 400 years, the status of global hegemon has passed from the Netherlands to the UK to the USA.

World Systems theory shows how different parts of states can be integrated with each other across national borders. The theory notes, for example, how some cities in peripheral countries can be more economically integrated with core zone countries than with the 'hinterlands' of their own countries. Also, it provides an historically informed globalist social theory of global inequality and exploitation. In this respect, theorisations of global inequality should be seen not just as the background context of GSPs. Rather, they become vital parts of the explanation of the forms that GSPs take and of their effects. In this regard, the UN, the World Bank, the IMF and the WTO reflect the interests of core zone political powers – they institutionalise these powers' economic and trade advantages – and therefore dominance – over peripheral and semi-peripheral zones.

Where this theory really comes into its own for GSP is its attention to macro-level global political shifts that result from world–system dynamism. It is not only that states that established their dominance in the world–system early on tend to remain dominant because they control the key economic IGOs (the IMF, the World Bank, the WTO), but that countries' upward or downward mobility within the world–system, combined with their international development strategies, unleash further dynamics that impact on the politics of GSP. For example, China pursues a markedly different way of 'doing' international development aid compared with the West, one that seems to give it much influence over the development of countries in which it has invested (Urbina-Ferretjans and Surender, 2013). It remains to be seen whether China or other emerging world powers will favour a more comprehensive approach to GSP, but there are few signs of this so far. China is an interesting case in these terms because it also demonstrates that it is possible for a country to break out of the periphery.

World Systems theory may cast critical light on how core zone states' extraction of productive resources from the periphery extends to the domain of social reproduction and social services. Yeates' work on global health worker **migration** and recruitment (Yeates, 2004, 2009, 2014) showed how the dominant direction of travel is from more peripheral zones to core ones, and how this systematic 'extraction' of human resources for health and development works primarily to the benefit of countries and populations in the core zone countries. Her later work (Yeates and Pillinger, 2019) connected this dynamic of social reproduction in the world–system and the development of post-war GSPs, concluding that the multilateralisation of social policy in this area (for example, the conclusion of ILO and WHO agreements ostensibly controlling such migration and recruitment) develops alongside the intensification of health labour recruitment and migration to core zone countries.

As a theory of domination and exploitation, World Systems theory has much in common with Marxist analyses that emphasise how global relations of inequality are the outcome of capitalist social relations on a global scale. However, Marxist theories of imperialism differ in various ways and contain various critiques of World Systems theory (see, for example, Brewer, 1980). Susan Soederberg (2006) offers a Marxist interpretation of the role of **global governance** in sustaining global relations of domination and exploitation, at the apex of which sits the USA. She argues that global policies on debt relief, **corporate social responsibility** (CSR) and development assistance fail to engage with the fundamental contradictions of global capitalism, and that they normalise austere forms of capitalist expansion. In a similar vein, Robert Cox applies the Gramscian notion of hegemony to international relations (Cox, 1983, p 164). In a hegemonic order, he argues, the structure of meaning, of values and understandings, is 'relatively stable and unquestioned'; it appears as 'the natural order' of things. Such an order cannot rely on one dominant state for its survival or reproduction, but is secured by the dominant social strata of the dominant states (Gill, 1993). There are few analyses of GSPs from these perspectives (although see Cox's earlier work on the ILO, for example Cox, 1977), but their focus on social inequalities, exploitation and power asymmetries within global capitalism has clear relevance for GSP, and there is much scope to apply and develop them.

## Conclusion

The academic analysis of GSP is a field whose social–theoretical basis is still under construction. A unified theory of GSP is neither desirable nor possible given the varied questions that GSP analysts ask, but better integration of social theory into GSP studies is needed and attainable. This integration is challenging because it involves working across disparate theoretical approaches rooted in explaining national welfare state development or processes of global social change. There is significant scope for new generations of GSP scholars to take forward this theoretical development. In this context, we have highlighted an array of theoretical approaches and specific social theories that may contribute to understanding better the origins, development and forms of GSP. **Table 5.1** summarises the key features of these theories.

Social theories of GSP will in future need to ensure they reflect the perspectives, circumstances and experiences of all countries and populations of the world, especially the countries and regions of the **Global South**, if they are to avoid replicating first–world and gender biases. Among other things, this would mean foregrounding connections between higher income and lower income parts of the world, as well as between lower income ones. Similarly, the ways in which certain Southern actors are developing capabilities of their own to shape norms and policies within their own 'neighbourhoods' and beyond are important (Yeates, 2018). There is ample scope to learn from theories of imperialism and social movements, from feminist and intersectional theories, and from Development Studies, Global Public Policy and Administration, and Global Political Economy. Comparative methodologies will also be of vital importance to answering questions about how different sorts of GSP are structured and by which transnational forces, under what conditions, and with what outcomes. Similarly, comparative methodologies can help us to better understand under what circumstances formerly global social policies may become **deglobalised** – a crucial question in a period when **populist** nationalism has become globally widespread.

Table 5.1: Summary features of social theories relevant to global social policy

| | Proponent(s) | Original focus | GSP focus | GSP as … |
|---|---|---|---|---|
| **Economic development and capitalism** | Wilensky<br>Offe<br>Gough | Relationship between the economy and welfare state | Relationship between economic globalisation and GSP | The outcome of the 'needs' of globalising economies, of global capitalism |
| **Class struggle and political mobilisation** | Korpi<br>Esping-Andersen<br>Gough | How social actors, class conflict and class alliances shape the timing and forms of welfare state development | The role of transnational social and political actors in GSP formation | The outcome of worldwide social and political contestation |
| **Political institutions** | Huber, Ragin and Stevens<br>P. Pierson<br>Bonoli | The role of differing political institutions on the development of welfare states | IGOs as global institutions shaping the forms that GSP takes | The outcome of institutional structures and orientations |
| **Organisational behaviour** | Kaasch and Martens | How (international) organisations work and interact with their different environments | How IGOs become meaningful actors, cooperate with other actors, and produce social policy knowledge and norms | The social policies of international bureaucracies |
| **Cultural diffusion and policy transfer** | Meyer<br>Jakobi<br>Tag | How global diffusion of norms, ideas and political practices become deeply institutionalised in world structures; how policy ideas travel between jurisdictions | The development and diffusion of global norms, policy ideas and models shaping welfare arrangements | The outcome of the worldwide diffusion and embeddedness of global cultural norms and policy ideas; IGO GSPs as channels for diffusion processes |
| **Global domination and exploitation** | Wallerstein<br>Chase-Dunn<br>Soederberg<br>Cox | How world-level structures and relations of inequality, exploitation and imperialism shape development and underdevelopment | How core–periphery and other global relationships of power shape the forms and outcomes of GSPs | The outcome of uneven patterns of development and power within the world order (world-system) |

## Summary

- We can distinguish between theories of global social welfare/policy, social theories of GSP and normative theories that have a strong affinity to the former.
- Two different approaches to developing social theories of GSP are to 'globalise' theories of national welfare state development and to 'welfarise' globalist social theories.
- No single theory is sufficient to fully explain GSP, but blending elements of different theories may prove useful as a basis for systematic theorisation of GSP. Such blending will be a multidisciplinary endeavour.
- A unified theory of GSP is neither desirable nor possible, but better integration of social theory into GSP studies is needed and attainable.
- This integration may draw on globalist social theories beyond those discussed in this chapter, such as theories of imperialism and of social movements, and from insights from Development Studies, Public Policy and Administration, and Global Political Economy, among others.
- Such theoretical development should give priority to different forms of global social inequality and avoid replicating rich-world biases. Comparative methods will also be vital.

## Questions for discussion

- What do different theories of welfare state development offer for GSP studies? What aspects of GSP do they offer good insights into and what do they miss?
- Compare two globalist social theories in terms of the insights they potentially provide for GSP studies.

## Follow-up activities

- Read as many of the texts cited in this chapter as possible and make notes about them in relation to the 'Questions for discussion'.
- Pick a topic or issue in GSP covered in this book that most interests you and try to apply the insights of one of the theories discussed in this chapter to it. Don't worry about being comprehensive – just having a go is important. Compare your answer(s) with those from other students in a discussion group.
- Select one or two articles from the journal *Global Social Policy* to see which theoretical approaches seem to have influenced the author(s).

## Further resources

There are no further specialist resources on social theories of GSP to consult. *The global social policy reader* (Yeates and Holden, 2009) provides an excellent sample of key GSP readings, many of which are considered theoretical classics in the field.

### References

Barnett, M. and Finnemore, M. (1999) 'The politics, power, and pathologies of international organizations', *International Organization*, 53(4), 699–732.

Barnett, M. and Finnemore, M. (2004) *Rules for the world: International organizations in global politics*, Ithaca, NY: Cornell University Press.

Boli, J., Gallo-Cruz, S. and Mathias, M. (2010) 'World society, world-polity theory, and international relations', *Oxford Research Encyclopedia of International Studies*, doi:10.1093/acrefore/9780190846626.013.495.

Bonoli, G. (2001) 'Political institutions, veto points, and the process of welfare state adaptation', in P. Pierson (ed) *The new politics of the welfare state*, New York: Oxford University Press, 238–64.

Brewer, A. (1980) *Marxist theories of imperialism: A critical survey*, London: Routledge & Kegan Paul.

Brosig, M. (2011) 'Overlap and interplay between international organisations: A question of institutional design?', *Governance*, 23, 385–410.

Chabbott, C. (2003) *Constructing education for development: International organizations and education for all*, New York: Routledge/Falmer.

Chase-Dunn, C. and Grimes, P. (1995) 'World-systems analysis', *Annual Review of Sociology*, 21, 387–417.

Chase-Dunn, C. and Hall, T. (1997) *Rise and demise: Comparing world-systems*, Boulder, CO: Westview Press.

Chirot, D. and Hall, T. (1982) 'World-system theory', *Annual Review of Sociology*, 8, 81–106.

Cox, R. (1977) 'Labor and hegemony', *International Organization*, 31(3), 385–424.

Cox, R. (1983) 'Gramsci, hegemony and international relations: An essay in method', *Millennium: Journal of International Studies*, 12(2), 162–75.

Deacon, B. (2007) *Global social policy and governance*, London: SAGE Publications.

Deacon, B., with Hulse, M. and Stubbs, P. (1997) *Global social policy: International organisations and the future of welfare*, London: SAGE Publications.

DiMaggio, P.J. and Powell, W.W. (1983) 'The iron cage revisited: Institutional isomorphism and collective rationality in organizational fields', *American Sociological Review*, 48, 147–60.

Dolowitz, D. and Marsh, D. (2000) 'Learning from abroad: The role of policy transfer in contemporary policy-making', *Governance*, 13(1), 5–23.

Esping-Andersen, G. (1990) *The three worlds of welfare capitalism*, Cambridge: Polity Press.

Flora, P. and Alber, J. (1984) 'Modernization, democratization, and the development of the welfare state in Western Europe', in P. Flora and A.J. Heidenheimer (eds) *The development of the welfare state in Europe and America*, New Brunswick, NJ: Transaction Publishers, 37–80.

Gill, S. (ed) (1993) *Gramsci, historical materialism and international relations*, Cambridge: Cambridge University Press.

Gough, I. (1979) *The political economy of the welfare state*, London: Macmillan.

Haas, E. (1990) *When knowledge is power: Three models of change in international organisations*, Berkeley, CA: University of California Press.

Hawkins, B. and Holden, C. (2016) 'A corporate veto on health policy? Global constitutionalism and investor–state dispute settlement', *Journal of Health Politics, Policy and Law*, 41(5), 969–95.

Hawkins, B., Holden, C. and Mackinder, S. (2020) *The battle for standardised cigarette packaging in Europe: Multi-level governance, policy transfer and the integrated strategy of the global tobacco industry*, London: Palgrave Macmillan.

Holden, C. (2017) 'Confronting Brexit and Trump: Towards a socially progressive globalization', in J. Hudson, C. Needham and E. Heins (eds) *Social policy review 29*, Bristol: Policy Press, 63–81.

Holden, C. (2018) 'Global social policy: An application of welfare state theory', *Journal of International and Comparative Social Policy*, 34(1), 40–57.

Huber, E., Ragin, C. and Stephens, J. (1993) 'Social democracy, Christian democracy, constitutional structure and the welfare state', *American Journal of Sociology*, 99(3), 711–49.

Hulme, R. (2005) 'Policy transfer and the internationalisation of social policy', *Social Policy & Society*, 4(4), 417–25.

Jakobi, A.P. (2009) *International organizations and lifelong learning: From global agendas to policy diffusion*, Basingstoke: Palgrave Macmillan.

Kaasch, A., Koch, M. and Martens, K. (2019) 'Exploring theoretical approaches to global social policy research: Learning from international relations and inter-organisational theory', *Global Social Policy*, 19(1–2), 87–104.

Koo, J.-W. and Ramirez, F.O. (2009) 'National incorporation of human rights: Worldwide expansion of national human rights institutions, 1966–2004', *Social Forces*, 87(3), 1321–54.

Korpi, W. (1983) *The democratic class struggle*, London: Routledge & Kegan Paul.

Krücken, G. and Drori, G.S. (eds) (2009) *World society: The writings of John W. Meyer*, Oxford and New York: Oxford University Press.

McNeely, C.L. (2012) 'World society theory', *The Wiley-Blackwell Encyclopedia of Globalization*, Oxford: Oxford University Press.

Marshall, T.H. (1950) *Citizenship and social class and other essays*, Cambridge: Cambridge University Press.

Meyer, J.W. (2009) 'Reflections: Institutional theory and world society', in G. Krücken and G.S. Drori (eds) *World society: The writings of John W. Meyer*, Oxford and New York: Oxford University Press, 36–63.

Meyer, J.W. (2010) 'World society, institutional theories, and the actor', *Annual Review of Sociology*, 36, 1–20.

Meyer, J.W., Ramirez, F.O. and Soysal, Y.N. (1992) 'World expansion of mass education, 1870–1970', *Sociology of Education*, 65(2), 128–49.

Meyer, J.W., Boli, J., Thomas, G.M. and Ramirez, F.O. (1997) 'World society and the nation-state', *American Journal of Sociology*, 103(1), 144–81.

Moos, K.A. (2021) 'The political economy of state regulation: The case of the British Factory Acts', *Cambridge Journal of Economics*, 45(1), 61–84.

Muller, W. and Neususs, C. (1978) 'The "welfare state illusion" and the contradiction between wage labour and capital', in J. Holloway and S. Picciotto (eds) *State and capital: A Marxist debate*, London: Edward Arnold, 32–9.

Niemann, D., Martens, K. and Kaasch, A. (2021) 'The architecture of arguments in global social governance: Examining populations and discourses of international organizations in social policies', in K. Martens, D. Niemann and A. Kaasch (eds) *International organizations in global social governance*, Cham, Switzerland: Palgrave Macmillan, 3–27.

O'Brien, M. and Penna, S. (1998) *Theorising welfare: Enlightenment and modern society*, London: SAGE Publications.

Offe, C. (1984) *Contradictions of the welfare state*, London: Hutchinson.

Orenstein, M. (2008) *Privatizing pensions: The transnational campaign for social security reform*, Princeton, NJ: Princeton University Press.

Patomaki, H. and Teivainen, T. (2004) *A possible world: Democratic transformation of global institutions*, London: Zed Books.

Pierson, C. (2006) *Beyond the welfare state? The new political economy of welfare*, Cambridge: Polity Press.

Pierson, P. (2004) *Politics in time: History, institutions and social analysis*, Princeton, NJ: Princeton University Press.

Reinalda, B. (2009) *Routledge history of international organisations: From 1815 to the present day*, London: Routledge.

Rose, R. (1991) 'What is lesson drawing?', *Journal of Public Policy*, 11(1), 1–22.

Schofer, E. and Meyer, J.W. (2005) 'The worldwide expansion of higher education in the twentieth century', *American Sociological Review*, 70, 898–920.

Soederberg, S. (2006) *Global governance in question: Empire, class and the new common sense in managing north–south relations*, London: Pluto.

Stone, D. (2004) 'Transfer agents and global networks in the "transnationalization" of policy', *Journal of European Public Policy*, 11(3), 545–66.

Tag, M. (2013) 'The cultural construction of global social policy: Theorizing formations and transformations', *Global Social Policy*, 13(1), 24–44.

Urbina–Ferretjans, M. and Surender, R. (2013) 'Social policy in the context of new global actors: How far is China's developmental model in Africa impacting traditional donors?', *Global Social Policy*, 13(3), 261–79.

Wallerstein, I.M. (1974) *The modern world-system*, New York: Academic Press.

Wallerstein, I.M. (2004) *World-systems analysis: An introduction*, Durham, NC: Duke University Press.

Wilensky, H. (1975) *The welfare state and equality: Structural and ideological roots of public expenditure*, Berkeley, CA: University of California Press.

Yeates, N. (1999) 'Social politics and policy in an era of globalisation', *Social Policy and Administration*, 33(4), 372–93.

Yeates, N. (2002) 'Globalization and social policy: From global neoliberal hegemony to global political pluralism', *Global Social Policy*, 2(1), 69–91.

Yeates, N. (2004) 'Global care chains: Critical reflections and lines of enquiry', *International Feminist Journal of Politics*, 6(3): 369–91.

Yeates, N. (2007) 'The global and supra–national dimensions of the welfare mix', in M. Powell (ed) *Understanding the mixed economy of welfare*, Bristol: Policy Press, 199–219.

Yeates, N. (2009) *Globalizing care economies and migrant workers: Explorations in global care chains*, Basingstoke: Palgrave Macmillan.

Yeates, N. (2014) 'Global care chains: Bringing in transnational reproductive labourer households', in W. Dunaway (ed) *Gendered commodity chains: Seeing women's work and households in global production*, Stanford, CA: Stanford University Press, 175–89.

Yeates, N. (2018) *Global approaches to social policy: A survey of analytical methods*, UNRISD Working Paper 2018–2, Geneva: UNRISD (http://oro.open.ac.uk/53709).

Yeates, N. (2019) 'World-regional social governance, policy and development', in J. Midgley, R. Surender and L. Alfers (eds) *Handbook of social policy and development*, Cheltenham: Edward Elgar, 224–45.

Yeates, N. and Holden, C. (eds) (2009) *The global social policy reader*, Bristol: Policy Press.

Yeates, N. and Pillinger, J. (2019) *International health worker migration and recruitment: Global governance, politics and policy*, London: Routledge.

# 6

# Global social justice

Theo Papaioannou

## Overview

Global justice is the extension of the theory and practice of social justice to the world. It is founded on the moral and political claim that, in today's globalising world, our duties and obligations to other people extend beyond state borders. This justifies global social policies that aim at eradicating global poverty and reducing inequality. This chapter examines key debates about global justice and reviews different schools of thought. The argument put forward is that global justice is both a normative claim and an instrument of global social policy. This is clearly reflected in emerging institutions of global redistribution that are underpinned by the idea of fairness.

**Key concepts**
Global justice; poverty alleviation; reduction of inequality; international action

## Introduction

One of the strong justifications of **global social policy** (GSP) is the growing theory and practice of **global justice**. The latter is founded on the moral and political claim that, in today's globalising world, our duties and obligations to other people extend beyond state borders. This implies that if people elsewhere (in other countries) find themselves in morally disturbing conditions due to unjust outcomes of **globalisation** or the dire consequences of global diseases such as COVID-19, we are obliged to act to mitigate existing injustices and prevent further injustice. International actions cannot be only by **civil society** mobilisations and advocacy campaigns. Rather, they can also take the form of institutional actions, including policies of global social redistribution, global social regulation and global social rights. These are GSPs that respond to global injustice, including health inequity and lack of social welfare (Deacon et al, 1997).

Global justice marks the shift from a Hobbesian perspective on international political morality to a Kantian one. The latter is more **cosmopolitan** and less statist than the former (see the next section). This implies that a Kantian perspective does not presuppose sovereign power for obliging people to follow moral principles. Indeed, some commentators on global justice, such as Amartya Sen (1999), Martha C. Nussbaum (2000), Gillian Brock (2009), Charles Beitz (1999) and Thomas Pogge (2002), argue that although we have special connections with those in close relation to us, we also have relations to humanity as a whole. These relations raise the issue of our obligations to the global citizen. The question is not only what our obligations are in the abstract, but also what we can practically do to help in terms of GSPs.

The current theory and practice of global justice is overwhelmingly focused on two issues: eradication of poverty and reduction of inequality. This is not surprising since both poverty and inequality constitute barriers to any plausible conception of the good life. Eradication of poverty is not just a necessity of socially just development but a fundamental presupposition of freedom. Reduction of inequality, on the other hand, is crucial for improving human welfare and wellbeing. Poverty and inequality problems are interrelated (see also **Chapter 8**, this volume). For instance, unequal distribution of global wealth and resources pushes communities behind and/or puts them under threat from famines and diseases such as COVID-19, malaria and cholera. However, claims for redistribution are often raised in conjunction with claims for care (Robinson, 1999) and recognition (Fraser and Honneth, 2003). The latter are for achieving equality of social relations. Fraser and Honneth (2003) point out that it is philosophically defensible to integrate redistribution, recognition and care into one normative paradigm that aims to equalise relations between people. This chapter is mainly focused on redistribution as a response to global poverty and inequality. As such, global poverty and inequality raise a number of questions: what does global justice require in terms of social policies for poverty eradication and equalisation of resources? How can the global justice requirements for reduction of poverty and inequality be practically met in the absence of a global political state? How can global justice reshape GSPs?

While **Chapter 8** discusses the measurement and politics of global poverty and inequality, the aim of this chapter is to provide some initial answers to the questions above, drawing on key perspectives and debates of global justice. These will offer insights into how a combination of normative and instrumental thinking about fairness on a global scale can influence the direction of GSP and facilitate social and economic change. The chapter begins with a discussion of the globalisation of social justice and related theoretical responses. It then moves on to explain **global social justice** in terms of moral obligations and rights. Such normative arguments tend to underpin the design and implementation of GSPs of redistribution. The final two sections answer the fundamental question of how global justice can be achieved in the absence of a world-state, and conclude that this is possible through institutions of global social transfers and social protections.

## Globalising social justice

The debate on global justice is relatively recent. Until some years ago, political theory and practice were mainly preoccupied with domestic social justice within the state (see **Box 6.1**). This is not to say that there was a total lack of interest in matters of international justice. For instance, as early as 1651, Thomas Hobbes (1991), in *Leviathan*, discussed the issue of legitimate state authority and rejected the idea of justice in international affairs on the grounds that the lack of a world-state makes the moral evaluation of nation-state actions impossible. Later, in 1795, Kant (2008), in *Perpetual peace*, argued that international justice is possible even in the absence of a world-state. However, what most political theorists after Hobbes and Kant had to say about justice and what policy-makers had to do in order to justify their policies for social welfare did not extend to considerations of global justice. Even utilitarian approaches to social policy, based on the maximisation of aggregate utility and welfare, did not explicitly require that the suffering from poverty and inequality of all human beings throughout the world should be reduced or, indeed, eliminated.

---

### Box 6.1: Social justice

Social justice can be defined as a moral and political standard of how people ought to live and relate to one another within a framework of fair institutions. The modern idea of social justice emerged as a critique of the industrialisation of Western societies in the 19th century. According to Barry (2005, p 5):

> The potentially revolutionary idea underlying the concept of social justice was that the justice of society's institutions could be challenged not merely at the margins but at the core. What this meant in practice was that a challenge could be mounted to the power of the owners of capital and to the dominance of the entire market system within which capitalism was embedded.

---

Only recently has the modern idea of social justice been extended to the whole of the world due to globalisation (see **Chapter 1**, this volume). Greater flows of capital and mobility of labour between nations, as well as cutting-edge transportation systems and information and communication technologies (ICTs), have strengthened global interactions between people and institutions, giving rise to a growing literature on questions of distributive justice in global civil society and the emergence of social policies based on principles of global justice. These questions include:

- Are there universal principles of global distributive justice?
- How should global society be structured in order to address issues of global distributive justice?
- How should global social justice be achieved? Should it be through states in charge of national social policies, or should there be supra–state institutions to design and implement GSPs designed to have a significant progressive redistributive outcome? Or should it be realised by systems affecting the primary distribution of resources, rather than focusing on the secondary system of redistribution? (This latter question points to how global economic justice must be considered integral to global social justice.)

In terms of theory, proponents of global justice derive their arguments from within competing ethical perspectives. Three of them are particularly important to mention: Kantianism, utilitarianism and liberal egalitarianism. Kantianism is a deontological ethical perspective that emphasises the relationship between moral duty and human action. That is to say, human action is considered to be right (or wrong) because of its relationship to a moral duty and not because of its consequences. By contrast, utilitarianism is a consequentialist ethical perspective that emphasises maximisation of happiness and aggregate utility. Human action is therefore considered to be right (or wrong) depending on whether its consequences maximise or reduce happiness and aggregate utility. Liberal egalitarianism is the ethical perspective that combines the values of social equality and individual freedom. This implies that each individual should be given an equal opportunity to flourish, exercising both agency and responsibility. Global justice theorists such as Thomas Pogge (2002), Charles Beitz (1999), Brian Barry (1995) and Onora O'Neill (2002) reconstruct the Kantian cosmopolitan perspective. For instance, O'Neill suggests looking beyond the boundaries of state, endorsing the Kantian principle of autonomy that demands actions be based on maxims that can be **universalised**. In her view, this does not imply that we should adopt a wholly abstract or moral **cosmopolitanism**, but rather more practical and more philosophically rigorous cosmopolitanism based on basic obligations instead of goods or rights. This type of cosmopolitanism presupposes a theory of agency that is practical and identifies where precisely obligations of justice should fall (O'Neill, 2010). Agents and agencies range from individuals and government agencies to **international non–governmental organisations** (INGOs) and **transnational corporations** (TNCs) whose actions impact on the distribution of resources.

Cosmopolitans such as O'Neill try to address three fundamental questions: who should be governed by a global theory of distributive justice? What should be fairly distributed? How should goods be distributed? Addressing the first question, cosmopolitans are clear that 'the duties are owed to individuals (and not to states)' (Caney, 2005, p 105). This is not surprising since most cosmopolitans are liberal thinkers who defend a package of civil and political human rights accompanied with an egalitarian distributive programme.

Addressing the second question, cosmopolitans divide into three schools of thought:

- *Kantian cosmopolitans* (Beitz, 1999; Pogge, 2002; O'Neill, 2010) argue that what should be fairly distributed are resources.
- *Utilitarian cosmopolitans* (Singer, 2008) insist that global principles of distributive justice should be concerned with maximising utility and welfare.
- *Capability cosmopolitans* (Sen, 1999; Nussbaum, 2000) maintain that global justice should be concerned with people's capabilities to function.

Addressing the third question, cosmopolitans find themselves in disagreement as to whether goods should be distributed equally to all or according to merit or according to basic human needs. For instance, Pogge (2002) defends a 'global resource dividend' that requires that people be taxed for using natural resources and that the proceeds be spent on the global poor. This justifies GSPs of redistribution based on taxation of those who appropriate and intensively exploit natural resources. Beitz (1999), on the other hand, maintains that John Rawls' 'difference principle', according to which 'social and economic inequalities are to be arranged so that they are both (a) reasonably expected to be to everyone's advantage, and (b) attached to positions and offices open to all' (Rawls, 1972, p 60), should be extended to the global level and guide social policies for achieving social justice (see **Box 6.2**). At the global level, in order for social and economic inequalities to be to everyone's advantage, social policy interventions are required to rectify injustice in the global distribution of income and wealth that makes the least advantaged worse off. Achieving economic justice through such interventions is an integral part of global social justice.

## Box 6.2: John Rawls

The key justice thinker of the 20th century is John Rawls. In *A theory of justice* (1972) he argued for a hypothetical contract (original position) in which people agree on fundamental principles of justice as fairness behind a 'veil of ignorance', that is, in abstraction from their individual, social and economic backgrounds. These principles are the equal right to basic liberty and the so-called 'difference principle':

1. Each person has an equal right to the most extensive scheme of equal basic liberties compatible with a similar scheme of liberties for all.
2. Social and economic inequalities are to satisfy two conditions: they must be (a) to the greatest benefit of the least advantaged members of society; and (b) attached to offices and positions open to all under conditions of fair equality of opportunity. (Rawls, 1999, p 362)

In a liberal scheme of social cooperation, a distributive practice is fair or just when it satisfies the two fundamental principles that people mutually accepted in the original position.

*The law of peoples* (Rawls, 1999) is Rawls' main work on international political theory. He was concerned with the political process through which representatives of 'peoples' (the actors in the international society) determine the principles that will govern their society (Society of Peoples). This process, he argued, derives its legitimacy from a second-level original position (Rawls, 1999, p 17). Although Rawls explicitly rejects the cosmopolitan relationship between 'global' and 'domestic' political theory, Pogge (2002) and Beitz (1999) insist that a global theory of justice can only be Rawlsian in its principles. This is a rather problematic position to hold since what matters for Rawls is justice within 'peoples' societies', or at least within nationally bounded concepts of society and not the wellbeing of individuals. Indeed, his theory is primarily concerned with the basic structure of 'peoples' societies' and not with furthering the standard of living of individual people. According to Rawls (1999), the final political end of 'peoples' societies' is to become fully just and stable. This illustrates the contrast between his theory and a cosmopolitan view. Criticising the latter, he argues that:

> The ultimate concern of a cosmopolitan view is the well-being of individuals and not the justice of societies. According to that view there is still a question concerning the need for further global distribution, even after each domestic society has achieved internally just institutions. (Rawls, 1999, p 119)

Clearly, in this argument Rawls defends a theoretical and **methodological nationalism** against cosmopolitanism.

Rawls' nationalism is accompanied by a 'reasonable pluralism' that does not allow the extension of his 'difference principle' to the global level. This pluralism is founded on the 'Law of Peoples' and not on universal liberal principles of justice as fairness. Thus, at the global level, Rawls seems to prioritise legal formalism over cosmopolitanism. This is clearly illustrated in his pluralist distinction between two kinds of 'peoples': 'liberal peoples' and 'decent peoples'. The first kind is liberal and has developed constitutional regimes, while the second kind is illiberal but has respect for the rule of law. 'Liberal peoples' and 'decent peoples' constitute what Rawls calls the 'Society of Peoples' that is bound by the 'Law of Peoples'. As he explains:

> By the "Law of Peoples" I mean a particular political conception of right and justice that applies to the principles and norms of international law and practice. I shall use the term "Society of Peoples" to mean all those peoples who follow the ideals and principles of the Law of Peoples' in their mutual relations. (Rawls, 1999, p 3)

In Rawls' account, the ideals and principles of the Law of Peoples are chosen by representatives of 'liberal peoples' in a second-level original position in which 'the only alternatives for the parties to pick from … are formulations of the Law of Peoples' (Rawls, 1999, p 40).

The question, of course, is how the chosen formulation of the Law of Peoples can be applied to the world as a whole. Rawls does not provide any clear answer to that question. Instead he insists on the general Kantian position that a world government is not necessary for the application of the chosen formulation of the Law of Peoples. As he says:

> Here I follow Kant's *Perpetual peace* (1795) in thinking that a world government – by which I mean a unified political regime with legal powers normally exercised by central governments – would either be a global despotism or else would rule over a fragile empire. (Rawls, 1999, p 36)

Other critiques of cosmopolitanism take clearer positions than Rawls on how laws and principles can be applied at the global level. For instance, Thomas Nagel argues that 'the requirements of justice themselves do not … apply to the world as a whole, unless and until, as a result of historical developments … the world comes to be governed by a unified sovereign power' (Nagel, 2005, p 121). From this it follows that enforcement of obligations of global justice could only be politically legitimised in terms of a unified sovereign power. As Nagel again stresses:

> Current international rules and institutions may be the thin end of a wedge that will eventually expand to seriously dislodge the dominant sovereignty of separate nation-states, both morally and politically, but for the moment they lack something that according to the political

conception is crucial for the application and implementation of standards of justice: they are not collectively enacted and coercively imposed in the name of all individuals whose lives they affect; and they do not ask for the kind of authorization by individuals that carries with it a responsibility to treat all those individuals in some sense equally. (Nagel, 2005, p 138)

Nagel leaves the door open to the future emergence of a world-state. No matter how unrealistic this possibility may seem to be for the current **international system**, he does not rule it out for the future. In this sense, Nagel's critique of cosmopolitanism draws on historical facts with regards to global politics. If those facts change, then the application of standards of social justice at the global level might be possible.

## Box 6.3: Marxist and nationalist critiques of cosmopolitanism

Rawls' and Nagel's critiques of cosmopolitanism are certainly not the only ones. Realists, Marxists and nationalists have also developed strong arguments *against* cosmopolitanism. Specifically, Morgenthau (1985) has consistently accused idealist views of global justice as being ignorant of the role of power in international relations. In his view, power should be used to promote national interest. This is what nation-states do in the global realm – they exercise their national interests through relations with other states, trying to establish an order that serves their interests. Other thinkers such as Mason and Wheeler (1996) have also stressed that states are obliged to pursue their national interests. For 'realists' the recent 'ethical turn' to global justice cannot be divorced from questions of interests and power in so-called 'real politics' (Kiely, 2007, p 108). Marxists also accept this position, but link it to their critique of global capitalism. Thus, theorists such as Rosenberg (1994) clearly explain the power relations between dominant capitalist states such as the USA and poor developing countries. Marxists and realists identify crucial weaknesses of the contemporary theory of global justice. However, most of them remain statists in that they understand global relations in terms of extended state interests.

In fact, only nationalists have produced non-statist critiques of cosmopolitanism (see **Box 6.3** for an overview of nationalist and Marxist critiques of cosmopolitanism). For instance, thinkers such as Miller (2008) insist on the 'ethical significance' of the nation. Membership of a nation generates special obligations to compatriots. Therefore, Miller argues for the primacy of the nation rather than the state. His argument justifies policies for the social redistribution of resources and welfare to fellow nationals but not to outsiders. Miller (2008), in order to mitigate cosmopolitan critiques of his argument, tries to compromise between *ethical particularism* and *ethical universalism*. For him, these are two competing accounts of ethical thought. Ethical universalism emphasises individuals with their generic human capacities abstracting from their particular relations and ties to other individuals. By contrast, ethical particularism holds that relations and ties and commitments to individuals and groups determine ethical reasoning about justice obligations. However, Miller argues that the division between ethical universalism and ethical particularism is not necessarily rigid. According to him, 'it is possible to start from a universalist position and then to move some considerable distance to accommodate particularist concerns and vice versa' (2008, p 284). This compromise is important for accepting the basic rights of individuals who are not in close relations or ties with us.

These critiques of cosmopolitanism are powerful but not, of course, without problems. For instance, cosmopolitans such as Caney insist that Rawls' position is rather difficult to maintain. According to Caney:

> … first we might ask why "peoples" occupy this special position in his theory in contrast with every other social organisation (such as family or a religious community or a federal unit in federation)?… Second, we might question whether it is coherent to care about intra-societal justice independently of, and rather than "the well-being of individuals". (Caney, 2005, p 272)

Both questions attack Rawls' preoccupation with the basic structure of social cooperation that cannot be extended to the global level. Cosmopolitans also reply to critiques of their global politics. Thus, for instance, Held (1995, p 279) and Caney (2005, p 161) stress that there are alternatives to a 'purely statist world order' and call 'for democratically elected global and regional supra-state political authorities standing over and above states'. They also suggest that the United Nations (UN) should be reformed so that a directly elected second assembly could be developed. Finally, cosmopolitans question nationalists' 'ethnic' conception. According to them, this conception is no more plausible than the statist conception. Caney provides two reasons for this:

> First there are many relatively uncontroversial cases of nations that share no common ethnicity. To be American, for example, is not to belong to any one ethnic group…. Second, the members of an ethnic group can include members of a number of different nations. Ethnic groups, such as Jews, can and do straddle numerous nations. (Caney, 2005, p 14)

From this, cosmopolitans conclude that nationalists fail to come up with a plausible 'disanalogy argument' about the relationship between the domestic and global realms.

## Global justice, obligations and rights

So far, we have seen that the increasing interactivity and close relationship between the domestic and the global realms as well as the common nature of humanity generates moral obligations of global justice. Such obligations translate into duties and rights that are interpreted differently by competing schools of cosmopolitan thought. Thus, for Kantian cosmopolitanism, individuals are potential rights holders and duty bearers who observe universal principles of justice as fairness. Followers of John Rawls, including Beitz and Pogge, insist that under the universal application of the difference principle, those left worst off by the global distribution of income hold the right to claim fair redistribution via global institutions and social policies. In contrast, those left better off have a duty towards the former not to cooperate in imposing an unjust institutional scheme on them, but to accept policies such as taxation for the purpose of achieving justice at the global level.

Kantian cosmopolitans defend institutionalism in the sense that they consider universal rule frameworks to be important for achieving a just outcome of the scheme of global cooperation. One of these frameworks is human rights. Kantian cosmopolitans argue that rights to liberty, security, equality before the law, freedom of expression, assembly, association, adequate standard of living and self-determination concern every individual human being. For this reason, they consider the Universal Declaration of Human Rights (UDHR) to be an essential historical step towards defending global justice. According to Beitz (2008, p 156), 'Human rights are standards intended to play a regulative role for a range of actors and political circumstances of the contemporary world'. The fast globalising world fails to meet some of these standards and therefore generates injustice. According to Pogge:

> Socioeconomic rights, such as that "to a standard of living adequate for health and well-being of oneself and one's family, including food, clothing, housing, and medical care" (UDHR, Article 25), are currently, and by far, the most frequently unfulfilled human rights. (Pogge, 2008, p 358)

Although Kantian cosmopolitans provide useful clarifications to the doctrine of universal human rights, they do not necessarily specify what type of just distribution might be possibly meeting human rights requirements. Most Kantian cosmopolitans focus on resources. Resources are conceived as material productive means, and for this reason they are distinguished from welfare (Dworkin, 2002).

For a competing school of cosmopolitan thought such as utilitarianism, neither human rights nor resources are as important as maximisation of aggregate utility and social welfare. Proponents of cosmopolitan utilitarianism recognise that the current global distribution of resources produces harm. It does so by leaving millions of people in poverty and by making them unable to meet basic needs such as adequate food, shelter, clothing, clean water and sanitation. Utilitarian thinkers such as Peter Singer (2008, p 388) endorse a position according to which 'if it is in our power to prevent something bad from happening without thereby sacrificing anything of comparable moral importance, we ought, morally to do it'. This position is predominantly utilitarian because it tells us that unless the prevention of human suffering at the global level can meet the condition of non-sacrifice at domestic level, no aggregate utility or social welfare can be possibly maximised. Clearly, then, for cosmopolitan utilitarians, achieving global justice, say, through redistribution of resources to those worse off, is conditional on whether the better-off would consider such redistribution to be a sacrifice and thereby fail to maximise aggregate utility. For thinkers like Singer (2008) who take this approach to cosmopolitanism, utility is about all sentient beings throughout the world and ought to be maximised (Caney, 2005).

Utilitarians reject the 'institutional' form of cosmopolitanism, namely that 'principles of justice concern the distribution of resources within institutions and the focus of attention is on the fairness of the institution(s)' (Caney, 2012, p 135). Instead, they defend what Pogge calls 'interactive' form of cosmopolitanism, namely that 'principles of justice concern the behaviour of individuals and one has obligations to other humans independently of whether they are members of the same institutions or not' (Caney, 2012, p 135). This reasoning places importance on the consequences of individual behaviour and actions, which tend to be evaluated according to whether they contribute to human happiness and/or human wellbeing. However, as O'Neill (2010) observes, utilitarianism has been used to support incompatible courses of GSP action:

> There are those who think that it requires the rich to transfer resources to the poor until further transfer would reduce aggregate well-being.... There are others, especially various neo-Malthusian writers, who … argue that the rich should transfer nothing to the poor: they claim that transfers of resources encourage the poor to have children they cannot support and so lead to "unsustainable" population growth and, eventually, to maximal aggregate harm. (O'Neill, 2010, p 65)

Although utilitarianism raises hopes with the prospect of calculating the consequential costs and benefits of actions and policies at the global level, its instruments of calculation often lead to disagreement and disputes.

Another cosmopolitan approach that might be regarded as 'interactive' is the **capability approach**. As has been already pointed out earlier in this chapter, capability cosmopolitans such as Sen (1999) and Nussbaum (2000) are not concerned with institutions but with people's capabilities, that is, what people are actually able to do and be. For Sen (1980), capabilities is the answer to the question 'equality of what?' In his view, equality of basic human capabilities is crucial for achieving global justice. The capability approach shifts focus from both institutions and utility to the basic freedoms of people. For example, Nussbaum (2008) argues that institutions of global justice based on indicators of economic growth fail to tell us how deprived people are doing. Thus, according to her, 'women figure in the argument as people who are often unable to enjoy the fruits of a nation's general prosperity' (Nussbaum, 2008, p 598). Similarly, she criticises the utilitarian perspective because, as she says, it:

> ... proves inadequate to confront the most pressing issues of gender justice. We can only have an adequate theory of gender justice, and social justice more generally, if we are willing to make claims about fundamental entitlements that are to some extent independent preferences shaped, often, by unjust background conditions. (Nussbaum, 2008, p 598)

These claims are universal and hence claims of global justice.

The distributive objective of the capability approach is to guarantee all individuals access to the basic abilities required for the achievement of essential functionings. By doing so, no one would fall below the relevant baseline into what Sen calls a state of 'capability deprivation'. Above that baseline individuals bear responsibility for their choice of non–essential functionings. Sen (1999, p 3) argues that global justice demands:

> ... the removal of major sources of unfreedom: poverty as well as tyranny, poor economic opportunities as well as systematic deprivation, neglect of public facilities as well as intolerance or overactivity of repressive states.

For Sen, freedom is both the primary end and the principle means of the ideals of global justice and development. By focusing on what people are actually able to do and to be, he affirms both 'first-generation rights', that is, political and civil liberties, and 'second-generation rights', that is, economic and social rights.

The idea of human rights such as the idea of capabilities aims to defend freedom against coercion from illegitimate institutions (for example, undemocratic states) and/or from unjust socioeconomic conditions (for example, poverty and inequality). Nussbaum also endorses this close connection between capabilities and rights. According to her:

> Rights language ... has value because of the emphasis it places on people's choice and autonomy. The language of capabilities ... is designed to leave room for choice and to communicate the idea that there is a big difference between pushing people into functioning in ways you consider valuable and leaving the choice up to them. (Nussbaum, 2008, p 603)

Although both Sen and Nussbaum combine the capabilities approach with the language of rights, the latter thinker endorses a more specific list of capabilities than the former. This list includes 10 basic capabilities: life; bodily health; bodily integrity; senses, imagination and thought; emotions; practical reason; affiliation; other species; play; and control over one's environment. Nussbaum considers her list of basic capabilities to be open–ended and abstract. This implies basic capabilities are constantly under revision. Also, Nussbaum's list leaves enough room for contextual specification of human activities.

From this brief review of contemporary cosmopolitan perspectives of global justice obligations and rights, it is clear that there is a variety of different cosmopolitan arguments for fair distribution of resources at the global level, but that there is also an agreement that people's entitlements are independent of their culture, gender, 'race', sexuality, age, (dis)ability and nationality. Depending on whether claims for global justice are based on Kantian, utilitarian or capability perspectives, they justify different GSPs. For example, a Kantian claim for rectifying unjust inequality could justify institutional developments at a global level that would ensure that the distribution of income benefits the least advantaged people through applying the global difference principle. By contrast, a utilitarian claim could justify policies of global **social insurance** or social regulations that could have the potential to maximise global social welfare. Finally, a capability claim might justify global social transfers and other mechanisms targeting individuals and groups that suffer from capability deprivation due to global inequality.

## Achieving global justice in the absence of a world-state

Global justice and related GSPs cannot take place in an institutional vacuum. As you have seen in the second section of this chapter, the main (realist and nationalist) critiques of cosmopolitanism have been that it underplays the importance of a unified sovereign state and the role of power in international relations. To put it another way, the question is: how can obligations of global justice be enforced in the absence of a world-state? This question is as old as modern political theory; it originates from Hobbes' political writings. In *Leviathan*, Hobbes argues that there is no justice in international affairs because there is no world body that can evaluate the actions of nation-states as right or wrong.

For Hobbes, the state has legitimate authority over its members only if the latter give their consent to the former through a **social contract**. But there is no world sovereign power over its members. As Brooks (2008, p xv) points out: 'This classical "realist" understanding of international politics continues to be highly influential to this day.' Indeed, neo-realist and nationalist critiques of cosmopolitanism reconstruct Hobbesian arguments to insist that there are no obligations of global justice without world-state enforcement. However, these critiques often underplay the fact that the international sphere is governed by a variety of norms that are observed by nation-states. This implies that the international sphere is not anarchical, in the sense that it is disordered. Indeed:

> The fact that we lack a world-state does not discredit the fact of the absence of anarchy in the international sphere: we are bound by rules that member states should recognise and uphold. (Brooks, 2008, p xvi)

These include rules of global justice. Kant, in *Perpetual peace*, defended the position that, in fact, achieving global justice in the absence of a world-state is a matter of global institutions (see **Box 6.4**).

## Box 6.4: Global institutions

Already established global institutions such as the UDHR as well as organisations such as the Global Fund to Fight AIDS, Tuberculosis and Malaria and the UN agencies, including the International Monetary Fund (IMF), the World Trade Organization (WTO), the World Bank, the World Health Organization (WHO) and the International Labour Organization (ILO), may be able to deal with injustice in the global distribution of resources. But doing so requires that they can operate as just schemes of global cooperation and be guided by moral principles such as the Rawlsian difference principle. To what extent is this actually the case?

Consider how some global institutions respond to high levels of vulnerability, risk and deprivation that are deemed socially unjust within the current scheme of global cooperation. **Intergovernmental organisations** (IGOs) such as the ILO, the World Bank and UNICEF have long experience in promoting global policy schemes of **social protection** that aim to deal with unjust deprivation and vulnerabilities of people, including the poor and the marginalised. Given that global injustice is mainly the outcome of contemporary processes of globalisation (for example, various economic and financial crises due to the growing integration of trade systems and capital markets), global programmes of social protection are needed to mitigate poverty and protect individuals and households against social risks (Norton et al, 2001; see **Chapter 15**, this volume). These schemes range from tax-financed benefits, in cash or kind, to insurance programmes that cover health, environment, production and other risks. Note, however, that the ILO sets standards for these schemes and programmes and does not venture into actual provision. One exception to this was the ILO's solidarity fund, the Global Social Trust (GST). The rationale behind this initiative was to support the development of national **social security** systems through international financing. Given that only about 20 per cent of the world's population has access to formal social security, in order to meet the requirements of global justice, richer countries have the moral obligation to contribute towards the development of social security systems in poorer countries. That was exactly the objective of the ILO initiative – to request that people in richer OECD countries contribute voluntarily to a GST initiative. The resources would be transferred to developing countries, for example Ghana, to help build social protection schemes (ILO, 2007). Another example of a GSP response to morally disturbing poverty and inequality is aid. As such, aid is a tax-financed benefit. Although since 1990 global poverty at US$1.90 per day has more than halved (from 1.9 billion to about 0.7 billion), in recent years more than 120 million people each year have needed **social assistance** and protection. In 2020 nearly 168 million people needed help, and UN agencies aimed to assist about 109 million of the most vulnerable. Global aid policies required annual funding of US$28.8 billion well into the foreseeable future. Even more might be needed because of the effects of climate change, conflict and pandemics such as COVID-19 (OCHA, 2020).

In most cases, the global justice foundations of social protection schemes are either Kantian cosmopolitan (for example, rights to social protection are embedded in the UDHR) or utilitarian cosmopolitan (for example, social protection reduces harm and thereby maximises worldwide aggregate utility). Both cosmopolitan perspectives justify a holistic approach to social protection that embraces **universalism** (that is, coverage of all social groups and risks) and emphasises the moral obligation to deal with social inequality and exclusion in developed and developing countries.

But what about more specific issues, which, even though related to poverty and economic inequality, go beyond that to threaten basic human rights such as health? One of them is the issue of unjust inequality in the generation and diffusion of global health goods, such as essential medicines, new drugs, therapies, vaccines, and so on. Again, here cosmopolitans offer institutional proposals and mechanisms for addressing the issues. By doing so, they believe that global justice-founded social policies can shape political, social and economic relations in terms of fairness. Take, for example, Pogge (2005). He offers an institutional proposal of a Health Impact Fund (HIF) that aims to address two aspects of current injustice in global health: the lack of equal access to essential medicines and the failure to develop innovative drugs for the poor (see **Box 6.5**). These aspects are due to the problem of lack of market demand for such innovations in low-income countries (Prahalad, 2005). To put it another way, given their low income, people in these countries are unable to buy expensive drugs and therapies, and therefore market demand for them remains low. Often the high price of pharmaceutical innovations is due to the intellectual property rights (IPRs) of big pharmaceutical companies. IPRs include patents, trade secrets and other regulations that enable innovative companies to privately own the information about their innovations and therefore set prices high. This is a huge problem for GSP in the area of health because it undermines universal access to healthcare (see **Chapter 13**, this volume).

## Box 6.5: Health Impact Fund (HIF)

As a solution to the problem of global health innovation, Pogge proposes an alternative IPR system (what he calls a 'Patent 2 option') that operates in parallel to the current IPR system (what he calls a 'Patent 1 option'), and that requires innovators to make public all information about their innovation, but that makes them eligible for reward from an international HIF in proportion to the positive impact of their innovation on increasing health and decreasing poverty. According to Hollis and Pogge:

> To be eligible to register a product under the HIF reward scheme, a company must hold a patent (on the product) from one of a set of patent offices specified by the HIF. It can then register its product with HIF and will then be rewarded on the basis of the product's global health impact in its first ten years following marketing approval. (2008, p 9)

## Box 6.6: A Global Institute for Justice in Innovation (GIJI)

A competing cosmopolitan proposal for dealing with injustice in global innovation comes from Buchanan et al (2011) who also propose a new global institution – a Global Institute for Justice in Innovation (GIJI). However, unlike Pogge, their concern lies with impediments to the diffusion of industrial innovation in general, and not just with health. Indeed, they are concerned that important innovations for GSP and sustainable futures, including health, are not diffused fast and equally enough, creating injustices in the world. Therefore, they propose 'to modify the IPR regime in a way that preserves its valuable functions while remedying or at least significantly ameliorating its institutional failures' (Buchanan et al, 2011, p 314). Specifically, they argue that the GIJI would be an organisation designed to construct and implement a set of rules and policies governing the just diffusion of innovations. This organisation would be similar to the WTO and would:

> ... encourage the creation of useful innovations, for example through prizes and grants for justice-promoting innovations and through offering extended patent life for innovations that have a positive impact on justice. But its major efforts would be directed toward the wider and faster diffusion of innovations in order to ameliorate extreme deprivations and reduce their negative impact on basic political and economic inequalities. (Buchanan et al, 2011, p 9)

Buchanan et al (2011) insist that the most important asset of GIJI would be the 'licensing option', that is, the option to authorise compulsory licensing of slowly diffusing innovations. Another asset would be the 'compensation option' through GIJI and not through royalties from the sales of licensed products.

Both proposals (**Boxes 6.5** and **6.6**) constitute examples of (direct and indirect) GSP because they promote redistribution of global resources, for example health innovation in order to rectify global social injustice. However, they are predominantly institutional and demonstrate how cosmopolitans put into practice their theories of global justice. Hollis and Pogge (2008) and Buchanan et al (2011) make a series of assumptions about their proposals. The former assume that innovators such as big pharmaceutical companies would voluntarily invoke the 'Patent 2 option'. In contrast, the latter assume that GIJI would receive political support to become a legitimate global institution. However, both assumptions might be invalid, given that it is neither certain that innovators would support HIF's 'Patent 2 option' nor that powerful nation–states (such as the USA and China) would support GIJI's compulsory licensing authority. GSP can derive justification from global justice principles but cannot be based on invalid assumptions about the global institutional structure. Otherwise it would remain just a theoretical possibility without practical implications or benefits for the lives of disadvantaged people.

## Conclusion

Global justice is not just an abstract ideal. Rather, it is a concrete concept with both instrumental and **normative power** that can justify GSP. Although cosmopolitan theorists provide different answers to questions of what and how goods should be fairly distributed and redistributed, they all agree that it is humans and their societies who should be governed by principles of global justice. For them, state borders are not of moral importance. Cosmopolitans call into question the historically developed dichotomy between moral principles appropriate to the domestic realm and those appropriate to the global realm (Caney, 2005). It is the negation of this dichotomy that justifies the development of global institutions in charge of design and implementation of social redistributive policies. However, global justice and related social policies must not be uncritically cosmopolitan. Whether Kantian, utilitarian or capability cosmopolitanism, there are weaknesses that have been exposed to a great extent by Marxists and realists. Global justice must take on board these critiques, but remain a normative and instrumental approach to GSP. In any case, global justice and related social policies require universality in order to be valid.

## Summary

- Extending social justice to the global realm results from globalisation processes and the increasing interactions between people and institutions worldwide. Global social justice demands addressing issues such as poverty and inequality in terms of fairness, leading to morally acceptable outcomes of global cooperation.
- There are competing schools of thought in the area of global justice. Within cosmopolitanism one can include Kantian, utilitarian and capability approaches to global justice obligations and rights.
- The growing theory and practice of global justice provides strong justification for GSPs. Whether such policies focus on redistribution of resources, welfare or capabilities is due to competing theoretical approaches. Different approaches to global justice tend to justify different GSPs.
- Achieving global justice does not necessarily presuppose the existence of a world-state. Proponents of global justice rely on global institutions to deliver social policies that successfully address issues of unfair distribution of resources and unequal treatment of people.

## Questions for discussion

- Why is it necessary to extend social justice from the domestic realm to the global realm?
- What do you think should be fairly distributed in the global realm? Resources, welfare, capabilities, or something else?
- Why do realists and nationalists raise the issue of the absence of a unified sovereign power in the global realm as an objection to the idea of global social justice? How important is addressing this issue for delivering GSP?

## Follow-up activities

- Take a closer look at the arguments of Kantian and utilitarian cosmopolitans. What are their differences?
- Think of a global justice issue, such as the unequal distribution of vaccines for combating COVID-19. What theory would you use to make sense of this issue? What GSPs would your theory justify for addressing it?

## Further resources

Caney (2005) and Brooks (2008) both provide good detailed introductions to global social justice. Another source on the idea of social justice in the global age is Cramme and Diamond (2009). Finally, Yeates (2022) provides a short introduction to globalisation, international organisations and social policy, in which she briefly considers what it might mean to globalise social justice.

**References**

Barry B. (1995) *Justice as impartiality: A treatise on social justice*, Vol II, Oxford: Oxford University Press.

Barry, B. (2005) *Why social justice matters*, Cambridge: Polity Press.

Beitz, C. (1999) *Political theory and international relations*, Princeton, NJ: Princeton University Press.

Beitz, C. (2008) 'Human rights as a common concern', in T. Brooks (ed) *The global justice reader*, Oxford: Blackwell, 145–66.

Brock, G. (2009) *Global social justice: A cosmopolitan account*, Oxford: Oxford University Press.

Brooks, T. (2008) 'Introduction', in T. Brooks (ed) *The global justice reader*, Oxford: Blackwell, xii–xxii.

Buchanan, A., Cole, T. and Keohane, R.O. (2011) 'Justice in the diffusion of innovation', *The Journal of Political Philosophy*, 19(3), 306–32.

Caney, S. (2005) *Justice beyond borders: A global political theory*, Oxford: Oxford University Press.

Caney, S. (2012) 'International distributive justice', in G.W. Brown and D. Held (eds) *The cosmopolitan reader*, Cambridge: Polity Press, 134–47.

Cramme, O. and Diamond, P. (eds) (2009) *Social justice in the global age*, Cambridge: Polity Press.

Deacon, B., Hulse, M. and Stubbs, P. (1997) *International organisations and the future of social policy*, London: SAGE Publications.

Dworkin, R. (2002) *Sovereign virtue: The theory and practice of equality*, Cambridge, MA: Harvard University Press.

Fraser, N. and Honneth, A. (2003) *Redistribution or recognition? A political-philosophical exchange*, London and New York: Verso.

Held, D. (1995) *Democracy and the global order: From modern state to cosmopolitan governance*, Cambridge: Polity Press.

Hobbes, T. (1991 [1651]) *Leviathan*, Cambridge: Cambridge University Press.

Hollis, A. and Pogge, T. (2008) 'Health Impact Fund: Making new medicines accessible for all' (https://healthimpactfund.org/pdf/hif_book.pdf).

ILO (International Labour Organization) (2007) *Progress evaluation of the Global Social Trust pilot project*, Geneva: ILO Governing Body (www.ilo.org/wcmsp5/groups/public/---ed_norm/---relconf/documents/meetingdocument/wcms_084171.pdf).

Kant, I. (2008 [1795]) '*Perpetual peace*', in T. Brooks (ed) *The global justice reader*, Oxford: Blackwell Publishing, 319–31.

Kiely, R. (2007) *The new political economy of development: Globalisation, imperialism and development*, Basingstoke and New York: Palgrave Macmillan.

Mason, A. and Wheeler, N. (1996) 'Realist objections to humanitarian intervention', in B. Holden (ed) *The ethical dimensions of global change*, London: Macmillan, 94–110.

Miller, D. (2008) 'The ethics of nationality', in T. Brooks (ed) *The global justice reader*, Oxford: Blackwell Publishing, 284–305.

Morgenthau, H.J. (1985) *Politics among nations: The struggle for power and peace*, New York: Alfred Knopf.

Nagel, T. (2005) 'The problem of global justice', *Philosophy and Public Affairs*, 33(2), 113–47.

Norton, A., Conway, T. and Foster, M. (2001) *Social protection concepts and approaches: Implications for policy and practice in international development*, Working Paper 143, ODI (https://gsdrc.org/document-library/social-protection-concepts-and-approaches-implications-for-policy-and-practice-in-international-development).

Nussbaum, M. (2000) *Women and human development: The capabilities approach*, Cambridge: Cambridge University Press.

Nussbaum, M. (2008) 'Capabilities as fundamental entitlements: Sen and social justice', in T. Brooks (ed) *The global justice reader*, Oxford: Blackwell Publishing, 598–614.

OCHA (United Nations Office for the Coordination of Humanitarian Affairs) (2020) *Global humanitarian overview 2020* (www.unocha.org/global-humanitarian-overview-2020).

O'Neill, O. (2002) 'Public health or clinical ethics: Thinking beyond borders', *Ethics and International Affairs*, 16(2), 35–45.

O'Neill, O. (2010) 'A Kantian approach to transnational justice', in G.W. Brown and D. Held (eds) *The cosmopolitan reader*, Cambridge: Polity Press, 61–80.

Pogge, T. (2002) *World poverty and human rights: Cosmopolitan responsibilities and reforms*, Cambridge: Polity Press.

Pogge, T. (2005) 'Human rights and global health: A research programme', *Metaphilosophy*, 36, 182–209.

Pogge, T. (2008) 'Moral universalism and global economic justice', in T. Brooks (ed) *The global justice reader*, Oxford: Blackwell Publishing, 358–81.

Prahalad, C.K. (2005) *The fortune of the bottom of the pyramid: Eradicating poverty through profits*, Upper Saddle River, NY: Pearson Education/Wharton School Publishing.

Rawls, J. (1972) *A theory of justice*, Oxford: Oxford University Press.

Rawls, J. (1999) *The law of peoples*, Cambridge, MA: Harvard University Press.

Robinson, F. (1999) *Globalising care: Ethics, feminist theory, and international relations*, New York and London: Routledge.

Rosenberg, J. (1994) *The empire of civil society*, London: Verso.

Sen, A. (1980) 'Equality of what?', *McMurrin S. Tanner lectures on human values*, Vol 1, Cambridge: Cambridge University Press.

Sen, A. (1999) *Development as freedom*, Oxford: Oxford University Press.

Singer, P. (2008) 'Famine, affluence, and morality', in T. Brooks (ed) *The global justice reader*, Oxford: Blackwell Publishing, 387–96.

Yeates, N. (2022) 'Globalism, international organisations and social policy', in P. Alcock, T. Haux, V. McCall and M. May (eds) *The student's companion to social policy* (6th edn), Oxford: Wiley-Blackwell.

# Part Two
## Cross-cutting policy fields and issues

# 7

# Global climate justice

Carolyn Snell

## Overview

The substantial threat to human life posed by climate change, the inherent social and economic inequalities associated with its causes and effects, and the challenges of collective policy action to address a truly global policy problem all make climate change an important issue for global social policy scholars. The chapter starts by briefly outlining the main concerns raised by social policy scholars. Then, using the concept of climate justice as a framing device, the chapter considers how the harmful effects of climate change tend to be felt most by communities, countries and populations that have contributed the least to the problem. The chapter then explores how questions of justice pervade the global policy-making process, leading to heated debates about which countries should be required to act, when and how. The chapter then considers how issues of climate injustice are also present as global-level agreements are implemented, exploring the claim that some of these processes are overly Western in outlook. Ways to address these injustices are considered, with an emphasis placed on the value of procedural and recognition justice. The chapter concludes by expressing concerns about current levels of action at the global level and the impact of the global COVID-19 pandemic. It also highlights the potential of the burgeoning climate movement.

**Key concepts**
Climate justice; climate change; global policy regime; climate policy

## Introduction

Increased awareness of, and alarm about, climate change gained momentum during the 1980s in tandem with the growth of green politics, political parties and policy agendas that emerged in the 1960s, which, among other things, conceptualised the world as a single ecosystem (Snell and Haq, 2013). While concerns about a changing climate were in part related to broader claims about the inherent value of the natural world, they were also increasingly related to a realisation about detrimental human impacts. As a policy problem, climate change is understood throughout the academic and policy community as being both global in scope and unprecedented in scale (UN, 2020). It is described by the United Nations (UN) as 'the defining issue of our time' (UN, 2020), with multiple risks to human life, including: 'shifting weather patterns that threaten food production [and] rising sea levels that increase the risk of catastrophic flooding' (UN, 2020). The most recent evidence on climate change from the fifth report of the International Panel on Climate Change (IPCC) (IPCC, 2018a, pp 6–8) highlights current and future risks to human life, occurring globally, with 'severe, pervasive, and irreversible' impacts that will occur without 'substantial and sustained' policy action.

Given these issues, climate change has been characterised as a 'wicked' policy problem (Cahill, 2001) that is 'truly complex and diabolical' (Steffen, 2011, cited in Gough, 2011) and 'big, global, long term, persistent and uncertain' (Stern, 2007, p 25). While most nations agree in principle that there is a need for global collective action (cf UNFCCC, 2020a), beyond this, there is far less agreement of what sort of action is needed, with much controversy over the action each nation should be required to take. As a result, despite the desperate need for global collective action, it is often difficult to secure meaningful global-level policy agreement.

Within the field of social policy a body of work slowly emerged during the late 1980s that considered the relationship between social and environmental policy issues. In the 1990s these debates were brought to the foreground by Huby (1998) and Cahill (2001), and more recently by Gough (2011, 2013a, b, 2014, 2015a, b), Fitzpatrick (2011), the United Nations Research Institute for Social Development (UNRISD) (2016), Banks et al (2014), and Nordensvard (2017). More specifically, Gough (2013a, b, 2014) has provided the most expansive argument to link climate change and **global social policy** (GSP) in both conceptual and empirical terms, highlighting the impact of climate change on human welfare and the new forms of 'distributional conflict' that have emerged in terms of who feels the effects of climate change and also who is required to pay to address these (Gough, 2014, pp 119–28). Furthermore, Gough led the way in terms of analysis of the institutions responsible for GSP and climate change, and, alongside UNRISD (2016), has discussed the potential of an 'eco-social policy' that integrates social and environmental concerns more coherently.

One central concern that links scholars of global climate policy and social policy is that of justice (see **Chapter 6**, this volume). Environmental and social theorists think about justice in quite different ways, and there is some way to go in incorporating environmentalism into theories of **global social justice**. From the perspective of this chapter, the justice frame provides a powerful analytic tool, allowing the impacts of both climate change and climate policy to be understood through a critical lens, offering insight into the global–level climate policy process and an understanding of policy failure. This chapter draws on the concept of climate (in)justice to critically assess the state of global climate policy.

## Climate science and climate change

The IPCC was established by the United Nations Environment Programme (UNEP) and the World Meteorological Organization (WMO) in 1988, and was endorsed by the UN General Assembly (UNGA) (IPCC, 2018b). An organisation described as 'unique and important' by Gough (2013a, p 194), its role is to assess the scientific evidence on climate change, its potential impacts and options for mitigation and adaptation (IPCC, 2018a). The most recent evidence from the IPCC identifies the causes of anthropogenic climate change (see **Box 7.1**).

---

### Box 7.1: The causes of anthropogenic climate change

The causes of climate change related to human activity are summarily set out by the IPCC in the following extract:

> Anthropogenic greenhouse gas emissions have increased since the pre-industrial era, driven largely by economic and population growth, and are now higher than ever. This has led to atmospheric concentrations of carbon dioxide, methane and nitrous oxide that are unprecedented in at least the last 800,000 years. Their effects, together with those of other anthropogenic drivers, have been detected throughout the climate system and are extremely likely to have been the dominant cause of the observed warming since the mid-20th century. (IPCC, 2018a, p 4)

---

The WMO (2020) identifies the breadth of areas of human life where climate-related events are already posing a threat, highlighting impacts on: health, food, water security, human security, livelihoods, economies, infrastructures and bio-diversity (see **Table 7.1**; see also **Chapter 12**, this volume).

When considering future impacts of climate change, scientists usually present a range of possible outcomes in order to take account of different scenarios (including successful policy interventions). Current scientific understanding is that:

> … human activities are estimated to have caused approximately 1.0C of global warming above pre industrial levels, with a likely range of

.08C–1.2C. Global warming is likely to reach 1.5C between 2030 and 2050 if it continues at the current rate. (IPCC, 2018a, p 4)

**Box 7.2** indicates the risks and/or impacts of an increase in global temperatures of 1–2 degrees. The infographic provides a stark indication of the future impacts of climate change (flooding, displacement, food insecurity, heat–related deaths, economic), even where temperature increases are limited to 1.5 degrees.

In broad terms, policy responses focus on mitigation (taking steps to reduce or prevent greenhouse gas [GHG] emissions) and adaptation (finding ways to live with climate change) (IPCC, 2014). The terms **decarbonisation** and the 'transition to a low/zero carbon economy' are increasingly common during discussions about mitigation. The extent of action necessary in order to limit warming to 2 degrees requires action throughout 'all sectors of all countries, with an aim for deep decarbonisation with the goal of reaching zero emissions' (Åhman et al, 2017, p 635). Decarbonisation requires widespread changes across the economy. While some systems such as zero–emission energy technologies are relatively well developed (for example, renewable energy sources), others, for example the cement industry, are harder to address (Åhman et al, 2017, p 635). Decarbonisation of the electricity sector has been central to most industrialised countries' transition to a **low carbon economy** given its high share of emissions,

*Table 7.1: Social impacts of climate change*

| Threats | Cause of threat |
| --- | --- |
| Health | Heat-related illness and death; injury/loss of life associated with severe weather events; vector-borne/water-borne diseases; exacerbation of cardiovascular/respiratory diseases through air pollution; mental trauma from displacement/loss of livelihoods and property |
| Food and water security | Climate variability and extreme weather are drivers of a rise in global hunger |
| | Losses to crops and livestock as a result of flooding and drought. Soil degradation with impacts on crop productivity. Impacts on fisheries as a result of increased temperatures and salinity |
| Loss of property, security and livelihoods | Loss of agricultural livelihoods |
| | Internal disaster displacements between January and June 2019 (close to 22 million in total for 2019). Displacement across borders also occurs, and may be interrelated with other reasons for migration, for example conflict. The Lake Chad region has seen movement of millions of people across borders due to environmental deterioration, water scarcity and mismanagement, population increase, scarce resources and conflict |

Source: Author's adaptation from WMO (2020, pp 27–32)

# Box 7.2: Risks and/or impacts of a 1.5–2 degree temperature increase

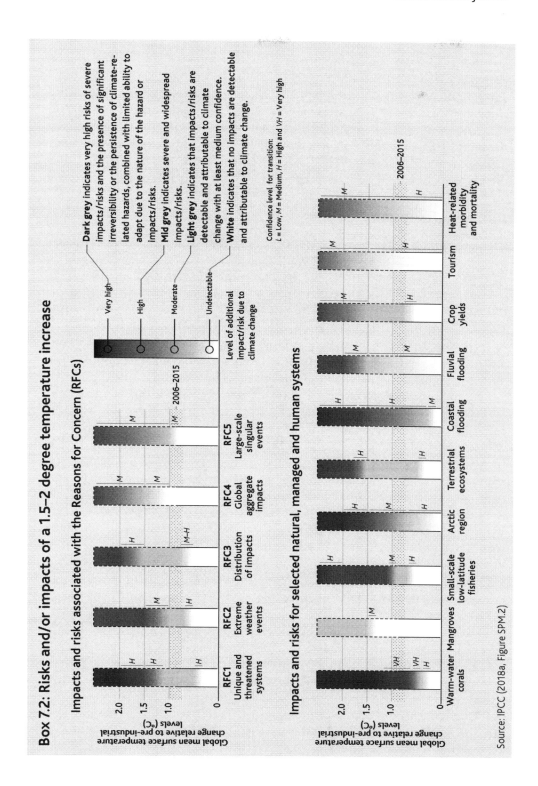

Source: IPCC (2018a, Figure SPM.2)

and the existence of alternative power generation sources and technology (for example, renewables) (Fankhauser, 2012, p 10).

While there is general agreement that these are two key ways of addressing climate change, this is where the consensus ends. The 'diabolical policy problem' of climate change is fraught with debates about who should be required to take the most stringent mitigation measures, and how both low-carbon development and adaptive measures should be funded. These debates are often framed using the language of justice, and this is considered in the next section.

## Climate change and justice

The term **climate justice** has a broad use and application. Its concerns reflect two key groups: the grassroots environmental justice movement that emerged in the 1970s linked to the civil rights movement in the USA, and, more recently, the work of elite environmental non-governmental organisations working on the international stage to influence policy-makers (Schlosberg and Collins, 2014; Jenkins, 2018; Tokar, 2018). As a result, discussions of climate justice are often broad in scope and can vary substantially in terms of aims and ambition, ranging from a rejection of capitalism and big business through to more pragmatic approaches aiming to reform existing policy and practice (Schlosberg and Collins, 2014).

At their broadest, concerns of climate justice reflect many of the moral and political questions of global social justice raised in **Chapter 6**. However, historically there has been limited interface between discourses of social justice and climate justice (see Banks et al, 2014, p 16, for details). Despite this, it is important to note that the principles of intergenerational equity, intragenerational equity, common but differentiated responsibilities, **gender equality** and participation were, and remain at the time of writing, central concepts of the original global-level environmental agreements of the early 1990s (Baker, 2006), and, implicit within each of these, are ideas of fairness and equity (see Pauw et al, 2014). As such, the core issues raised by climate justice are:

- That the nations or populations feeling the effects of climate change most keenly are often not those contributing towards the problem (Roberts and Parks, 2006, p 7).
- That future generations may feel the effects of climate change despite having contributed little to the problem (intergenerational equity) (see Caney, 2005).
- How GHG emissions might be reduced and vulnerable populations protected in the fairest way (Roberts and Parks, 2006, p 7).

Aside from the issue of **distributional justice**, most discussions of climate justice also consider notions of **procedural justice**, for example, stressing the importance of working with communities rather than imposing policy interventions on them (Robinson and Shine, 2018). Some approaches go further, highlighting the idea of **recognition justice**, on the basis that: 'climate justice requires considerations beyond the fair distribution of rights and responsibilities or the procedural requirements for participation and access to decision making ... it also entails recognising existing forms of inequality and how climate change actions exacerbate or entrench underlying structural disadvantages' (Chu and Michael, 2019, p 141).

This chapter considers issues of injustice in the broadest understanding and use of the term considering:

• issues of global-level distributive (in)justice;
• concerns of equity and justice within global climate policy-making;
• issues of distributional, procedural and recognition justice in the implementation of global climate policy.

These points are addressed over the course of the remaining sections.

## Issues of distributional injustice at the global scale

### Unequal emissions across time and space?

Historically, Organisation for Economic Co-operation and Development (OECD) countries have had both the highest overall emissions as well as the highest per capita emissions (see **Figure 7.1**). Conversely, the poorest countries, especially those in Africa, have had the lowest overall and per capita emissions. However, in some regions there have been substantial increases in GHG emissions over the past two decades, especially in Asia.

Between 2005 and 2015 India and China increased their emissions (compared to the EU28 and USA, which saw reductions), and in 2006 China overtook the USA as the greatest producer of $CO_2$ (Levine and Aden, 2008). While these increases can, in part, be attributed to rapid industrialisation and urbanisation (Levine and Aden, 2008; Zheng et al, 2019), they are also attributed to a shift in production patterns, with emissions embodied in international trade being said to account for more than 20 per cent of global emissions (Mi et al, 2018). For example, in 2015, OECD countries were found to be net importers of embodied carbon, and non-OECD countries were generally found to be net exporters (OECD, 2019). Data from 2012 found China to be the largest contributor to $CO_2$ emission flows from developing to developed countries (Mi et al, 2018, p 4309, citing Peters et al, 2012), with the authors voicing concerns that as China takes action to reduce its emissions, other developing countries with low wages and large labour forces will 'vi[e] ... to replace China as the world's factory' (Mi et al, 2018, pp 4316–17).

*Figure 7.1: Emissions over time and space*

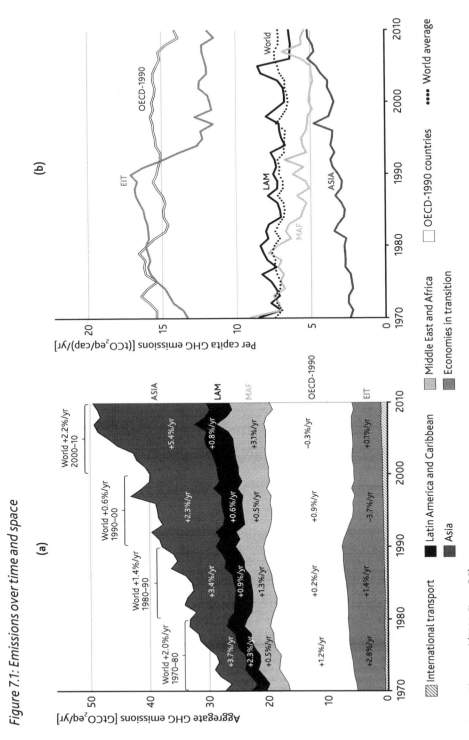

Source: Blanco et al (2014, Figure 5.2)

## Unequal impacts of climate change

As indicated, climate change and climate-related events are already posing a risk to human life. There is a substantial evidence base that indicates that the impacts of climate change are felt unequally by both populations and nations (UNFCCC, 2020a). For example, the UN's Office of the High Representative for the least developed countries (LeDC), landlocked developing countries (LaDC) and small island developing states (SIDS) (UN-OHRLLS) highlights the current and potential impact of climate change on these three groups of countries with a combined population of around 1.1 billion: 'They face intricate and multiple challenges related to structural issues and geographical disadvantage.... In 2016, the 15 countries with the highest levels of vulnerability to natural hazards were either [LeDCs], [LaDCs] or SIDS' (IOM, 2019, p v).

For the LeDCs,

> … limited productive capacity, lack of economic diversification, inadequate infrastructure and public services, stagnant trade and investment, and limited institutional capacity … makes them more vulnerable to systemic shocks including economic crises, commodity price volatility, health epidemics, natural hazards and environmental shocks. (IOM, 2019, p 4)

These factors make it harder for a country to manage problems directly associated with climate change, such as drought or food insecurity. For example, the WMO suggests that climate variability and extreme weather are among the drivers of a rise in global hunger, something that is felt most acutely in Sub-Saharan Africa (WMO, 2020, p 29).

Furthermore, these factors may also make it harder for LeDCs to deal with the knock-on effects of climate change, for example displaced internal migrants, and increased levels of conflict over natural resources such as that occurring in some West and Central African LeDCs (IOM, 2019). The Lake Chad region has seen the movement of millions of people across borders due to environmental deterioration, water scarcity and mismanagement, population increase, scarce resources and conflict (WMO, 2020, p 30). Here, climate change is described as a 'threat multiplier', where the lack of food security and threat to livelihoods can act as a driver for 'membership of armed groups' and 'insurgent activity', which is, in turn, linked to even more rapid environmental damage (UNODC, 2019).

While certain regions and nations are vulnerable to the impacts of climate change, so, too, are particular populations and groupings of people, regardless of where they live. The World Health Organization (WHO) lists some of the most vulnerable groups as:

- People living in ... other coastal regions, megacities, and mountainous and polar regions.
- Children, especially those in poor countries.
- Elderly people and those with infirmities or pre-existing medical conditions.
- Areas with weak health infrastructure – mostly in developing countries who will be the least able to cope without assistance to prepare and respond (WHO, 2018).

For many (for example, Roberts and Park, 2006; Gough, 2013b; Robinson and Shine, 2018), these distributional inequalities embody the issue of climate injustice. For Mary Robinson (former President of Ireland, Chair of the Elders), a move from climate injustice to climate justice 'insists on a shift from a discourse on greenhouse gases and melting ice caps into a civil rights movement with the people and communities most vulnerable to climate impacts at its heart' (UN, 2019a). These issues sit at the heart of climate politics and negotiations.

## Justice in decision-making? The development of a global climate policy

Climate change is, by nature, a GSP problem that requires a global, coordinated response. There have been a number of key events that have shaped the development of global climate policy, starting with the establishment of the IPCC by UNEP/WMO in 1988. Following this, one of the most notable events was the ground-breaking Rio Earth Summit in 1992, which was attended by 172 nations, including many heads of state. One of its major outputs was the United Nations Framework Convention on Climate Change (UNFCCC), which laid out the legal structure for global cooperation on climate change (Selin and Najam, 2015; see also UNFCCC, 2020a). As such, the work of UNEP/WMO and the Rio Earth Summit made way for a number of institutions that take an active role in the **governance** of global climate policy (see **Table 7.2**). **Table 7.3** outlines some of the key milestones associated with climate policy.

The parties to the UNFCCC, the Conference of the Parties (COP), have met annually since 1995 in their capacity as the 'supreme decision-making body of the UNFCCC' (UNFCCC, 2020b). In 1997, the Kyoto Protocol, which set out legally binding emission reduction targets for developed countries ('Annex 1, countries'), was agreed, coming into force in 2005 with the commitment period running between 2008 and 2012. While the term 'climate justice' was not used within the wording of the Kyoto Protocol, it embodied its concerns. The Protocol required developed countries to take action in recognition that collectively these countries had had the longest and greatest contribution to the problem, in line with one of the key principles outlined in the 1992 UNFCCC treaty – *common but differentiated responsibilities* – recognising the different capacities and responsibilities

*Table 7.2: Main climate policy-related institutions*

| Institution | Global climate policy |
| --- | --- |
| UN – multilateral | United Nations Environment Programme (UNEP), United Nations Framework Convention on Climate Change (UNFCCC), Conference of the Parties (COP) |
| Bretton Woods institutions and WTO | UNFCCC adapts to World Trade Organization (WTO) trading regime |
| Country groupings | G7, G77, BASIC (Brazil, South Africa, China, India) group, European Union (EU) |
| Business interests | Cooperation Council for the Arab States of the Gulf Brown business, green business |
| Other non-state actors | International non-governmental organisations (INGOs), global campaigns, green parties |
| Scientific bodies | Independent Panel on Climate Change (IPCC) |

Source: Adapted from Gough (2013a, p 195) and IPCC (2010)

*Table 7.3: Significant global climate policy milestones*

| Date | Event |
| --- | --- |
| 1988 | IPCC is set up |
| 1992 | UNFCCC is adopted at the Rio Earth Summit |
| 1997 | Kyoto Protocol: the world's first GHG emissions reduction treaty. Emphasis on 'common but differentiated responsibilities' |
| 2009 | COP15 results in the Copenhagen Accord. This endorsed the extension of the Kyoto Protocol and represents an informal agreement between the USA, China, India, Brazil and South Africa. The Green Climate Fund (GCF) is proposed |
| 2010 | COP16 leads to the Cancun Agreement. This establishes the Green Climate Fund (with 84 partners) for projects in developing countries. It is adopted the following year in Durban at COP17 |
| 2012 | COP18 leads to the Doha Amendment to the Kyoto Protocol, establishing a second commitment period (2013–20) |
| 2015 | COP21 leads to the Paris Agreement, which is adopted by 197 nations, including the USA. Ratified in 2016 following 55 signatories. All parties are to put forward their 'best efforts' through voluntary 'nationally determined contributions' |
| 2018 | COP24 Katowice 54 countries signed the 'Just Transition Declaration' |

Source: Author's adaptation from: BBC News (2009); IPCC (2015, p 23); UNFCCC (2015); GCF (2020a); UN (2020)

of countries to act (UNFCCC, 2011, p 1). This principle also required developed countries to support developing countries, either financially, through technology transfer or via other means (Nordensvard, 2017). Implicit in this is the idea of fairness and equity (see Pauw et al, 2014).

However, while the USA's Clinton–Gore Administration was considered a main player in the lead up to the Kyoto Protocol, there was less support at national level (Hovi et al, 2013), with increased debate about the burden placed on rich countries, especially the impact on industrial competitiveness and the cost-effectiveness of policies (Jotzo, 2005, p 78). Five months before the signing of the Kyoto Protocol the US Senate unilaterally approved the 'Byrd–Hagel' Resolution, which stated that the USA would not sign a climate treaty without participation from developing countries. This meant that the ratification of Kyoto was effectively prohibited. Following his election in 2000, President Bush withdrew the USA from the Kyoto Protocol in 2001 on the basis that 'it was not in US interests' (Lisowski, 2002, p 101). In a White House address in 2001, while he recognised the USA's responsibility for emissions, Bush questioned the omission of China and India from binding reduction targets, and raised concerns about damage to the national economy.

While COP18 in 2012 led to the Doha Amendment to the Kyoto Protocol establishing a second commitment period of 2013–20, this required ratification by 144 governments to take effect. At the time of writing only 137 parties had done so (UNFCCC, 2020c), with numerous countries, including Canada, announcing their withdrawal from it.

**The Copenhagen Accord:** Following the Kyoto Protocol, the debate concerning the responsibility of countries such as China and India continued, and this was a central element of COP15 in 2009. This COP was considered significant given the political attention it received compared to previous conferences, with attendance from over 100 heads of state (C2ES, 2009). The Accord announced at COP15 embodied these concerns – with the USA, India, China, Brazil and South Africa at the heart of negotiations. These were controversial negotiations that sidestepped the formal UN process, effectively freezing out countries with no negotiating power outside the UN establishment (Brown/ODI, 2009). Lumumba Di-Aping, chief negotiator of the G77 group of nations, described it in the following terms: '[as having] asked Africa to sign a suicide pact, an incineration pact, in order to maintain the economic dominance of a few countries' (cited in EUobserver, 2009).

The Accord was largely described as 'disappointing' (European Commission President José Manuel Barroso, cited in EUobserver, 2009), 'Brokenhagen' (Andy Atkins, Friends of the Earth [FOE] Executive Director until 2015, cited in EUobserver, 2009), and for some, 'a shameful and monumental failure' (Tim Jones, Climate Policy Officer at the World Development Movement [WDM], cited in EUobserver, 2009), providing no tangible, concrete way forward that would lead to a reduction in carbon emissions despite two years of negotiations prior to the conference. However, while the Accord had no substantive outputs, it did set some actions in motion. For example, it proposed the Green Climate Fund (GCF) for developing countries, the details of which were established at COP16 and adopted at COP17, and which included the aspiration of keeping temperature increases below 2 degrees centigrade.

**The Paris Agreement:** COP21 was attended by 'the biggest gathering ever of world leaders' (Harvey, 2015). It was ratified in 2016 following 55 signatories, and the details were outlined at COP24 in 2018. The conference and its outcomes were received in a stark contrast to Copenhagen. One journalist described the response to it in the following terms: 'The delegates were clapping, cheering and whistling wildly, embracing and weeping. Even the normally reserved economist Lord Stern was whooping' (Harvey, 2015).

The strengths of the Agreement were said to be that all countries were included in the effort to reduce emissions through the creation of 'nationally determined contributions' (NDCs) (in comparison to the Kyoto Protocol, which focused on wealthy nations), that all countries were involved in the negotiations (compared to Copenhagen), the support offered to developing countries, and the ambition to pursue efforts to limit temperature increases to 1.5 degrees (UNFCCC, 2020d). The Paris Agreement used the term 'just transition' (see **Box 7.3**) for the first time (UNFCCC, 2015).

## Box 7.3: The 'just transition'

The term 'just transition' has been used since the 1970s in the context of the US trade union movement and concerns over protecting both jobs and the environment (Just Transition Centre, 2017, p 2; UNRISD, 2018a, p 6). Its use has become more diffuse, and it is now used in a variety of contexts, including global climate agreements. Within global climate policy discourse, it is most commonly used to recognise the interests of workers and communities exposed to potential economic risks during the transition to a low carbon economy (UNRISD, 2018b), and to identify the positive opportunities associated with early action (IISD, 2020). While most commonly used within the Global North, it is slowly being used within the Global South too (UNRISD, 2018b). At COP24 in '2018 54 countries signed the "Just Transition Declaration" which recognised the importance of workers and communities during a rapid shift to a zero carbon economy' (UNFCCC, 2020d).

While the Agreement was positively received, this was not universal; for example, its voluntary nature has been heavily criticised. Equally, while most countries have ratified the Agreement it did not have the backing of the USA. Donald Trump formally announced the country's withdrawal in November 2020, something that has had an impact on climate finance (to be discussed later).

Since Paris, other than advancements that support the 'just transition' to a low carbon economy, attempts to make further progress have been what many regard as 'disappointing' (António Guterres, UN Secretary-General, cited in *The New York Times* by Sengupta, 2019), with a press release from the Coalition of Small Island States describing its reaction as 'appalled and dismayed' (Sengupta, 2019) about a lack of decision-making.

## Justice in policy implementation

The most common policy approaches to climate change are 'adaptation' and 'mitigation'. Adaptation to climate change is necessary because 'reducing carbon emissions is no longer enough to halt [its] impacts' (UNEP, 2020). It has been a significant part of global-level discussion since the adoption of the UNFCCC, largely as a result of Article 4.4, which stated: 'The developed country parties ... shall also assist the developing country parties that are particularly vulnerable to the adverse effects of climate change in meeting costs of adaptation to those adverse effects' (UNFCCC, 2020a, p 9). The Paris Agreement set out the Global Adaptation Goal; at the time of writing UNEP had implemented 50 adaptation projects across 40 countries through the GCF, funded in part by developed countries (UNFCCC, 2020a, p 9). An example of an adaptation project funded through the GCF is outlined in **Box 7.4**.

---

### Box 7.4: Providing safe and secure freshwater to 105,000 people on the outer islands of the Maldives – an adaptation project

The Maldives consists of 1,190 small, low-lying coral islands spread over 90,000 square kilometres. There are high levels of poverty on the outer islands, which experience drinking water shortages during the dry season causing significant human, environmental, and social impacts. Groundwater becomes increasingly saline as a result of climate change-induced sea level rise (3.1 mm/year) and variable rainfall patterns. Responses are constrained by remoteness and limitations on land space.

The project will scale up an integrated water supply system based on rainwater, groundwater, and desalinated water into a low-cost delivery

---

system for vulnerable households. This will provide uninterrupted supply to 49 islands that currently rely on emergency water deliveries for three months of each year. Decentralized and cost-effective dry season water supply systems will also be introduced. Water desalination production plants will be built on four larger islands that will contribute to this improved dry season water distribution network to outer atolls and local supply systems. Increased capacity of local and central government authorities will strengthen the management and efficiency of these systems. Groundwater quality will be improved for long-term resilience. Groundwater recharge systems and improved water resource management capacity will contribute to improved groundwater quality. (GCF, 2020b)

While adaptation projects are more likely to be found in developing countries with greater overall vulnerability to climate change, mitigation projects exist throughout a wide range of countries. Some aim to reduce carbon emissions, for example through the improved energy efficiency of public sector buildings in Bosnia–Herzegovina, whereas others seek to develop green infrastructure where little or none existed previously. Mitigation projects of this kind aim to 'leapfrog' the 'polluting stages of historical industrial development' (Nordensvärd, 2017, p 13). **Box 7.5** provides an example of a GCF-funded project in Mali.

## Box 7.5: Rural electrification through isolated solar photovoltaic green mini-grid systems (Mali)

This first phase of the project will promote rural electrification through isolated solar photovoltaic (PV) green mini-grid systems as a low-carbon and resilient solution to the effects of climate change in the energy sector of Mali.

This would be achieved by: increasing the rural population's access to electricity in 50 identified communities by (a) switching energy demand from diesel generators, kerosene lamps, paraffin candles and other emitting sources; and (b) by installing 4.83 megawatts of isolated solar PV mini-grid systems. In addition this project will strengthen the capacity of public institutions engaged in rural electrification; catalyse the development of an efficient solar market that will enable Mali to meet its renewable energy and greenhouse gas (GHG) reduction targets; contribute to the regulatory

> framework through capacity-building and putting in place an institutional
> framework to further promote the deployment of renewable energy; and
> catalyse the inclusion of the private sector in the programme through the
> incentivisation of workable and long-term operation and maintenance
> concessions. (GCF, 2020c)

As highlighted by UNRISD (2016, p 4), this approach has the hallmarks of
eco-social policy, with the potential to challenge structural inequalities through
redistribution, and to promote new (green) patterns of production, consumption
and investment. However, climate finance mechanisms such as the GCF and its
predecessors have received a mixed reception. On the one hand, Fonta et al (2018)
indicate some of the positives of the mechanism – that without it, countries such
as Ghana would be unable to meet their NDCs or play a role in climate change
mitigation. As such, the mechanism presents an opportunity for a paradigm shift
in Africa (for example) to a green economy that would not otherwise be possible
(Fonta et al, 2018).

However, on the other hand, while the GCF embodies the principle of
redistributive justice, it also captures the ongoing disagreement about what
common but differentiated responsibilities should look like. The scheme is
based on voluntary contributions (Okereke and Coventry, 2016, p 844), and in
2020 there was a gap between amounts pledged in 2014 and money transferred
(Okereke and Coventry, 2016, p 837), with US$10.3 billion pledged in 2014,
and only US$7.2 billion made available by 2020 (Chaudhury, 2020, p 5). Where
shortfalls exist, there are no enforcement mechanisms to address them (Okereke
and Coventry, 2016). Unsurprisingly, then, key criticisms of the GCF include
limited availability of funds (Chaudhury, 2020) and low commitment of funds
from developed countries (Okereke and Coventry, 2016; Chaudhury, 2020).
Additional concerns relate to the unequal allocation of mitigation and adaptation
funds despite a promise to split funds equally; skewed allocation of funding to
International Accredited Entities (IAEs); and, closely related, a stringent process
for accreditation that makes it hard for some countries to obtain direct funding
(Chaudhury, 2020, p 5; see also Fonta et al, 2018).

The allocation of funding to IAEs is worthy of further exploration. While
the GCF is meant to be country-driven, this is often not the case (Okereke and
Coventry, 2016; Fonta et al, 2018). The majority of funding goes to IAEs such
as UN agencies, development banks and finance institutions, rather than national
or regional organisations from the public or private sector (Flood Resilience
Alliance, 2019, p 3). The IAEs then work alongside countries to submit funding
applications for projects (GCF, 2020a). While nations can seek accredited status,
this process is regarded as stringent.

Criticism of the role of IAEs and lack of country-level autonomy reflects broader concerns that have been present throughout the history of global climate policy. Critics have expressed unease over the dominance of Western governance regimes and a lack of cultural alignment with recipient-country values (Nursey-Bray and Palmer, 2018; Chu and Michael, 2019). This risks a lack of recognition of specific community needs and involvement in decision-making processes that may 'create and sustain inequalities within a country' (Colenbrander et al, 2018, p 902; see also Okereke and Coventry, 2016). Specifically, this approach may reinforce the invisibility of some communities, as routine exclusion (deliberate or accidental) or stereotyping by national policy-makers and IAEs may lead to some communities being left behind (or even harmed) by policy measures (Chu and Michael, 2019). Indeed, climate measures such as those supported by the GCF are identified throughout the literature as having failed to recognise local conditions and needs, and in some instances as having worsened vulnerability to climate change as a result (Robinson and Shine, 2018). Unsurprisingly, the critics argue, projects that are not tailored to community needs, that are implemented in spite of, rather than with, communities, are far less successful (Robinson and Shine, 2018).

These criticisms could lead to the suggestion that the approach taken by the GCF is too top-down and removed from the communities that it is attempting to support. Robinson and Shine (2018) indicate the importance of working with communities, stressing the importance of procedural justice to ensure that measures are developed with communities rather than imposed on them. Beyond the moral arguments implicit in discussions of justice, this is important for a variety of practical reasons. Developing measures with communities makes them more likely to suit the local conditions, it means that risks of measures can be reduced, certain groups are less likely to be ignored or hidden, and communities are more likely to accept measures (Robinson and Shine, 2018).

## Conclusion

In 2019 the UN warned that there were just '11 years to prevent irreversible climate change' (UN, 2019b). Despite this, this chapter has identified relatively limited action at the global policy level and problems with the measures that have been introduced in terms of their ambition and implementation.

This chapter has identified some of the key issues that make climate change a diabolical policy problem. Most notably these include the global nature of the problem, especially that effects of climate change may be felt more severely by regions, countries and populations that have contributed little to the problem. Moreover, there is a temporal issue, with the full extent of the problem being felt some time after the pollution has occurred. This can also lead to uncertainty about what the future effects of climate change will be, leading to a reliance on predictive models, such as those indicated in **Box 7.2**.

These issues raise fundamental questions of justice. Scholars have typically focused on concerns of distributional justice (the distribution of environmental goods and bads), procedural justice (access to decision-making processes, inclusion within decision-making), and recognition justice (including, acknowledging and addressing the needs of a diverse range of people). These underlying questions of justice have led to heated global-level debate about where responsibility for the problem lies, which countries should be making the greatest emission reductions, who should pay, and how much. Further questions are raised about how adaptation and mitigation projects are best designed and implemented so that they work in the interests of the communities affected by them, with concerns raised over the dominance of Western governance regimes and a lack of cultural alignment with recipient-country values (Nursey-Bray and Palmer, 2018). However, what is clear is that there is also potential for appropriately aligned adaptation and mitigation projects. While the gap between promised and received funds must be addressed and overall commitments increased, the best, most successful projects are those that are culturally appropriate and engage with affected communities or populations.

Finally, it is important to recognise that while there may be political resistance to making climate agreements and taking national action, the resurgence of climate movements – for example, Extinction Rebellion and the climate strikes – has played a role in keeping climate change on national and global policy agendas. In September 2019 the largest ever global climate protest took place (Laville and Watts, 2019), with millions of participants from an estimated 185 countries taking part.

Climate policy is a long-term policy issue of great significance to GSP. It is one that continues to be negotiated and implemented from the global through to the community level, and illustrates the importance of multilevel and interconnected action. The COVID-19 pandemic and the shape of the associated economic recovery, how the USA and other most-polluting nations choose to engage with climate change and **global governance** more broadly, and the state of relations between the USA and China will have an impact on future global climate policy, as will the burgeoning climate justice movement. While the global policy outlook may be unclear, what is certain is the stark, urgent need for action.

## Summary

- Climate change has profound implications for the wellbeing of billions of people and impacts on a range of social issues.
- There is an urgent need for stronger and more coordinated action to address climate change, and to think through the relationship between the social and the environmental, in terms of justice and policy.

- Given the global nature of the problem, global-level agreements are indispensable, but are very complex and slow to negotiate and agree on.
- There are inherent issues of justice in all aspects of climate policy including: cause and effect, how to take action, who should take action, and who should pay.
- There are also justice concerns as global-level climate policies are implemented in regions, countries, localities and communities. Some argue that climate policies are too top-down and Western in nature.
- Despite the desperate need for action, this has been slow-moving and stalled by concerns about national interests. However, the burgeoning climate movement and increased public interest in environmental issues present a glimmer of hope that could provide new insights for and challenges to social policy.

## Questions for discussion

- Why should countries that have contributed little to climate change be required to take action to limit their carbon emissions?
- Voluntary nationally determined contributions make the action agreed at Paris meaningless: discuss.
- Bearing in mind the themes of justice discussed throughout this chapter, what would the key features of a socially just mitigation and/or adaptation project in a least developed country be?

## Follow-up activities

- Choose an adaptation and/or mitigation project that is listed on the GCF website (www.greenclimate.fund/projects). Consider how issues of distributional, procedural and recognition injustice might arise. How would you address these injustices?
- Summarise what happened at the most recent Conference of the Parties (COP) (https://unfccc.int/process/bodies/supreme-bodies/conference-of-the-parties-cop). Consider:
  - What was agreed?
  - What does this mean for climate change mitigation?
  - What does this mean for the countries most vulnerable to climate change?

## Further resources

The web pages of the UNFCCC (https://unfccc.int) and the IPCC (www.ipcc.ch) provide extensive information about climate science, predictions and policy developments. A full timeline of global climate policy-making can be accessed at https://unfccc.int/timeline

## References

Åhman, M., Nilsson, L. and Johansson, B. (2017) 'Global climate policy and deep decarbonization of energy-intensive industries', *Climate Policy*, 17(5), 634–49.

Baker, S. (2006) *Sustainable development*, London: Routledge.

Banks, N., Preston, I., Hargreaves, K., Kazmierczak, A., Lucas, K., Mayne, R., Downing, C. and Street, R. (2014) *Climate change and social justice: An evidence review*, York: Joseph Rowntree Foundation.

BBC News (2009) 'Copenhagen deal: Key points', 19 December (http://news.bbc.co.uk/1/hi/sci/tech/8422307.stm).

Blanco, G., Gerlagh, R., Suh, S., Barrett, J., de Coninck, H.C., Diaz Morejon, C.F., et al (2014) 'Drivers, trends and mitigation', in O. Edenhofer, R. Pichs-Madruga, Y. Sokona, E. Farahani, S. Kadner, K. Seyboth, et al (eds) *Climate change 2014: Mitigation of climate change, Contribution of Working Group III to the Fifth Assessment Report of the Intergovernmental Panel on Climate Change*, Cambridge: Cambridge University Press.

Brown, J. and ODI (Office for Disability Issues) (2009) 'The Copenhagen Accord: Lofty plans and blurred allegiances', 21 December (https://odi.org/en/insights/the-copenhagen-accord-lofty-plans-and-blurred-allegiances).

C2ES (Centre for Climate and Energy Solutions) (2009) *15th session of the Conference of the Parties to the United Nations Framework Convention on Climate Change* (www.c2es.org/content/cop-15-copenhagen).

Cahill, M. (2001) *The environment and social policy*, London: Routledge.

Caney, S. (2005) 'Cosmopolitan justice, responsibility, and global climate change', *Leiden Journal of International Law*, 18(4), 747–76.

Chaudhury, A. (2020) 'Role of intermediaries in shaping climate finance in developing countries: Lessons from the Green Climate Fund', *Sustainability*, 12(14), 5507.

Chu, E. and Michael, K. (2019) 'Recognition in urban climate justice: Marginality and exclusion of migrants in Indian cities', *Environment and Urbanization*, 31(1), 139–56.

Colenbrander, S., Dodman, D. and Mitlin, D. (2018) 'Using climate finance to advance climate justice: The politics and practice of channelling resources to the local level', *Climate Policy*, 18(7), 902–15.

EUobserver (2009) 'Copenhagen failure "disappointing", "shameful", 20 December (https://euobserver.com/environment/29181).

Fankhauser, S. (2012) *A practitioner's guide to a low-carbon economy: Lessons from the UK*, London: Grantham Research Institute on Climate Change and the Environment.

Flood Resilience Alliance (2019) *The Green Climate Fund: Recommendations for meeting climate change adaption needs*, Zurich: Flood Resistance Alliance.

Fonta, W., Ayuk, E. and van Huysen, T. (2018) 'Africa and the Green Climate Fund: Current challenges and future opportunities', *Climate Policy*, 18(9), 1210–25.

Fitzpatrick, T. (2011) *Understanding social policy and the environment*, Bristol: Policy Press.

GCF (Green Climate Fund) (2020a) 'About GCF' (www.greenclimate.fund/about).

GCF (2020b) FP007, 'Supporting vulnerable communities in Maldives to manage climate change–induced water shortages' (www.greenclimate.fund/project/fp007).

GCF (2020c) FP102, 'Mali solar rural electrification project' (www.greenclimate.fund/project/fp102).

Gough, I. (2011) *New paradigms in public policy: Climate change and public policy futures*, London: British Academy Policy Centre.

Gough, I. (2013a) 'Climate change, social policy, and global governance', *Journal of International and Comparative Social Policy*, 29(3), 185–203.

Gough, I. (2013b) 'Carbon mitigation policies, distributional dilemmas and social policies', *Journal of Social Policy*, 42(2), 191–213.

Gough I. (2014) 'Climate change, social policy, and global governance', in A. Kaasch and P. Stubbs (eds) *Transformations in global and regional social policies*, London: Palgrave Macmillan, 108–33.

Gough, I. (2015a) 'Climate change and sustainable welfare: The centrality of human needs', *Cambridge Journal of Economics*, 39(5), 1191–214.

Gough, I. (2015b) 'Can growth be green?', *International Journal of Health Services*, 45(3), 443–52.

Harvey, F. (2015) 'Paris climate change agreement: The world's greatest diplomatic success', *The Guardian*, 14 December (www.theguardian.com/environment/2015/dec/13/paris-climate-deal-cop-diplomacy-developing-united-nations).

Hovi, J., Sprinz, D.F. and Bang, G. (2013) 'Why the United States did not become a party to the Kyoto Protocol: German, Norwegian, and US perspectives', *European Journal of International Relations*, 18(1), 129–50.

Huby, M. (1998) *Social policy and the environment*, Buckingham and Philadelphia, PA: Open University Press.

IISD (International Institute for Sustainable Development) (2020) *Just transition* (www.iisd.org/topic/just-transition).

IOM (International Organization for Migration) (2019) *Climate change and migration in vulnerable countries*, Geneva: UN Migration.

IPCC (Intergovernmental Panel on Climate Change) (2010) 'The role of the IPCC and key elements of the IPCC assessment process' (www.ipcc.ch/2010/02/04/the-role-of-the-ipcc-and-key-elements-of-the-ipcc-assessment-process).

IPCC (2014) *Climate change 2014 synthesis report: Fifth assessment report* (https://ar5-syr.ipcc.ch/topic_adaptation.php).

IPCC (2015) 'The Doha Amendment' (https://unfccc.int/process/the-kyoto-protocol/the-doha-amendment).

IPCC (2018a) 'Summary for policymakers', in V. Masson-Delmotte, P. Zhai, H.O. Pörtner, D. Roberts, J. Skea, P.R. Shukla, et al (eds) *Global warming of 1.5°C. An IPCC Special Report on the impacts of global warming of 1.5°C above pre-industrial levels and related global greenhouse gas emission pathways, in the context of strengthening the global response to the threat of climate change, sustainable development, and efforts to eradicate poverty*, Geneva: World Meteorological Organization.

IPCC (2018b) *IPCC timeline: Highlights of IPCC history*, Geneva: IPCC.

Jenkins, K. (2018) 'Setting energy justice apart from the crowd: Lessons from environmental and climate justice', *Energy Research and Social Science*, 39, 117–21.

Jotzo, F. (2005) 'Developing countries and the future of the Kyoto protocol', *Global Change, Peace & Security*, 17(1), 77–86.

Just Transition Centre (2017) *Just transition: A report for the OECD*.

Laville, S. and Watts, J. (2019) 'Across the globe, millions join biggest climate protest ever', *The Guardian*, 21 September (www.theguardian.com/environment/2019/sep/21/across-the-globe-millions-join-biggest-climate-protest-ever).

Levine, M. and Aden, N. (2008) 'Global carbon emissions in the coming decades: The case of China', *Annual Review of Environment and Resources*, 33, 19–38.

Lisowski, M. (2002) 'Playing the two-level game: US President Bush's decision to repudiate the Kyoto Protocol', *Environmental Politics*, 11(4), 101–19.

Mi, Z., Meng, J., Green, F., Coffman, D'M. and Guan, D. (2018) 'China's "exported carbon" peak: Patterns, drivers, and implications', *Geophysical Research Letters*, 45(9), 4309–18.

Nordensvärd, J. (2017) *The social challenges of low carbon development*, Abingdon: Routledge.

Nursey-Bray, M. and Palmer, R. (2018) 'Country, climate change adaptation and colonisation: Insights from an Indigenous adaptation planning process, Australia', *Heliyon*, 4(3).

OECD (Organisation for Economic Co-operation and Development) (2019) *Trade in embodied $CO_2$ database (TECO$_2$)* (www.oecd.org/sti/ind/carbondioxideemissionsembodiedininternationaltrade.htm).

Okereke, C. and Coventry, P. (2016) 'Climate justice and the international regime: Before, during, and after Paris', *WIREs Climate Change*, 7, 834–51.

Pauw, P., Brandi, C., Richerzhagen, C., Bauer, S. and Schmole, H. (2014) *Different perspectives on differentiated responsibilities: A state-of-the-art review of the notion of common but differentiated responsibilities in international negotiations*, Discussion Papers 6/2014, Bonn: German Development Institute.

Peters, G.P., Davis, S.J. and Andrew, R. (2012) 'A synthesis of carbon in international trade', *Biogeosciences*, 9(8), 3247–76.

Roberts, T. and Parks, B. (2006) *A climate of injustice: Global inequality, north–south politics, and climate policy*, London and Cambridge, MA: The MIT Press.

Robinson, M. and Shine, T. (2018) 'Achieving a climate justice pathway to 1.5°C', *Nature Climate Change*, 8, 564–69.

Schlosberg, D. and Collins, L.B. (2014) 'From environmental to climate justice: Climate change and the discourse of environmental justice', *WIREs Climate Change*, 5, 359–74.

Selin, H. and Najam, A. (2015) 'Paris Agreement on Climate Change: The good, the bad and the ugly', *The Conversation*, 14 December (https://theconversation.com/paris-agreement-on-climate-change-the-good-the-bad-and-the-ugly-52242).

Sengupta, S. (2019) 'UN climate talks end with few commitments and a "lost" opportunity', *The New York Times*, 15 December (www.nytimes.com/2019/12/15/climate/cop25-un-climate-talks-madrid.html%202019).

Snell, C. and Haq, G. (2013) *The short guide to environmental policy*, Bristol: Policy Press.

Steffen, W. (2011) 'A truly complex and diabolical policy problem' in J.S. Dryzek, R. Norgaard and D. Schlosberg (eds) *The Oxford handbook of climate change and society*, Oxford University Press, 21–37.

Stern, N. (2007) *The economics of climate change: The Stern review*, London: Grantham Research Institute on Climate Change and the Environment, London School of Economics and Political Science.

Tokar, B. (2018) 'On the evolution and continuing development of the climate justice movement', in T. Jafrey (ed) *Routledge handbook of climate justice*, London: Routledge, 13–25.

UN (United Nations) (2019a) 'Climate justice – Interview with Mary Robinson' (www.un.org/sustainabledevelopment/blog/2019/05/climate-justice).

UN (2019b) 'Only 11 years left to prevent irreversible damage from climate change, speakers warn during General Assembly High-Level Meeting', 28 March (www.un.org/press/en/2019/ga12131.doc.htm).

UN (2020) *Climate change* (www.un.org/en/climatechange).

UNEP (United Nations Environment Programme) (2020) *Climate adaptation*, Geneva: United Nations.

UNFCCC (United Nations Framework Convention on Climate Change) (2011) *Fact sheet: The Kyoto Protocol*, Geneva: United Nations.

UNFCCC (2015) *The Paris Agreement*, Geneva: United Nations.

UNFCCC (2020a) *UN Framework Convention on Climate Change*, Geneva: United Nations.

UNFCCC (2020b) *Supreme bodies: Conference of the Parties* (https://unfccc.int/process/bodies/supreme-bodies/conference-of-the-parties-cop).

UNFCCC (2020c) *The Doha Amendment*, Geneva: United Nations.

UNFCCC (2020d) *The Paris Agreement*, Geneva: United Nations.

UNODC (United Nations Office on Drugs and Crime) (2019) *Climate change could mean more terrorism in the future* (www.unodc.org/nigeria/en/climate-change-could-mean-more-terrorism-in-the-future.html).

UNRISD (United Nations Research Institute for Social Development) (2016) *Implementing eco-social policies: Barriers and opportunities – A preliminary comparative analysis*, Geneva: United Nations.

UNRISD (2018a) *Mapping just transition(s) to a low-carbon world*, Geneva: United Nations.

UNRISD (2018b) *Lessons learnt and guiding principles for a just transition in the Global South*, Geneva: United Nations.

WHO (World Health Organization) (2018) *Climate change and health*, Geneva: WHO.

WMO (World Meteorological Organization) (2020) *WMO statement on the state of the global climate in 2019*, Geneva: WMO.

Zheng, J., Mi, Z., Coffman, D'M., Milcheva, S., Shan, Y., Guan, D. and Wang, S. (2019) 'Regional development and carbon emissions in China', *Energy Economics*, 81(C), 25–36.

# 8

# Global poverty and inequality

## Chris Holden

### Overview

Global poverty reduction has been a key goal of intergovernmental organisations within the United Nations system for some time. However, the World Bank has tended to dominate discourses on the measurement and mitigation of global poverty, and global inequality has received less attention. While it is crucial to understand how global poverty and inequality are measured, these are not simply technical problems but are also fiercely contested political issues. This chapter therefore outlines some of the main ways in which global poverty and inequality have been measured; explains why these are so politically contested; presents some key data; and considers the broader politics of poverty and inequality in the context of globalisation processes.

**Key concepts**
Global poverty; global inequality

## Introduction

The goal of global poverty reduction is now at the heart of an international consensus, enshrined within the **Sustainable Development Goals** (SDGs), and pursued by international institutions such as the World Bank and governments in **high-** and **low-income countries** alike. But deciding what poverty is, how it should be measured and the best ways to reduce it are not straightforward. Furthermore, related phenomena also demand our attention, particularly the current degree of global inequality and its causes and consequences. In addressing these issues, the aim of this chapter is not to summarise the huge volume of literature on poverty and inequality that now exists, or to explain basic concepts relating to poverty and inequality, which can be found elsewhere. Rather, it aims to explore and explain the challenges of measuring and tackling poverty and inequality at the global level. It will discuss some national-level concepts and data for various countries, but its chief aim in doing so is to explain how these are related to processes of **globalisation** and how they are incomplete without a global analysis.

The chapter discusses global poverty and inequality in turn. In both cases, it discusses issues of measurement first before going on to discuss the politics and policies related to tackling the problem. It is worth noting from the beginning, however, that measurement issues are not purely technical matters, but are themselves highly political.

## Measuring global poverty

Ruth Lister (2021, pp 3–4) argues that 'there is no single concept of poverty that stands outside history and culture. It is a construction of specific societies.' But if society is becoming more global, with people's reference points being people in other countries as well as in their own, how should we think about poverty? Should we think of ourselves as living within nationally circumscribed societies, or in different countries that are nevertheless part of one global society? Each country usually has its own national poverty line, but these may be derived from different principles or methodologies. If we want to count how many people in the world are living in poverty, we need an agreed methodology for doing so (Townsend, 2009).

If we use an 'absolute' definition of poverty, we could try to count all the poor people in the world according to one common measure, regardless of where they happened to reside. This is what the World Bank does when it applies its common measure of 'extreme' poverty throughout the world. This measure of global poverty has been highly influential, and the World Bank is the foremost provider of global poverty statistics and analyses, so it is worth taking some time to examine it more closely. Although it is a global measure of poverty, this measure, in fact, estimates the total number of extremely poor people in low- and **middle-income countries**, since it is assumed (not necessarily correctly) that negligible numbers of people in high-income countries fall below the **extreme poverty** line (see **Box 8.1**).

---

### Box 8.1: Country income groups

The World Bank classifies countries into the broad categories of 'low-', 'lower-middle-', 'upper-middle-' or 'high'-income countries according to their **gross national income (GNI) per capita**. GNI per capita is the annual gross national income of a country divided by its population, or, in other words, the average yearly income of each person in that country. Thus, in 2021, 'low'-income countries were those with a GNI per capita of US$1,045 or less; 'lower-middle'-income countries were those with a GNI per capita of US$1,046–US$4,095; 'upper-middle'-income countries were those with a GNI per capita of US$4,096–US$12,695; and 'high'-income countries were those with a GNI per capita of US$12,696 or more.

The World Bank has defined poverty as 'the inability to attain a minimal standard of living' (1990) and as 'pronounced deprivation in wellbeing' (2000). This is measured by setting a poverty line based on the expenditure necessary to buy a minimum standard of nutrition and other necessities. Although low-income countries, often acting with the advice and assistance of the World Bank, usually have their own national poverty lines based on these principles, the World Bank has built on these to derive measures of **absolute poverty** that can be applied on a global basis to count the total number of poor people in the world. The most well known of these is the 'international poverty line', which aims to measure extreme poverty globally. Sometimes referred to as the 'dollar a day' measure, the current version of this is set at US$1.90 a day, calculated as the mean of the national poverty lines of the poorest 15 countries in the world.

Since the measure is expressed in US dollars, a method is needed to convert each national currency into US dollars. This is not done using market exchange rates but rather through the use of **purchasing power parity** (PPP) exchange rates. This is because a dollar converted into the currency of a low-income country at market exchange rates is likely to be able to buy significantly more than the same dollar if spent in the USA. By contrast, a dollar converted at the PPP rate buys about the same in a low-income country that a dollar buys in the USA. This is important because incomes in low-income countries 'can be three or four times higher when measured at PPP exchange rates than when measured at market exchange rates' (Anand et al, 2010b, p 10).

Using PPP exchange rates, the World Bank currently measures poverty globally according to two further poverty thresholds, in addition to the main US$1.90 a day line. Currently these are US$3.20 a day and US$5.50 a day, derived from the median values of national poverty lines in lower-middle-income countries and upper-middle-income countries respectively. Estimations of the extent of poverty at each threshold are based on data collected from periodic household surveys, carried out by governments in each country. Obviously, the higher the threshold is set, the greater number of people globally fall below it and are thus counted as poor.

World Bank poverty measures have been criticised for being both minimalist and arbitrary (see, for example, Gordon, 2009). Using a poverty threshold like the US$1.90 a day line tells us nothing about the duration of spells of poverty, since people's income tends to move upwards and downwards at different times. Furthermore, the crisp distinction made between poor and non-poor tells us nothing about how many people are just over the line or about the depth of poverty of people who are under the line. At worst, '[a] simple binary measure that classifies households as either poor or non-poor incentivizes policy makers to prioritise people just below the poverty line' (Cimadamore et al, 2013, p 2). These problems can be mitigated somewhat by comparing the numbers of poor people identified at each of the different poverty lines used by the World Bank. Additionally, we can measure the 'poverty gap', a way of measuring the depth of poverty using the mean shortfall from any given poverty line (counting the non-poor as having zero shortfall), expressed as a percentage of the poverty line. However, a further problem, which may lead to underestimations of the extent of female and child poverty, relates to the way that households are assumed to share resources between their members (see **Box 8.2**).

## Box 8.2: Gender and household surveys

The surveys that the World Bank relies on for its poverty data usually employ a unitary model of the household. As Falkingham and Baschieri (2009, p 123) explain, this model 'envisages the household as a single unit, implying the existence of a single household welfare function reflecting the preferences of *all* its members, and assumes that all members of the household pool their resources' (original emphasis). However, in practice, members of the household are likely to have different preferences and rarely pool all of their resources. Men tend to spend some of their income on themselves, whereas women are more likely to spend it on their children or general household consumption. The unitary model makes an assumption that the (usually male) household head acts altruistically on behalf of the household as a whole, but we know that this is not always the case. The upshot is that 'gender differentials in welfare are often hidden with the result that policies to combat poverty may be poorly targeted on women and children' (Falkingham and Baschieri, 2009, p 123). Recognising this problem, the World Bank has recently tried to develop new ways of understanding the distribution of resources and wellbeing within households (World Bank, 2018, chapter 5).

Despite their weaknesses, the poverty measurements provided by the World Bank do provide us with one way to estimate the number of extremely poor people in the world at any given time; to see how the numbers of extremely poor vary by country or region; and to see how poverty rates have changed over time. As the Commission on Global Poverty put it, 'The estimates of global poverty are flawed but not useless' (World Bank, 2017, p xvi; we will discuss the Commission on Global Poverty in the next section). Focusing on the World Bank's main measure of US$1.90 a day, **Figure 8.1** shows that the numbers of extremely poor people in the world fell from 1.9 billion in 1990 to an estimated 736 million in 2015. So, according to the World Bank, 'Despite the world population increasing by more than 2 billion people over this period, more than a billion fewer people lived in extreme poverty in 2015 than in 1990' (World Bank, 2018, p 19).

However, the rate of extreme poverty reduction began to fall after 2013, even before the effects of the COVID-19 pandemic were felt (World Bank, 2020, p 2). SDG 1, Target 1.1, aims to 'eradicate extreme poverty for all people everywhere by 2030', which the World Bank operationalises at the global level as reducing the number of people living below the US$1.90 a day line to less than 3 per cent. Prior to the pandemic, forecasts based on historical rates of growth in **gross domestic product** (GDP) indicated that levels of extreme poverty would be substantially above this in 2030, at about 6 per cent, with the majority of extremely poor people residing in Sub-Saharan Africa (World Bank, 2018, pp 23–4). **Figure 8.2** illustrates these trends for the total number of extremely poor people. Of the 28 countries with the highest rates of poverty, 27 were in Sub-Saharan Africa. In

*Figure 8.1: Global extreme poverty rate and headcount, 1990–2015*

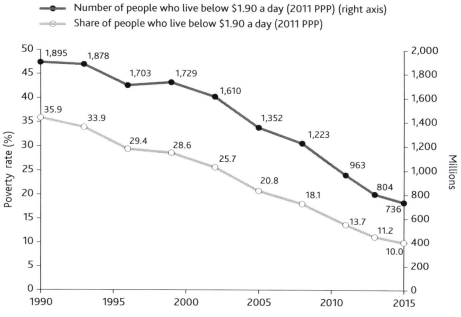

Note: PPP = purchasing power parity.

Source: World Bank (2018, p 21)

*Figure 8.2: Number of extreme poor by region, 1990–2030*

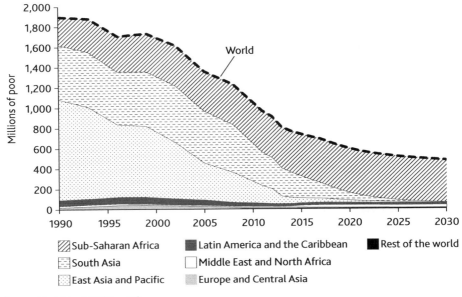

Source: World Bank (2018, p 25)

11 Sub-Saharan countries, more than half the population lived in extreme poverty in 2015 (World Bank, 2018, p 27). Global extreme poverty rates were expected to be even higher as a result of the pandemic (World Bank, 2020).

To understand trends in different regions, and why the further reduction of extreme poverty will be so difficult, we first need to understand why extreme poverty fell so sharply after 1990. **Figure 8.3** shows that the reduction in overall global poverty after 1990 was due overwhelmingly to poverty reduction in the East Asia and Pacific region, which itself was due predominantly to poverty reduction in China following that country's integration into the world market after the 1980s. China was able to grow its economy at consistently high rates as a result of various policies to facilitate foreign investment and boost export-based trade, leading to high rates of extreme poverty reduction. South Asia, and particularly India, was also able to make substantial progress in reducing extreme poverty through economic growth, although large numbers of extremely poor people still reside there. The numbers of extremely poor people were expected to remain high in Sub-Saharan Africa even prior to the COVID-19 pandemic, so that the share of the global poor residing there was forecast to be about 87 per cent in 2030 (World Bank, 2018, p 25).

There are many reasons why extreme poverty has remained high in Sub-Saharan Africa. Per capita GDP growth has been relatively low in a context where the population has been increasing quickly. Furthermore, economic growth

*Figure 8.3: Extreme poverty, regional and world trends, 1990–2015*

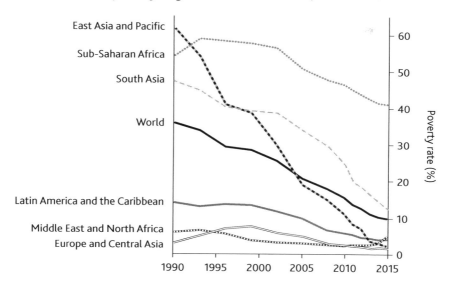

Note: The regional estimates for Europe and Central Asia in 1990 and South Asia in 1999 and 2015 are based on regional population coverage of less than 40 per cent. The criterion for estimating survey population coverage is whether at least one survey used in the reference year estimate was conducted within two years of the reference year. Because of the low coverage, these numbers are censored in PovcalNet.

Source: World Bank (2018, p 29)

has been less effective at reducing poverty due to high levels of inequality. Of particular importance is the prevalence of conflict and what the World Bank calls 'institutional fragility', with 54 per cent of all people living in fragile and conflict-affected situations in 2015 residing in Sub-Saharan Africa (World Bank, 2018, p 35). Countries in fragile and conflict-affected situations had just 6.6 per cent of the global population in 2015, but 23 per cent of the global extreme poor (World Bank, 2018, p 36). World Bank analysis shows that there is a correlation between poverty rates and the strength of institutions – countries with high poverty rates have a weaker rule of law and higher perceived corruption, among other indicators (World Bank, 2018, p 36). This means that issues of conflict and **governance** must increasingly attract our attention if we are to reduce extreme poverty to negligible levels by 2030 (Mackinder, 2020). Added to this will be the profoundly negative effects of the COVID-19 pandemic and the economic recessions that it engendered, as well as the negative impacts of climate change on many countries (World Bank, 2020).

The US$1.90 a day measure is relatively easy to understand, and the numbers produced by the World Bank allow us to see how global poverty has changed over time. However, this approach to measuring poverty is a very narrow one, and it produces a very conservative estimate of the number of poor people in the world. One problem is that it does not take into account non–monetary features that are necessary for wellbeing, including access to health and education services, which may (or may not) be provided by governments.

One approach to human wellbeing and development that overcomes some of the limitations of the purely consumption/income-based approach of the World Bank is that taken by the United Nations Development Programme (UNDP) in compiling the Human Development Report each year since 1990. This is based on the **capability approach** of Amartya Sen (2001), in which human development is defined as 'the process of enlarging people's choices' (UNDP, 1997, p 15; see also **Chapter 6**, this volume). Poverty is thus characterised by a lack of real opportunity to achieve the things a person can do or be and which they value, such as living a long and healthy life, being educated and enjoying a decent standard of living (UNDP, 1997, pp 15–16). On the basis of this premise, the UNDP's **Human Development Index** (HDI) allows us to compare overall levels of human development within each country with those in other countries. It does so by combining indicators of health (life expectancy), education (mean and expected years of schooling) and living standards (GNI per capita) for each country.

However, while extremely useful in allowing us to compare mean rates of human development between countries, the HDI does not allow us to measure the total number of poor people in the world, or even in any given country. The Multidimensional Poverty Index (MPI) was therefore created in 2010 (UNDP, 2010). This is based on survey data in a similar way to that of the World Bank's poverty measures. However, unlike monetary income or consumption–based measures such as the World Bank's US\$1.90 a day measure, the MPI considers multiple deprivations and their overlap. It sets deprivation thresholds across the same three dimensions as the HDI, that is, health, education and living standards (see **Box 8.3**). Those suffering deprivations in at least 33 per cent of these weighted indicators are considered to be 'multidimensionally poor'. As well as providing a headcount of the number of multidimensionally poor people in a country, an MPI value is assigned to each country. This value represents both the incidence of multidimensional poverty in the country (how many people experience overlapping deprivations) and its intensity (how many deprivations they face on average). Importantly, the MPI allows not only the ranking of countries in a similar way to the HDI, but also the estimation of the number of people who are 'multidimensionally poor' for the developing world as a whole and by region.

Globally, 1.3 billion people in the 105 developing countries for which the MPI was estimated in 2018 lived in multidimensional poverty, equal to 23 per cent of those countries' population (OPHI, 2018, p 11). For most countries, the MPI indicates a greater number of poor people than the World Bank's US\$1.90 a day measure, but some countries with relatively good access to public services have

## Box 8.3: Deprivation thresholds in the Multidimensional Poverty Index (MPI)

The MPI identifies multiple deprivations at the individual level in health, education and standard of living, using micro data from household surveys. Each person in a given household is classified as poor or non-poor depending on the number of deprivations their household experiences.

The health thresholds are having at least one household member under the age of 70 who is undernourished and having had one or more children die in the five-year period preceding the survey. The education thresholds are having no household member aged 10 or over who has completed six years of schooling and having at least one school-age child who is not attending school. The standard of living thresholds relate to not having electricity; not having access to clean drinking water; not having access to adequate sanitation; using 'dirty' cooking fuel (for example, dung, wood or charcoal); having inadequate housing; and owning no car, truck or similar motorised vehicle, and owning at most one of a list of assets (for example, radio, TV, refrigerator).

Source: OPHI (2018)

an MPI significantly below the World Bank's monetary–based estimate of poverty (OPHI, 2018, p 15). This is an indication of the importance of access to public services in mitigating poverty, not just the need for better incomes. The MPI is an important innovation in the measurement of poverty, but because it only began in 2010, we cannot yet see how global poverty has changed over time using this measure, and even comparisons between countries must be made with caution, since available data cover various years (the 2018 estimate, for example, draws on data ranging from 2006 to 2016) (OPHI, 2018, p 7). In 2018, in response to the Commission on Global Poverty's recommendation that it adopt complementary poverty measures, including multidimensional indicators, the World Bank adopted its own version of the MPI (World Bank, 2018).

The US$1.90 a day measure and the MPI are alternative ways of measuring *extreme* or *absolute* global poverty. How might we go about measuring global poverty according to a *relative* definition? If we understand poverty in 'relative' rather than 'absolute' terms, we are likely to want to agree on a methodology that would allow us to determine the minimum necessary for a person to sustain themselves and participate adequately in the social life of the country or particular location where they live. This minimum might vary from place to place, but if we can agree on a common definition and means of measurement, we could establish the total number of poor people in the world using this relative approach. Gordon, for example, cites a Council of Europe definition of poverty as 'individuals or families whose resources are so small as to exclude them from a minimum acceptable way of life *in the Member State in which they live*' (EEC, 1981, cited by Gordon, 2009, p 95; emphasis added).

This is effectively the approach the World Bank now takes with its new 'societal poverty line' (SPL), although the SPL is, strictly speaking, a hybrid of absolute and relative measures. The World Bank's introduction of the SPL in 2018 was a response to the Commission on Global Poverty's recommendation that it 'introduce a societal head count measure of global consumption poverty that takes account, above an appropriate level, of the standard of living in the country in question, thus combining fixed and relative elements of poverty' (World Bank, 2017, p xxi). The introduction of the SPL represents an acknowledgement by the World Bank that the US$1.90 measure is increasingly less relevant for many countries, given that the extreme poverty rate by this measure was less than 3 per cent in 2015 in more than half the 164 countries that the World Bank monitors (World Bank, 2018, p 72). It is also a belated acknowledgement of the point long made by those like Peter Townsend (2009) that needs change as societies become richer. The minimum monetary amount needed to fully participate in a country that is on average richer is likely to be significantly greater than that needed in a poorer country.

The SPL is measured as follows. First, anyone living below the US$1.90 measure is considered also to be societally poor. Second, anyone living on less than US$1.00 a day plus half of the value of median consumption (or income) per day in that country is also considered to be societally poor. As the World Bank puts it, 'societal poverty represents a combination of extreme poverty, which is fixed for everyone, and a relative dimension of well-being that differs in every country depending on the median level of consumption in that country' (2018, p 74). Just as the US$1.90, US$3.20 and US$5.50 a day lines are derived from national poverty lines that are widely used in low-, lower-middle- and upper-middle-income countries respectively, 50 per cent of median income reflects **relative poverty** lines that are widely used in high-income countries, as well as by the Organisation for Economic Co-operation and Development (OECD) (World Bank, 2018, p 75).

The global headcount of societal poverty by this measure was about 2.1 billion people in 2015, almost three times higher than the number of people living on US$1.90 a day (World Bank, 2018, p 76). **Figure 8.4** shows that, while the societal poverty rate declined between 1990 and 2015 (panel a), the overall number of poor people in the world by this measure did not much change during the same period (panel b). For those countries that have moved from low-income or lower-middle-income country status to become upper-middle-income countries during the period, economic growth was able to lift substantial numbers of people out of societal poverty, since at lower levels of median income the SPL value is close to

*Figure 8.4: Societal and extreme poverty, global estimates, 1990–2015*

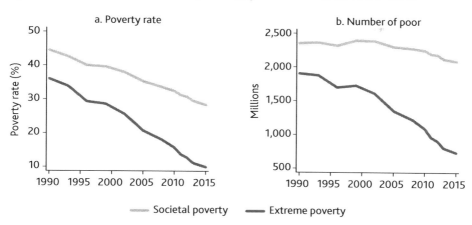

Note: Panel a shows the rate of extreme poverty based on the international poverty line (US$1.90, 2011 PPP) and societal poverty based on the societal poverty line. Panel b shows the corresponding number of people who are poor by both lines. PPP = purchasing power parity.

Source: World Bank (2018, p 77)

the US$1.90 a day measure. In these countries, societal poverty has been reduced by reducing extreme poverty, as measured by the US$1.90 component of the SPL. But at higher levels of median income, economic growth alone is insufficient to reduce societal poverty. In high–income countries, the value of the SPL increases at around the same rate as median income. This means that reductions in societal poverty (or what at this level of median income is effectively relative poverty) require policy action to reduce *inequality*. We will discuss inequality below, but first we consider the politics of global poverty.

## The politics of global poverty

Ultimately, there is only a point in measuring poverty if we then want to do something about it. Measuring poverty is important because we need to see how poverty changes over time, particularly in response to policy change and political action. The lived experiences of millions of people depend on the actions taken to reduce poverty by governments, **intergovernmental organisations** (IGOs) and other social actors.

As we have seen, the primary IGO influencing the measurement of poverty is the World Bank. The World Bank's approach to poverty, and to the appropriate policies for its mitigation, has developed considerably over time. The key shift came in the 1990s with the initiation of the World Bank's Comprehensive Development Framework (Pender, 2001; Cammack, 2004) and the Poverty Reduction Strategy Paper process (Deacon, 2007, p 29). The latter involves governments of countries in receipt of loans from the World Bank drawing up strategy papers, alongside **civil society** organisations (CSOs) and World Bank and International Monetary Fund (IMF) staff, detailing how they plan to monitor and reduce poverty. The driver of this new process was widespread criticism of the World Bank and the IMF for the negative social consequences of the **structural adjustment programmes** (SAPs) they had imposed on debtor countries as a condition of loans in the 1980s, which involved harsh economic **austerity** measures.

The World Bank and the IMF have continued with pro-market policy prescriptions as conditions for debtor countries, premised on the fundamental belief that only economic **liberalisation** will lead to economic growth, and thus poverty reduction in the long term, but there is now also an emphasis on the provision of targeted safety nets as a means to protect the poor and the most vulnerable during the economic transition. The World Bank's *2012–2022 Social protection and labour strategy* (World Bank, 2012) aimed to increase the coherence of **social protection** systems in low- and middle-income countries, which suffered from the fragmentation of constituent programmes, and to emphasise three key principles: expanding and better targeting social protection coverage; ensuring that social protection programmes enhance workers' productive potential; and ensuring that systems are able to respond rapidly to economic crises and other shocks. This represents in some ways a maturing of the World Bank's approach to social protection, recognising, as it does, the need for comprehensive social protection systems rather than simply poverty alleviation programmes, the importance of social protection systems in underpinning economic growth, and the need to learn lessons from the **global financial crisis** (GFC) of 2007–09. Yet critics have long argued that the emphasis on *targeted* safety nets risks undermining attempts to build more **universal** social protection systems (see Deacon, 2007, pp 24–45).

Cammack (2004) argues that the World Bank's commitment to poverty reduction was developed during the 1990s as part of a broader strategy, which aimed to situate the World Bank as the foremost, if not monopoly, provider of development knowledge. The success of this strategy, and the consequent predominance of its ideas within global anti–poverty discourses, is demonstrated by the situation of its poverty measures at the heart of the United Nations (UN) SDGs and their forerunner, the **Millennium Development Goals** (MDGs). Nevertheless, the Commission on Global Poverty and the World Bank's response to it demonstrate that the Bank is willing to develop its poverty indicators beyond simple consumption/income measures of extreme poverty, but that the proper measurement of global poverty remains contested. The Commission, chaired by the eminent economist Sir Anthony Atkinson, was convened in 2015 and asked by the World Bank to advise on how it could improve its practices and procedures for measuring and monitoring global poverty. Its report contained a number of recommendations, including the adoption of complementary multidimensional and societal poverty indicators, as discussed above (World Bank, 2017). Although many of these have been adopted by the World Bank, some have been partially or wholly rejected, including the recommendation that the Bank's poverty indicators should be audited on a regular basis by a body 'fully external' to the Bank, and that this body should be consulted about major changes in methodology (World Bank, 2016; Moatsos, 2018).

As a number of critics have argued, choices about poverty lines can be political, and too much focus on the World Bank's 'extreme' poverty line can distract us from the suffering of those who may be above this line. Such people may still be poor by many definitions and may be living highly precarious lives with a risk of sliding back into extreme poverty, and their numbers may have been increasing even before the COVID-19 pandemic (Edward and Sumner, 2017; Hickel, 2019). This can be seen in the World Bank's own poverty statistics. We have already seen that the number of poor people, as measured by the SPL, remained stubbornly high; using the World Bank's US$5.50 line, we find that the total number of poor people in the world was actually *increasing* for much of the period from 1990 to 2015, even if the percentage was decreasing (World Bank, 2018, p 83; see also Edward and Sumner, 2017). Even using the World Bank's 'extreme' measure, but particularly when measured by these higher lines, it will be very difficult to reduce poverty within an acceptable time frame without also reducing inequality. This was the case even before the COVID-19 pandemic hit the world. We discuss the measurement and politics of global inequality in the next two sections.

## Measuring global inequality

If poverty is about the lack of certain things that people need for a minimum acceptable level of wellbeing, inequality is about the distribution of resources (or some other thing that is valued). Discussions of inequality, whether at the national level (that is, within a country) or the global level (that is, within the world taken as a whole), often focus on inequality of *income*, although inequality of *wealth* is just as important. While sufficient income is clearly necessary for people to support themselves on a day-to-day basis, wealth has a disproportionate impact on household wellbeing over time (Davies et al, 2009), and is in itself an important source of income (World Inequality Lab, 2018). However, in this chapter we focus only on income inequality.

Income inequality can be measured in a number of different ways (Foster and Lustig, 2019). The most commonly used measure is the **Gini coefficient**, which allocates a score between 1 and 0 (or 100 and 0), where 1 (100) equals absolute inequality and 0 equals absolute equality, so the higher the score, the higher the inequality. However, the Gini index tends to downplay changes occurring at the top and bottom ends of the distribution, which is where the most significant changes have taken place over recent decades (World Inequality Lab, 2018, p 27;

see also Palma, 2011). In order to get an accurate picture of changes to inequality, we might therefore need to look at the income share of the top of the distribution (the top 1 per cent or the top 10 per cent, for example) and/or the bottom of the distribution (such as the bottom 40 per cent). So we will see, for example, that the top 10 per cent in most countries have a larger share of total income than the bottom 40 per cent.

Data sources are also important. Whereas household surveys may be sufficient to estimate poverty levels, they are less adequate for inequality analysis, since they rely on self-reported information and are therefore likely to underestimate top income and wealth levels. We also need to take account of the fact that there is no transparent data on the significant proportion of income and wealth that is sheltered in tax havens. The World Inequality Lab therefore combines survey data with tax data and national accounts data to arrive at a more accurate estimate of inequality levels (World Inequality Lab, 2018, p 29).

In a globalising world, how should we approach the study of income inequality? Should we be attempting to measure inequality between individuals (or households) within countries, or between the average incomes of countries, or between individuals (or households) in the world as a whole, regardless of where people live? Income inequality within countries remains important for political, economic and social outcomes, and may be influenced by processes of globalisation, so it is perhaps useful to start by comparing how income inequality has changed within various countries.

Using the income shares of the top 10 per cent in key countries and regions since 1980, **Figure 8.5** shows that inequality has been rising in most countries. Only in the countries with the most extreme levels of inequality has there been any reduction at all. However, inequality has increased at different speeds, indicating the importance of institutions and government policy in determining outcomes (World Inequality Lab, 2018). This can be seen in the difference between Russia and China, which pursued very different forms of opening up to the world economy, leading to an abrupt and dramatic increase in inequality in Russia and a more gradual increase in China. It can also be seen in the difference between Europe and the USA, which have pursued different social policies. While Europe has also become more unequal, most European countries retained fairer educational systems and higher real minimum wages than the USA, and tax progressivity was reduced less than in the USA (**Figure 8.5** shows pre-tax income; see World Inequality Lab, 2018). As we will discuss below, income inequality has risen most dramatically at the very top of the distribution, particularly in Anglophone countries.

However, while these trends in within-country inequality are important, they tell us little about trends in global inequality, that is, for the world taken as a whole. In examining global inequality, it is useful to follow Milanovic's work, who makes a distinction between *international* and *global* measures of inequality,

*Figure 8.5: Top 10 per cent income shares across the world, 1980–2016*

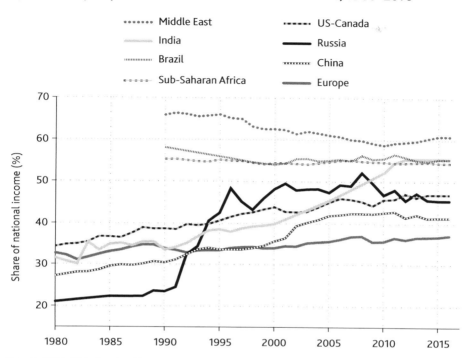

Note: In 2016, 55% of national income was received by the Top 10% earners in India, against 31% in 1980.
Source: World Inequality Lab (2018, p 11)

using three 'concepts'. We can measure inequality between nations (international inequality) by comparing the gross domestic income (GDI) per capita of each country. This tells us what the differences are between the mean incomes of people in different countries, but it tells us nothing about the distribution of income within those countries. This is what Milanovic calls 'concept 1 inequality' or 'unweighted international inequality' (Milanovic, 2009). 'Concept 2 inequality', or 'weighted international inequality', is the same as concept 1 inequality, except that each country is represented in accordance with its population, but still with mean incomes rather than the actual incomes of the people who live there. So, for example, whereas in concept 1 China's weight is the same as any other country, in concept 2 China's weight is approximately 20 per cent of the world because of its large population. Nevertheless, concept 2 still relies on the representative (mean) incomes of people in each country (that is, GDI per capita) rather than their actual incomes, so differences in incomes within countries are still not taken into account (Milanovic, 2009, p 130). 'Concept 3 inequality' measures 'global inequality', that is, inequality between all individuals in the world, regardless of where they live. The data requirements for measuring concept 3 inequality are much more challenging than for the other two concepts, since rather than simply calculating GDI per capita from data in national accounts, it relies on collating data from household surveys undertaken in different countries (Milanovic, 2009, p 130).

Milanovic (2012a) is able to show how inequality has changed over time using these different approaches. **Figure 8.6** illustrates these changes. It is clear from **Figure 8.6** that unweighted international inequality (concept 1) increased substantially between 1950 and 2000 (measured using the Gini coefficient), but dropped off after that. Weighted international inequality (concept 2) appears to have reduced throughout the period, particularly after 1990. However, the bulk of that recent reduction is explained by economic growth in China, and, to a lesser extent, India, which account for a large segment of the developing world's population. The challenges of data collection for global inequality (concept 3) mean that there are fewer data points for this. These show no clear trend, although there seems to be a small decrease in the latter years. What is clear is that global inequality is much higher than international inequality, a fact explained primarily by high levels of within–country inequality (Milanovic, 2012a). Global inequality is also considerably higher than inequality within any given country, with a Gini of about 0.7 (see **Figure 8.7**).

*Figure 8.6: Milanovic's three concepts of inequality*

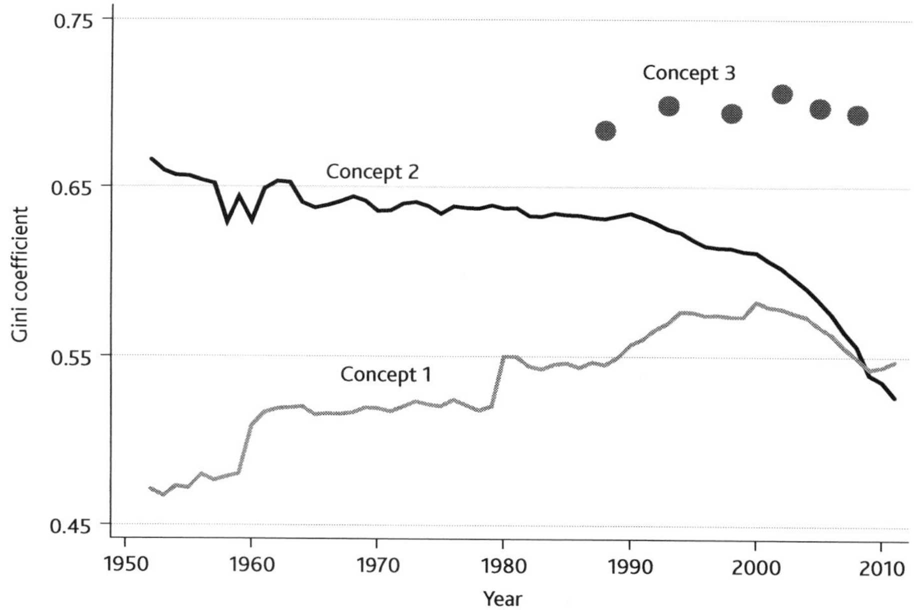

Source: Milanovic (2012a, p 6)

*Figure 8.7: Global Gini coefficient compared to the Ginis of selected countries*

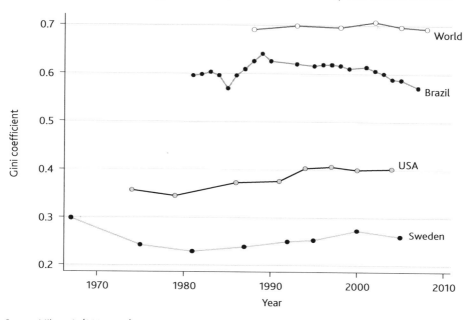

Source: Milanovic (2012a, p 9)

A crucial issue in understanding the relationship between **neoliberal** globalisation and poverty and inequality concerns the extent to which economic liberalisation has led to growth. We have seen in the previous sections that China was able to integrate into the global economy, grow its economy and thereby substantially reduce extreme poverty. One way of understanding the dynamics of global income inequality is to look at who has benefited from economic growth across the world population. We can illustrate this via the 'elephant curve' (so called because the original version of this resembled the shape of an elephant; see Milanovic, 2012a, p 13). The World Inequality Lab's version of this is shown in **Figure 8.8** (2018, p 51). This plots each percentile of the global population in ascending order on the horizontal axis, from the poorest on the left of the graph to the richest on the right. In this version, rather than being represented on the same scale as the rest of the population, the global top 1 per cent is disaggregated in order to capture the extent to which those at the very top of the distribution have benefited from income growth, which is plotted on the vertical axis. What this and other versions of the graph illustrate is that two big groups have gained disproportionately from economic growth since the 1980s: an emerging middle class in fast-growing countries such as China and India, and the global elite of the top 1 per cent, located in the USA and Europe, but with members from other parts of the world too, including the Middle East, Latin America and China.

*Figure 8.8: Total income growth by percentile across all world regions, 1980–2016*

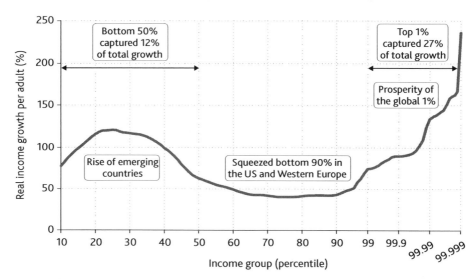

Note: On the horizontal axis, the world population is divided into a hundred groups of equal population size and sorted in ascending order from left to right, according to each group's income level. The Top 1% group is divided into ten groups, the richest of these groups is also divided into ten groups, and the very top group is again divided into ten groups of equal population size. The vertical axis shows the total income growth of an average individual in each group between 1980 and 2016. For percentile group p99p99.1 (the poorest 10% among the world's richest 1%), growth was 74% between 1980 and 2016. The Top 1% captured 27% of total growth over this period. Income estimates account for differences in the cost of living between countries. Values are net of inflation.

Source: World Inequality Lab (2018, p 51)

Poorer people in emerging countries have gained too, as we saw with China's reduction of extreme poverty. But what Milanovic (2012a, p 13) calls the 'global upper middle class' saw their incomes grow only slowly or even stagnate. As the World Inequality Lab (2018, p 7) points out, this segment of the world population includes 'all North American and European lower-and-middle-income groups', which perhaps goes some way to explain the votes for Brexit in the UK and Trump in the USA in 2016 (see Holden, 2017).

## The politics of global inequality

We can see that there are extremes of inequality within countries, between the mean incomes of different countries, and between people in the world taken as a whole. For the most part these inequalities have increased substantially over recent decades. The extent of inequality has become a contentious political issue at the national level in high-, middle- and low-income countries alike, especially following the GFC of 2007–09. One key debate has been about the impact of economic liberalisation on inequality. Globalisation has often been thought to affect inequality through impacting workers with different skill levels differently, as well as because competition between countries seeking foreign investment leads to a '**race to the bottom**' in tax rates and social protection.

Empirical research has produced no consensus on these issues, in part because researchers do not always focus on the same aspects of globalisation when attempting to understand its impact on inequality (they may choose to focus on **tariff** reductions, increases in the volume of trade or increases in **foreign direct investment** [FDI], for example, or some combination of these or other variables) (Milanovic and Squires, 2005; Dreher and Gaston, 2008). Similarly, they may focus on different aspects of inequality (within–country income inequality or wage inequality, or global income inequality, for example) (Milanovic and Squires, 2005). Furthermore, it is extremely difficult to disentangle the effects of trade and investment liberalisation, reforms to labour laws and technological advances, since these often happen at the same time and each may affect the rewards accruing to different groups of workers (Milanovic and Squires, 2005; OECD, 2011). In particular, increasing openness to the world market through trade and investment liberalisation is often accompanied by liberalisation of labour markets through reforms to make labour contracts more 'flexible'; in other words, both types of liberalisation are often part of a 'package' of neoliberal reforms.

What is clear is the profound effect that government policy can have, for better or worse, on inequality within countries. Effective and well–designed policies on taxation, social transfers and public services, on education, and on employment protection can play a major role in mitigating inequality (OECD, 2011). Thus, the question for governments is not simply whether they should open their economies to the world market, but if they do, how they should combine economic policies of openness with tax and social policies (see **Chapter 3**, this volume). China's economy, for example, has grown dramatically during the period of its opening up, but inequality has also increased, making decisions about how to expand **social security** and other redistributive policies of the utmost importance. Furthermore, Hacker and Pierson (2010) show how government policies on these issues are not simply the result of a rational, evidence-based process, or of the inevitable effects of globalisation, but rather, the outcome of long–term struggles between social groups and political actors. In particular, they argue, it is the growing power of business that has facilitated the dramatic increase in inequality in the case of the USA (Hacker and Pierson, 2010; see also **Chapter 4**, this volume).

The World Inequality Lab (2018) reinforces the importance of national institutions, politics and policies. It notes that, while inequality has increased everywhere, it has done so at different speeds and to different extents, often between countries that have very similar levels of integration into the world market. In particular, diversity in changes at the top of the income distribution in different countries can best be accounted for by changes in tax progressivity, with drastic reductions in progressive income taxes for the richest in some high-income countries, such as the USA, facilitating the growth of inequality in those countries (World Inequality Lab, 2018, pp 257–8).

However, it is not only national-level policy that is important for inequality, but also how effectively governments coordinate policies through **world-regional** or **intergovernmental organisations**. As Dreher (2006) points out, supranational political integration might effectively counter the 'race to the bottom' (see **Chapter 3**, this volume). Inequality therefore needs to be tackled at multiple levels – national, regional and global. At the global level, the focus of the MDGs was very much on combating extreme poverty, while inequalities of income and wealth were largely ignored. By contrast, SDG 10 is to 'Reduce inequality within and among countries', while Target 10.1 is as follows: 'By 2030, progressively achieve and sustain income growth of the bottom 40 per cent of the population [within each country] at a rate higher than the national average.' While, if achieved, this would reduce inequality by one measure, it is a fairly weak target, ignoring as it does the top of the income distribution and the need for redistribution. As we have seen, it is the concentration of income and wealth at the very top of the distribution that has driven inequality in recent decades. Calls for the adoption of the Palma ratio, which is the ratio of the income share of the top 10 per cent to that of the bottom 40 per cent, were not heeded during the process of drawing up the SDGs (Anderson, 2016; see also Palma, 2011). The World Bank's operationalisation of Target 10.1 is even weaker than the target itself. Alongside its main goal of ending extreme poverty, the World Bank has now also adopted the goal of promoting 'shared prosperity', defined as 'the growth in the average consumption or income of the poorest 40 percent of the population' in each country (World Bank, 2018, p 49). This does not actually operationalise Target 10.1, since it simply requires that the consumption or income of the bottom 40 per cent grows, not that it does so at a faster rate than the average. Target 10.1 is instead operationalised by the World Bank as what it calls the 'shared prosperity premium'.

Inequality is important for many reasons. Not least of these is that, as the World Bank's own data demonstrate, on the basis of existing economic growth trends it would have been impossible to eradicate extreme poverty and meet SDG Target 1.1 without the redistribution of resources, even before the economic shock of the 2020 COVID-19 pandemic hit. The effects of the pandemic are likely to substantially worsen both poverty and inequality. Furthermore, as Milanovic argues (2012b), global and international inequalities give rise to large **migration** flows, which politicians in the rich countries cannot ignore. Migration could be a key mechanism for reducing global poverty and inequality and facilitating the economic growth of poorer countries (including through **remittances**), and should be seen as similar to trade policies in this respect (Milanovic, 2012b). Like trade policy and other aspects of economic globalisation, however, migration gives rise to a number of contentious political issues that require careful management, and which have become even more salient with the rise of nationalist **populism** (see **Chapters 3 and 9**, this volume). Aid, trade and migration ought therefore to be seen as complementary means for reducing global poverty and inequality, especially since if migration flows are to be reduced, the economies of poorer countries need to be helped to grow faster (Milanovic, 2012b).

## Conclusion

This chapter has explained some of the basic measurement issues relating to both global poverty and inequality because an appreciation of these is important to understanding the scale of these interrelated problems, how they have changed over time, and what might therefore be done about them. Yet, necessary as the proper measurement of both is, an overemphasis on this risks promoting the fallacy that these are essentially technical problems with technical solutions. Indeed, the debate about how we can best measure global poverty is as fierce as it is only because these are at root deeply political problems that implicitly, if not explicitly, challenge dominant power structures. Meanwhile, the debate about inequality, particularly within countries, has intensified over the last decade, as median incomes in many countries have stagnated following the 2007–09 GFC, the scale of inequality has become more apparent, and neoliberal forms of globalisation have increasingly been challenged.

### Summary

- The goal of global poverty reduction has been central to the activities of IGOs for some time, but global inequality has received less attention.
- The World Bank's measures of extreme poverty have been at the heart of international poverty reduction initiatives, but the measurement of global poverty remains contested.
- Progress on reducing extreme poverty has been made in recent years, but this has varied greatly between different regions, and the COVID-19 pandemic has had a negative impact on poverty reduction.
- The best means for reducing both global poverty and inequality have been highly contested, with some arguing that liberalisation usually brings economic growth and subsequent poverty reduction. Others question this and highlight the increases in inequality, nationally and globally, that have often accompanied economic liberalisation.
- Comprehensive social policies, designed to complement carefully chosen economic policies, can play a major role in reducing both poverty and inequality. However, differing interests and unequal power relations give rise to intense political struggles over the shape of these policies.

## Questions for discussion

- Why is the measurement of global poverty so contested?
- What are the relationships between trade and investment liberalisation, economic growth, poverty alleviation and changes in levels of inequality?
- Are reductions in inequality, nationally and/or globally, as important as the reduction of global poverty? Why (not)?

## Follow-up activities

- Explore the World Bank's poverty data pages (http://data.worldbank.org/topic/poverty), and look in more detail at the up-to-date data for different countries and regions and for the world as a whole using different monetary poverty lines. What impact did the COVID-19 pandemic have on global poverty rates?
- Explore the World Inequality Database (https://wid.world).
- Compare relevant goals and targets related to poverty and inequality in the MDGs (www.un.org/millenniumgoals) and the SDGs (www.un.org/sustainabledevelopment).

## Further resources

Lister (2021) provides a good general introduction to poverty. Yeates and Holden (2009), Section 2, contains a number of chapters on both the measurement and politics of global poverty and inequality. Anand, Segal and Stiglitz's book (2010a) contains a number of chapters on debates about how global poverty should be measured. Sen (2001) explains his theory of capabilities, which underpins the UN's HDI and provides a theoretical foundation for rejecting an approach to poverty that relies solely on the measurement of income or consumption. See also the World Bank's website (www.worldbank.org), particularly its pages on 'Poverty' (www.worldbank.org/en/topic/poverty), the UNDP's website (www.undp.org/content/undp/en/home.html), the Oxford Poverty & Human Development Initiative's MPI website (https://ophi.org.uk/multidimensional-poverty-index) and the World Inequality Report (https://wir2018.wid.world).

### References

Anand, S., Segal, P. and Stiglitz, J.E. (2010a) (eds) *Debates on the measurement of global poverty*, Oxford Scholarship Online, doi:10.1093/acprof:oso/9780199558032.001.0001.

Anand, S., Segal, P. and Stiglitz, J.E. (2010b) 'Introduction', in S. Anand, P. Segal and J.E. Stiglitz (eds) *Debates on the measurement of global poverty*, Oxford Scholarship Online, doi:10.1093/acprof:oso/9780199558032.001.0001.

Anderson, E. (2016) 'Equality as a global goal', *Ethics & International Affairs*, 30(2), 189–200.

Cammack, P. (2004) 'What the World Bank means by poverty reduction, and why it matters', *New Political Economy*, 9(2), 189–211.

Cimadamore, A.D., Deacon, B., Gronmo, S., Koehler, G., Lie, G.T., O'Brien, K., et al (2013) *Poverty and the Millennium Development Goals: A critical assessment and a look forward*, CROP Poverty Brief, January (www.crop.org/viewfile. aspx?id=422).

Davies, J.B., Sandstrom, S., Shorrocks, A. and Wolff, E.N. (2009) 'The world distribution of household wealth', in N. Yeates and C. Holden (eds) *The global social policy reader*, Bristol: Policy Press, 149–62.

Deacon, B. (2007) *Global social policy and governance*, London: SAGE Publications.

Dreher, A. (2006) 'The influence of globalization on taxes and social policy: An empirical analysis for OECD countries', *European Journal of Political Economy*, 22(1), 179–201.

Dreher, A. and Gaston, N. (2008) 'Has globalization increased inequality?', *Review of International Economics*, 16(3), 516–36.

Edward, P. and Sumner, A. (2017) 'Global inequality and global poverty since the Cold War: How robust is the optimistic narrative?', in P.A.G. van Bergeijk and R. van der Hoeven (eds) *Sustainable Development Goals and income inequality*, Cheltenham: Edward Elgar, 74–97.

Falkingham, J. and Baschieri, A. (2009) 'Gender and poverty: How misleading is the unitary model of household resources?', in N. Yeates and C. Holden (eds) *The global social policy reader*, Bristol: Policy Press, 123–7.

Foster, J. and Lustig, N. (2019) 'Spotlight 3.2: Choosing an inequality index', in UNDP, *Human development report 2019*, New York: United Nations Development Programme.

Gordon, D. (2009) 'The international measurement of poverty and anti–poverty policies', in N. Yeates and C. Holden (eds) *The global social policy reader*, Bristol: Policy Press, 91–114.

Hacker, J.S. and Pierson, P. (2010) 'Winner–take–all politics: Public policy, political organization and the precipitous rise of top incomes in the United States', *Politics & Society*, 38(2), 152–204.

Hickel, J. (2019) 'Progress and its discontents', *New Internationalist*, July–August.

Holden, C. (2017) 'Confronting Brexit and Trump: Towards a socially progressive globalisation', in J. Hudson, C. Needham and E. Heins (eds) *Social policy review 29*, Bristol: Policy Press, 65–83.

Lister, R. (2021) *Poverty* (2nd edn), Cambridge: Polity Press.

Mackinder, S. (2020) 'Ideas, institutions and the World Bank: The social protection and fragile states agendas', *Global Policy*, 11(1), 26–35.

Milanovic, B. (2009) 'Globalization and inequality', in N. Yeates and C. Holden (eds) *The global social policy reader*, Bristol: Policy Press, 129–47.

Milanovic, B. (2012a) *Global income inequality by the numbers: In history and now*, Policy Research Working Paper 6259, Washington, DC: World Bank.

Milanovic, B. (2012b) 'Global inequality: From class to location, from proletarians to migrants', *Global Policy*, 3(2), 125–34.

Milanovic, B. and Squires, L. (2005) *Does tariff liberalization increase wage inequality? Some empirical evidence*, Policy Research Working Paper 3571, Washington, DC: World Bank.

Moatsos, M. (2018) 'The unbearable errorlessness of global poverty estimates', *The Economists' Voice*, doi:10.1515/ev-2018-0004.

OECD (Organisation for Economic Co-operation and Development) (2011) *Divided we stand: Why inequality keeps rising*, Paris: OECD Publishing (http://dx.doi.org/10.1787/9789264119536-en).

OPHI (Oxford Poverty & Human Development Initiative) (2018) *Global multidimensional poverty index 2018: The most detailed picture to date of the world's poorest people*, Oxford: University of Oxford.

Palma, J.G. (2011) 'Homogeneous middles vs heterogeneous tails, and the end of the "inverted-U": It's all about the share of the rich', *Development and Change*, 42(1), 87–153.

Pender, J. (2001) 'From "structural adjustment" to "comprehensive development framework": Conditionality transformed?', *Third World Quarterly*, 22(3), 397–411.

Sen, A. (2001) *Development as freedom*, Oxford: Oxford University Press.

Townsend, P. (2009) 'Poverty, social exclusion and social polarization: The need to construct an international welfare state', in N. Yeates and C. Holden (eds) *The global social policy reader*, Bristol: Policy Press, 81–9.

UNDP (United Nations Development Programme) (1997) *Human development report 1997*, New York: UNDP.

UNDP (2010) *Human development report 2010*, New York: UNDP.

World Bank (1990) *World development report: Poverty*, Oxford: Oxford University Press.

World Bank (2000) *World development report 2000/2001: Attacking poverty*, Washington, DC: World Bank.

World Bank (2012) *Resilience, equity and opportunity: The World Bank 2012–2022 social protection and labor strategy*, Washington, DC: World Bank.

World Bank (2016) *Monitoring global poverty: A cover note to the report of the Commission on Global Poverty*, 18 October (http://pubdocs.worldbank.org/en/733161476724983858/MonitoringGlobalPovertyCoverNote.pdf).

World Bank (2017) *Monitoring global poverty: Report of the Commission on Global Poverty*, Washington, DC: World Bank.

World Bank (2018) *Poverty and shared prosperity 2018: Piecing together the poverty puzzle*, Washington, DC: World Bank.

World Bank (2020) *Poverty and shared prosperity 2020: Reversals of fortune*, Washington, DC: World Bank.

World Inequality Lab (2018) *World inequality report 2018* (https://wir2018.wid.world).

Yeates, N. and Holden, C. (eds) (2009) *The global social policy reader*, Bristol: Policy Press.

# 9

# Global migrations and global social policy

Nicola Yeates and Nicola Piper

## Overview

Migration has featured in global social policy debate and action for the best part of a century. Key global social policy issues include the relationship between migration and development, labour exploitation and portability of rights and justice. This chapter focuses on issues that are of special relevance to migrant women. These include domestic and health work. We illustrate differences among women as well as between women and men in global social policy in terms of how global migration policy is defined, priorities, institutional design and the policy-making process. Political contestation over global migration governance and policy is, we suggest, a struggle over the conditions of development, state sovereignty, rights and resources.

**Key concepts**
Managed migration; portability; feminisation; development; rights; care work

## Introduction

For as long as humankind has existed, we have migrated. Whether in flight from persecution, war, conflict or poverty, or in search of peace, work, a career, a better climate or for love, **migration** is a normal part of everyday life. At another level, international migration is exceptional, in that international migrants account for just 3.5 per cent of the world's population. This has remained the case for much of the last century (IOM, 2019, p 3).

Even though the aggregate number of migrants globally is actually rather small, migrants tend to be concentrated in certain areas of the world, hence the socioeconomic and political impacts of migration in relation to global policy-making and global social welfare are substantial, if unevenly distributed and experienced. At one level, migration is a major flashpoint in contemporary global politics, and a factor in widening global inequalities and the growth of political **populism** worldwide. At another level, migration gives rise to new social formations and welfare arrangements. Transnational connections among people include the sending of **remittances**, which play a crucial role in sustaining welfare and financing development. Migrant advocacy groups exhibit high degrees of political agency and policy activism. The effects of repeated, continuous movements of people over time impact on social structures, forging multistranded personal and social networks that give rise to diasporic families and communities, linking people and places, societies and economies, and health and welfare systems around the world.

For all these reasons and more besides, migration opens a fascinating vista on to the state of the world's welfare, the contested politics of **global social policy** (GSP)-making, and political struggles over global development, state sovereignty, rights and resources.

## Globalisations, migrations and social development

There is general agreement that migration is inextricably entwined with **globalisation** processes, and that the causes of migration are found in border-spanning processes, rather than purely national ones. Principally, uneven development, inequality and poverty are major factors spurring migration (UNDP, 2009). Economic restructuring releases people from their traditional livelihoods and from their means of economic security. This prompts relocation initially from rural to urban areas before moving abroad in search of the economic opportunity and security that may no longer be available to them at home. Environmental degradation as a result of climate change adds to the destruction of livelihoods for many farmers, and renders coastal towns and islands uninhabitable due to floods, fires or storms. In all of this, cheaper and more accessible transport and communications technologies make **emigration** possible for more people while allowing them to maintain family and cultural contact with those 'back home'.

Two narratives about the impacts of global restructuring dominate global policy discourses on migration. On the one hand, new possibilities for personal adventure, increased income, educational, skills and career advancement are opened by global economic restructuring and the internationalisation of labour markets. Those who are prepared to move overseas and, more importantly, have the resources to do so, can take advantage of these opportunities for their own personal benefit and for the benefit of their families and communities. Migration can increase access to education and economic resources, and improve migrants' autonomy and social status. By this account, international migrants are entrepreneurs in the 'new' global economy, responding to opportunities, moving where labour is needed, reaping the benefits from it and passing those benefits on to others.

On the other hand, much international migration is involuntary and risky, whether due to being drawn into labour-trafficking operations, or needing to emigrate to survive. Far from constituting a privileged elite able to freely travel on diplomatic or corporate passports, most migrants face great difficulty in entering richer countries and remaining there. Many enter global circuits of 'invisible', precarious and hazardous (and often fatal) work, whether in global factories, agriculture and mariculture, or servicing the personal and care needs of the rich and other local populations. In this account, international migration heralds the 'globalisation' of exploitation and servitude (Lutz, 2002; Sassen, 2002; Piper, 2011), with migrants denied the respect and rights that many people in rich countries take for granted.

Global migration affects men and women differently. Feminist researchers have long understood that migration decisions, processes and practices are ones in which female (constrained) agency plays a decisive role. For example, it is the 'motherly' care labour that women provide to children and elders in their capacity as family members, friends or neighbours that enables and sustains male (and other female) emigration. But women also participate directly in international migration streams. The phrase '**feminisation** of migration' has become widely used in recent years in policy debates, in part due to the efforts of feminist scholars and activists to get policy-makers to pay greater attention to the experiences of women as primary migrants (as opposed to 'trailing wives') and workers. This has highlighted the significant rise in demand for migrant female workers in the expanding health, social and domestic services sectors, especially in the rich 'developed' countries. It has revealed how, across the migration process, women are more vulnerable to exploitation, abuse and violence, including trafficking, as they face double discrimination as migrants *and* as women. Migrant stocks are also being feminised, which is attributed to migrant population ageing following the same patterns as for non-migrants, in that women enjoy greater longevity than men (Donato and Gabaccia, 2015). Feminist scholars highlight that global policies need to better reflect gender differences among migrants and that gender intersects with other social attributes (for example, class, 'skill', age, social background, country of origin), and shapes different migrants' needs over the life course (Bastia and Piper, 2019).

Migrant men and women tend to occupy different roles in labour markets, working in entirely different sectors or in different roles within the same job category. Gendered labour market segmentation seen in national labour markets is thus also apparent in international ones. Much of the work most female migrants carry out is low-wage, informal or under-regulated. Some feminist economists argue that this is a major feature of the **neoliberal** macroeconomic development project (Peterson, 2012). Women's position in the labour market is constrained by gender divisions of labour and gender inequality all over the world (Piper, 2011). Thus, women migrant workers face additional restrictions around recruitment dynamics, which, again, are gendered (Hennebry et al, 2018).

The impacts of the emigration of skilled labour (**brain drain**) on countries of origin have long been considered a major issue for global development. In social policy much of this discussion has revolved around health workers who have a significant presence in international migration streams (health workers account for about one in three international migrants) (Bach, 2003; Yeates, 2008, 2009, 2011). Individual migrants benefit from enhanced wages and career prospects, and their families benefit from the financial remittances they receive. Economies prosper from the general buoyancy generated by remittances and other aspects of the migration economy (for example, commercial businesses in recruiting, transporting workers). International remittances are one of the few means by which some states can generate much-needed foreign currency or a means of securing loans. For poorer labour-exporting countries, migrants' remittances may exceed the value of exports and official aid. But critics argue that the losses to the country of origin from emigration – and consequently the loss of investment in education and of intellectual capital, as well as reduced services capacity – outweigh the gains (Ahmad, 2005; Yeates, 2011). Furthermore, the net benefits accrue disproportionately to richer (destination) countries. In the case of health worker migration, the cost is counted in human lives since the loss of health workers through emigration impairs the ability of countries of origin to fight against life-destroying diseases and causes excess deaths (Chen and Boufford, 2005; Mensah et al, 2005; Yeates, 2011). Such impacts are especially pronounced in the poorest countries, notably in Sub-Saharan Africa and parts of Southeast Asia, where, in some instances, there is not even enough human capacity to use substantial additional funds that could improve health there (Kinfu et al, 2008; Yeates, 2008, 2009; Yeates and Pillinger, 2018).

This raises questions about whether the competing interests of state, commercial, professional, labour and household actors can be reconciled, and how far international migration should be regulated in the interests of public health, welfare and wider social development (Yeates, 2008, 2009). What *is* the right balance between the *collective right* to health and development and the *individual right* to migrate? These questions touch on the matter of whether the recruitment and employment of overseas workers can ever be 'ethical' and if so, what an ethical global policy on migration would 'look' like (**Box 9.1**).

## Box 9.1: Balancing rights – ethical recruitment of health workers in global social policy

The question of what constitutes 'ethical recruitment' in relation to health workers such as physicians, nurses, midwives, surgeons, paramedics and so on has been addressed at various times in GSP. The growing scale of trained, qualified and experienced health worker emigration from 'developing' countries to 'developed' ones has been identified as a major factor in the acute shortages of health workers in countries of emigration, and their inability to address the high burden of disease and poor health outcomes there. The global policy question is how to avoid the adverse human and social development consequences of excessive recruitment of overseas health workers. Global policy responses have, at various times, tried to restrict the circumstances under which countries can recruit each other's health workers in order to fill vacancies in their own health workforces.

The International Labour Organization's (ILO) Nursing Personnel Recommendation (1977) was the first multilateral policy instrument to codify principles of ethical recruitment. It stated that countries should not rely on overseas nursing personnel to staff their health services. The presumption was that international recruitment would be permissible if there was a lack of qualified personnel for the posts to be filled in the country of employment, and/or if there was no shortage of nursing personnel with the qualifications sought in the source country. These conditions were, in some ways, more stringent than the more recent World Health Organization (WHO) Global Code of Practice on the Ethical Recruitment of Health Personnel, signed in 2010. This referred only to the avoidance of recruitment from countries suffering from serious health personnel shortages. Otherwise, the Global Code encourages member states to 'strive to create a self-sufficient health workforce and work towards establishing effective health workforce planning that will reduce their need to recruit migrant health personnel' (WHO, 2010).

Although all WHO members are required to comply with the Global Code, its effectiveness is limited because there are no mechanisms for enforcement beyond reporting and monitoring. That said, the ILO has not monitored the implementation of its Nursing Personnel Recommendation, even though it has the institutional mechanisms at its disposal to do so.

Source: Yeates and Pillinger (2019)

## Global migration governance

Global migration **governance** is a multi-actor field, characterised by a fragmented legal and institutional framework (see **Table 9.1**).

The predominant regulatory mode – especially in relation to South–South migration – takes the form of **bilateral** agreements. The various bilateral agreements on **domestic worker** migration rarely include clauses on protecting their rights (Lee and Piper, 2017). The same goes for bilateral agreements on health workers, where commitments to equal treatment of migrant health workers, decent work and building the health sector capacity of the countries of origin are almost wholly absent (Yeates and Pillinger, 2018, 2019). More generally, states tend to refrain from instituting gender-sensitive migration policies that facilitate women's cross-border labour mobility. They are more likely to impose legal restrictions (such as bans) on women's labour migration, typically under the guise of protecting women (Hennebry et al, 2017). Yet labour laws in most host countries often poorly protect the rights of women migrants or exclude the type of work women migrants do (such as **domestic work**) altogether (Piper, 2013).

Historically, international migration has been among the first areas identified as an issue for **multilateral** attention and inter-state cooperation. The founding constitution of the first norm-setting international governmental organisation – the ILO – refers to the 'protection of the interests of workers when employed in countries other than their own'. Created in 1919 at the end of the First World War, its work on 'orderly' migration was seen as a contribution to the overarching goal of realising peace and social justice. At that time, a clear distinction between **refugees** and migrant workers in institutional and legal terms was not made. The bifurcation of migration into 'forced' and 'voluntary' came in the 1950s as the result of the Cold War (see Karatani, 2005, for a detailed historical discussion). Since that time, refugees and (labour) migrants have been presented as different groups, subject to separate global regimes. Ever since this split, there has been no single, lead organisation with a normative mandate on migration as a whole. Labour migrants have historically been subject to a much weaker system of global governance, characterised as 'thin multilateralism' by Betts (2011). This takes the form of low pooling of sovereign powers by states, low ratification rates of global migration **conventions** (UN human rights and ILO conventions) and institutional fragmentation.

The ILO, the IOM and the UNHCR were historically the lead actors in global migration governance, but recent decades have witnessed the development of greater involvement by many other IGOs. This is reflected in the (not exclusive) membership of the Global Migration Group (which was originally set up in 2003 under the name of the Geneva Migration Group), comprising 10 global agencies. Those agencies deal with different aspects of migration. For example, the United Nations Development Programme (UNDP) and the World Bank are concerned

*Table 9.1: Migration-relevant intergovernmental organisations*

| IGO | Type of organisation | Migration-related remit/focus |
|---|---|---|
| International Labour Organization (ILO) | UN specialised agency, norm-setting | International labour standards and social protection coverage for migrant workers and workers in sectors where migrant workforce is highly represented |
| International Organization for Migration (IOM) | Project-oriented, established in 1951 as an intergovernmental UN Migration Agency; since 2016 a related organisation of the UN | All aspects of migration but particularly migration management; **immigration**, emigration policy |
| United Nations Educational, Scientific and Cultural Organization (UNESCO) | UN specialised agency, norm-setting | Promotion of intercultural understanding, anti-racism and social integration of migrants; international students |
| United Nations High Commissioner on Refugees (UNHCR) | UN Commission, custodian of 1951 Geneva Convention, direct provision | International standards for the protection of refugees; provision of humanitarian assistance to refugees (eg, running refugee camps); repatriation and resettlement |
| United Nations Children's Fund (UNICEF) | UN specialised agency, norm-setting, direct provision | Rights and services for migrant children |
| UN Women | UN specialised office, norm-setting, coordination of standards | All aspects of female migration, particularly gender impacts of migration management, including impacts on female labour migration, families |
| World Bank | Provider of development finance | Migration as a factor of development; remittances as development finance |
| World Health Organization (WHO) | UN specialised agency, norm-setting | Migrant health workers, health of migrants, impacts of migration on health systems |
| World Trade Organization (WTO) | Regulator of international trade | Temporary international labour migration ('mobility') as factors of international trade (General Agreement on Trade in Services, GATS) |

with development aspects of migration, while UNICEF deals with child migrants and UN Women with female migrants (Grugel and Piper, 2007). There are also overlapping interests between different **international organisations** (IOs). For example, the WHO and the ILO take a common interest in the migration of health workers (Yeates and Pillinger, 2019). Various forums discussing migration matters sit on this institutional landscape. Since 2007 the Global Forum on Migration and Development (GFMD) has taken place on an annual basis, and so-called 'Regional Consultative Processes' have been established around the world (Grugel and Piper, 2007). The EU holds regular meetings with Asian nations via the trans-regional Asia–Europe Meeting framework. These initiatives manifest the importance accorded to migration as an issue in and for global and regional governance (Lavenex and Piper, 2019). As a result, multiple regimes and discourses have emerged, albeit along common binaries such as low-skilled/highly skilled, regular/irregular and voluntary/forced. Such discourses are mostly not borne out by migrants' actual experiences.

UN agencies' involvement in migration tends to take the form of standard setting, and focuses on developing global norms on 'best' approaches to migration and the treatment of migrants (see **Table 9.1**). Such norms are anchored in the international human rights regime (laws, standards).

Many **international non-governmental organisations** (INGOs) are involved in lobbying or advocating for particular policy directions on migration. Examples of these include global union confederations, global employer associations, global professional bodies, global **civil society** and faith-based organisations (such as Caritas Internationalis and the International Detention Coalition). For many of these, international migration may be just one issue among many others. There has been an emergence of migration-specific civil society organisations (CSOs), notably the Global Coalition on Migration, which is formed of national migrant and migration-related associations. Migration and migration-related INGOs/CSOs have played a crucial role in GSP initiatives (see **Box 9.2**).

## Box 9.2: Migration campaign coalitions and global policy reform – the case of the ILO Convention on Decent Work for Domestic Workers (No 189)

In 2011 the new ILO Convention on Decent Work for Domestic Workers (No 189) was adopted. The fact that the ILO's Governing Body agreed to table such a convention at its annual congress in 2010 is testimony to the effectiveness of advocacy campaigns by cross-organisational and transnational networks. Such networking activities among migrant and non-migrant domestic worker associations intensified in the lead-up to the ILO congress in 2010 (see www.domesticworkerrights.org).

Throughout the globe, national domestic workers associations and unions had extended their work to foreign workers. Regional networks, such as CONLACTRAHO (Confederación Latinoamericana y del Caribe de Trabajadoras del Hogar, the Latin American and Caribbean Confederation of Women Domestic Workers), the Asian Domestic Workers Network, as well as European networks such as RESPECT and SOLIDAR, joined advocacy efforts. The integration of foreign domestic workers in national and transnational organising campaigns indicates the trend among many **trade unions** towards treating foreign migrant workers first and foremost as workers, regardless of their migration status, and thus indicates an understanding of workers' rights beyond the nation-state citizenship framework.

Given the tripartite nature of the ILO, which allows representation of worker interests through formal trade unions only, migrant associations had to channel their advocacy through unions. To this end, a new network grew out of a conference held in 2006 on 'Respect and Rights: Protection for Domestic Workers' led by the International Union of Food, Agricultural, Hotel, Restaurant, Catering, Tobacco and Allied Workers' Association (see www.domesticworkerrights.org for the conference report). Together, they constitute an example of alliances and networks working towards greater respect for gender equity, decent work, informal worker and migrant justice in one of those sectors that have been historically outside the purview of conventional trade unionism – domestic work. Domestic workers have traditionally lacked union organising or organised at the margin of 'malestream' labour politics. As a result of the success of ILO Convention No 189, a **global union federation** (GUF) established for and by domestic workers came into being, the first of its kind: the International Domestic Workers' Federation (IDWF).

Source: Piper (2013)

Barriers to organisational participation pose a major challenge for migrant workers in influencing global policy. The most democratic process is embodied in the ILO. Its tripartite processes allow employer and worker representation alongside governments (Hurd, 2014), and this has been a principal route through which migrant political agency in global governance has been realised. Still, many migrant workers, especially women, are concentrated in the **informal economy** around the world and are, in labour activism terms, disorganised (Ford and Piper, 2007). New representative groups have been created where necessary to campaign for greater attention to migrant work, health and welfare issues in GSP. Such political agency is also seen in migrant organisations' campaigns to implement global agreements (see **Box 9.2**). Protecting the human rights of migrants depends not only on building robust **supranational institutions**, but also on 'bottom–up' transnational coalition building and activism (Piper, 2015).

Such 'bottom–up' global policy campaigns have been an essential ingredient in efforts to place migrant welfare at the centre of global migration governance (Grugel and Piper, 2007).

## Global social policy on migration

In this section we look more closely at the content of GSP on migration, consider some achievements regarding female migrants, and identify some outstanding issues yet to be addressed.

Global social *policy* on migration has historically gravitated around the civil 'right' to move across borders, but has come to expand to a wide range of other areas, such as employment/labour markets, development/poverty alleviation, **gender equality**, protection of children and so on. For much of the post-Second World War period, little actual progress was made on turning the right to migrate into tangible actual global policies. However, over the last 20 years, the UN has made efforts to arrive at a truly global framework on migration that would comprehensively cover those intersecting policy areas and organisational mandates, and to ensure multistakeholder buy-in. The climax to these efforts is the **Sustainable Development Goals** (SDGs). Unlike their predecessors, the **Millennium Development Goals** (MDGs), these make explicit reference to migration (Piper, 2017) as well as the means of implementation. The 2018 Global Compact on Migration, which has been described as a guide to 'action' rather than a normative framework, assists the implementation of the migration-relevant SDGs.

In relation to worker mobility, the dominant paradigm has been that of managed temporary labour migration (Chi, 2008), which builds on guest worker programmes practised in Europe and the USA over the last century. Promoted by various global institutions (UN, IOM), this **managed migration** discourse places great emphasis on the design of formal policies by which origin and destination countries try to assert control over migratory flows and employment (Grugel and Piper, 2007). This framework claims to constitute a 'triple win' solution, benefiting host and source countries as well as individual migrants and their families (GCIM, 2005), although critics doubt that such claims bear much resemblance to reality (Lee and Piper, 2017; Yeates, 2021). Considering that, for a long time, migration had predominantly been framed as a threat to security, national identity or social welfare systems, the positive connotations of migrants as 'agents of development' in countries of origin and destination may indicate a more balanced perspective on migration. However, this perspective is open to contestation, since this discourse largely ignores the more far-reaching concept of **human development** and, in doing so, overlooks the significant costs of migration for the majority of those who labour in the bottom rungs of the global economy, typically on time-limited contracts or without regular status (Piper et al, 2017).

Although the 'migration–development nexus' frame has helped integrate migration into a globally interconnected policy field, in practice, the focus has been on a narrow range of issues: first and foremost, recruitment, remittances and return migration. This was evident during the negotiation of the Global Compact on Migration that followed from various GFMDs, and is the product of the UN High Level Dialogue on International Migration and Development in 2006. The topic of 'costs of migration' regularly appeared on the agenda of those forums, but only narrowly so – in relation to remittance transfer and recruitment fees, not in the form of transnationally split family life and other social rights issues related to temporary contract migration (Grugel and Piper, 2011). Such global forums typically celebrate **diaspora** engagement and migrant entrepreneurship, and idealise forms of return migration involving the accumulation of savings and acquisition of new skills, which are then transferred 'back' into the 'home' country's economy. This has politicised the 'migration management' discourse and instrumentalised migration for economic development at the expense of improving **labour standards** and conditions for the millions of low-wage migrant workers (Piper and Rother, 2014). Other than under the rubric of trafficking, the reality of globalisation for the many low-wage workers has rarely been topicalised. The 'new normal' of low-wage care and agricultural work performed in social isolation, the long working hours and hardship of construction workers, indebtedness, exorbitant recruitment fees, under- or non-payment of wages, lack of channels for legal recourse, failed migration projects due to premature (voluntary or forced) return – all pressing issues highlighted by trade unions and migrant rights organisations – are largely missing from such agendas.

Labour migration has demonstrated the importance of **universal** social rights and access to basic healthcare for all, and how the linking of social rights to permanent residency no longer works well (if it ever did). Indeed, many argue that a highly internationally mobile world requires that social rights are genuinely universal, that is, that they can be enjoyed by everyone, everywhere. Civil society has been at the forefront of advocating for and assisting migrant workers lacking social rights and social safety nets. A GSP issue in this regard is the inadequacy of labour protection for migrant workers. Lower skilled migrants are more likely to be concentrated in precarious forms of work, and are far less likely to be unionised or to work in unionised sectors, so they are more likely to be exploited by employers and less likely to access the same labour rights and **social protections** as non-migrant workers or migrant workers in other sectors. Women migrants experience additional risks of exploitation in this regard. They are more likely than men to migrate via lower skilled temporary worker schemes or undocumented channels. This means they are even more concentrated in feminised and therefore precarious sectors of the economy, and are particularly politically disenfranchised (Piper et al, 2017). Such work exposes them to gendered forms of exploitation and violence (Pillinger et al, 2021). The extent of this was amplified by the COVID-19 crisis, which left many migrants stranded without an income or access to healthcare, and very vulnerable to abuse and exploitation.

The degree to which social, civil and political rights and justice are 'portable' between states and jurisdictions is a further major GSP issue. National legal systems do not have international jurisdictional reach, and justice is not 'portable'. For example, contracts signed in the country of origin can only be legally contested under that country's legal system. This means that migrants need to break their work and residence in the country of employment to return to the country of origin in order to contest any breach of their rights. Doing so is expensive and may breach their conditions of residence and rights of return. Under such circumstances, seeking redress for the widespread problem of non-payment or underpayment of wages ('wage theft') has become a huge issue (Foley and Piper, 2021). The fact that governments typically allocate more resources to border management than to labour inspectorates compounds this problem (Berg and Farbenblum, 2017).

Many migrants have very restricted access to **social security** benefits. The reality, especially in the context of temporary contract migration, is that migrants do not qualify for child benefit in the country of destination when their children remain in the country of origin. Transnational living does not translate into access to transnational social benefits. For the individual migrant, unless their government has entered into a social security agreement with the government of the country of employment that allows their prior contributions to be 'ported' (recognised), they will have to leave behind their entitlements and rights to social security support on moving abroad. Migrants also face obstacles in accessing social security, healthcare and labour protection in the country of destination, especially those on temporary contracts. For example, many migrants do not make the minimum contributions needed in order to qualify for benefits. This is a particular problem when it comes to retirement pensions, where many decades of contributions are required. Temporary migrants are also discriminated against by the requirement that benefit claimants be permanent residents of the country. In some cases, migrant temporary workers will be 'taxed' twice, continuing to pay social security contributions at home as well as abroad.

These and other social security 'losses' are often greatest for migrants from developing countries, which are less likely to be party to totalisation agreements that permit their nationals to receive benefits based on their combined employment history, whether at home or abroad (Desai et al, 2000; Yeates, 2005, 2018). This lack of coordination among social security and healthcare systems, combined with an increased emphasis on temporary migration schemes that restrict access to citizenship rights, imposes significant additional costs on migrants.

This issue of portability has been a driver behind calls for more globalist conceptions of social policy, underpinned by ideals of **cosmopolitan** citizenship and 'one worldism'. Such ideals enshrine genuinely universal rights, available to all on a basis of equality, irrespective of country of birth and residence. The UN's human rights framework for migration and migrants is in a sense a tangible expression of this one worldism (see **Box 9.3**), although its effectiveness is undermined by poor implementation. The creation of world–regional forms of citizenship enshrining rights of citizenship for the nationals of its **member states** is another example. Such citizenship projects are seen in the European, Asian, African and South American contexts. Critics argue, however, that such transnational rights tend to be limited to minimal labour rights necessary to facilitate the 'free' movement of labour. Regional groupings, especially those with concentrations of economic wealth, have also maintained highly controlled access, work and residency regimes for non–nationals (for example, Southeast Asia, North America, South America). Such delineations sit uneasily with the more genuinely universal UN concept of human rights, which asserts the right to human dignity and equality irrespective of national origin (see **Box 9.3**).

## Box 9.3: Migration and human rights

The right to migrate has been defined as a human right by the UN since its foundation. The Universal Declaration of Human Rights (UDHR) (1948) set out rights that are universally recognised as benefiting all human beings. This proclaims that human beings are born free and equal in dignity and rights, and that everyone is entitled to all the rights and freedoms set out in the Declaration, irrespective of social origin, including race, colour or national origin. Some exceptions to this principle exist, notably where rights are restricted to nationals. These exceptions do not exclude migrant workers from protections granted, but they limit this protection in certain cases.

Migration features in several international human rights conventions that give concrete meaning to the UDHR:

- International Convention on the Elimination of All Forms of Racial Discrimination (ICERD) (1965)
- International Covenant on Civil and Political Rights (ICCPR) (1966)
- International Convention on Economic, Social and Cultural Rights (ICESCR) (1966)
- Convention on the Elimination of All Forms of Discrimination Against Women (CEDAW) (1979)
- Convention Against Torture, and Other Cruel, Inhuman or Degrading Treatment or Punishment (CAT) (1984)
- Convention on the Rights of the Child (CRC) (1989)
- International Convention on the Rights of Migrant Workers (ICRMW) (1990)

The last of these, the ICRMW, aims specifically at the protection of migrant workers. It reflects the need for specific protection of migrant workers that is not fully provided by the previous six conventions. In this, it offers new perspectives on migrants' rights and the Committee on Migrant Workers set up under the convention provides a dedicated focus on migrant workers and an expert understanding of the specificities of the situation of migrants. Together, these seven conventions set out international standards for regulatory frameworks as regards the human rights of migrant workers and members of their families.

The ICRMW is the most poorly ratified of all, numbering only 41 states. Countries of destination, which employ migrant workers, have been reluctant to ratify it, and this leaves migrant workers and their families without full human rights protection. Undocumented workers are especially vulnerable in this regard. The many states that have not ratified this convention so far are still bound by some or all of the other six conventions.

ILO conventions and **recommendations** give further expression to the rights of migrants and their families in relation to industries, occupations and labour issues.

Source: Slinckx (2009)

Despite advances in international law to protect migrant workers through UN human rights conventions (see **Box 9.3**), under present institutional arrangements, no international body can directly intervene in cases of violations of migrants' rights. Only the states that have ratified the ICRMW can take action against the offending party (for example, the employer or recruitment agency). The Global Compact on Migration does not fundamentally alter this situation, being non-binding.

There have been more promising developments in GSP pertaining to female migrants. Feminists regard ILO Convention No 189 on Decent Work for Domestic Workers as a great success story (Fish, 2017). The Convention was adopted in 2011 after a two-year negotiation process and several years of concerted advocacy by trade unions and other CSOs around the world, especially those situated in the **Global South** (Piper, 2013; see **Box 9.2**). The adoption in 2019 of the ILO Violence and Harassment Convention (No 190), which includes gender-based violence and harassment, is similarly lauded for the additional protections it affords migrant women at work as well as for the decade of concerted advocacy by transnational feminist networks that led to it (Pillinger et al, 2021). UN Women has also carried out important work on empowering migrant domestic workers, targeting in particular the migration corridor between the Middle Eastern countries and South Asia (Piper and Lee, 2013). In addition, there are now some good practice examples of bilateral agreements between some countries in the Middle East and South Asia, promising unified contracts and minimum standards.

The existence of an ever-greater number of CSOs and their expanding regional and global networks that place gender equality and non-discrimination at the core of their advocacy efforts are also promising factors. The advocacy actions of these policy actors are important in reminding governments of their commitments, and holding governments accountable for not fulfilling them.

## Global social welfare by migrants

Migrants are not just on the receiving end of GSPs; they are directly involved in providing global social welfare. Women play a central role in providing care through transnational families and communities that migration engenders. Members of family and/or communities residing in different countries sustain active, regular links and connections with one another, often across large geographical distances, and make mutual social and economic provision. Such multistranded relations continue to be vital in the working of the 'real' global economy, because they constitute a key channel in accessing and distributing valuable economic assets.

Financial and care provision necessary for economic and social development are provided through such transnational networks. Regarding care, children's care (see, for example, Parreñas, 2005) and elder care (see, for example, Baldock, 2000) have been central focal points in research on how transnational families 'do' care. The key point is that whether the subject of care is young or elderly, emigration does not close down migrants' roles or identities as carers. Instead, it transforms them into 'distant carers' who are incorporated into informal care networks that plug gaps in public social care services in most countries of the world (Yeates, 2009). Regarding finance, migrant remittances are a major financial flow in the global economy. They are variously heralded as 'ideal neoliberal currency' that can be leveraged to fund development initiatives and as 'alternative forms of finance' utilised to fulfil the basic welfare needs of poor families, enable the purchase of essential goods and services (food, medical costs, school fees, house building and repairs) and support family businesses (Ratha, 2005; Datta et al, 2007). Yeates and Owusu-Sekyere (2019) argue that migrant remittances are a central means of global social welfare provisioning and financing.

Most financial and care remittances are provided on an informal familial basis, but diasporic formations also play a key role in financing communal economic and social welfare worldwide – be it through raising funds for community health, education and welfare projects, local enterprise initiatives or the purchasing of land for house building in the area. Hometown associations link emigrants with their communities in their country of origin, and are important in channelling these funds (Terrazas et al, 2008). The remittances sent back from generations of Keralese overseas contract workers are attributed as a major factor in the relatively high standard of living in the Indian state of Kerala. They are also important in raising funds at times of humanitarian disasters, significantly supplementing international relief efforts by NGOs and governments.

Maintaining constancy in remittance flows is not without its costs, however. Sustaining regular and reliable payments over the long term to families and communities overseas can be a heavy burden on many senders' health and wellbeing, to the extent that many of them talk about the sacrifices they must make in meeting their own needs (Yeates and Owusu-Sekyere, 2019). This attention to the experiences of senders of remittances has led many to question the assumptions of the World Bank (see, for example, Ratha, 2005) that remittances are a stable and reliable form of international development finance (Yeates and Owusu-Sekyere, 2019).

## Conclusion

International migration has been a key subject of global governance since the early 20th century, although the most significant efforts to give tangible meaning to the 'right to migrate' and to migrants' work and welfare rights have occurred over the last two decades. Global migration governance and policy is characterised by a high level of politicisation that reflects the reluctance by governments to cede sovereignty over rights of entry and residence, and the different experiences, perspectives and interests of sending and receiving countries.

Just as there are many different reasons for and experiences of migration, there are many aspects of its governance at global level and policy responses to it. We see a mixture of policy approaches and responses, ranging from the humanitarian to the economic, and exhibiting different degrees of compassion, instrumentalism and punitivity.

Institutionally, global migration governance is characterised by 'thin multilateralism', an institutional divide between migrants and refugees, multiple policy actors, a fragmented legal framework and a weak system of enforcement of migrants' human rights. Managed temporary migration is the dominant global policy paradigm. Still, global migration policy is no longer just about the right to 'free movement'; it covers all aspects of migration and migrants' lives, and considerable progress has been made in recognising the distinctive experiences and positions of migrant women in recent years. Advocacy activists and policy-makers continually grapple with the tension between the individual right to migrate and collective rights to decent work, health and development. These tensions massively complicate what counts as socially just global migration policy.

Over the coming years, we can expect migration to require globally coordinated social policy responses through multilateral institutions at the same time as migrants continue to work at the 'front line' of delivering global social welfare. One question is whether populism and economic nationalism will further undermine movement towards a more coherent and fairer multilateral migration governance, and/or whether there will be a hardening of punitive responses to migrants and a strengthened focus on temporary migration. This will bear on institutional capacity to operate effectively in a transnational sphere of jurisdiction and welfare. Portability of rights and justice will remain a central issue for GSP. Global debate will also likely focus on the *extent* to which the SDG targets regarding migrants and migration are realised in practice, *how* they are realised, and what impacts they have on the socioeconomic security of migrants and their families.

## Summary

- International migration currently accounts for 3.5 per cent of the world's population, and is a high-profile area of GSP.
- The main flows of international migrants are from poorer to richer countries, but most migrants stay within their home region. Most attention focuses on South–North migration, but South–South migration is of major importance.
- Migration raises questions about cosmopolitan citizenship, social equity and justice on a global scale, about how the individual right to migrate can be balanced against collective rights to health and development, and how to ensure migrants have the same rights to decent work, social protection and health as non-migrants and on the basis of equality.
- Global migration governance is characterised by 'thin multilateralism', extensive use of 'soft' global social laws, multi-actor participation, weak enforcement powers and a track record of states not ratifying international conventions.
- Migrants are not just objects of GSP-making; they are involved in delivering global social welfare. They help 'square the circle' of welfare finance and care provision around the world, and are vital to humanitarian and disaster responses. They are major actors in achieving the social policy SDGs.
- Transnational coalition-based political activism demonstrates the power of **non-state actors** in GSP – how their advocacy is levered in support of recognising migrant work, care and welfare issues in GSP, and holding governments to account in implementing international conventions.

## Questions for discussion

- What GSP issues arise from international migration? How might these differ for countries of origin compared with countries of destination?

- How are women's migration experiences different from those of men? And how do migration experiences differ among women?
- Has the international community failed to uphold migrants' human rights?

## Follow-up activities

- Do some research into how global human rights conventions relating to migration and migrants have been implemented in your country. Which conventions have been ratified and implemented? What are the obstacles to the implementation of those that have not been ratified?
- Familiarise yourself with campaigns to support migrants' rights (the december18 portal [see below] provides a list of campaigning organisations in different countries). Research the social policy issues they take up on behalf of migrants.

## Further resources

*International Migration* (a publication of the IOM) and *Global Social Policy* publish research articles on social policy and global migrations. The OECD's *Migration Outlook* is worth consulting, although it is not freely available. Data, research studies and policy briefs on migration can be downloaded for free from IGOs' own websites. The UN's designated site contains comprehensive information (www.un.org/en/development/desa/population/migration/data/index.asp). Also worth consulting are:

december18, a 'portal' for the promotion and protection of the rights of migrants:
    www.december18.net
Migration Information Source: www.migrationinformation.org
Forced Migration Online: www.forcedmigration.org
Human Rights Watch: www.hrw.org/doc/?t=migrants and http://hrw.org/
    doc/?t=refugees&document_limit=0,2
Migration Dialogue: http://migration.ucdavis.edu

### References

Ahmad, O.B. (2005) 'Managing medical migration from poor countries', *British Medical Journal*, 331, 43–5.

Bach, S. (2003) *International migration of health workers: Labour and social issues*, Sectoral Activities Programme Working Paper WP209, Geneva: International Labour Office.

Baldock, C.V. (2000) 'Migrants and their parents: Caregiving from a distance', *Journal of Family Issues*, 21(2), 205–24.

Bastia, T. and Piper, N. (2019) 'Women migrants in the global economy: A global overview (and regional perspectives)', *Gender & Development*, 27(1), 15–30.

Berg, L. and Farbenblum, B. (2017) 'Wage theft in Australia: Findings of the national temporary migrant work survey', Migrant Worker Justice Initiative, November (www.mwji.org/highlights/2017/11/14/report-released-wage-theft-in-australia-findings-of-the-national-temporary-migrant-work-survey).

Betts, A. (2011) *Global migration governance*, Oxford: University of Oxford Press.

Chen, L.C. and Boufford, J.I. (2005) 'Fatal flows: Doctors on the move', *New England Journal of Medicine*, 353(17), 1850–2.

Chi, X. (2008) 'Challenging managed temporary labor migration as a model for rights and development for labor-sending countries', *New York University Journal of International Law and Politics*, 40, 497–540.

Datta, K., McIlwaine, C., Wills, J., Evans, Y., Herbert, J. and May, J. (2007) 'The new development finance or exploiting migrant labour?', *International Development Planning Review*, 29(1), 43–67.

Desai, M.A., Kapur, D. and McHale, J. (2000) 'Sharing the spoils: Taxing international human capital flows', Mimeo, Harvard University (https://ideas.repec.org/a/kap/itaxpf/v11y2004i5p663-693.html).

Donato, K. and Gabaccia, D. (2015) *Gender and international migration*, New York: Russell Sage Foundation.

Fish, J. (2017) *Domestic workers of the world unite! A global movement for dignity and human rights*, New York: New York University Press.

Foley, L. and Piper, N. (2021) 'Returning home empty-handed: Examining how COVID-19 exacerbates the non-payment of temporary migrant workers' wages', *Global Social Policy*, 7 May (https://doi.org/10.1177/14680181211012958).

Ford, M. and Piper, N. (2007) 'Southern sites of female agency: Informal regimes and female migrant labour resistance in East and Southeast Asia', in J.H. Dobson and L. Seabrooke (eds) *Everyday politics of the world economy*, Cambridge: Cambridge University Press, 63–80.

GCIM (Global Commission on International Migration) (2005) *Migration in an interconnected world: New directions for action*, Geneva: GCIM.

Grugel, J.B. and Piper, N. (2007) *Critical perspectives on global governance: Rights and regulation in governing regimes*, London: Routledge.

Grugel, J.B. and Piper, N. (2011) 'Global governance, economic migration and the difficulties of social activism', *International Sociology*, 26(4), 435–54.

Hennebry, J., Hari, K.C. and Piper, N. (2018) 'Not without them: Realising the sustainable development goals for women migrant workers', *Journal of Ethnic and Migration Studies*, 45(14), 2621–37.

Hennebry, J., Holliday, J. and Moniruzzaman, M. (2017) *At what cost? Women migrant workers, remittances and development*, United Nations Entity for Gender Equality and the Empowerment of Women (UN Women), New York: United Nations.

Hurd, I. (2014) *International organizations*, Cambridge: Cambridge University Press.

IOM (International Organization for Migration) (2019) *World migration report 2020*, Geneva: IOM.

Karatani, R. (2005) 'How history separated refugee and migrant regimes: In search of their institutional origins', *International Journal of Refugee Law*, 17(3), 517–41.

Kinfu, Y., Dal Poz, M.R., Mercer, H. and Evans, D.B. (2008) 'The health worker shortage in Africa: Are enough physicians and nurses being trained?', *Bulletin of the World Health Organization*, 87, 225–30.

Lavenex, S. and Piper, N. (2019) 'Regional migration governance: Perspectives "from above" and "from below"', in A. Geddes, M.V. Espinoza, L.H. Abdou and L. Brumat (eds) *The dynamics of regional migration governance*, Cheltenham: Edward Elgar, 15–35.

Lee, S. and Piper, N. (2017) 'Migrant domestic workers as "agents of development"', *European Journal of East Asian Studies*, 16(2), 220–47.

Lutz, H. (2002) 'At your service madam! The globalization of domestic service', *Feminist Review*, 70(1), 89–104.

Mensah, K., Mackintosh, M. and Henry, L. (2005) *The 'skills drain' of health professionals from the developing world: A framework for policy formation*, London: Medact (www.medact.org/wp-content/uploads/2014/03/2.-the-skills-drain-of-health-professionals.pdf).

Parreñas, R.S. (2005) *Children of global migration: Transnational families and gender woes*, Stanford, CA: Stanford University Press.

Peterson, V.S. (2012) 'Rethinking theory: Inequalities, informalization and feminist quandaries', *International Feminist Journal of Politics*, 14(1), 1–31.

Pillinger, J., Runge, R. and King, C. (2021) *Stopping gender violence at work*, Newcastle upon Tyne: Agenda.

Piper, N. (2011) 'Towards a gendered political economy of migration: The "feminizations" of migration, work and poverty', in N. Phillips (ed) *Migration in the global political economy*, Boulder, CO: Lynne Rienner, 61–82.

Piper, N. (2013) 'Resisting inequality: Global migrant rights activism', in T. Bastia (ed) *Migration and inequality*, London: Routledge, 45–64.

Piper, N. (2015) 'Democratising migration from the bottom up: The rise of the Global Migrant Rights Movement', *Globalizations*, 12(5), 788–802.

Piper, N. (2017) 'Migration and the SDGs', *Global Social Policy*, 17(2), 231–8.

Piper, N. and Lee, S. (2013) *Contributions of migrant domestic workers to sustainable development*, Policy Report prepared for UN Women, Regional Office for Asia and the Pacific (http://asiapacific.unwomen.org/publications/2013/5/policy-paper-for-the-pregfmd-vi-high-level-regional-meeting-on-migrant-dw).

Piper, N. and Rother, S. (2014) 'More than remittances – Resisting the global governance of migration', *Journal für Entwicklungspolitik/Austrian Journal for Development Studies*, 30(1), 30–45.

Piper, N., Rosewarne, S. and Withers, M. (2017) 'Migrant precarity: "Networks of labour" for a rights-based governance of migration', *Development and Change*, 48(5), 1089–110.

Ratha, D. (2005) 'Workers' remittances: An important and stable source of external development finance', in S.M. Maimbo and D. Ratha (eds) *Remittances: Development impact and future prospects*, Washington, DC: World Bank, 19–51.

Sassen, S. (2002) 'Global city and survival circuits', in B. Ehrenreich B. and A.R. Hochschild (eds) *Global woman: Nannies, maids and sex workers in the new economy*, New York: Metropolitan/Owl Books, 254–74.

Slinckx, I. (2009) 'Migrants' rights in UN human rights conventions', in R. Cholewinski, P. de Guchteneire and A. Pecoud (eds) *Migration and human rights: The United Nations Convention on Migrant Workers' Rights*, Cambridge: United Nations Educational, Scientific and Cultural Organization/Cambridge University Press.

Terrazas, A., Durana, J. and Somerville, W. (2008) *Hometown associations: An untapped resource for immigrant integration?*, Policy Brief, Migration Policy Institute (www.migrationpolicy.org/research/hometown–associations–untapped–resource–immigrant–integration).

UNDP (United Nations Development Programme) (2009) *Overcoming barriers: Human mobility and development*, New York: UNDP.

WHO (World Health Organization) (2010) *WHO global code of practice on the international recruitment of health personnel*, Geneva: WHO.

Yeates, N. (2005) 'Extending social security for temporary migrant workers: What role for the General Agreement on Trade in Services (GATS)', *Global Social Policy*, 'Forum', 5(3), 271–4.

Yeates, N. (2008) 'Transnationalism, social reproduction and social policy: International migration of care workers', in C. Moser and A. Dani (eds) *Assets, livelihoods and social policy*, Washington, DC: World Bank, 149–68.

Yeates, N. (2009) *Globalising care economies and migrant workers: Explorations in global care chains*, Palgrave: Basingstoke.

Yeates, N. (2011) 'Ireland's contributions to the global nursing and health crises', in B. Fanning and R. Munck (eds) *Globalization, migration and social transformation: Ireland in Europe and the world*, Farnham: Ashgate, 35–50.

Yeates, N. (2018) 'Social security in global context', in J. Millar and R. Sainsbury (eds) *Understanding social security* (3rd edn), Bristol: Policy Press, pp 141–58.

Yeates, N. (2021) 'Global union federations and temporary and circular labour migration', in ILO/ACTRAV, *Temporary labour migration: Two studies on workers' perspectives and actions*, Geneva: ILO/ACTRAV.

Yeates, N. and Owusu-Sekyere, F. (2019) 'The financialisation of transnational family care: A study of UK-based senders of remittances to Ghana and Nigeria', *Journal of International and Comparative Social Policy*, 35(2), 137–56.

Yeates, N. and Pillinger, P. (2018) 'International healthcare worker migration in Asia Pacific: International policy responses', *Asia Pacific Viewpoint*, 59(1), 92–106.

Yeates, N. and Pillinger, J. (2019) *International health worker migration and recruitment: Global governance, politics and policy*, London: Routledge.

# 10

# Gender and global social policy

Rianne Mahon

## Overview

The study of global social policy has largely been silent when it comes to gender. Nevertheless, gender has long been a factor, albeit often marginalised, in global social policy practices. Since the four United Nations Conferences on Women (1975–95), moreover, gender equality and women's empowerment have been recognised as a global norm, supported by a United Nations-centred institutional architecture. This chapter describes the core elements of that architecture. It examines gender as a dimension of labour policy, the 'discovery' of the unequal burden of unpaid domestic work and care, and the deepening of global understandings of sexual and reproductive health and rights.

## Key concepts
Gender equality and women's empowerment; informal economy; domestic work and care; care economy; sexual and reproductive health and rights (SRHR)

## Introduction

In contrast to the study of national welfare regimes, **global social policy** (GSP) studies have largely invisibilised gender. The same cannot be said for GSP as practice. '**Gender equality** and women's empowerment' has become an established (if still contested) global norm, with an institutional architecture dedicated to making gender inequalities visible and promoting policies to address these. Various United Nations (UN) agencies and other **intergovernmental organisations** (IGOs), together with transnational feminist networks (TFNs), have worked to gender understandings of global poverty and inequality, labour policy, health, **social protection** and **migration**.

This chapter outlines ways of thinking about how GSP, as a field of academic study and as political practice, incorporates a gender lens. It begins with an overview of the global institutional architecture developed to make visible the gender dimensions of GSP issues. UN agencies and UN treaty bodies like the Convention on the Elimination of All Forms of Discrimination Against Women (CEDAW) play a critical role, but they do not work in isolation. Of critical importance are their links with feminist **epistemic communities** and TFNs. The second section looks at gender and labour policy, highlighting the International Labour Organization's (ILO) standard-setting work. It shows that the ILO's understanding has evolved, influenced by developments in the wider environment and the actions of TFNs.

Identification of women's reproductive roles in the biological sense of women as bearers of children and in **social reproduction** understood as 'the processes involved in maintaining and reproducing people ... on a daily and generational basis' (Bezanson and Luxton, 2006, p 3) contributes to the gendering of social policy practice. The third section focuses on social reproduction policy – both women's unpaid **domestic work** and the broader **care economy**. The latter conception focuses attention on social services, which are attracting increased attention in the wake of gendered COVID-19 impacts. The fourth section turns to **sexual and reproductive health and rights** (SRHR), a concept that emerged from the 1994 International Conference on Population and Development (ICPD). Originally focused on women's sexual and reproductive rights, the concept has expanded to include sexual orientation and gender identities. This section highlights the growing conflict between those seeking to defend SRHR and those who oppose it as an attack on the family.

## Making gender visible: the global institutional architecture

IGOs play a key role in the practice of GSP, especially UN agencies, for example UN Women and its predecessors, such as the UN Development Fund for Women (UNIFEM) (see **Box 10.1**). These organisations have sponsored research, developing tools to make visible gender inequalities and policies to address these. In doing so they rely on pressure/support from feminist transnational networks such as Development Alternatives for Women for a New Era (DAWN) and Women in Informal Employment: Globalizing and Organizing (WIEGO) to develop ideas and to maintain a forward momentum. The annual meetings of the Commission on the Status of Women (CSW) and IGO-organised conferences build on this knowledge, providing forums for negotiating programmes of action and identifying common objectives for states. The CSW, the Committee on the Elimination of Discrimination Against Women and TFNs are also involved in monitoring progress towards these objectives.

Gender has been part of GSP debates for over a century, although often marginal to the main business. Feminists fought to make women's issues a concern for the League of Nations (Stienstra, 1994), establishing a Joint Standing Committee of Women's International Organisations to monitor the League's operations. The

ILO's tripartite structure gave women **trade unionists** a means to place their issues on the agenda (this point is discussed further in the next section).

The naming of 1975 as International Women's Year, the first UN Conference on Women and the identification of 1975–85 as the UN Decade for Women critically advanced the gendering of global policy discourse and practice. The Conferences built on the CSW's work on a **convention** to eliminate discrimination against women, through the creation of the CEDAW. The three first UN conferences on women spawned the creation of UNIFEM and the International Research and Training Institute for the Advancement of Women (INSTRAW), and on the eve of the third conference, feminist scholars and activists from the **Global South** launched DAWN. These organisations would become important sites for the incorporation and dissemination of feminist knowledge (see **Box 10.2**).

---

## Box 10.1: The main United Nations agencies focused on women

*CSW (Commission on the Status of Women):* Established as part of the UN in 1946, from the outset it functioned as 'an institutional and movement-oriented women's space' (Caglar et al, 2013, p 8), asserting women's unequal status a matter of global concern. Although initially focused on legal impediments to women's equality, in the 1960s it turned to socioeconomic issues. In recent years CSW has become a site of contestation between TFNs and conservative forces.

*UNIFEM (Le Fonds de développement des Nations Unies pour la femme/United Nations Development Fund for Women):* Established in 1976, UNIFEM supported gender equality through links with official women's agencies and women's organisations in the major regions of the world. In 2010 it was incorporated into the new UN Entity for Gender Equality and the Empowerment of Women (UN Women).

*CEDAW (Convention on the Elimination of All Forms of Discrimination Against Women):* This brings out the gender dimensions of numerous global social policy issues. Article 11 reiterated women's right to equal pay for equal work and to equality in social security, and called for the introduction of maternity leave with pay and supporting social services to enable parents to combine family obligations with work requirements. Article 12 dealt with women's equal rights to healthcare, including family planning. The CEDAW is one of the most widely ratified UN conventions.

*UN Women:* The UN Entity For Gender Equality and the Empowerment of Women was created in 2010 out of the merger of UNIFEM, the Division for the Advancement of Women (Secretariat to the CSW), INSTRAW and the Office of the Special Advisor on Gender Issues and the Advancement of Women (OSAGI).

---

UNIFEM commissioned one of the leading feminist economists, Diane Elson, to edit the first two editions (2000 and 2002) of what would become its flagship publication, *The progress of the world's women*. The first edition criticised the invisibilisation of women's *unpaid care work* in the System of National Accounts. Feminist economists made visible women's domestic work by identifying a tool (time use surveys) for its quantification. The idea of women's unpaid domestic work and the broader issue of care (or the *care economy*) – who performs it, where, for whom and under what circumstances – is gaining global traction in the wake of COVID-19.

---

## Box 10.2: Several key transnational feminist networks (TFNs)

*DAWN (Development Alternatives for Women for a New Era):* A South-centred TFN brought its vision of an alternative to neoliberal globalisation to the Third UN Conference on Women in Nairobi, later published as *Development crises and alternative visions* (Sen and Grown, 1988). Since then DAWN has given voice to Southern women's critique of 'development' as practised by Northern donors, and sought to offer a gender egalitarian alternative. Among other things, it has been an important advocate for SRHR.

*WIEGO (Women in Informal Employment: Globalizing and Organizing):* Founded in 1997, WIEGO brings together researchers, organisations of informal workers and development practitioners to make visible the contributions of informal workers to all economies, and to assist their organisations in gaining voice in the rule-making bodies that affect their lives.

*IWHC (International Women's Health Coalition):* Founded in 1984, IWHC has become a leading voice for women's health and rights across the world. Its publication, *Population policies reconsidered*, edited by Gita Sen, Adrienne Germain and Lincoln Chen (Sen et al, 1994), played a key role in defining the feminist alternative at the 1994 ICPD. It has since become a key actor in the field of SRHR.

---

DAWN and WIEGO played an important part in making visible the preponderance of women in the **informal economy**. At Nairobi, DAWN criticised Northern feminists' focus on equal pay for work of equal value for assuming women had jobs in the formal sector, so little attention was paid to the informal sector where most women worked. UNIFEM learned from this critique and invited Marty Chen and other key people at WIEGO to edit the third *Progress of the world's women* (2005) focused on this issue. The volume linked women's unpaid domestic labour and their 'choice' of jobs in the informal economy, and advanced a statistical method to assess the poverty risk associated with employment status by sex, constructed a typology of informal employment and developed a new policy tool (an informal economy budget analysis). The issue of women in the informal economy comes up again in the next section.

The 1990s proved an especially important decade for making gender equality and women's empowerment a global norm, with the Vienna Conference on Human Rights in 1993, the Cairo Conference on Population and Development in 1994, the World Summit on Social Development in Copenhagen in 1995, culminating in the Fourth UN Conference on Women, also in 1995, which resulted in the Beijing Platform for Action (BPfA).

The Commission on Population and Development (CPD) was subsequently designated as the review agency on progress towards the ICPD Programme of Action while the CSW was charged with reviewing progress on the BPfA (see **Box 10.3**).

---

### Box 10.3: Elements of the Beijing Platform for Action (BPfA) pertinent to global social policy

The BPfA identified the need for states to tackle the 'feminisation of poverty' by reviewing the impact of neoliberal macroeconomic policies on women's poverty, and called for the research and the development of methodologies to illuminate the gender dimensions of poverty. It identified violence against women as an important global problem.

The BPfA took up the issue of women's equal access to employment and resources, expanding on the ideas embedded in ILO conventions and CEDAW, but it also took on 'new' ideas like that of women's unpaid care work and the consequent need to adjust employment policies to promote the sharing of family responsibility.

The BPfA called for analyses of gender impacts in the development of macro- and microeconomic policy and social policies – or gender mainstreaming – and, recognising that this is more likely to happen when women have 'voice', it called on state parties to 'devise mechanisms and take positive action to enable women to gain access to full and equal participation in the formulation of policies and the definition of structures through such bodies as ministries of finance and trade, national economic commissions, economic research institutes and other key agencies, as well as through their participation in appropriate international bodies' (UN, 1995, p 68).

---

The Beijing conference is often seen as a high point for transnational feminism. However, feminists were not the only ones galvanised by the conferences. So, too, were those opposed to measures that they perceived as threatening to undermine 'the family'. In the 1990s the Holy See played a key role in building these alliances, focused on the issue of reproductive rights. As the new millennium dawned, the US government became its powerful ally. The Trump administration (2017–21) opposed women's rights globally even more actively.

## Gendering global labour policy

Global **labour standards** are set through the conventions and resolutions passed at the ILO's annual International Labour Conferences (ILCs). For most of the 20th century, however, the ILO vision of the 'ideal worker' was a male, unionised, industrial worker, located in the **Global North**. As it gradually attempted to come to grips with an increasingly globalised world, however, the ILO began to consider 'the variety of employment patterns in the economy, which included precarious employment such as casual labour, work in the informal sector, various types of home work and contract work' (O'Brien, 2014, 139–40) (see **Box 10.4**). Below we examine the making of two conventions – ILO Convention No 177 on Home Work and ILO Convention No 189 on Decent Work for Domestic Workers – that reflect this new understanding and its gendered implications. First, however, it is important to trace the ILO's evolving view of women workers.

---

**Box 10.4: The main International Labour Organization (ILO) conventions and recommendations dealing with gender**

*ILO Convention No 100: Equal Remuneration for Men and Women Workers (1951).* Although ratified by 173 of the ILO's 187 member states, the principle of equal pay for work of equal value has been difficult to implement, and the gap between men and women's wages persists.

*ILO Convention No 156: Equal Opportunity and Treatment of Men and Women Workers with Family Responsibilities (1981).* This replaced the 1965 Recommendation on Women with Family Responsibilities, officially recognising that men also had family responsibilities. It was, *however, silent on the unequal division of household work.*

*ILO Convention No 177: Home Work (1996).* This signalled the ILO's recognition of workers in the informal economy. *Conclusions Concerning Decent Work and the Informal Economy* (2002) and *ILO Recommendation No 204: Concerning Transitioning from the Informal to the Formal Economy (2014)* built on these foundations.

---

*ILO Convention No 183 and Recommendation No 191: Maternity Protection (2000).* Like its predecessors ILO Convention Nos 3 and 103, ILO Convention No 183 included provision for maternity leave, employment protection, cash and medical benefits, and protection from work harmful to the mother or child. Accompanying Recommendation No 191 suggested employed mothers *or* fathers be entitled to parental leave following the expiry of maternity leave.

*ILO Convention No 189: Decent Work for Domestic Workers and Recommendation No 201 (2011).* These focused on the rights to decent work of a particularly vulnerable category of workers in the informal economy, a group that is predominantly composed of women.

*ILO Convention No 190: Violence and Harassment at Work (2019).* This attempts to come to grips with violence against women in the workplace.

Although the ILO focused on the male breadwinner, from the outset it was aware that women were workers too. One of the first conventions the ILC passed was Convention No 3 (1919) on maternity protection. This appealed to both sides of the then-current debate that pitted protectionists, who felt women's reproductive role required special protections, against equal rights feminists. Although the balance shifted in favour of the latter, during the ILO's first years, the ILC tended to side with the protectionists, as reflected in ILO Convention No 4, prohibiting night work, and Convention No 13, prohibiting women from working in industries using white lead paint. Convention No 45 sought to ban women's work underground.

As women's labour force participation began to rise in the 1960s, the ILC began to reflect on the challenges women face in reconciling work and family life. In 1965 it agreed on Recommendation No 123, encouraging states to facilitate the development of supportive services, such as childcare. The ILO's position further evolved in response to the UN Conferences on Women. On the eve of the first such conference, it passed a Declaration on Equality of Opportunity and Treatment for Women Workers. Following the Second UN Conference on Women, the ILC adopted Convention No 156, Equal Opportunities and Equal Treatment for Men and Women Workers: Workers with Family Responsibilities. Although this formally identified male workers' family responsibilities, it failed to acknowledge the unequal sharing of unpaid domestic and care work, which would only come later.

The Declaration also reiterated women's right to equal pay for work of equal value (Article 7), and the same Conference noted the ILO's responsibility to collect statistics to make visible the gap between men and women's wages (Neunsinger, 2018, p 145). The equal pay principle had actually been affirmed in the 1919

ILO Constitution (Whitworth, 1997, p 128), but it was only in 1951 that the ILC passed Convention No 100, Equal Remuneration. Progress towards the development of techniques to measure 'equal value' has been slow. Moreover, its conception of equality continued to ignore those in the informal economy, which remains 'a more important source of non-agricultural employment for women than for men' (Bonner et al, 2018, p 176).

The ILO began to be aware of the informal economy through its World Employment Programme, via its field offices in the South. Thus, ILO-India worked with the Self Employed Women's Association (SEWA) to document the extent of home-based work, a project later replicated in several other Southeast Asian countries (Bonner et al, 2018, p 182). SEWA, HomeNet, the International Union of Food, Agricultural, Hotel, Restaurant, Catering, Tobacco and Allied Workers (IUF), and other unions helped put ILO Convention No 177 (1996) on Home Work on the ILC's agenda a decade later. To provide critical material for the ILC's resolution on *Conclusions concerning decent work and the informal economy*, the Secretariat engaged WIEGO's international coordinator to produce the first ILO report *Women and men in the informal economy: A statistical picture* (2002). In addition to recognising self-employed home workers as workers, the resolution committed the ILO to ongoing collection of statistics, enabling it to make visible the extent and gendered nature of home work. In 2014, the ILC went a step further, passing Recommendation No 204: Concerning the Transition from the Informal to the Formal Economy. More recently, Sustainable Development Goal (SDG) indicator 8.3.1 calls for the measurement of the proportion of informal employment in the non-agricultural sector, by sex, to monitor progress in making such a transition.

The ILO also moved to regulate an area of the informal economy dominated by women – paid domestic work. **Domestic workers** fill the gaps, enabling other women to combine work and family life when neither men nor states (in the form of care services and leave arrangements) have stepped in to help. As a substitute for women's hitherto unpaid domestic labour, such work is undervalued and often not regarded as work. Domestic workers are typically excluded from protective legislation and **social security** systems. They are especially vulnerable as their work is hidden in the household. This is particularly true for many migrant domestic workers who are frequently denied any of the rights associated with citizenship.

In 2011, the ILC passed Convention No 189 and Recommendation No 201 on Decent Work for Domestic Workers. The International Domestic Workers' Federation (IDWF), in alliance with the IUF and WIEGO, played an important part (Boris and Fish, 2014; Bonner et al, 2018) in making visible domestic work and the often exploitative conditions under which it is performed. The ILO, which now publishes data on domestic work, estimates that there are 67 million domestic workers across the world, 80 per cent of whom are women (see www.ilo.org/global/topics/domestic-workers/lang--en/index.htm). Since the passage of Convention No 189, the ILO has worked with the IDWF and the International Trade Union Confederation (ITUC) at the regional and national scales to promote decent work for domestic workers. Although only 29 countries have ratified it, such work has helped to bring about improvements even in countries that have not ratified it.

## Unpaid domestic work: recognise, reduce and redistribute

Since Waring's path-breaking work (1988), feminist economists have endeavoured to make visible the extent and the unequal distribution of unpaid domestic and care work and its importance to economic development and human wellbeing. This has led to a call to recognise, reduce and redistribute unpaid domestic and care work. To these original '3 Rs' can be added two additional 'Rs': rewarding care workers properly, and representing them via social dialogue and collective bargaining (Esquivel and Rodriguez Enriquez, 2020, pp 289–90) (see **Box 10.5**). Together the '5 Rs' hold the promise of formalising informal work and generating jobs that are comprehensively covered by social protection and offer good working conditions.

Recognition of women's continued responsibility across the world for unpaid domestic work did not happen overnight. ILO Convention No 156: Workers with Family Responsibilities encouraged provision of social services to enable women to reconcile work and family life, but this left untouched the remaining domestic work, carried out by women as part of their 'double burden', or passed on to other women, often from less powerful socioeconomic groups as paid domestic work. Shortages of licensed childcare have also fuelled the growth of care services in the informal economy in both North and South.

Feminist mobilisation at the Beijing Conference on Women resulted in unpaid domestic work being taken up in the BPfA, which called for the development of methods to quantify the value 'of unremunerated work … such as caring for dependents and preparing food … with a view to recognizing the economic contribution of women and making visible the unequal distribution of remunerated and unremunerated work between women and men' (UN, 1995, pp 87–8). The first issue of UNIFEM's *The progress of the world's women* sought to make visible 'women's provision of services within households for other household members' (2000, p 9). It is only in the last decade, however, that women's unpaid domestic work has come to be widely recognised in GSP practice.

Not surprisingly, UN Women has taken up the call to 'recognise, reduce and redistribute' domestic work. Thus, *The progress of the world's women 2015–16* highlighted the importance of the unpaid care and domestic work to human wellbeing and economic development, and embraced the '3 Rs'. Mobilising around the **Sustainable Development Goals** (SDGs), the Women's Major Group

## Box 10.5: The '5 Rs' of the care economy

*Recognition:* acknowledging the fundamental contribution of care work within a household to the production of human capabilities. This does not mean 'wages for housework', as demanded by the International Wages for Housework campaign, as this would simply entrench women's unequal share of domestic work. Rather, it is a question of making visible the contribution to the daily and intergenerational reproduction of society and its unequal division. This can be done through time use surveys and the introduction of satellite accounts.

*Reduction:* involves investment in physical infrastructure (water, sanitation, clean energy) to reduce domestic work that persists in many parts of the world as well as investment in care services. Attention has often focused on childcare as this can increase women's labour force participation, boost fertility levels, prevent the intergenerational transmission of poverty and improve (future) **human capital**. In addition to daily care for able-bodied adults, the care agenda encompasses care for frail elderly people, and those with severe illnesses and disabilities.

*Redistribution:* there are limits to the 'defamilialisation' of domestic work and care. Maternity leave reinforces the idea that it is a woman's job to care for very young children. Parental leave, when it is accompanied by incentives to get both parents to share the leave, contributes to redistribution. Leave insurance to care for a sick or dying relative and flexible work schedules also facilitate redistribution. Yet it is important to go beyond these to include measures to make men's working lives more like those of women's via reductions in normal working time.

*Reward:* domestic work is part of a larger 'care economy', which includes 'economic activities in the home, market, community and state that fit loosely under the rubric of human services and have a particularly strong personal and emotional dimension: activities such as child rearing, childcare, healthcare, elder care, social work and education' (Folbre, 2006, p 12). Women typically predominate in these fields. In the absence of adequate public investment, these labour-intensive services often generate low pay as higher wages mean higher prices for those using the services. Depressing wages, however, is not a solution as this results in lower quality of care, again, as conditions in long-term care homes have been revealed by COVID-19. Fair wages for care workers contribute to quality care that also benefits recipients.

*Representation:* reinforces reward by giving both care workers and recipients a voice, that is, the capacity and space to participate in the debate. Rights mean little without the ability to claim them. Organisations like trade unions and organisations representing care recipients thus have a crucial role to play.

used the '3 Rs' framework to secure SDG Target 5.4: 'Recognize and value unpaid care and domestic work through the provision of public services, infrastructure and social protection policies, and the promotion of shared responsibility within the household and the family as nationally appropriate' (https://indicators.reports/targets/5-4). Similarly, the Agreed Conclusions to the 61st Session of the CSW included demands for 'decent paid care and domestic work for women and men' as well as for adequately reimbursed parental leave (CSW, 2017).

*Reward* and *representation* came up in the reports of the two working groups for the UN Secretary-General's High-Level Panel on Women's Economic Empowerment. The Working Group on Driver 3 (the '3 Rs') argued that 'Where care services are offered, they should be of high quality and protect the rights and dignity of those cared for and the workers that care for them' (UN Secretary-General's High-Level Panel on Women's Economic Empowerment, 2017a, p 1). The Working Group on Driver 7, 'Strengthening visibility, collective voice and representation', argued that 'Collective organization through trade unions and other membership-based organizations and collectives enhances women's ability ... to negotiate terms and conditions of employment; to access markets and supply chains; and to influence policies that may have a direct bearing on their lives, through tripartite dialogue and through collective bargaining and other forms of negotiations' (UN Secretary-General's High-Level Panel on Women's Economic Empowerment, 2017b, p 1). In addition to urging ratification of ILO Convention No 87: Right to Organise and No 98: Right to Organise and Collective Bargaining, it urged the reform of legal frameworks to protect informal workers and promote the formalisation of their work in line with ILO Recommendation No 204: Concerning Transitioning from the Informal to the Formal Economy.

The issue has also been taken up at the regional scale. Through documents prepared for the biennial conferences, the commissioning of studies by feminist scholars in the region and work with technical experts on projects such as the time use survey, the UN Economic Commission for Latin America and the Caribbean (ECLAC) began to develop the idea of the care economy as early as 2004. In Sub-Saharan Africa, transnational women's networks like Solidarity for African Women's Rights and the African Women's Development and Communication Network have actively pushed for the recognition and reduction of women's unpaid domestic and care work. At the Asia-Pacific preparatory meetings for Beijing+25, DAWN and other TFNs fought hard to advance women's rights against opposition, securing agreement to 'accelerate efforts to reduce and redistribute unpaid care and domestic work, recognizing that failing to act contributes to placement of informal domestic worker and migrant workers in precarious environments' (Kowalski, 2020).

It is not only IGOs with strong links to feminist epistemic communities that have taken up the idea of paid and unpaid care work. In 2013, the International

Conference of Labour Statisticians adopted a resolution that redefined work activities 'to include all forms of work, including the unpaid care work performed by women and girls in households' (Razavi, 2015, pp 434–5). The United Nations Development Programme's (UNDP) 2015 Human Development Report noted that work includes care work, which may or may not be paid and may be carried out in the formal or informal economy. UNDP devoted Chapter Four of its 2015 report to exploring the gendered imbalance in paid and unpaid work, noting with particular concern a global shortage of 13.6 million care workers, especially in long-term care. It, too, concluded the need to reduce and redistribute the burden of unpaid care while improving the outcomes for care workers by introducing legislation prohibiting sexual harassment at work, promoting equal pay and introducing mandatory parental leave (UNDP, 2015, p 122).

Outside the UN, the Organisation for Economic Co-operation and Development (OECD) moved from a narrow concern to increase women's labour force participation to incorporate insights from feminists like Janet Gornick as well as from ongoing debates in several of the countries studied. Although its *Babies and bosses* study (2001–07) originally focused on work–family reconciliation, as the study progressed, the OECD learned that it was important to get fathers to take their share of parental leave (Mahon, 2009). By the time it published *Closing the gender gap* (OECD, 2012), it had also incorporated the concept of unpaid domestic work. The OECD's gender database includes 'time spent in unpaid, paid and total work, by sex' (www.oecd.org/gender/data/employment). Nor has the OECD focused solely on the care needs of working parents. It recently published *Who cares? Attracting and retaining care workers for the elderly* (2020), in which it argues that the COVID-19-induced crisis in long-term care is simply making visible pre-existing structural problems in a sector where 90 per cent of the workers are women. The World Bank's 2012 *World development report: Gender equality and development* acknowledged the importance of access to clean water and sanitation to the reduction of women's unpaid work. The World Economic Forum's (WEF) 'dialogue' on Gender and Work, headed by Caren Grown of the World Bank, Monika Queisser from the OECD and Phumzile Mlambo-Ngcuka, Executive Director for UN Women, also took up the question of 'What are the key features of a robust care economy sector?' (WEF, 2015). Although the WEF dialogue reiterated the importance of 'the 3 Rs', like the World Bank, it put less weight on reward and representation.

The gendered care economy has thus entered the lexicon and practices of a range of international organisations (IOs) and the formal architecture of **global social governance** and policy through the work of feminist scholars and activists. For the most part, the original '3 Rs' have come to be seen as a gender-responsive solution to growing care needs across the globe. Differences remain over the auspices of care (public and non-profit vs for-profit; formal vs informal) as well as how to promote fathers taking up their share of **domestic work and care**.

Thus far, little consideration has been given to redefining the normal work day so that men's work hours become more like women's, although in her plans for post–COVID-19 recovery, Jacinda Ardern, Prime Minister of New Zealand, has floated the idea of a four-day work week.

## Sexual and reproductive health and rights: contested terrain

Since the 1990s, women's right to control their fertility, so critical to their ability to enjoy other rights, has been recognised at the global scale, most notably through the 1994 International Conference on Population and Development (ICPD) in Cairo and the BPfA. In the new millennium headway was also made for the broader idea of sexual and reproductive health and rights (SRHR). It has never been uncontested, however. The Holy See long opposed birth control (beyond the rhythm method), and it has found new allies. The UN Human Rights Council, the ICPD and the CSW are important sites for engagement of the opposing forces, especially during the quinquennial reviews of the ICPD Programme of Action and the BPfA. While TFNs like DAWN and the IWHC played a critical role in promoting SRHR from the outset, they have been joined by a new generation that places greater emphasis on sexualities, gender identities, violence against sex workers and the rights of indigenous and racialised women.

Women's rights advocates were by no means the only ones initially promoting birth control. Support from more powerful quarters came in the name of a neo-Malthusian concern to control population increase, especially among the poor. As Hendrixson et al note, 'From Malthus' time onward, the implied "over" in population has invariably referred to poorer people, people from black and disadvantaged groups or people from the colonies or countries of the South' (2014, p 265). As decolonisation gained pace in the 1950s, the issue of population control was taken up at the 1954 World Population Conference in Rome, which focused on the demographic situation of developing countries (www.un.org/en/development/devagenda/population.shtml). The second conference coincided with the US government's adoption of population policy as part of its 'war on poverty'. That government's aim was to promote population control in the South as a way to simultaneously combat poverty and the spread of communism (Whitworth, 1997, p 87). By the end of the decade, 'the UNFPA, the World Bank, USAID, and a range of non-governmental organizations such as International Planned Parenthood Federation, as well as national organizations, were all … involved in refining, establishing and administering family planning programmes' (Sending, 2004, p 63). Northern family planning advocates faced ongoing opposition from the Holy See and certain Latin American countries, and at the 1974 Population Conference they encountered broader pushback from the South, arguing 'development is the best contraceptive'.

In the 1980s the global alignment of forces on the issue shifted. Reagan's election resulted in the USA taking a clear anti-abortion position. At the 1984 Population Conference in Mexico City, the US government introduced a 'global gag' rule, denying funds to any non-governmental organisation (NGO) advocating decriminalisation of abortion or providing abortion counselling, referrals or services. The same year, however, the first international reproductive rights conference resulted in a consensus around the concept of reproductive rights (Corrêa, 2015, p 458). At the Third UN Conference on Women, the two sides clashed openly as abortion opponents mobilised under the 'right to life' banner (Corrêa et al, 2016, p 8), while DAWN countered with the argument that 'Control over reproduction is a basic need and a basic rights for all women.... But our bodies have become a pawn in the struggle among states, religions, male heads of households and private corporations' (Sen and Grown, 1988, p 49).

In Latin America, feminists like Brazilian Sonia Corrêa engaged in the struggle for reproductive rights as part of the broader process of democratisation (Corrêa et al, 2016, p 8). In New York, Joan Dunlop and Adrienne Germain formed the IWHC, and began to frame the struggle for birth control as part of a broader health programme including maternal and child health, safe motherhood and child survival. The IWHC would go on to play an important role in making women's reproductive health and rights globally visible, gathering 'feminist professionals and activists ... along with top researchers and policy makers from many countries of the North and South to contribute dozens of publications and policy debates on neglected core elements of SRHR', such as safe abortion, contraceptive choices, quality of family planning services and the issue of sexually transmitted infections (Corrêa et al, 2016, p 7).

While transnational feminist mobilisation in advance of the 1994 UN Conference on Population and Development and the Fourth UN Conference on Women has been well described elsewhere, the key points to emphasise here are as follows. First, the strategy of the emerging women's reproductive health movement 'took the form of strategically commissioning and using research to establish a different problem-definition of fertility behaviour, one that emphasized the importance of paying more attention to the socio-economic status, rights and health needs of women' (Sending, 2004, p 64). In other words, they produced the knowledge to make the importance of women's reproductive health and rights visible. Second, reproductive rights activists secured important allies like the Women's Environment and Development Organisation (WEDO), which enabled them to garner support for reproductive rights at the 1992 UN Conference on the Environment in Rio and taught them to work effectively within the UN system (Corrêa et al, 2016, p 11). And third, their research and the broader (reproductive health and rights) framing helped gain allies within key IOs such as the World Health Organization (WHO) and United Nations Population Fund (UNFPA) (Corrêa et al, 2016, p 8).

The ICPD is widely considered to have produced a new rights–based and gendered population paradigm. The BPfA built on TFN gains in Cairo. Paragraph 223:

> … reaffirms that reproductive rights rest on the recognition of the basic right of all couples and individuals to decide freely and responsibly the number, spacing and timing of their children and to have the information and means to do so, and the right to attain the highest standard of sexual and reproductive health … free of discrimination, coercion and violence. (UN, 1995, p 91)

It also repudiated the thinking behind the USA's gag law (withdrawn by the Clinton administration): Paragraph 106(k) notes, 'in all cases, women should have access to quality services for the management of complications arising from abortion', and that countries should consider reviewing laws that criminalise abortion (UN, 1995, p 40). While these can be seen as important gains for women's reproductive rights, the BPfA was criticised for its heteronormative assumptions. Lesbian rights had already been placed on the global agenda by the first UN Special Rapporteur on Violence Against Women, who was critical of violence against women 'who live out their sexuality in ways other than heterosexual', as was her successor (Saiz, 2004, p 58). In Beijing, however, such efforts were defeated:

> … four references to the persecution of women for their sexual orientation in the draft Platform for Action were dropped after the Vatican and some Islamic states, supported by organizations of the Christian right, decried the "hijacking of human rights" by feminists and lesbian rights activists as a major threat to fundamental religious and cultural values. (Saiz, 2004, p 58)

The same forces mobilised at the ICPD5 meetings of the CPD, and in 2000, several states successfully opposed insertion into the BPfA reference to prohibition of discrimination on the basis of sexual orientation. At this point, under the George W. Bush administration, the USA restored the 'gag' law and went on to play an instrumental role in keeping reproductive health out of the original **Millennium Development Goals** (MDGs) (Corrêa, 2015, p 463). However, the Women's Major Group and UN Women and their state party allies were able to ensure that reproductive rights were included in the SDGs, although there is no reference to abortion, and the SDGs are silent on the rights of LGBTQI people (**Box 10.6**).

---

**Box 10.6: Sexual and reproductive health and rights (SRHR) in the Sustainable Development Goals (SDGs)**

*SDG 3.7*: Ensure universal access to sexual and reproductive healthcare services, including for family planning, information and education and the integration of reproductive health into national strategies and programmes.

*SDG 5.6*: Ensure universal access to sexual and reproductive health and reproductive rights as agreed in accordance with the Programme of Action of the ICPD and BPfA, and the outcome documents of their review conferences.

---

Although there has been a stalemate on reproductive rights and abortion, proponents of sexual rights have made some headway. UN treaty bodies like the Human Rights Committee, the Committee on Economic, Social and Cultural Rights, the Committee on the Elimination of Discrimination Against Women and the Committee on the Rights of the Child have all upheld LGBTQI rights (Saiz, 2004; Aylward and Halford, 2020). In 2004 the UN Special Rapporteur for Health released *The right of everyone to the enjoyment of the highest attainable standard of physical and mental health,* Article 55 of which clearly staked out the importance of *sexual* as well as reproductive rights: 'Since many expressions of sexuality are non-reproductive, it is misguided to subsume sexual rights, including the right to sexual health, under reproductive rights and reproductive health.' In 2006, the WHO, the International Planned Parenthood Federation and the World Association for Sexual Health all endorsed a similar definition of sexual rights (Dandan and Yiping, 2018, p 5). That same year, a meeting of human rights experts developed the Yogyakarta Principles, which affirmed binding international legal standards behind the right to one's sexual orientation or gender identity.

TFNs like DAWN and IWHC have been working with younger generations concerned to make visible the plight of marginalised groups, including Indigenous and Afro-Descendant women, **refugees** and migrants, and sex workers. At the same time, the USA's Trump administration reinstated the 'gag' rule, and installed social and religious conservatives in influential positions in the State Department and the Agency for International Development (USAID) to make global the fight against abortion and LGBTQI rights (Gramer, 2019). The ICPD Programme of Action and the BPfA may have been reaffirmed in SDG 5.6, but there is no mention of LGBTQI rights.

Opponents of SRHR were also visible at the ICPD25 Summit in Nairobi, but the 12 commitments made in Nairobi included investment in sexual and reproductive health services for adolescents and youth; that no one is left behind because of race, religion, disability, sex, sexual orientation and gender identity or expression; and 'nothing about young people's health and wellbeing can be discussed and decided upon without their meaningful involvement and participation' (www.nairobisummiticpd.org/content/icpd25–commitments). In other words, SRHR has become a global norm, upheld by UN treaty bodies like the Human Rights Council and the Committee on Economic and Social Rights, which can draw on a deepening pool of expertise. INGOs like the IWHC have contributed to that knowledge. In the process, the concepts of gender and sexuality have been enriched. To be sure, SRHR remains a contested norm in GSP, but that very contestation has heightened its visibility.

## Conclusion

Women's demand for equality has long been on the international agenda and part of GSP practice. March 8, International Women's Day, was first celebrated in 1911 by a transnational women's movement demanding the right to vote, hold public office and enter the labour force without facing discrimination. The League of Nations and one of its most important creatures, the ILO, were also forced to acknowledge these claims. The four UN Conferences on Women, and the transnational women's movements they helped to form, have made gender equality and women's empowerment a global norm, with ramifications for many areas of GSP. They also served to establish key elements of a gender equality institutional architecture. At the same time, conservative states and social movements now confront feminists within their 'own' spaces like the CSW. Such opposition has grown to the point that Sandler and Goetz (2020) question whether the UN can indeed deliver 'a feminist future', although they find grounds for cautious optimism in UN Women and its connections with vibrant transnational feminist networks and epistemic communities. The former provides an important space for feminist activists to counter misogynist and homophobic forces, while the latter can offer their critical knowledge and grassroots support.

If gender is thus recognised as an important if contested aspect of GSP practice, the same cannot be said of the study of GSP. This chapter has outlined some of the ways *the study* of GSP can incorporate a gender lens. While this chapter focused on labour policy, the push to recognise, reward and redistribute unpaid domestic and care work and SRHR, poverty, social protection, education, migration, food security as well as less obvious areas like trade policy and the environment can also fruitfully be viewed through a gender lens.

## Summary

- GSP has been gendered through the formation of an institutional architecture developed especially since the UN Conferences on Women (1975–95).
- The ILO grasped the importance of gender differences from the outset, but its understanding has evolved in response to changes in labour markets and families, growing awareness of the specific challenges women face in the Global South, and the work of TFNs like WIEGO and DAWN.
- Feminist scholarship and advocacy helped identify the unequal sharing of domestic work and care, leading to the call to recognise, reduce, redistribute, reward and represent care work.
- As paid domestic work has grown in the absence of measures to redistribute domestic and care work, ILO Convention No 189 aims to secure decent work for domestic workers.
- SRHR has expanded from a focus on women to encompass sexual orientations and gender identities. Both versions have met with resistance from the Holy See, some Islamic countries and conservative states. However, the generation of feminists that pushed for the original version are working with younger activists at the ICPD+25 (Nairobi, 2019) and Beijing+25 (Paris, 2021).

## Questions for discussion

- How might gender be better woven into the study of GSP? What impact would the incorporation of a gender lens have on how we see various GSP issues?
- Has COVID-19 added new urgency to the demand to recognise, reduce and redistribute care? How important are the other two Rs – reward and representation – to the achievement of the first three?
- The current debate on SRHR has troubled the concept of 'gender', going beyond the male–female binary. How might this broader understanding affect a range of GSP issues beyond health?

## Follow-up activities

- Has there been any debate in your country about the newer ILO conventions – No 189 on Decent Work for Domestic Workers and No 190 on Violence and Harassment at Work? Has your country ratified either?
- Most countries, having ratified the CEDAW, must regularly report on progress to the Committee on the Elimination of Discrimination Against Women. What did CEDAW say about your country's progress on gender equality? What issues did your country emphasise in its report? Did women's organisations submit shadow reports to the Committee? What were their concerns?

• The SDGs took up a number of the issues covered in this chapter. How has your country been doing with regard to these? How did your country deal with gender issues at home and abroad in its report to the High-Level Political Forum on Sustainable Development?

## Further resources

TFNs play an important role in making the gender dimensions of global social policy issues visible. Check out the websites of one of the following: DAWN (https://dawnnet.org), WIEGO (https://wiego.org) or IWHC (https://iwhc.org). In addition to *Global Social Policy* and the *Journal of International and Comparative Social Policy*, journals like *Feminist Economics*, *Signs* and the *International Journal of Feminist Politics* offer insights into the work being done within these feminist epistemic communities relevant to the gendering of global social policy studies.

## References

Aylward, E. and Halford, S. (2020) 'How gains for SRHR in the UN have remained possible in a changing political climate', *Sexual and Reproductive Health Matters*, 28(1).

Bezanson, K. and Luxton, M. (2006) 'Social reproduction: Feminist political economy', in K. Bezanson and M. Luxton (eds) *Social reproduction: Feminist political economy challenges neo-liberalism*, Montreal: McGill-Queen's University Press, 3–10.

Bonner, C., Horn, P. and Jhabvala, R. (2018) 'Informal women workers open ILO doors through transnational organizing', in E. Boris, D. Hoehtker and S. Zimmerman (eds) *Women's ILO: Transnational networks, global labour standards and gender equity 1919 to the present*, Geneva and Leiden: ILO and Brill, 176–201.

Boris, E. and Fish, J.N. (2014) '"Slaves no more": Making global standards for domestic workers', *Feminist Studies*, 40(2), 411–43.

Caglar, G., Prügl, E. and Zwingel, S. (2013) 'Introducing feminist strategies in international governance', in G. Caglar, E. Prügl and S. Zwingel (eds) *Feminist strategies in international governance*, London and New York: Routledge, 1–18.

Corrêa, S. (2015) 'Reproductive and sexual rights: Transnational trends from a global south perspective', in J.D. Write (ed) *International encyclopedia of the social and behavioral sciences* (2nd edn), Amsterdam: Elsevier, 457–67.

Corrêa, S., Germain, A. and Sen, G. (2016) 'Feminist mobilizing for global commitments to the sexual and reproductive health and rights of women and girls', in E. Chesler and T. McGovern (eds) *Women and girls arising: Progress and resistance around the world*, London: Routledge, Chapter 4.

CSW (Commission on the Status of Women) (2017) *Women's economic empowerment in a changing world of work. Agreed conclusions of the 61st session of the CSW*, New York: United Nations.

Dandan, Z. and Yiping, C. (2018) 'Body, sexuality and reproduction in a changing context: Advocacy notes from DAWN', DAWN (Development Alternatives with Women for a New Era), 12 October (https://dawnnet.org/publication/body-sexuality-and-reproduction-in-a-changing-context).

Esquivel, V. and Rodriguez Enriquez, C. (2020) 'The Beijing Platform for Action charted a future we still need to bring up: Building feminist economic policy', *Gender & Development*, 28(2), 281–98.

Folbre, N. (2006) 'Demanding quality: Worker/consumer coalitions and the "high road" strategy in the care sector', *Politics and Society*, 34(1), 11–31.

Gramer, R. (2019) 'US quietly waters down another communique on gender equality', FP, 17 May (https://foreignpolicy.com/2019/05/17/united-states-waters-down-G7-communique-gender-equality-international-organizations-womens-rights-sexual-reproductive-health).

Hendrixson, A., Hildyard, N., Lohmann, L. and Sexton, S. (2014) 'Global population policy', in N. Yeates (ed) *Understanding global social policy* (2nd edn), Bristol: Policy Press, 261–84.

ILO (International Labour Organization) (1975) *Declaration on Equality of Opportunity and Treatment for Women Workers*, Official Bulletin, vol LVIII, Series A.

ILO (2002) *Women and men in the informal economy: A statistical picture*, Geneva: ILO.

Kowalski, S. (2020) '"Beijing+25" US objections can't stifle progress in Asia-Pacific', International Women's Health Coalition, 26 February (https://iwhc.org/2020/02/beijing25-us-objections-cant-stifle-progress-in-asia-pacific).

Mahon, R. (2009) 'The OECD's discourse on the reconciliation of work and family life', *Global Social Policy*, 9(2), 183–203.

Neunsinger, S. (2018) 'The unobtainable magic of numbers: Equal remuneration, the ILO and the international trade union movement 1950s–1980s', in E. Boris, D. Hoehtker and S. Zimmermann (eds) *Women's ILO: Transnational networks, global labour standards and gender equity, 1919 to present*, Geneva and Leiden: ILO/Brill, 121–49.

O'Brien, R. (2014) 'Global labour policy', in N. Yeates (ed) *Understanding global social policy* (2nd edn), Bristol: Policy Press, 131–58.

OECD (Organisation for Economic Co-operation and Development) (2012) *Closing the gender gap: Act now*, Paris: OECD.

OECD (2020) *Who cares? Attracting and retaining care workers for the elderly*, Paris: OECD.

Razavi, S. (2015) 'Care and social reproduction: Some reflections on concepts, policies and politics from a development perspective', in D. Béland, C. Howard and K. Morgan (eds) *The Oxford handbook of transnational feminist movements*, Oxford: Oxford University Press, 422–42.

Saiz, I. (2004) 'Bracketing sexuality: Human rights and sexual orientation: A decade of development and denial at the UN', *Health and Human Rights*, 7(2), 48–80.

Sandler, J. and Goetz, A.M. (2020) 'Can the United Nations deliver a feminist future?', *Gender and Development*, 20(2), 239–63.

Sen, G. and Grown, C. (1988) *Development, crises and alternatives vision: Third world women's perspectives*, London and Washington, DC: Earthscan.

Sen, G., Germain, A. and Chen, L. (1994) *Population policies reconsidered*, New York: International Women's Health Coalition.

Sending, J.O. (2004) 'Policy stories and knowledge-based regimes: The case of international population policy', in M. Bøås and D. McNeill (eds) *Global institutions and development: Framing the world?*, London: Routledge, 56–72.

Stienstra, D. (1994) *Women's movements and international organizations*, New York: St Martin's Press.

UN (United Nations) (1995) *Beijing Declaration and Platform for Action at the Fourth World Conference on Women* (www.un.org/womenwatch/daw/beijing/platform).

UN Secretary-General's High-Level Panel on Women's Economic Empowerment (2017a) *Recognize, reward and redistribute unpaid work and care*, Driver 3 Working Group, Report to the UN Secretary-General's High-Level Panel (https://hlp-wee.unwomen.org/en/reports-toolkits).

UN Secretary-General's High-Level Panel on Women's Economic Empowerment (2017b) *Strengthening visibility, collective voice and representation*, Driver 7 Working Group, Report to the UN Secretary-General's High-Level Panel (https://hlp-wee.unwomen.org/en/reports-toolkit).

UNDP (United Nations Development Programme) (2015) *Human development report 2015: Work for human development*, New York: UNDP.

UNIFEM (United Nations Development Fund for Women) (2000) *The progress of the world's women*, New York: UNIFEM.

UNIFEM (2002) *The progress of the world's women: Gender equality and the Millennium Development Goals*, New York: UNIFEM.

UNIFEM (2005) *The progress of the world's women: Women, work and poverty*, New York: UNIFEM.

Waring, M. (1988) *If women counted: A new feminist economics*, New York: Harper & Row.

WEF (World Economic Forum) (2015) *Global gender gap report*, Geneva: WEF (www3.weforum.org/docs/WEF_GGGR_2020.pdf).

Whitworth, S. (1997) *Feminism and international relations*, New York: St Martins Press.

World Bank (2012) *World development report: Gender equality and development*, Washington, DC: World Bank.

# 11

# Young people and global social policy

Ross Fergusson

## Overview

As a field of study, global social policy has been largely silent about the social relations and political-economic relations of age regarding young people. But global social policy as a political practice has long been attentive to young people, since the foundation of the League of Nations in 1920. The core of global social policy regarding young people has revolved around the education–employment nexus within a wider field spanning social protection, health, social inclusion, economic security and participation in international development. This chapter traces core elements of the global institutional architecture of governance concerning young people, the growing understanding of their position in the world economy, and the normative power of the youth transitions discourse in global policy-making. It examines key tensions between 'protectionism' and 'economism' in relation to young people, global policy concerning young people's participation, and the powers and activities of international organisations.

## Key concepts

Young people; education; employment and unemployment; economism and protectionism; transitions discourse; NEET ('not in education, employment or training'); demand-side failures; supply-side failures

## Introduction

Young people worldwide are typically the objects of care, protection, nurture, development and preparation for independent adulthood. Most social policies exist primarily in recognition of their vulnerability and of their need for protection from many potential harms: physical and mental neglect; exploitation; emotional, physical and/or sexual abuse; forced labour and economic exploitation;

victimisation; and criminal acts. But this emphasis on protection is not universal, and young people's development between childhood and adulthood is experienced in such diverse ways across countries and types of society and economy as to make sweeping generalisations about the state of the world's youth misleading.

In almost all countries the processes of young people's care, nurture and personal development, and of exploitation, violence and harm are, to differing degrees, influenced by *global* as well as national social policy. The work of **intergovernmental** and **international non-governmental organisations** (IGOs and INGOs) and the processes of **global governance** have produced a wide array of international standards and normative frameworks guiding national policies. This chapter outlines how **global social policy** (GSP) has incorporated attention to young people aged 15–24 years into social policy development. It begins with definitional issues concerning young people, highlighting key features of a century of the global institutional architecture concerning them. It then focuses on young people's 'transitions', the concept of being 'not in education, employment or training' (NEET), and conflicting interpretations of causes of youth unemployment. The final section reviews how GSP and IGOs have responded to mass youth unemployment.

## Young people and social policy: definitions and distinctions

A key challenge for GSP concerning young people's wellbeing and development is that 'youth' is not a self-evident category. According to country, culture and religion, distinctions between 'child' and 'young person', and 'young person' and '(young) adult' can be ambiguous or variable. Biological age alone does not define these categories.

One useful way of identifying international differences between these age groups and categories is to view them in terms of participation (or non-participation) in education or employment. These two policy fields mark critical junctures in children's and young people's development: starting school (typically ages 3–6), electing to continue education and training beyond the legal requirement (14–18), and starting 'work' – or facing unemployment (14+). These junctures that mark growth towards autonomy and independence apply in most societies, but specific age ranges vary – for example, according to whether they are compulsory or elective, and whether according to national law, custom and practice, or variations of entitlement or obligation (accepting employment contracts and receiving welfare benefits, for example). Whether we focus on chronological age, legal statuses and obligations or perceived social, cognitive, physical or sexual maturity, the categories of child, youth/young person and adult elude universal definition.

While this 'state of ambiguity' poses difficulties when comparing countries, these distinctions between childhood dependence, young people's progressively developing independence and full adult independence are useful because they signify crucial *transitions* in everyone's 'life course' (MacDonald and Marsh, 2005; Jones, 2009; Shildrick et al, 2012; Furlong, 2013; MacDonald and Shildrick, 2018). Starting school, leaving education and beginning paid work are widely understood as *the* important markers of developing autonomy and independence. They provide convenient lenses for interpreting the significance and insights of GSP for understanding young people across countries (see **Box 11.1**). But they are not the whole story: they describe transitions in the countries of the **Global North** better than those of the **Global South**, where, for example, for young women in some cultures early childbirth and motherhood are not just complicating factors, but also crucial status markers of greater significance than schooling or employment.

## Box 11.1: Global definition of young people

For statistical purposes, the United Nations (UN) defines 'youth' as those between the ages of 15 and 24, without prejudice to other definitions by member states. This definition was established during preparations for the International Youth Year (1985), and endorsed by the UN General Assembly (UNGA) (see A/36/215 and Resolution 36/28, 1981). All UN statistics of demography, education, employment and health are based on this definition. Children are therefore those age 14 years or under. However, Article 1 of the UN Convention on the Rights of the Child (CRC) defines children as those up to the age of 18. This difference was intentional, as it was hoped that the resolution would provide protection for and the rights of young people.

Many countries demarcate youth by the age at which a person is given equal treatment under the law – often referred to as the 'age of majority' (18 years in most countries). Once a person passes this age, they are considered to be an adult. However, regardless of these international definitions, operational definitions of 'youth' vary between countries, depending on sociocultural, economic and political factors. Within the category 'youth', it is also important to distinguish between teenagers (13–19) and young adults (20–24), since the sociological, psychological and other influences they experience differ.

Nevertheless, however we define youth, the world's population has never been so young: there are approximately a *billion* young people. Although this is the highest number in history, the global *proportion* of young people is in decline. In 1985 it was 19 per cent of the total population, 18 per cent in 1995, and by 2025, it is expected to decline to 15 per cent. Much of this change occurred in the 1990s, when annual growth in the world's youth population slowed almost everywhere except in Africa. Eighty-five per cent of young people live in developing countries; approximately 60 per cent live in Asia, the remainder in Africa, and Latin America and the Caribbean. UN demographic projections show that by 2025, the number of young people living in developing countries will grow to 90 per cent. The resulting policy challenges are to establish the most conducive conditions in which young people can thrive, socially and economically – conditions that ensure productive transitions from dependency on parents to social and economic independence, social inclusion and participation, and economic security. Labour market participation has therefore been a central preoccupation of policy-makers, and how to ensure sufficient youth labour to meet employers' specific needs without harming young people looms large in GSP debates. These issues are sources of continuous major tension and contestation in GSP. One approach prioritises care for and nurture and protection of children and young people – captured in the term **protectionism**. The other prioritises economic growth and competitive economic success as the primary source of young people's security and prosperity, and the freedom of employers and businesses to promote both – captured in the term **economism**. These often-competing priorities run throughout GSP concerning young people, and are an important theme throughout this chapter.

## A very brief history of the global institutional architecture of youth policy

International concern for the wellbeing and protection of children and young people has a century-long honourable history, dating from the League of Nations (LoN) (founded in 1920 to deal with the devastating damage of the First World War) and spanning the whole post-Second World War history, from the foundation of the UN onwards. These, and many other IGOs, have been concerned with young people and their education, health, physical and mental protection, and their neglect, exploitation and importance as key sources of labour. IGOs have also made the world aware of the weakness of national borders as barriers to the spread of abuse, exploitation and disease. In a world in which international trade, **migration**, pandemics and the movement of goods and information are ubiquitous, ensuring the protection of juveniles and securing the conditions of their development towards independent adulthood have long been identified as inherently *global* social policy priorities.

The LoN was the first **governance** organisation to work at global scope and scale, including in relation to young people. Education, health, welfare and labour issues regarding young people were considered by its Child Welfare, Unemployment and International Intellectual Cooperation Committees, supported by vibrant international **civil society** organisations (CSOs) concerned with youth, peace and social justice issues (Fergusson and Yeates, 2021). The

LoN initiated the world's first-ever international **convention**, which resulted in the 1924 Geneva Declaration of the Rights of the Child, which asserted that 'men and women of all nations' should 'declare and accept it as their duty' to protect and provide for children across several social policy fields concerning their health, nourishment, shelter and 'relief in times of distress'. It was a remarkable intervention, unprecedented in its ambition and scope. However, although the Declaration asserted that 'the child must be put in a position to earn a livelihood, and must be protected against every form of exploitation' (LoN, 1924), it provided no age definition of childhood, and it was internationally legally non-binding (Buck, 2014). In some ways, the LoN's work was soon overtaken by the International Labour Organization's (ILO). By 1924 the ILO had already instituted international standards on child and young people's employment, including in relation to unemployment (1919), the 'night work of young persons' (1919), several minimum working age conventions (1919–21) and vocational education (1921). Most ILO interventions were clearly *protectionist* rather than *economistic*, intended to combat child labour and prevent children from being required to earn a living. In doing so, the ILO started to define an age group – 'young people' – that was clearly distinct from children and adults, and that required special consideration.

In the interwar years, the ILO established protectionist policies that defined international standards regarding the rights of young people at work (minimum working age in non-industrial sectors, 1932; maximum working hours, 1935–36; and their post-school development and vocational training, 1939). Of particular interest is that the Unemployment (Young Persons) Recommendation (1935) promoted extensive provision across education, vocational guidance and employment centres as well as addressing unemployment itself. ILO **labour standards** aimed to set the school leaving age at 15, with guaranteed further provision up to the age of 18, supported by maintenance allowances and a requirement for attendance among unemployed youth, and special youth placement services in employment exchanges. Most of these ILO **recommendations** were decades ahead of their time.

After the Second World War the ILO and the UN Educational, Scientific and Cultural Organization (UNESCO) worked to strengthen national employment and education policies, developing complementary agendas on age norms for compulsory education worldwide, recommendations on preventing child labour and premature youth employment, and shaping a programme for global full employment. This work was captured in the UN's Declaration of the Rights of the Child (1959), which asserted that all children:

> … shall enjoy the benefits of social security … [and] … the right to adequate nutrition, housing, recreation and medical services … [and] … *shall not be permitted to employment before an appropriate minimum*

*age ... [or to] ... any occupation or employment that would prejudice* [their] *health....* (UN, 1959, Principles 4 and 9; emphasis added)

These emblematic themes epitomised the ILO's and UNESCO's *protectionist* work in pursuit of care for and development of children and young people worldwide. They *both* sought to set standards and universalise expectations of their basic needs, entitlements and rights, *and* attempted to do so globally, across all countries, irrespective of national social norms, cultures, religions, wealth and poverty, to prevent nation–states gaining competitive economic advantage over other nation–states by exploiting the cheapest, most vulnerable human labour, that of young people.

These themes represented extraordinary aspiration, in particular to secure key aspects of children's and young women's wellbeing. But IGOs' resolutions, declarations, conventions and recommendations did not translate easily into social policy reforms among **member states**. By 1971 a new focus on young people was emerging within the UN. The UNGA emphasised that 'serious problems still exist for the individual and social needs of many of the world's youth regarding health, education, training, employment and housing and social services' (1971, p 76). Worldwide youth protests and rebellions in the 1960s led to belated recognition that 'youth' had become a political and economic as well as a social force that the UN should no longer ignore (Rosenmayr, 1972). By 1979, the UNGA had established a Task Force on Youth Policies and Programmes focused on better communication between the UN and youth organisations; employment-oriented national youth service programmes; a Directory of Youth Organisations; a programme of environmental education for youth; and crucially, the first UN resolution on youth unemployment (UNGA, 1981).

The UN's multi-issue, multisector approach was in part a response to transformative economic, social and welfare policies. In the period 1980–85 unemployment among 15- to 19-year-olds reached heights not seen since the 1930s (exceeding 15 per cent in the USA and Canada, 20 per cent in Australia and the UK, 30 per cent in France and Ireland, 40 per cent in Italy, and 50 per cent in Spain). Post-war **Keynesian** demand management, public sector growth and state intervention in advanced economies gave way to the **Washington Consensus** – that **neoliberalism** would liberate dynamic market forces and economic growth. These policies were to be realised through the International Monetary Fund (IMF) and the World Bank, thereby partially sidelining the ILO.

The UN's broad-based approach to young people in GSP, especially regarding poverty and their participation in the international development process, defined its work, initially through the 1995 UN 'World Programme of Action for Youth to the Year 2000 and Beyond', which defined education and employment as its leading priorities. The UN's Copenhagen Declaration on Social Development, and its Programme of Action at the World Summit for Social Development, identified young people as its leading social development priority. In 1998, 146 governments committed to the Lisbon Declaration on Youth Policies and Programmes addressing youth participation, development, peace, education, employment, health, and drug and substance abuse.

These and subsequent endeavours culminated in the UN's **Millennium Development Goals** (MDGs) in 2000 (see **Box 11.2**), updated in the **Sustainable Development Goals** (SDGs) in 2015.

---

## Box 11.2: Millennium Development Goals (MDGs) and outcomes

MDG Target 1.B pursued full employment and decent work for all, including women and young people. But by 2015, only four in ten 15- to 24-year-olds were fully employed worldwide.

MDG Target 2.A specified that all boys and girls should complete a full course of primary schooling. But by 2015, 9 per cent of the world's 57 million primary school age children did not do so. Furthermore, although gender differences in education had been largely eliminated in developing countries by 2015, only half of working age women worldwide were employed, compared to three-quarters of men (UN, 2015).

---

The SDGs extended the MDG targets to include secondary education, employment for people with disabilities, and new targets and indicators that included literacy and numeracy, secondary education completion rates, average earnings and unemployment rates across all groups, and abolition of all forms of gender discrimination and inequality in these fields. The leading priority targets of the UN Youth Strategy 2030 are to provide greater access to quality education, health services, decent work and productive employment (UN, 2018, p 11).

In 2009, in the wake of the **global financial crisis** (GFC), the ILO and the World Health Organization (WHO) developed Social Protection Floors (SPFs), nationally defined guarantees of **social security** based on essential healthcare and basic income security for children, young people and adults experiencing sickness or unemployment, all intended to promote 'decent work' (SDG Target 8.5). Progress towards SDG targets is monitored through the ILO's World Social Protection Database. Young people seeking employment are widely excluded from social protection schemes, and required instead to join work experience or training for minimal allowances. Barely one in ten countries provide unemployment benefits for first-time jobseekers, and many refuse to provide them if young workers make insufficient contributions to insurance schemes (ILO, 2014, pp 37–8). One in five unemployed youth and adult workers (152 million) lack unemployment benefits (ILO, 2017, p xxxi).

In all, the institutional architecture of global youth policy is complex, comprising multiple **international organisations** (IOs) spanning many social sectors and encompassing many social policy issues. The dominant actors since the 1950s have been UN agencies (ILO, UNESCO, UNICEF, WHO), and latterly, the World Bank. INGOs have played a key role since the LoN era, and continue to be very active in youth–related fields. International charities and youth–specific non–governmental organisations (NGOs) are also key global civil society actors, alongside many global corporate actors in the youth (un)employment policy field. Workers' groups have played a far less significant role compared with other social groups. GSP regarding young people is multisectoral, spanning an extensive range of social policy fields: education, employment, poverty, health, but also 'social inclusion', social security, housing, self–harm and mental health, and criminal justice.

## Young people's 'transitions': the global reach of a concept and a discourse

Tensions between protectionist and economistic priorities concerning young people continue undiminished at national and international levels, and in GSP itself. They are visible in accounts of how young people navigate their own individual *transitions* between their fluid statuses as children, youths and young adults (see **Box 11.3**). How successful transitions are achieved or fail partly reflects the relative power of economistic and protectionist policies to shape young people's lives.

### Box 11.3: Young people's transitions – concept and discourse

The *concept* of 'transition' is based on the social-psychological concept of young people's 'life courses', which model the sequences of human development that occur between birth and independent adulthood, moving through predicted episodes of personal growth and autonomy (Hamilton and Crouter, 1980; Buchmann, 1989; Farmer, 1993; Fend, 1994). All tend to draw on ideas of 'age and stage', incorporating biological and social-psychological trajectories of the 'life course' as well as key 'transition junctures' around leaving school or college and starting work. There are many versions and variants of these trajectories, some of which focus on personal characteristics while others prioritise fixed categories like gaining employment and leaving the parental home.

The *discourse* of young people's 'transitions' greatly extends ideas of biological and social stages of development by making them normative. That is to say, the *transitions discourse* (a particular way of interpreting young people's successful or failed progress towards employment) builds in expectations of standards, ideals or required behaviours and progress, which may include sanctions of some kind if the norm is not adhered to. The discourse had its origins in the 1960s in the USA and in the 1970s in the UK (Wolfbein, 1959; Ashton, 1973), and is now internationally deployed in the research literature and in social policy and practice (Heinz and Heinz, 1999; Helve and Evans, 2013). There is also a strong countervailing literature that challenges the premises and applications of the transitions discourse (Bates et al, 1984; Miles, 2000; see also MacDonald et al, 2001; Craig, 2008; Fergusson, 2016).

The great majority of children and young people typically follow the almost-universal established pathways through the stages of the life course. But the transitions discourse identifies these stages as norms from which some young people are deemed to stray or actively deviate. Not achieving smooth passage from education or training into employment is then seen less as a result of limited ability or lack of jobs than as shortcomings or personal failures on the part of young people who do not 'progress' to the next 'stage' of their life. Compensatory interventions may then be called for by teachers, social workers or youth justice workers, for example. Recurrent non-progress along 'normal' routes may be interpreted as a need for help *or* as an active refusal to adapt. If the latter, it may result in being labelled as 'unemployable', 'recalcitrant' or 'deviant'.

'Transitions studies' has become a recognised research field (Raffe, 1984; Courtenay and McAleese, 1986). Researchers typically observe that young people who struggle or fail to 'make the transition' – into employment particularly – are, unsurprisingly, from lower socioeconomic groups, from Black, Asian and minority ethnic (BAME) communities and from deindustrialised regions. Certainly, 'poor' and 'failed' transitions typically proliferate in adverse economic conditions. Deep economic recessions in the UK, North America, Japan and parts of Europe in the early 1980s, and the recessions triggered by the 1990s international oil crisis, produced major spikes in youth unemployment as labour markets collapsed. Between 1980 and 1994, youth unemployment rates increased substantially, exceeding 10 per cent in most years in **high-income countries** (20 per cent in Northern Europe and 30–40 per cent in Southern Europe). Many governments withdrew unemployment benefits for young people *and* options to extend schooling beyond age 16 among low-achievers. For them, welfare-to-work ('workfare') schemes offered 'work experience' with pitifully small training allowances (rather than wages) (Peck, 2001; MacDonald and Marsh, 2005; Blossfeld et al, 2008; Simmons and Thompson, 2011).

These events were significant international watersheds. They redefined the status of young people who fell between categories (juvenile/adult, pupil/worker, employed/unemployed), as now epitomised in the internationally recognised category 'NEET' that redefined the status of millions of 15- to 18-year-olds and others (see **Box 11.4**). Its speedily recognised usefulness to many governments was that, presentationally, the category 'NEET' *masked* unemployment rates by excluding unemployed youth from national unemployment data. But 'being NEET' also *highlights* the number of young people who are neither studying nor earning. NEETs are often assumed to be unwilling (or have been deemed unfit) to study, train or work. They are, as a result, often vilified as self-determined non-participants who rely on parental provision or subsist on undeclared earnings or crime. Young people become labelled as a result of a transitions discourse that makes adverse judgements on their status and its causes. In effect, most NEETs occupy a liminal place between education and employment that is both usefully vague and typically beyond the immediate responsibilities of governments.

---

### Box 11.4: 'Not in education, employment or training' (NEET) rates among young women

Internationally, women are more likely to be NEET than men. According to ILO data for 2017, globally, one in three 15- to 24-year-old women were NEET compared to one in ten men. Women's highest NEET rates are in Asia and Northern Africa. And although the lowest rates are in Europe, EU data shows that one in five young women aged 20–24 were NEET in 2019. In one in four high-income countries, NEET rates among women aged 20–24 ranged between 20 and 45 per cent (OECD, 2020). These women constitute a large cohort of the 'hidden unemployed'.

---

Consistent with the claims of the transitions discourse and high NEET rates, employers and governments frequently claim that young people are ill qualified for and ill adjusted to the evolving needs of businesses. Many of them typically view high rates of youth unemployment as indicative of **supply-side** failures – that is, failures of preparing young people to 'supply' the needs of local labour markets. Schools, colleges, their curricula and teaching staff are sometimes also implicated: poor preparation for employment is seen not only as a cause of youth unemployment, but also as holding back the capabilities of enterprising businesses that would excel if young people were more skilled, knowledgeable and adaptive. Employers advocate vocational training to strengthen young people's 'employability'. These responses reflect the influence of **human capital** theory, which claims that investment in education and training supports economic growth and global competitiveness (Schultz, 1971; Carnoy and Levin, 1985), and that the 'vocationalisation' of education serves the purposes of human capital development (Hussain, 1976). All this typifies the approach favoured by economism, as new 'learning regimes' begin to reconfigure the purposes and priorities of education and training (see **Chapter 14**, this volume).

But there are equally strongly held contrary views that attribute raised NEET levels and high youth unemployment rates to **demand–side** failures – that is, failures of governments to foster jobs growth and to distribute work more equitably, and failures of employers to make the best use of their employees, including by investing in training. NEET and youth unemployment rates persist, even during upturns in the business cycle and periods of expanding global trade. Much of the expanded provision in schools and colleges instituted by successive UK governments to absorb young unemployed people is characterised as 'warehousing'. Young people lacking alternatives are sometimes reluctantly 'retained' in schools and colleges beyond the minimum school leaving age when labour market demand is low, to be 'released' to jobs when and if economies eventually recover (Roberts and Parsell, 1992; Simmons and Thompson, 2011; Fergusson, 2014). These recurrent cycles of growing and shrinking demand for young people's labour become exaggerated during and after crises like the GFC – and prospectively, the COVID-19 pandemic. In most advanced economies and many others, the supply of youth labour typically exceeds demand. Only in low–income countries (one in seven countries worldwide, mostly in Africa) do poverty and subsistence agriculture mean that almost all young people (and many children) are nominally 'employed', even if they are only paid 'in kind' by parents or neighbours. Elsewhere, the mismatch between supply of and demand for young labour is largely attributable to over–supply *or to* insufficient demand – depending on how each is understood and interpreted in the conflicted views among and between employers, governments, researchers and IGOs.

It is therefore of considerable significance that the UN's Youth Strategy 2030 aims to:

> … engage Member States and other partners to advocate for a balanced approach to *stimulate the youth labour demand* and prompt improvements in skills development systems, with the objective of *easing the school-to-work transition and reducing the youth NEET rate, particularly among young women* and disadvantaged youth… [and] …support Member States and other partners in their efforts to *create youth employment and self-employment ecosystems*. (UN, 2018, p 11; emphasis added)

These aims typify the 'protectionist' position, representing unprecedented major shifts towards demand–side strategies, and recognise young women's particular post-school vulnerability in labour markets. However, it is notable that Youth Strategy 2030 never refers to youth *un*employment, perhaps because the prospects for reducing NEET rates are considerably better than those for meeting the infinitely greater challenge of reducing and eliminating *global* youth unemployment.

## Global social policy and youth unemployment

The GFC of 2007–09 and its aftermath resulted in the most compelling evidence since reliable global data became available that 'economism trumps protectionism' in shaping the prospects and future trajectories of young people internationally. Youth employment rates plummeted, and millions of young people aged up to 24 years were left without incomes, except in the minority of countries providing unemployment benefits for those aged 15+. Imbalances between the supply of young people's labour and the demand for it manifested themselves in high youth unemployment *rates* and unemployment *totals* across almost all world regions. According to the ILO's data, since 1991 the annual *totals* of the world's unemployed 15- to 24-year-olds have fluctuated between 57 and 78 million. This constitutes up to one in seven of the global youth population. However, it is highly variable across countries: differences in youth unemployment *rates* between countries, according to their wealth and between young women and men, are remarkably large (see **Box 11.5**).

As we saw earlier, NEET rates among young women are even higher than among young men, if compared to the ILO's 'not in the labour force' rates. While young women may choose to be 'not in', many have had little choice other than to be home-based workers or primary carers. If we add these 'not in' figures to the unemployed population, young women appear to be doubly excluded from employment compared to young men. These inequalities are particularly exaggerated in the Arab States, Northern Africa, Latin America, the Caribbean and Eastern Europe, where averaged youth unemployment rates rose to between 20 and 40 per cent year-on-year to 2019. Overall, young women were very much more likely than young men to have been excluded from formal employment during the GFC period.

These extremes since the onset of the GFC raised major concerns in UN organisations, the World Bank, the IMF and regional organisations worldwide. The ILO and the World Bank took leading positions on the causes of mass youth unemployment and on appropriate responses to the GFC, often reflecting their 'supply-side versus demand-side' disagreements about those causes. Although it had been *the* key youth employment player among IGOs since 1919, the ILO (and its partner UNESCO) took much less active leadership roles between the

## Box 11.5: Employment inequalities, country income groups and gender

**Figure 11.1** shows unemployment rates according to groups of countries, classified by the World Bank into four income groups: the most affluent (high-income) countries, the least affluent (low-income) countries, and upper-middle and lower-middle income groups between them.

*Figure 11.1: Unemployment rates by World Bank country income group, 15- to 24-year-olds, 1991–2021 (%)*

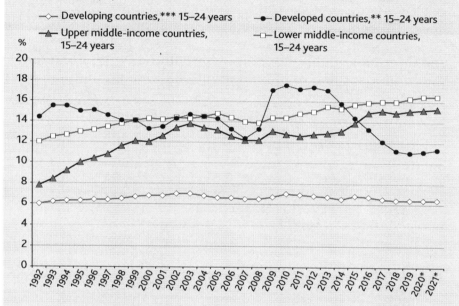

Note: * Projected data; **Also known as high-income countries (HICs); *** Also known as low-income countries (LICs).

Source: Adapted from Fergusson and Yeates (2021, Figure 5.8). Based on data derived from International Labour Organization Statistics (ILOSTAT) and ILO World Employment and Social Outlook Data (WESODATA) 2020 (data for 2020–21 are projections)

Counterintuitively, youth unemployment rates in developing (low-income) countries are by far the lowest of the four groups, while the average rate for developed (high-income) countries is often the highest, but also the most volatile. This is explained by multiple factors – in particular better unemployment data recording and more extensive welfare entitlements in more developed countries, and different economic and labour force structures across all types of countries.

Unemployment rates are much more heavily affected by global economic cycles among younger than older age groups. The rising rate to 1993 in **Figure 11.1** coincided with early 1990s recessions in many developed countries. The huge increase between 2007 and 2013 coincided with the GFC, but was followed by a very speedy recovery by 2019, in contrast to the middle-income countries where rates rose continuously over the same period. It is clear that the GFC had a huge impact in all except developing countries, but only in developed countries did unemployment decline. In lower-middle-income countries it doubled between 1991 and 2019, and was projected to continue upwards even before the impact of COVID-19 – a trajectory that was increasingly closely matched by upper-middle-income countries. The advanced economies alone, it seems, are particularly sensitive to economic crises, but they recover from them much more quickly and fully.

These extreme differences are even starker if we view gender differences in global youth labour market participation data. ILO data divides populations between those who are 'in the labour force' (that is, available to work, but unemployed) and those who are not. Worldwide, **Figure 11.2** shows that the proportion of 15- to 24-year-olds who are in the labour force has been declining steeply and steadily for 30 years among both women and men, at similar rates.

*Figure 11.2: Gender and labour force: men and women aged 15–24, labour force and not in the labour force, 1991–2021 (%)*

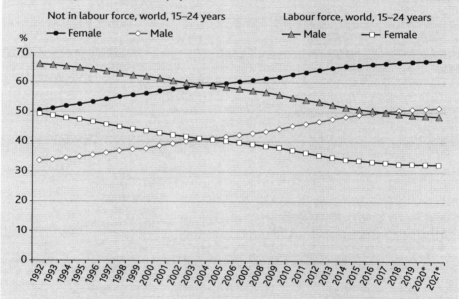

Note: * Projected data.

Source: Adapted from Fergusson and Yeates (2021, Figure 5.6). Based on data derived from ILO WESODATA (2020) (data for 2020–21 are projections)

Despite similar trends affecting young women and men, there is a huge gender gap between those 'in' and those 'not in' the labour force. By 2019, two-thirds of young women were 'not in' the labour force compared to half of young men.

1970s and 2000. The transformative global forces of the Washington Consensus and neoliberalisation were antithetical to their priorities and objectives concerning the protection and wellbeing of children and young people at work. The World Bank and the IMF were dominant forces in global political economy during this period, extolling the virtues of competition and reward of enterprise among businesses, and advocating deregulation and voluntary self-regulation by businesses internationally, especially in the field of labour (see **Chapter 4**, this volume). Some of the 'slack' of the ILO and UNESCO's marginalisation was taken up through the UNGA, but it faced a hard struggle. New UNGA resolutions and reports every year between 1981 and 1989 highlighted the extreme concerns of the UN Economic and Social Council (ECOSOC), the ILO and UNESCO regarding the vulnerability and injustices of mass youth unemployment at internationally extreme scales, as well as the social and political risks of huge cohorts of young people without occupations or incomes. Yet, the issue of booming youth unemployment was not 'on the radar' of the World Bank and the IMF, and unwillingness to tackle the central ostensible defining issue – lack of *demand* for youth labour – remained 'the elephant in the IGO room' throughout this period, until the GFC. Almost invariably, debates and reports during the 1980s and 1990s defaulted towards the 'standard' responses to mass youth unemployment, namely the supposed need for supply–side measures that were, incongruously, expected to make young people more skilful and more employable in jobs that did not exist, and that were exceedingly unlikely to be created in a period of economic decline. The ILO was the IGO that most fully appreciated the contradictions of the 'supply–side vs demand–side' impasse over youth unemployment. With UNESCO and ECOSOC, before 2008 the ILO *sometimes* succeeded in injecting into global debates *some* recognition of the great potential of creating genuine new jobs through public spending on infrastructure while also ensuring their equitable distribution. But the ILO was less than assertive in pressing this priority, constrained and diminished as it was by the power of the World Bank and the IMF.

By 2001 the World Bank was making major incursions into youth unemployment policy, invited by the UN. In response to MDG Target 1.B's commitment to full employment and 'decent work' for young people, the UNGA called on IOs to form partnerships with private sector global corporate bodies, NGOs and civil society bodies. The ILO entered into partnership with the World Bank; their Youth Employment Network (YEN) aimed to improve work opportunities for young people in selected countries. This partnership was to be the first of several over two decades in which one took the lead and the other contributed to varying degrees. The ILO's earlier marginalisation from this global policy field in which it had long-standing deep knowledge and expertise highlighted the tensions from the outset. On two defining issues the ILO and the World Bank began from very different positions. Historically, the ILO predominantly favoured demand-side solutions to youth unemployment, while the World Bank favoured supply-side approaches. Although both IGOs adjusted and occasionally shifted position on this core issue, differences prevailed. The second issue was their respective predispositions towards the **social protection** of young people, especially those without work. Since 1919, much of the ILO's most progressive pioneering work had been to deploy its 'soft' powers of global governance by building consensus between member states towards protecting children and young people from workplace exploitation, and to advocate social security provision for those without incomes (priorities that remain prominent in the ILO's Social Protection Floors). In contrast, the World Bank was highly conditional in its attitude to social protection for unemployed youth, limiting it to the poorest people, on condition that they adapted to workplace norms.

These contrasting positions and enduring tensions were visible in the ILO's and the World Bank's work throughout five partnerships in 17 years (see **Table 11.1**). Incrementally, these partnerships resulted in increasingly outward-facing connections with other organisations rather than with each other. From 2012 onwards, the ILO and the World Bank were 'separating partners'. Following the SDG that strengthened the MDG by adding the important goal of 'equal pay for work of equal value' (see **Box 11.2**), the UN 'raised its game' by creating 'Generation Unlimited' (GenU) as part of its Youth Strategy 2030. GenU was a partnership with a major difference – UNICEF (not the field leaders, the ILO or UNESCO) was to be the World Bank's partner and, in effect, GenU's programme lead, with a particular emphasis on significantly reducing NEET rates (as distinct from youth unemployment). Tellingly, the ILO was excluded from GenU's Executive and assigned a role as part of its very large 53-member board, where its influence would be weakened. In the same year, 2015, this transformation of previous partnership models coincided with the ILO establishing its own major new programme, 'Decent Jobs for Youth', drawing in a great many UN and other IGO co-partners but *excluding* the World Bank (Fergusson, 2021; Fergusson and Yeates, 2021).

*Table 11.1: Youth employment partnerships, 2001–18*

| Year initiated | Lead IGO + other IGOs | Title of partnership |
| --- | --- | --- |
| 2001 | UNESCO + ILO + World Bank | Youth Employment Network (YEN) |
| 2008 | World Bank + ILO | Global Partnership for Youth Employment (GPYE) |
| 2015 | World Bank + ILO | Solutions for Youth Employment (S4YE) |
| 2015 | ILO + other UN IGOs | Global Initiative on Decent Jobs for Youth (GDJY) |
| 2018 | World Bank + UNICEF | Generation Unlimited (GenU) |

The global politics of collaboration, coexistence and contestation between these various partners is complex and opaque. For almost six decades the global governance of policy in this field predominantly operated through the quasi-legislative processes of conventions, recommendations and declarations. Outcomes were transparent; member states accepted internationally agreed decisions and IGOs monitored them through reports and data gathering. At the ILO these processes dwindled during the 1980s, and were largely superseded by UNGA resolutions that had less oversight of member states' acceptance and implementation of their priorities. The neoliberalisation of the 1980s and 1990s had the effect of removing ILO's quasi-legislative governance powers and diminishing its effectiveness in relation to youth unemployment more generally.

From 2000 onwards, the ILO's youth employment work was confined to designing and overseeing programmes of direct intervention, using its worldwide regional networks to alleviate youth unemployment locally. In effect, the ILO was reduced from global leader and bastion of the global governance of youth labour policies to being an international organiser and overseer of relatively small 'ground-level' programmes. It lost its once-dominant global strategic role and was confined to tactical local interventions. Its diminished power and reach will never affect more than a tiny fraction of the 70 million young people who are known to be unemployed (and the hundreds of millions more whose unemployment is 'invisible'; see Fergusson and Yeates, 2021). The decades-long weakening of UN agencies and the powers and reach of the World Bank appear to have immeasurably diminished the possibilities for genuinely strategic interventions capable of substantially reducing youth unemployment globally.

Ten years after the GFC economists had already predicted a new financial crisis. The global COVID-19 pandemic subsequently triggered widespread predictions that its adverse economic effects would raise unemployment rates further, and that young people, as before, would be among the worst affected, worldwide, especially in some middle-income countries (Fergusson and Yeates, 2021).

## Conclusion

As a field of political practice, GSP has embraced a wide range of concerns that shape young people's lives and prospects. Central to these have been their needs for education and employment as fundamental determinants of their development towards adult independence, social and economic security and autonomy. Both have been major preoccupations of the work of IGOs since 1919. Both have also been deeply entangled in debates and conflicts between global policy actors about how to ensure young people's progress towards independent adulthood. It is clear that there remain major obstacles to the opportunities for tens – perhaps hundreds – of millions of young people worldwide to do so. It is also clear that these obstacles have become greater, more common and harsher. There are strong grounds for concluding that the necessary conditions for *all* young people worldwide to progress towards independent adulthood are repeatedly blocked by adverse national and international conditions, and by political and economic priorities that are allowed to take precedence over their protection and development – especially wherever national economies are weak or prone to crises. Such crises are increasingly inherently global in their origins and impacts, and protecting young people from the harms these impacts may cause them presents profound challenges to GSP, especially in the Global South, but also in advanced economies in which many young people's prospects currently also look uncertain. The daunting central challenge to GSP and to the IGOs that play major roles in driving it is to (re-)establish protectionist over economistic priorities, in the interests of young people's growth and development as independent citizens, everywhere.

## Summary

- Global youth policy covers a wide range of issues spanning many sectors and involving a strong element of participation in social development generally. Participation in UN processes has been a mainstay of UN youth policy. Education and employment are fundamental determinants of young people's independence as autonomous adults, and are, accordingly, among the most developed areas of GSP in practice.
- The global institutional architecture of social policy concerning young people is multisectoral, spanning many social policy fields, key UN agencies, the World Bank, international charities, NGOs and global corporate actors.
- A key question for GSP is how to produce sufficient youth labour capable of meeting employer and national needs without harming young people's autonomous development. There are tensions and conflicts between economistic approaches and policies that prioritise the former, and protectionist approaches and policies that prioritise the latter.
- The last decade has seen the 'transitions' discourse being globalised, especially through the policy category of 'NEET' and its inclusion in the SDGs. This normalises expectations of young people's ideal and expected progress from dependency to independence, especially through employment.
- High NEET and youth unemployment rates can be attributed either to 'supply-side failures' or 'demand-side failures' in labour markets; which of the two explains them better is another major source of dispute between global policy actors.
- The necessary conditions for *all* young people worldwide to progress towards adult independence through employment have been hampered by economic priorities that have taken precedence over the protection and development of young people, especially following global crises.

## Questions for discussion

- Why is defining the category 'young people' a complex task, from a global perspective?
- What are the sources of tension between protectionist and economistic priorities with regard to young people's education and employment?
- What might be the possible reasons for youth unemployment being higher among women than men, and lower in developing countries than developed countries?

## Follow-up activities

- Use the ILO's WESODATA (World Employment and Social Outlook Data Finder) facility (www.ilo.org/wesodata) to help address any of the questions above (or questions of your own), and to explore worldwide data on youth unemployment.
- Choose one of the readings or sources listed below to explore an aspect of global youth unemployment and why it matters, and/or to answer one or more of the questions above.
- Consider how much the arguments and information in this chapter fit with what you understand about youth unemployment in a country or countries you know well.

## Further resources

For a general introduction to young people and social policy, see Coles (1995). Fergusson and Yeates (2021) provide a century-long perspective on youth unemployment worldwide and the ways in which IGOs have responded to it. World Social Protection Reports and World Youth Reports are major sources of up-to-date information on the current position of young people in a range of policy fields, including unemployment, but also beyond it (see www. ilo.org and www.un.org/esa/socdev). For detailed up-to-date information on the effects of the COVID-19 pandemic on youth unemployment globally, regionally and nationally, go to www.ilo.org and search for 'COVID-19 youth unemployment'.

**References**

Ashton, D.N. (1973) 'The transition from school to work: Notes on the development of different frames of reference among young male workers', *The Sociological Review*, 21(1), 101–25.

Bates, I., Clarke, J., Cohen, P., Finn, D. and Moore, R. (1984) *Schooling for the dole? The new vocationalism*, Basingstoke: Macmillan.

Blossfeld, H-P., Buchholz, S., Bukodi, E. and Kurz, K. (eds) (2008) *Young workers, globalization and the labour market: Comparing early working life in eleven countries*, Cheltenham: Edward Elgar.

Buchmann, M. (1989) *The script of life in modern society: Entry into adulthood*, Chicago, IL: University of Chicago Press.

Buck, T. (2014) *International child law*, London: Routledge.

Carnoy, M. and Levin, H. (1985) *Schooling and work in the democratic state*, Redwood City, CA: Stanford University Press.

Coles, B. (1995) *Youth and social policy*, London: UCL Press.

Courtenay, G. and McAleese, I. (1986) *England and Wales Youth Cohort Study: First summary report*, London: Social and Community Planning and Research.

Craig, G. (2008) 'Social exclusion', in B. Goldson (ed) *Dictionary of youth justice*, Cullompton: Willan, 328–9.

Farmer, E. (1993) 'Externalising behaviour in the life-course', *Journal of Emotional and Behavioral Disorders*, 1(3), 179–88.

Fend, H. (1994) 'The historical context of transition to work and youth unemployment', in A.C. Petersen and J.T. Mortimer (eds) *Youth, unemployment and society*, New York: Cambridge University Press, 77–94.

Fergusson, R. (2014) 'Warehouse, marketise, shelter, juridify: On the political economy and governance of extending school participation in England', in K. Farnsworth, Z. Irving and M. Fenger (eds) *Social policy review 26: Analysis and debate in social policy*, Bristol: Policy Press, 47–64.

Fergusson, R. (2016) *Young people, welfare and crime: Governing non-participation*, Bristol: Policy Press.

Fergusson, R. (2021) 'International organisations' involvement in youth unemployment as a global policy field, and the global financial crisis', in K. Martens, D. Niemann and A. Kaasch (eds) *International organisations in global social governance*, Basingstoke: Palgrave, 31–56.

Fergusson, R. and Yeates, N. (2021) *Global youth unemployment: History, governance and policy*, Cheltenham: Edward Elgar.

Furlong, A. (2013) *Youth studies: An introduction*, Abingdon: Routledge.

Hamilton, S.F. and Crouter A.C. (1980) 'Work and growth: A review of research on the impact of work experience on adolescents', *Journal of Youth and Adolescence*, 9(4), 323–38.

Heinz, W.R. and Heinz, W.R. (eds) (1999) *From education to work: Cross national perspectives*, Cambridge: Cambridge University Press.

Helve, H. and Evans, K. (eds) (2013) *Youth and work transitions in changing social landscapes*, London: Tufnell Press.

Hussain, A. (1976) 'The economy and the educational system in capitalistic societies', *Economy and Society*, 5(4), 413–34.

ILO (International Labour Organization) (2014) *World social protection report 2014/15: Building economic recovery, inclusive development and social justice*, Geneva: ILO (www.ilo.org/wcmsp5/groups/public/---dgreports/---dcomm/documents/publication/wcms_245201.pdf).

ILO (2017) *World social protection report 2017–19: Universal social protection to achieve the Sustainable Development Goals*, Geneva: ILO (www.ilo.org/wcmsp5/groups/public/---dgreports/---dcomm/---publ/documents/publication/wcms_604882.pdf).

Jones, G. (2009) *Youth*, Cambridge: Polity Press.

LoN (League of Nations) (1924) *Geneva Declaration of the Rights of the Child*, Adopted on 26 September, 1924, by League of Nations General Assembly, Geneva: LoN.

MacDonald, R. and Marsh, J. (2005) *Disconnected youth? Growing up in Britain's poor neighbourhoods*, Basingstoke: Palgrave Macmillan.

MacDonald, R. and Shildrick, T. (2018) 'Biography, history and place: Understanding youth transitions in Teesside', in S. Irwin and A. Nilsen (eds) *Transitions to adulthood through recession: Youth and inequality in a European comparative perspective*, London: Routledge, 74–96.

MacDonald, R., Mason, P., Shildrick, T., Webster, C., Johnston, L. and Ridley, L. (2001) 'Snakes and ladders: In defence of studies of youth transition', *Sociological Research Online*, 5(4), 1–13.

Miles, S. (2000) *Youth lifestyles in a changing world*, Buckingham: Open University Press.

Peck, J. (2001) *Workfare states*, New York: Guilford Press.

OECD (Organisation for Economic Co-operation and Development) (2020) 'Youth not in employment, education or training (NEET)', OECD Data (https://data.oecd.org/youthinac/youth-not-in-employment-education-or-training-neet.htm).

Raffe, D. (1984) 'The transition from school to work and the recession: Evidence from the Scottish school leavers' survey', *British Journal of Sociology of Education*, 5(3), 247–65.

Roberts, K. and Parsell, G. (1992) 'The stratification of youth training', *British Journal of Education and Work*, 5(1), 65–83.

Rosenmayr, L. (1972) 'Editorial: Youth: A social force?', *International Social Science Journal*, 24(2), 215.

Schultz, T. (1971) *Investment in human capital: The role of education and of research*, New York: Free Press.

Shildrick, T., McDonald, R., Webster, C. and Garthwaite, K. (2012) *Poverty and insecurity: Life in 'low-pay, no-pay' Britain*, Bristol: Policy Press.

Simmons, R. and Thompson, R. (2011) *NEET young people and training for work: Learning on the margins*, Stoke-on-Trent: Trentham Books.

UN (United Nations) (1959) *Declaration of the Rights of the Child*, New York: UN.

UN (2015) *End poverty: Millennium Development Goals and beyond 2015*, New York: UN (www.un.org/millenniumgoals/poverty.shtml).

UN (2018) *Youth 2030: Working with and for young people: UN Youth Strategy*, New York: UN (www.un.org/youthenvoy/youth-un).

UNGA (United Nations General Assembly) (1971) *Youth, its problems and needs, and its participation in social development*, A/RES/2770(XXVI), New York: UN.

UNGA (1981) *Efforts and measures for securing the implementation and the enjoyment by youth of human rights, particularly the right to education and to work*, A/RES/36/29, New York: UNGA.

Wolfbein, S.L. (1959) 'The transition from school to work: A study of the school leaver', *Personnel and Guidance Journal*, 38(2), 98–105

# Part Three
## Global social policy domains

# 12

# Global social policy at the nexus of water, energy and food

Jeremy J. Schmidt

## Overview

Water, energy and food have historically been governed as related yet discrete domains of social policy at local or national scales. Over the past two decades, however, this situation has significantly changed. This chapter examines how water, energy and food are increasingly understood and governed as interconnected domains of global social policy. The chapter shows how initial attempts to integrate these domains of social policy in sustainable development programmes were not wholly successful. Despite shortcomings, initial efforts towards policy integration shaped subsequent recognition of the nexus of concerns linking water, energy and food. The governance of this nexus is characterised by political and environmental considerations of complexity and change. Further, the water–energy–food nexus is indicative of how global social policy, such as the Sustainable Development Goals, seeks to enhance the resilience of both people and planet.

## Key concepts
Complexity; resilience; nexus; sustainability; water; energy; food

## Introduction

Water, energy and food are fundamental to individual and collective welfare. They focus attention on the mismatch between resource needs and the social systems through which resources are distributed. Some of this mismatch arises from environmental variability, but significant components are shaped by **global social policy** (GSP). For instance, the large energy inputs required to produce synthetic fertilisers and pesticides for industrial agriculture require international networks for monetary investment and infrastructures to move food for billions of people daily. Likewise, the tens of thousands of large dams that now block rivers around the world to create reservoirs for irrigation, cities and hydropower require global networks of engineering expertise and supply chains for construction materials like sand and cement. The energy extracted from fossil fuels requires significant water inputs, while energy use is the dominant contributor to climate change, the adverse impacts of which disproportionately affect those least responsible for the rapidly warming planet.

Water, food and energy have each long been significant areas of GSP, such as in international development, foreign aid and global trade (Schmidt, 2021). Perhaps surprisingly, however, the *connections* between water, energy and food, and their impact on human welfare and environmental health, have not always been fully recognised. That changed in the years between 2005 and 2008, when global food prices skyrocketed even though there was no physical shortage. Riots broke out in nearly two-dozen countries as the cost of wheat rose by 130 per cent and the price of rice doubled (Bush, 2010). At the same time, strong economic growth from 2003 to 2008 pushed oil prices to uncharted heights (Lutz and Hicks, 2013). Then, even more suddenly, food and energy prices collapsed alongside the **global financial crisis** (GFC) in 2008. The rapid surge and downward spike raised critical questions for GSP: what are the biophysical, social and economic connections among water, energy and food? How can these connections be better governed, globally, in the interests of socially equitable outcomes for human welfare and environmental sustainability?

This chapter explains how, in response to multiple crises, the water–energy–food nexus emerged as a key area of GSP. As **Box 12.1** indicates, the challenges facing food, water and energy are staggering. In this context, a key lesson that global policy actors took from food and energy price shocks was that recent crises were exacerbated by treating water, energy and food as discrete domains of local or national policy. This interpretation was not automatic. It was an outcome of three converging factors that structure this chapter, which traces the processes, actors and forms of knowledge that have shaped the water–energy–food nexus in global policy.

The first factor was recognition that the **sustainable development** policies of the 1980s and 1990s had not delivered on the promise of mutually beneficial environmental and economic policy. This historical context underscores the power of discourse in shaping how policy problems are framed and understood. The second factor was a search for a new policy framework that would retain the consensus on sustainability, but which could also equip decision-makers for complex realities across multiple geographic scales, international locales and economic sectors. Ultimately, the water–energy–food nexus provided a framework for social policy that was both integrative and global. The third factor was how to connect the water–energy–food nexus to policies that did not repeat past mistakes, and which could enhance the capacity of societies and ecosystems to adapt to a volatile global economy and a planet increasingly altered by human actions, especially climate change. The focus on enhancing capacity drew on ecological ideas of **resilience** to position the water–energy–food nexus prominently in the **Sustainable Development Goals** (SDGs).

## Box 12.1: Food, water and energy challenges

- Even before COVID-19, 821 million people went undernourished with poor nutrition, causing nearly 45 per cent of the deaths worldwide in children under the age of five.
- Freshwater species have declined by 84 per cent since 1970.
- Energy contributes 60 per cent of greenhouse gas emissions.
- Four billion people experience severe physical water scarcity for at least one month per year.
- Three billion people rely on wood, coal, charcoal or animal waste for cooking, leading to 3.8 million premature deaths each year, primarily women and children, from exposure to household air pollution.
- 2.2 billion people lack safe water supplies and 4.2 billion lack sanitation services that meet the standards set for the SDGs.

Sources: International Energy Agency et al (2019); High-Level Panel on Energy (2020); UNESCO and UN Water (2020)

## The unmet promise of sustainable development

Officially, sustainable development began with the publication of *Our common future* by the World Commission on Environment and Development in 1987, which defined it as development that 'meets the needs of the present without compromising the ability of future generations to meet their own needs'. But what does this mean, exactly? As with many statements of global policy, ambiguity over sustainable development was the result of contest, negotiation and dissent. Nevertheless, even tentative consensus carried significant weight, as agencies like the UN Development Programme (UNDP), the UN Environment Programme (UNEP) and the World Bank developed and funded sustainable development projects. Often, these agencies partnered with scientific networks to tackle a debate that swirled around *Our common future* regarding how to reconcile economic development premised on continued growth with limited material resources and the negative social and environmental impacts of industrialisation. Historically situating this debate helps explain how sustainable development took shape as a compromise over how to integrate environmental and economic policy to address water, energy and food challenges.

After the Second World War, and as many postcolonial nations achieved independence, the USA and other **Global North** powers launched international development programmes. These frequently tied development aid to natural resource extraction, such as for agricultural products, hydropower, mining and fossil fuels. Many of the first loans of the World Bank, for instance, funded large dams in South and Latin America. At the same time, recently decolonised countries were in a weakened economic position after Euro–American owners divested from newly independent nations in the 1950s and 1960s (Ogle, 2020). Much of the subsequent financial aid to developing nations flowed through unequal conditions linking water, food and energy to development policies. For instance, the USA withheld food from India in 1966 on the condition that aid would only flow if measures of population control and family planning were established (Sabin, 2013). Although the right to food was recognised by the UN in 1948, it was only in 1976 that the International Covenant on Economic, Social and Cultural Rights (ICESCR) came into force and established rights to an adequate standard of living, including for housing and food.

The 1950s and 1960s also saw a surge in Western environmentalism. Among the most famous were Aldo Leopold's *A Sand County almanac* and Rachel Carson's *Silent spring*. Leopold argued for a land ethic that would enhance ecological integrity. Carson decried the effects of chemical pollution on the environment, especially the pesticide applications of industrial agriculture. Environmental arguments, combined with the first images of Earth from space, changed Western perceptions of the planet in ways that frequently reproduced colonial inequality. For instance, Western environmentalists claimed species and landscapes in the **Global South** were not the sovereign domain of decolonised nations in Africa or South America. Rather, these species and landscapes were of global significance. Soon, environmental non–governmental organisations like the World Wildlife Fund (WWF) organised campaigns to conserve biodiversity. Many of these projects evicted local populations or prevented resource access crucial to local lives and livelihoods. The upshot was that even though state sovereignty over resources was international law, Western environmentalism often produced inequalities through conservation programmes (Macekura, 2015).

In this context, *Our common future* was anticipated by several decades of global institution building. In 1972, the first UN Conference on the Human Environment was held in Stockholm, Sweden. There, the first ideas of a right to a healthy environment were raised in global policy. Subsequently, arguments regarding 'basic rights' to food, water and clean air were promoted by proponents of sustainable development, such as Barbara Ward, and defended by philosophers like Henry Shue in his influential book *Basic rights* (1980). As environmental concerns rose on UN agendas, scientists forged transnational networks on environmental concerns. For example, from 1965–74, UNESCO sponsored the International Hydrological Decade. This culminated in a global assessment of human needs, notably for agriculture, and led to the first UN Conference on Water in 1977 (Schmidt, 2017). Assessments of water scarcity were made at a country scale, and were an environmental form of **methodological nationalism**. Transnational scientific networks, however, provided a form of soft diplomacy, such as between the USA and the United Soviet Socialist Republic (USSR), sharing some technical data despite competing economics and politics. For instance, the International Institute of Applied Systems Analysis (IIASA) was a key centre of knowledge exchange regarding the Earth's biophysical and social systems. In 1986, the year before *Our common future* was released, collaborators with IIASA published a landmark scientific assessment entitled *Sustainable development of the biosphere* (Clark and Munn, 1986). This covered everything from atmospheric chemistry and natural resources to the introduction of new concepts to global policy, such as the ecologist C.S. Holling's work on ecological resilience, thresholds and tipping points (see **Box 12.2**).

## Box 12.2: What is ecological resilience? An overview

In 1973, the ecologist C.S. 'Buzz' Holling introduced the scientific idea of 'resilience'. Holling's insight was that ecological systems are characterised by change, not stability. Previously, ecological systems were seen as seeking equilibrium, and ideas of the 'balance of nature' were used to justify policies that maximised extraction from what were presumed to be stable environments.

Resilience upends this way of thinking. Ecological systems are dynamic and evolve in complex, often surprising ways that do not 'naturally' balance. Further, changes to ecological systems can be irreversible, not because they push nature 'off balance', but because they exceed the capacity of a system to respond to disturbances.

As resilience developed, it was defined as the capacity of a system to respond to disturbances while still maintaining its functions, feedbacks and identity (Folke, 2006). Resilience is now used in many areas of policy, from urban planning and global finance to climate change.

When *Our common future* was published, many scientists and experts criticised its lack of attention to water. In response, they organised a conference in

Dublin, Ireland to amplify key messages before the planned UN Conference on Environment and Development in Rio de Janeiro in 1992. Water professionals argued that an integrated approach to water management was needed if demands for food and energy were to be met (Conca, 2006). They had a good case to make. Over the preceding decades, enormous pressure had been put on water through local and national policies that treated it discretely in agricultural and industrial policy. Thousands of large dams had been built for flood protection, irrigation and electricity. Many of these dams were part of geopolitical exchanges, where international aid was tied to Cold War strategies in South and East Asia, the Middle East and elsewhere. In agriculture, the 'green revolution' enhanced food production but also increased energy requirements for the production of synthetic fertilisers. Similarly, subsidies for fossil fuels in agriculture encouraged farmers to run diesel pumps that could irrigate cash crops for sale in the global economy. These were not uncontested forms of development. Many were tied to **structural adjustment programmes** (SAPs) of the World Bank and the International Monetary Fund (IMF), and indebted farmers through the high costs of patented seeds, fertilisers and pesticides. Complicating the picture further was the rise of fossil fuel consumption. As **Figure 12.1** illustrates, scientists now refer to the latter half of the 20th century as 'The Great Acceleration' owing to the rapid rate at which humanity – cumulatively, but unequally – appropriated Earth's material and energy resources (Steffen et al, 2015).

The 1992 Rio Conference established sustainable development as central to global environmental policy. Water did not achieve a binding international agreement, such as that of the Framework Convention on Climate Change or the Convention on Biodiversity. Instead, the Rio Conference came to anchor what is now known as 'integrated water resources management' (IWRM). In the 1990s, IWRM was promoted by development agencies such as UNESCO, UNDP, UNEP and the World Bank to such an extent that it became virtually hegemonic in development (Conca, 2006). New **international organisations** (IOs) were also formed to promote IWRM. The Global Water Partnership, for instance, launched in 1996 as a collaboration of UNDP and the World Bank and defined IWRM in terms congruent with sustainable development to maximise social welfare without compromising environmental health. A secretariat was established in Stockholm at the Swedish International Development Cooperation Agency, and experts began defining and promoting IWRM as a way to coordinate demands on water for food, energy and ecosystem health. Today, 172 countries promote IWRM in some capacity.

*Figure 12.1: The Great Acceleration at the nexus of water, energy, and food*

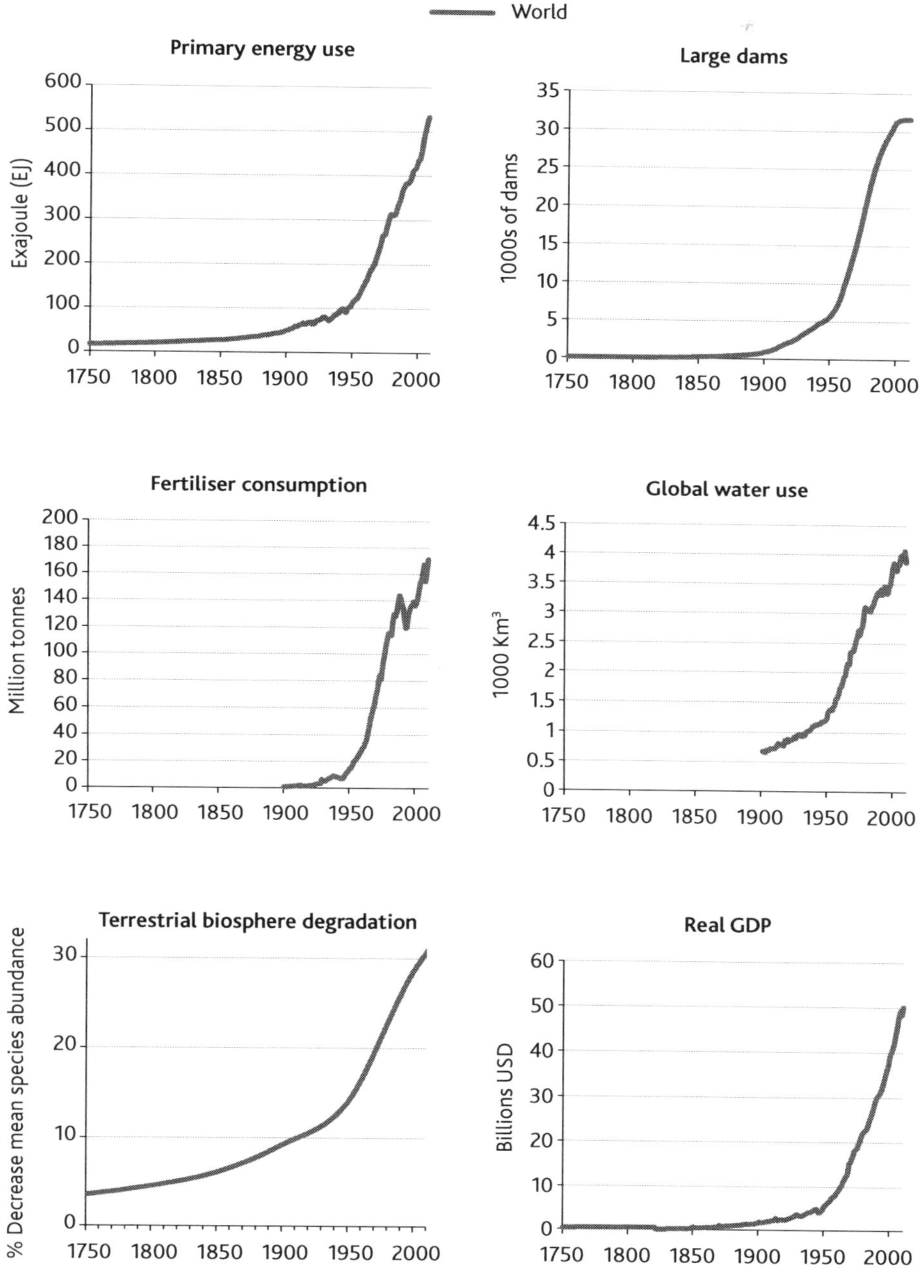

Source: Data from the International Geosphere-Biosphere Programme (IGBP) (www.igbp.net), courtesy of Wendy Broadgate, Owen Gaffney, Lisa Deutsch, Cornelia Ludwig and Will Steffen

## Global risks to water, energy and food

By the mid–1990s humans had transformed over a third of the Earth's land surface and were appropriating over half the annual available water supply (Postel et al, 1996; Vitousek et al, 1997). The distribution of basic goods for human welfare, however, was deeply unequal. Hundreds of millions lacked access to adequate drinking water or sanitation. At the 1996 World Food Summit, the malnutrition that disproportionately affects landless people, women and girls led to a new agreement to halve the number of undernourished people by 2015. Added to resource scarcity concerns were matters of environmental security that arose as energy demands on water, and water demands for food and energy, mutually reinforced growing concerns over climate change (Gleick, 1994). By the turn of the millennium, food, water and environmental security concerns were inseparable (Falkenmark, 2001). As this section shows, sustainable development policies that used markets to allocate scarce resources did not adequately address issues of water, food or energy security across the range of ways they matter for livelihoods, ecosystems or justice. Further, the form of 'integration' provided by economic tools carried its own security concerns. Although security concerns were not new, discourses of environmental security expanded significantly in the new millennium, from a focus on resource scarcity and conflict to concerns regarding human impacts on the planet. In 2004, Earth scientists published landmark findings that showed how, as the result of accelerating human impacts, Earth had entered a 'no analogue' state (Steffen et al, 2004). Since then, global policy has been grappling with the fact there is no precedent in Earth's history for the scale of human impacts on the planet. In particular, sustainable development has moved from seeking to 'integrate' environment and economy to governing global risks to water, energy and food that are *already* connected.

In a detailed history, Steven Bernstein (2001) describes the 'compromise of liberal environmentalism' through which sustainable development policies of the 1990s promoted economic tools as the primary instrument for environmental relief. This compromise was an effect of **neoliberalism**, which critiqued state–led development programmes as inefficient in comparison to free markets. However, owing to the place of water and food in social, political and moral relationships, the challenges in these sectors are not reducible to matters of economy alone (see **Box 12.3**). Many developing nations, such as Bolivia, rejected attempts to privatise water service delivery. There, and elsewhere, a backlash was due to the fact that basic rights to public water utilities and food aid had often been part of the exchange of development aid for liberalised trade. Other challenges arose regarding social and economic justice. Dams and industrial agriculture had displaced hundreds of thousands of people across the Global South, such as in India and Brazil. In response, international networks, like Via Campesina, advocated against policies that pursued market efficiencies that dispossessed small–holder farmers by developing counter-movements emphasising food sovereignty and human rights (see Weis, 2007).

## Box 12.3: Social rights to food and water

Water and food are social rights – rights that are basic to human dignity and part of the full suite of social and cultural rights recognised by the UN. This means that meeting obligations regarding food and water are not merely technical matters; they are normative challenges that require principles and practices that respect social and cultural differences.

For instance, the 'right to food' is not merely a right to a quantity of calories. It is a right to 'quantitatively and qualitatively adequate and sufficient food corresponding to the cultural traditions of the people to which the consumer belongs, and which ensures a physical and mental, individual and collective, fulfilling and dignified life free of fear' (Jean Ziegler, UN Special Rapporteur on the Right to Food, 2008, p 9).

Similarly, the 'right to water and sanitation' is defined in terms of sufficient, accessible, safe and acceptable to culturally appropriate norms of gender, lifecycle and privacy. These parameters situate 'the right to safe and clean drinking water and sanitation as a human right that is essential for the full enjoyment of life and all human rights' (UN, 2010a, p 2).

Neoliberal approaches to sustainable development failed to enhance the environment. The result was that accelerating social and ecological risks prompted two shifts in global policy. The first was a shift from management to **governance**. Whereas resource management focused on the site of decisions, such as irrigation timing, governance focused on the institutional structures affecting decisions. For instance, critics argued policy decisions that ignored social structures often further marginalised particular social groups, especially women, by reinforcing unequal institutions of property or land tenure. The second shift was that policy practitioners added security concerns to vernaculars of resource scarcity. In individual sectors, this was not new. Water, food and energy each have genealogies of security stretching back decades. What was unique was recognition of connections among food, water and energy security as *intersecting* concerns of *global policy*. This expanded sustainable development from policies focused nationally to global assessments of water and food security. One consequence was that when food and energy price shocks were followed by the 2008 GFC, there was already an appetite for a new framework for GSP.

How should connections of water, energy and food be understood under conditions of accelerating impacts of people on the planet? In 2008, the World Economic Forum (WEF) argued in a report titled *Thirsty energy* that connections of water and energy might not resonate as strongly as issues of drinking water, but that water consumption in energy production was critical to climate change policy. In 2009, Ban Ki-moon, the-then UN Secretary-General, asked the global financial community to focus on issues of water security at the WEF annual meeting in Davos, Switzerland. Two years later, the WEF (2011) published its response in *Water security: The water–energy–food–climate nexus*. The volume argued that water was structurally mismanaged across the global economy in ways that led to security concerns for food and energy in a warming world.

A good question here is: why would the UN seek advice from the WEF? Aside from the WEF's economic influence, an important part of the answer is that it had begun publishing annual *Global risk reports* in the mid–2000s. Through these reports, as **Figure 12.2** shows, the WEF defined what counted as a global risk. Global risk reports combined with a second consideration: after the UN launched the **Millennium Development Goals** (MDGs) in 2000, the WEF

*Figure 12.2: The World Economic Forum's Global Risk Criteria*

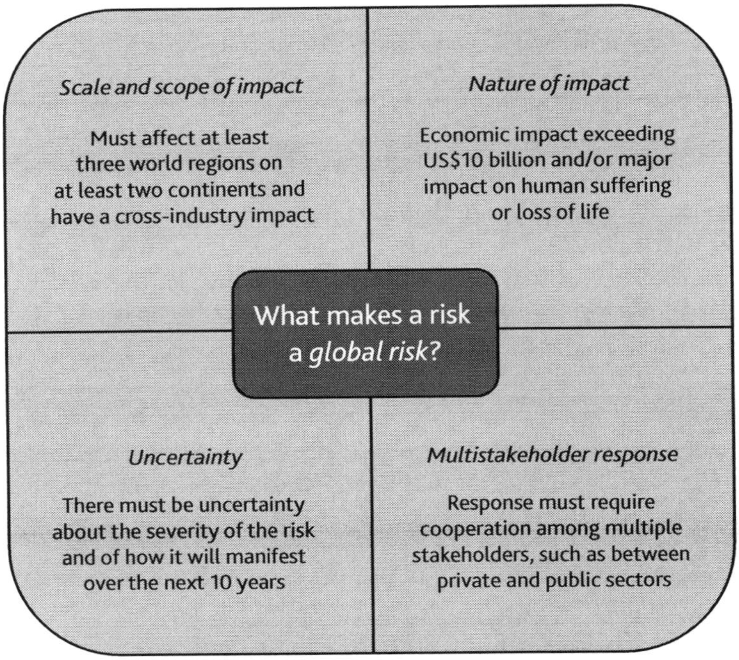

**Scale and scope of impact**

Must affect at least three world regions on at least two continents and have a cross-industry impact

**Nature of impact**

Economic impact exceeding US$10 billion and/or major impact on human suffering or loss of life

What makes a risk a *global risk?*

**Uncertainty**

There must be uncertainty about the severity of the risk and of how it will manifest over the next 10 years

**Multistakeholder response**

Response must require cooperation among multiple stakeholders, such as between private and public sectors

Source: Image created from the unabridged WEF (2006)

had positioned itself as an independent network for assessing progress towards sustainability (Pigman, 2007).

After the WEF report, the water–energy–food nexus quickly became a preferred framework for GSP. Ironically, the work experts had done to make water central to 'integration' in sustainable development was now critiqued for being too water-centric. Even the World Bank (2004), once a staunch advocate of IWRM, now considered it impractical. But IWRM was not abandoned. Rather, the consensus formed around 'integration' was renovated to link the nexus of food, water and energy security to risks to the global economy. To accomplish this policy shift, ideas of resilience were used to explain connections among *already integrated* domains of water, energy and food. Resilience offered three advantages. First, resilience had ascended from explanations of local ecology to form the basis for the Millennium Ecosystem Assessment, which published one of the largest ever scientific appraisals of the planetary environment in 2005. Second, resilience explained the dynamics of changing, interconnected and complex systems. As a policy concept, resilience provided a way to meaningfully discuss complexity, tipping points and surprising dynamics. Third, resilience was already being used in reference to economic risks after the 2008 GFC, and to explain the behaviour of a global economic system that had its own tipping points and surprises (Cooper, 2011). Taken together, the history of resilience in sustainable development, its use in global scientific assessments and its uptake in finance provided a common policy framework for governing complex relationships linking water, energy and food to global economic and environmental risks (Schmidt and Matthews, 2018).

## Resilience and the water–energy–food nexus

The WEF's 2011 report came a year before Rio+20, a conference marking the 20-year anniversary of the original UN Conference on Environment and Development. By this time, it was not only the WEF advancing the nexus. At a 2011 conference in Bonn, Germany, the water–energy–food nexus was advanced to connect policy challenges in a globalised world (Hoff, 2011). After Rio+20, the water–energy–food nexus ascended rapidly in global policy. By 2014, the water–energy nexus was the theme of World Water Day. As the nexus ascended, global supply chains were identified as key sites where security risks linking water, energy and food coalesced. Governing supply chains provided concrete sites to affect local, regional and global systems of water, food and energy. As this section shows, and as summarised in **Table 12.1**, multiple policy actors – private and public, policy and scientific – explained risks to the nexus in terms of resilience. Through this process, resilience moved from an organising framework to a policy goal.

'Nexus thinking' starts from the premise that water, energy and food systems are *already* integrated. But how, exactly, could these complex connections be

*Table 12.1: Discursive timeline on resilience and the water–energy–food nexus*

**Selected reports on the water–energy–food nexus, 2008–20**

| Organisation | Report title | Year |
|---|---|---|
| World Economic Forum | *Thirsty energy* | 2008 |
| World Economic Forum | *Water security: The water–energy–food–climate nexus* | 2011 |
| Stockholm Environment Institute | *Bonn2011 Conference: The water, energy and food security nexus* | 2011 |
| Food and Agriculture Organization | *Coping with water scarcity: An action framework for agriculture and food security* | 2012 |
| Food and Agriculture Organization | *Water, food security and human dignity: A nutrition perspective* | 2012 |
| Global Water Partnership | *Water security and climate resilient development* | 2012 |
| World Economic Forum | *Building resilience in supply chains* | 2013 |
| International Institute of Sustainable Development | *The water–energy–food security nexus* | 2013 |
| World Bank | *Thirsty energy* | 2013 |
| World Wildlife Fund and SABMiller | *The water–food–energy nexus: Insights into resilient development* | 2014 |
| World Economic Forum | *The water–energy nexus: Strategic considerations for energy policy-makers* | 2014 |
| Food and Agriculture Organization | *The water–food–energy nexus: A new approach in support of food security* | 2014 |
| UN Water | *World water development report: Water and energy* | 2014 |
| United States Geological Survey | *The water–energy nexus: An earth science perspective* | 2015 |
| World Economic Forum | *Resilience insights* | 2016 |
| World Bank | *High and dry: Climate change, water, and the economy* | 2016 |
| Organisation for Economic Co-operation and Development | *The land–water–energy nexus* | 2017 |
| Food and Agricultural Organization | *Policy brief: Water–energy–food nexus for the review of SDG 7* | 2018 |
| UNESCO and UN Water | *World water development report: Water and climate change* | 2020 |

translated into something actionable for policy? One answer was to use supply chains. These provide a ready fit with existing policy frameworks since, at each step of a supply chain, it is necessary to think about connections of food, water and energy as well as inputs like labour, manufacturing and logistics. Again, global actors like the WEF (2013) shaped this policy framing through arguments that supply chains presented sites where resilience could be enhanced. But the water–energy–food nexus wasn't just another supply chain issue faced by firms; it was also an issue linked to political decisions and macroeconomic policies regarding trade and development. One concept that sought to capture this expansive set of concerns was 'virtual water', a term introduced by Tony Allan (2003). The idea of virtual water is that states should consider how much water is 'embedded' in the production of different goods in calculations of political economy. Countries in water-scarce regions might import water–intensive products like rice while using limited domestic water supplies to produce high-value exports, like mangoes. Calculations of 'virtual water' could allow states to develop policies that 'virtually' import water to enhance food and water security.

Despite the appeal of using supply chains to frame policy challenges, the idea did not find consensus. Focusing on supply chains, many argued, too narrowly construed the policy challenges affecting the water–energy–food nexus. For instance, enhancing the resilience of existing supply chains does not necessarily address concerns of social justice that those same supply chains produce through extraction, labour conditions or trade. The Food and Agriculture Organization (FAO) (2012) argued that, given the potential for shocks and extreme events, a broader approach to enhancing resilience was needed. Other organisations, like the Global Water Partnership (2012), argued that mainstreaming resilience also required appreciating risks to finance and climate. These were also not adequately addressed through an exclusive focus on supply chains. Rather, the FAO (2014) recommended the broader goals of sustainable development should provide the framework for policies regarding the nexus. Similarly, the WWF, together with global beverage corporation SABMiller, argued that resilient development demanded strengthening the institutions that govern the complex connections between water, energy and food (WWF and SABMiller, 2014). How could this complex array of concerns be tackled? The FAO suggested one way forward would be to use scenario modelling to identify areas in which to enhance adaptive capacity. The next year, the German Federal Ministry for Economic Cooperation and Development and the European Union co-sponsored a new Water–Energy–Food Nexus Platform and developed a scenario planning tool for policy-makers, researchers and **civil society**.

The policy target that accompanied resilience was to enhance adaptive capacity. This is defined in terms of preparation for surprises, shocks and other disturbances by strengthening institutions, governance partnerships and economic relationships. As with other areas of GSP, **public–private partnerships** were identified as key to enhancing the resilience of the water–energy–food nexus. Adjacent themes of enhancing governance transparency were also promoted. Critics pointed out, however, that enhancing the capacity of the poor to deal with large disturbances, such as price shocks or extreme events, is not the same thing as policies oriented to reducing poverty or to addressing practices that generate poverty or environmental risks. So, resilience was not a neutral description of security challenges. Rather, it was a way of framing and interpreting risks, but this is not the same as global policy that addresses the equitable distribution of social and environmental goods (Leese and Meisch, 2015).

Concerns over social equity and social justice also arose as other international actors aligned the nexus with resilience. The FAO argued that governing the water–energy–food nexus was key to the resilience of the global food system and to human dignity (Lundqvist et al, 2015). These concerns were significant for agriculture. Land grabs, where states or corporations purchase agricultural land in foreign countries to secure their own supply chains, became more common after the 2008 GFC; the number and scale of international land transactions rose significantly, reaching into tens of millions of hectares (von Braun and Meinzen-Dick, 2009). The term 'land grabs' became a catch-all for transactions of various types: some were sales, others were contracts for particular products, still others were long-term leases that depended on what sort of security firms or states sought. Many land grabs targeted states with weak governance institutions. Often, the terms were not subject to public scrutiny. This sparked intense debate over the economic effects of international land deals and impacts on local communities (Cotula et al, 2009). While land conflicts intensified, critics argued that the water–energy–food nexus aligned too closely with economic systems rather than with development priorities focused on local livelihoods (Biggs et al, 2015).

Although the water–energy–food nexus was contested, it was ultimately the work of financial networks that influenced how it came to be used in policy (Schmidt and Matthews, 2018). The WEF and the World Bank, for instance, argued that the reliance of the global economy on hydrocarbon fuels entangled water, energy, food and climate change with financial risks. Some political theorists and ecologists similarly argued that environmental and economic systems were integrated to such an extent that a crisis in either domain could lead to the synchronic collapse of both (Homer-Dixon et al, 2015). Resisting the framing of global policy in terms of risk and resilience, others argue that attempts to make all values regarding water, energy and food commensurate with monetary values is a category error. That is, the type of error that arises from mistakes in understanding the kind of thing goods like water, energy or food are in different social, political and ecological contexts.

Parallel to the work of global financial actors developing the nexus, civil society actors pushed for water to be recognised as a human right. In 2010, the UN passed the resolution on human rights obligations related to safe drinking water and sanitation. Even the UN resolution, however, tied the right to water to the 'onset of the global financial and economic crisis' and the need to address intersecting food and climate crises (UN, 2010b, p 5). So, even as civil society celebrated the declaration of the right to water, the success was not exactly as hoped. A short time later, Ban Ki-moon even stated that the best way to achieve the right to water would be through enhanced use of market mechanisms (Schmidt, 2017, 2021). What has often passed unnoticed, however, is that the UN referenced the right to water in the MDGs. This had important implications as the MDGs were set to expire in 2015, at which time a new global agenda for sustainability would be put in place.

## The Sustainable Development Goals and the water–energy–food nexus

In 2015, the UN adopted the Sustainable Development Goals (SDGs). The same year, the Paris Agreement on Climate Change identified concerns of intergenerational equity as central to meeting the demands for economic development without dangerous global warming (see **Chapter 7**, this volume). In this context, the SDGs set ambitious targets that were only achievable through an integrated, global approach to policy. As the SDGs began to run from 2015–30, planning on how to achieve them focused on the nexus of water–energy–food, which became the 'most commonly discussed set of interactions' owing to their direct and indirect effects on multiple other SDGs (ESCAP, 2017, p 15). For example, hydroelectric dams on the Mekong River shared by China, Myanmar, Laos PDR, Cambodia and Vietnam may provide energy security for one country but negatively affect the large freshwater fishery downstream. At the level of GSP, decisions about development aid or financial investment are often discussed in terms of 'trade-offs' that leave significant roles for judgement in weighing social, scientific, political and economic factors.

When the SDGs were adopted, recognition of the nexus was an outcome of global risk reports, conferences and publications. With the SDGs in place, it was now time to move from framework to action. To this end, the OECD modelled the water–energy–food nexus in scenarios running to 2060. The OECD scenarios presented potential 'bottlenecks' as biophysical limits and economic systems would create 'hot spots' at the transnational level of particular regions. These bottlenecks were evident in the material water demands for agriculture, but also affected other policy objectives regarding 'welfare, environmental quality, food, water, and energy security' (OECD, 2017, p 13). Perhaps surprisingly, given earlier food and energy price shocks, the OECD scenario assessment exercise did not find significant *global* bottlenecks owing to how global trade could meet regional challenges. Perhaps unsurprisingly, however, the non-substitutable aspects of scarce resources like water meant that enhanced global trade would be unlikely to compensate for inequalities that would most negatively affect the welfare of the poorest households, especially as regional bottlenecks increased risks from climate change, drought or flood.

The OECD scenarios provide one model of a highly complex set of interactions. When considering other policy factors, however, global 'bottlenecks' do present key constraints. For instance, from a planetary perspective, contemporary societies have evolved in a narrow regime of climate stability that humans are now pushing off balance. In 2018, the Intergovernmental Panel on Climate Change (IPCC) released a special report demonstrating that key tipping points for the climate will be overshot well before the OECD scenario end point in 2060. What this means is that modern agriculture, social institutions, infrastructure and economic systems all face novel systemic risks as the climate moves beyond the normal bounds of variability. For instance, the McKinsey Global Institute identified how an increase in lethal heat waves (extreme heat lasting more than three days) will disrupt infrastructure across the world's mega-cities in North America, Europe, Africa and Asia, and alter the labour conditions by rendering daylight hours unworkable (Woetzel et al, 2020). Similarly, large disruptions are anticipated owing to extreme hydrological events of drought and flood associated with climate change.

The climate bottleneck is critical to GSPs linking water, energy and food. In 2018, the FAO's policy brief on SDG 7 (affordable and clean energy) argued that the water–energy–food nexus was closely connected to climate change concerns. As the FAO (2018) identifies, effective governance of the water–energy–food nexus under climate change is critically important to agricultural production and energy extraction. Both energy and agriculture are key contributors to climate change, which will necessitate careful assessments regarding how trade-offs in these sectors affect social policies regarding gender, race and social equity. What is noteworthy, however, is a policy conundrum the FAO identified: although the water–energy–food nexus emerged with an explicitly global orientation, the FAO found successful governance has largely been at the project level. Challenges remain, therefore, over how to scale up local water–energy–food dynamics to global policy. At the same time, a key recommendation of the FAO was to strengthen decentralised governance, which is, by definition, non-global. How can this circle be squared? One way is to think critically about the kind of work that concepts like the water–energy–food nexus do in global policy. In one sense, as the FAO identifies, the nexus provides a framework in which to assemble policy challenges of considerable diversity across economies, cultures and environments. In another sense, however, different uses of the nexus frame the terms on which trade-offs are made in particular ways, such as by including or excluding different factors of social justice, supply chains or climate change in scenario modelling exercises. How these terms are set matters crucially – from the data used in model scenarios to the language through which risks are interpreted.

Another bottleneck to the water–energy–food nexus is political. In particular, the SDGs are the first global sustainability agenda to have been agreed after the

UN Declaration on the Rights of Indigenous Peoples (UNDRIP). Passed in 2007, the UNDRIP resolution was the result of a long struggle that began when Indigenous peoples were excluded from the 1960 UN Declaration on the Granting of Independence to Colonial Countries and Peoples. In the decades since that time, and while postcolonial nations fought for sovereignty over their resources, Indigenous peoples lacked formal status in international politics. This issue is also global, from Inuit in northern Canada to Adivasis in India and Indigenous peoples across Latin and South America (and elsewhere). Through transnational action by Indigenous peoples, in 1989 the ILO adopted the Indigenous and Tribal Peoples Convention, known as Convention No 169. This was an important step towards the right to 'free, prior, and informed consent' on resource policies affecting Indigenous lands passed under the UNDRIP. The growing recognition of Indigenous rights presents a different kind of challenge for global policy – sustainable development included – that historically has not put Indigenous rights on a par with others. In effect, this means Indigenous peoples and lands have subsidised economic growth since colonisation began and through to today. The World Trade Organization has accepted this argument at least once, when it acknowledged that Canada's failure to uphold Indigenous rights constituted an unfair subsidy in its free trade agreement (NAFTA) with the USA and Mexico (Manuel, 2017).

Global scenarios that exclude climate risks or downplay Indigenous rights do not adequately or equitably capture policy challenges at the nexus of water, energy and food. By contrast, the 2020 *World water development report* by the UN examined the challenges of governing the water–energy–food nexus in view of climate change and social inequality, both for Indigenous peoples and others, impoverished or marginalised. The report noted that global challenges come from several directions: roughly 58 per cent of global water withdrawals from the energy sector are for fossil fuels that drive global warming, while water demands for agriculture require significant energy to move water to where it is needed, predominantly for irrigation (UNESCO and UN Water, 2020). The report makes social equity and **climate justice** central to its analysis of the water–energy–food nexus by identifying how the uneven impacts of climate change will affect those least responsible for greenhouse gas emissions. Indigenous peoples, and Indigenous knowledge in particular, feature prominently in the report as global policies promoting sustainable development continue to grapple with colonisation.

## Conclusion

A key policy horizon for the water–energy–food–climate nexus is 2030. The SDGs are set for renewal then, and the IPCC predicts that by then the Earth's climate will be at a threshold where the stable conditions in which human societies have evolved will, without rapid reduction of greenhouse gas emissions, be left behind. Between now and then, intersectional calls for social justice that link multiple domains of GSP – race, class, gender – are likely to intensify. These dynamics will compound issues at the nexus of water, energy and food. First, the complexity of environmental change will affect supply chains that link water, energy and food to the global economy. Second, the institutional and governance structures linking water, energy and food will continue to affect the unequal conditions that marginalise many of the world's poor and contribute to climate change. Third, climate change is likely to amplify concerns of resource security and social justice, especially in the context of historic and ongoing appropriation of land and ecosystems that come at the expense of postcolonial sovereignty and Indigenous rights. Discourses of security, risk, complexity and change are not neutral, yet are likely to be advocated, and contested, as ways to frame the water–energy–food nexus in GSP.

## Summary

- The water–energy–food nexus is a multi-actor policy field linking trade, development, environment and industrial policy sectors with IOs across scientific, environmental, political and economic domains.
- The water–energy–food nexus is beset by trade-offs over the resources necessary for human welfare and social justice, and sustainable approaches that respect livelihoods, environments and human dignity.
- Concepts of resilience and security are central to contests over how to meet rights to resources (water, energy, food), sovereignty and political self-determination.
- Global policy on the water–energy–food nexus that enhances adaptive capacity is not the same as policies that address causes of risk or disturbance in terms of social equity or justice.
- Linking different scales of risk at the local, regional or national level (that is, through supply chains) to global policy is a key site of politics and central to social conflict and struggle.
- Alongside development challenges of poverty, gender inequalities and social inequity, future policy on the water–energy–food nexus must address climate change and Indigenous rights.

## Questions for discussion

- Imagine you were presenting a three-minute policy brief on the water–energy–food nexus. What historical lesson(s) from sustainable development would you focus on, and why?
- After a talk on the water–energy–food nexus, you're asked: what alternatives to supply chains exist for linking local and global risk? What elements would you draw on to answer this question?

- At a citizen's forum, how would you differentiate resilience-based approaches to the water–energy–food nexus from those based on rights?

## Follow-up activities

- Want to govern the water–energy–food nexus? A scenario modelling tool that is part of the SDGs is accessible at: www.water-energy-food.org/resources/resources-detail/water-energy-and-food-nexus-tool-2-0 (it is free, but does require registration).
- 'Land grabs' come in many shapes, sizes and types. Use the Land Matrix database to download data, or generate infographics to examine them: https://landmatrix.org
- 'Remunicipalisation' is the term for returning water infrastructure to public governance after privatisation. Use the Water Remunicipalisation Tracker to compare policies, actors and local politics: www.remunicipalisation.org

## Further resources

*An unfinished foundation* (Conca, 2015) carefully appraises multiple UN environmental programmes that shape the global institutions now grappling with intersecting issues of water, energy and food. The edited collection *The water, food, energy and climate nexus* (Dodds and Bartram, 2016) provides an overview of how 'nexus thinking' is being taken up in global policy. By contrast, Sultana and Loftus (2020) think through global policy 'from below' in their edited collection, *Water politics*, which looks at issues intersecting with water, such as food, in the context of rights and justice.

See also the following websites:

The Water, Energy & Food Security Resource Platform: www.water-energy-food.org
UN Water: www.unwater.org
UN Energy: www.un-energy.org
UN World Food Programme: www.wfp.org
Environmental Justice Atlas: https://ejatlas.org

## References
Allan, J. (2003) 'Virtual water – The water, food, and trade nexus: Useful concept or misleading metaphor?', *Water International*, 28(1), 4–10.
Bernstein, S. (2001) *The compromise of liberal environmentalism*, New York: Columbia University Press.
Biggs, E., Bruce, E., Boruff, B., Duncan, J., Horsley, J., Pauli, N., et al (2015) 'Sustainable development and the water–energy–food nexus: A perspective on livelihoods', *Environmental Science & Policy*, 54, 389–97.

Bush, R. (2010) 'Food riots: Poverty, power, and protest', *Journal of Agrarian Change*, 10(1), 119–29.

Carson, R. (1962) *Silent spring*, New York: Houghton Mifflin.

Clark, W. and Munn, R. (eds) (1986) *Sustainable development of the biosphere*, Cambridge: Cambridge University Press.

Conca, K. (2006) *Governing water: Contentious transnational politics and global institution building*, Cambridge, MA: The MIT Press.

Conca, K. (2015) *An unfinished foundation: The United Nations and global environmental governance*, Oxford: Oxford University Press.

Cooper, M. (2011) 'Complexity theory after the financial crisis', *Journal of Cultural Economy*, 4(4), 371–85.

Cotula, L., Vermeulen, A., Leonard, R. and Keeley, J. (2009) *Land grab or development opportunity? Agricultural investment and international land deals in Africa*, London: Food and Agriculture Organization, International Institute for Environment and Development and International Fund for Agricultural Development.

Dodds, F. and Bartram, J. (eds) (2016) *The water, food, energy and climate nexus: Challenges and an agenda for action*, London: Routledge.

ESCAP (Economic and Social Commission for Asia and the Pacific) (2017) *Integrated approaches for Sustainable Development Goals planning: The case of Goal 6 on water and sanitation*, Bangkok: United Nations.

Falkenmark, M. (2001) 'The greatest water problem: The inability to link environmental security, water security and food security', *International Journal of Water Resources Development*, 17(4), 539–54.

FAO (Food and Agriculture Organization) (2012) *Coping with water scarcity: An action framework for agriculture and food security*, Rome: FAO.

FAO (2014) *The water–energy–food nexus: A new approach in support of food security and sustainable agriculture*, Rome: FAO.

FAO (2018) *Policy brief 09: Water–energy–food nexus for the review of SDG 7*, Geneva: United Nations.

Folke, C. (2006) 'Resilience: The emergence of a perspective for social–ecological systems analyses', *Global Environmental Change*, 16, 253–67.

Gleick, P. (1994) 'Water and energy', *Annual Review of Energy and Environment*, 19, 267–99.

Global Water Partnership (2012) *Water security and climate resilient development: Technical background document*, Stockholm: Global Water Partnership.

High-Level Panel on Energy (2020) *Food security and nutrition: Building a global narrative towards 2030*, Rome: High-Level Panel of Experts on Food Security and Nutrition of the Committee on Food Security.

Hoff, H. (2011) *Understanding the nexus: Background paper for the Bonn2011 Conference: The water, energy and food security nexus*, Stockholm: Stockholm Environment Institute.

Homer-Dixon, T., Walker, B., Biggs, R., Crépin, A.-S., Folke, C., Lambin, E.F., et al (2015) 'Synchronous failure: The emerging causal architecture of global crisis', *Ecology and Society*, 20(3), article 6.

International Energy Agency, International Renewable Energy Agency, United Nations Statistics Division, World Bank Group and World Health Organization (2019) *Tracking SDG 7: The energy progress report 2019*, Washington, DC: World Bank.

Leese, M. and Meisch, S. (2015) 'Securitising sustainability? Questioning the "water–energy and food–security nexus"', *Water Alternatives*, 8(1), 695–709.

Leopold, A. (1966) *A Sand County almanac: With essays on conservation from Round River*, New York: Oxford University Press.

Lundqvist, J., Grönwall, J. and Jägerskog, A. (2015) *Water, food security and human dignity – A nutrition perspective*, Stockholm: Ministry of Enterprise and Innovation, Swedish Food and Agriculture Organization Committee.

Lutz, K. and Hicks, B. (2013) 'Did unexpectedly strong economic growth cause the oil price shock of 2003–2008?', *Journal of Forecasting*, 32(5), 385–94.

Macekura, S. (2015) *Of limits and growth: The rise of global sustainable development in the twentieth century*, Cambridge: Cambridge University Press.

Manuel, A. (2017) *The reconciliation manifesto: Rediscovering the land, rebuilding the economy*, Toronto: James Lorimer & Company Ltd.

OECD (Organisation for Economic Co-operation and Development) (2017) *The land–water–energy nexus: Biophysical and economic consequences*, Paris: OECD.

Ogle, V. (2020) '"Funk money": The end of empires, the expansion of tax havens, and decolonization as an economic and financial event', *Past & Present*, 249(1), 213–49.

Pigman, G. (2007) *The World Economic Forum: A multi-stakeholder approach to global governance*, London: Routledge.

Postel, S., Daily, G. and Ehrlich, P. (1996) 'Human appropriation of renewable fresh water', *Science*, 271(5250), 785–88.

Sabin, P. (2013) *The bet: Paul Ehrlich, Julian Simon, and our gamble over earth's future*, New Haven, CT: Yale University Press.

Schmidt, J.J. (2017) *Water: Abundance, scarcity, and security in the age of humanity*, New York: New York University Press.

Schmidt, J.J. (2021) 'Water as global social policy: International organizations, resource scarcity, and environmental security', in K. Martens, D. Niemann and A. Kaasch (eds) *International organizations in global social governance: Global dynamics of social policy*, London: Palgrave Macmillan, 275–96.

Schmidt, J.J. and Matthews, N. (2018) 'From state to system: Financialization and the water–energy–food–climate nexus', *Geoforum*, 91, 151–9.

Shue, H. (1980) *Basic rights: Subsistence, affluence, and US foreign policy*, Princeton, NJ: Princeton University Press.

Steffen, W., Broadgate, W., Deutsch, L., Gaffney, O. and Ludwig, C. (2015) 'The trajectory of the Anthropocene: The Great Acceleration', *The Anthropocene Review*, 2(1), 81–98.

Steffen, W., Tyson, A., Jäger, P., Matson, J., Moore, P., Oldfield, B., et al (2004) *Global change and the earth system: A planet under pressure*, Berlin: Springer.

Sultana, F. and Loftus, A. (eds) (2020) *Water politics: Governance, justice, and the right to water*, London: Routledge.

UN (United Nations) (2010a) *The human right to water and sanitation*, A/64/292, New York: UN.

UN (2010b) Human rights obligations related to access to safe drinking water and sanitation (A/65/254), New York: UN.

UNESCO (United Nations Educational, Scientific and Cultural Organization) and UN Water (2020) *United Nations world water development report 2020*, Paris: UNESCO.

Vitousek, P., Mooney, H., Lubchenco, J. and Melillo, J. (1997) 'Human domination of Earth's ecosystems', *Science*, 277(5325), 494–9.

von Braun, J. and Meinzen-Dick, R. (2009) *'Land grabbing' by foreign investors in developing countries: Risks and opportunities*, Washington, DC: International Food Policy Research Institute.

WEF (World Economic Forum) (2006) *Global risk report*, Geneva: WEF.

WEF (2008) *Thirsty energy: Water and energy in the 21st century*, Geneva: WEF.

WEF (2011) *Water security: The water–food–energy–climate nexus*, Washington, DC: Island Press.

WEF (2013) *Building resilience in supply chains*, Geneva: WEF.

Weis, T. (2007) *The global food economy: The battle for the future of farming*, London: Zed Books.

Woetzel, J., Pinner, D., Samandari, H., Engel, H., Krishnan, M., Boland, B. and Powis, C. (2020) *Climate risk and response: Physical hazards and socioeconomic impacts*, McKinsey Global Institute (www.mckinsey.com/business-functions/sustainability/our-insights/climate-risk-and-response-physical-hazards-and-socioeconomic-impacts).

World Bank (2004) *Water resources sector strategy: Strategic directions for World Bank engagement*, Washington, DC: World Bank.

World Commission on Environment and Development (1987) *Our common future* (Brundtland Report), Oxford: Oxford University Press.

WWF (World Wildlife Fund) and SABMiller (2014) *The water–food–energy nexus: Insights into resilient development* (http://assets.wwf.org.uk/downloads/sab03_01_sab_wwf_project_nexus_final.pdf).

Ziegler, J. (2008) *Promotion and protection of all human rights, civil, political, economic, social and cultural rights, including the right to development*, Geneva: UN General Assembly Seventh Session, Resolution A/HRC/7/5.

# 13

# Global health policy

Meri Koivusalo and Eeva Ollila

## Overview

Global health policy is concerned with global agreements, financing, policies and practices of global actors, structures and measures that affect health, as well as the ways in which national health policies are shaped by global health issues and other global agreements, actors and processes. This chapter focuses on three main domains: first, agendas related to health systems, including health-related products and technologies, and how health systems are organised and financed; second, agendas concerned with how health security and protection are addressed at the global level; and third, agendas seeking to improve health, health-related social equity and the social determinants of health. The chapter reviews these domains and discusses key policy issues and challenges.

**Key concepts**
Health policy; health security; health systems; global health governance; health protection; social determinants of health

## Introduction

Health is of particular relevance to **global social policy** (GSP) for three reasons. First, it is a universal human right, and gross social inequalities in health undermine this right. Health inequalities have been addressed to reduce unequal health outcomes across countries and regions as well as to ensure equity in access to health services and medicines. Traditionally, this has been sought through development assistance for health, focused especially on international disease- or action-specific programmes such as those on HIV/AIDS, vaccinations or maternal and child health. Second, global health concerns have been identified by their potential to transcend national borders, in particular the risks of epidemics and contagious diseases, which can spread to/from the **Global South** to/from the **Global North**.

Coordinating action and ensuring resources has therefore required action at a global level to mitigate or contain these public health risks. The health security threats of severe acute respiratory syndrome (SARS), global pandemic influenza and COVID-19 are good examples of this type of global health concern. Third, promoting health and preventing diseases requires protection from harmful or unsafe products and practices. These activities are influenced by **transnational corporations** (TNCs) and shaped by global markets. Global agreements and policy frameworks to tackle, for example, tobacco and alcohol consumption, and to ensure food security, food safety and nutritional quality, may be necessary for national policy measures to be effective.

Global health policy analysis draws from the understanding of global health as a multidisciplinary and multisectoral practice (Koplan et al, 2009). It is concerned with global agreements, financing, policies and practices of global actors, structures and measures that focus on health and health service provision, as well as the ways in which national and global health policies are shaped by global health issues and other global agreements, actors and processes. Furthermore, global health policy includes impacts of transnational forms of collective action (Deacon et al, 1997).

While some measures of health policy directly address health through health sector-based interventions, others are more geared towards addressing the organising and financing of healthcare, or towards the protection and promotion of health extending outside the health sector. Knowledge about health determinants outside the healthcare sector is long established (Rosen, 1993). This is recognised in the field of infectious diseases, but has become reflected in the understanding of health determinants and the **social determinants of health** (SDH) that focus on broader determinants of health (see **Box 13.1** and **Figure 13.1**), including socioeconomic circumstances, cultural norms and practices, and the quality of diet, education, sanitation and housing. These determinants may, in turn, be influenced by combinations of factors at any one or all of the global, national, regional or local levels. It is important, therefore, to recognise that health is also influenced by policies and actions in sectors other than health and at different levels of **governance**. Health policies as a whole consist of measures:

- relating to health systems and **universal health coverage** (UHC) as part of **social protection**. This covers the health workforce, UHC and access, and the rational use and financing of health services and products, such as medicines;
- addressing specific health issues, such as control of **communicable diseases**, access to sexual and reproductive health services, maternal care and early childhood support;
- protecting health by environmental, sanitary and occupational health measures and standards;

- addressing social, political and **commercial determinants of health**, for example, through measures concerning properties, availability and taxation of tobacco, alcohol and food stuffs, as well as regulations concerning their labelling and advertising;
- relating to health research, surveillance, training and access to knowledge.

## Box 13.1: Determinants of health

The health of individuals is not only a product of genetic inheritance and biological factors, the functioning of health systems or lifestyle choices. Rather, our capacity to become and stay healthy is affected by a range of public policies and wider social conditions. These socioeconomic, cultural and environmental conditions are traditionally articulated as *determinants of health*. Social determinants of health describe in particular those that contribute to inequalities in health (WHO, 2008) (see also **Figure 13.1**).

*Figure 13.1: Determinants of health – the Dahlgren–Whitehead 'rainbow'*

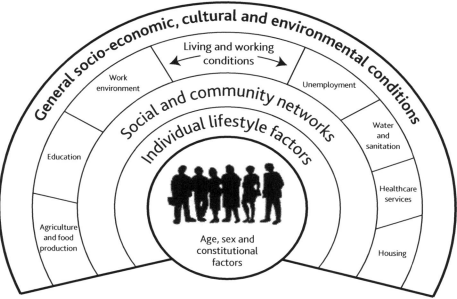

Source: Dahlgren and Whitehead (1991, Figure A-3)

## Global health issues require global health policy

Global health policies draw legitimacy both from international legal and institutional obligations as well as from emerging problems and concerns that emphasise the need for action on a global scale and through global institutions. Global health issues may present as local or national policy issues, yet effective responses at national and local level can be undermined by lack of global action. Infectious diseases have been particularly important in global health as they can cause epidemics and pandemics. The urgency of global action is underpinned by the fact that infectious diseases tend to be more common in parts of the world that lack resources for health. Such scarcity makes global action to address them even more important. The need for global action has become painstakingly clear as the COVID-19 outbreak quickly became a pandemic in 2020.

Emerging global health challenges include pandemics, antimicrobial resistance and **zoonoses** (diseases moving from animals to humans). More recently, the importance of non-communicable diseases (NCDs) has increased for global health agendas in all countries, including in the Global South. The need to regulate harmful commodities and address commercial policies of TNCs and their marketing practices thus applies to all countries (Ollila, 2005). The first global binding health agreement – the Framework Convention on Tobacco Control (FCTC) – was negotiated to support tobacco control within countries (see also **Chapter 3**, this volume).

The organisation and financing of national public health policies and health systems is influenced by **globalisation** and global economic integration with new and pressing issues coming on to the global health policy agenda. Globalisation increases business power to shape public policies (see **Chapter 4**, this volume). It influences broader policies affecting the determinants of health and has direct implications for health systems. A major global health issue is the governance of access to and research and development (R&D) for new medicines, which has gained recognition particularly for HIV/AIDS medicines, antimicrobials and cancer medicines. Health systems are also affected by, for example, the availability of a suitably qualified health workforce as well as the financing of national healthcare systems. Socially just health financing policies should mean that people who fall ill and need care do not incur excessive charges or face catastrophic repayment schedules. These issues are reflected in the global policy agenda through the World Health Organization's (WHO) *Global code of practice on the ethical recruitment of health personnel* (WHO, 2010) and the WHO's focus on UHC (UN, 2012).

Global climate change has major health implications (see **Chapter 7**, this volume), not only for the spectrum of communicable diseases and prevalence of a variety of determinants of health, but also for the resulting increase in needs and for the capacities of national health systems to respond to rising challenges. Health systems need to adjust and mitigate the effects of climate change, including their energy and waste management, and address the health effects of changed climate and increased temperatures. Water and sanitation have been part of traditional broader global health policy and epidemic control (see **Chapter 12**, this volume), but the range of global environmental health issues extends more broadly, encompassing zoonotic diseases and air and chemical pollution. Challenges of **sustainable development**, biodiversity and planetary boundaries form an emerging global health concern. Natural crises, conflicts and related **migrations** (see **Chapter 9**, this volume) also bring up global health issues including hunger and malnutrition, which require concerted action.

## Global health governance and global health policy

Global health governance is relevant to how global health policy issues are dealt with and what kind of institutions frame and shape global health policy, but we also need to examine the underpinning assumptions. Rushton and Williams (2012) have emphasised how global health policy is based on embedded **neoliberalism**, shaping how and where global health policy is addressed. One of the key elements of the institutional architecture is the WHO and its constitutional, normative and political role in global health policy (see also **Chapter 2**, this volume).

### The World Health Organization

Responsibility for global health, health policy-making and standard setting has traditionally been invested in the WHO, a United Nations (UN) specialised agency. Its constitution is broad and essentially sets it a mission of 'attainment by all peoples of the highest possible level of health'.

Given that the WHO came into existence as a result of international cooperation over cholera epidemics and the International Sanitary Conferences, it is not surprising that its work started with a disease-based focus (Cueto et al, 2019), in particular, with major campaigns on the eradication of diseases, notably of smallpox. The failure of the 'vertical' malaria programme led to recognition of the importance of health systems and broader intersectoral health policies in the Alma Ata Declaration (1978), which also emphasised primary healthcare. In the early 1980s, the emergence of the HIV/AIDS epidemic was first reflected in the Global Programme on HIV/AIDS under the WHO, and since 1996, via the UN Programme on HIV/AIDS (UNAIDS) (Knight, 2008). More recently, many disease- or issue-specific interventions have become established as new initiatives or institutions outside the WHO. Single-issue initiatives and programmes operate in the form of 'vertical' programmes. This means they are often maintained as separate structures rather than working through more 'horizontal' programmes focusing on health systems within countries.

As the UN specialised agency for health, the WHO is mandated to operate as the global regulatory and normative health agency. It is accountable to national ministries of health, which represent **member states** in the World Health Assembly (WHA). The WHO's regular budget comes from the assessed contributions of the member states' health ministries. However, additional resources mainly come from government development aid budgets and development-related sources, foundations and private sector sources. While the WHO's core funding has been in decline in real terms, the share of extra-budgetary resources, mostly ear-marked to specific purposes, has increased sharply. This has meant that while voting power within the WHO lies with ministries of health on the basis of 'one country, one vote', they have less power to control which WHO activities are funded through external funds. In 2020–21 the WHO's programmes budget was about US$5,840 million (WHA, 2019), but only about US$1,000 million resulted from assessed contributions (WHO, 2020a).

A large share of WHO activity relates to technical standards, guidelines, diagnostic criteria and undertaking reference work. The WHO also issues 'soft' guidance and guidelines that provide a basis for benchmarking and the setting of national policy priorities (see **Chapter 2**, this volume). The strongest and perhaps most contested form of global regulatory focus and guidance is that of negotiation of **conventions**. The WHO can negotiate conventions and has done so in the case of the FCTC. It is so far the only convention negotiated under the auspices of the WHO, although proposals have been made for other areas (for example, alcohol, R&D and trade in substandard and falsified medicines).

The WHO's role in global health was strengthened as a result of the negotiation of the new International Health Regulations (IHR) in 2005 (Fidler and Gostin, 2006). The IHR is not a convention, but a legal agreement, which seeks to prevent and respond to acute public health problems and emergencies, which could cross borders and be of importance for a larger number of countries. The IHR provide the WHO with limited rights to intervene, but essential legitimacy to act on international public health threats. This is essential to international travel and trade, which can be affected by epidemics. The IHR give the WHO the right to declare a Public Health Emergency of International Concern, which allows governments legitimately to restrict trade and travel to countries. However, the WHO has been criticised for acting too early on the H1N1 pandemic declaration and too late on Ebola in 2014.

Although the role of the WHO in curbing the COVID-19 pandemic has been crucial, WHO capacities to act on the IHR have been seriously affected as a result of lack of funding over and above membership fees. Faster decision-making and political influence can often be sought through funding of new agencies and initiatives, as was the case for the IHR and the 2014 Global Health Security Agenda, funded by the USA.

Other WHO normative policy measures have focused on the International Code of Marketing of Breastmilk Substitutes (1981) and later, *The WHO global code of practice on the international recruitment of health personnel* (Yeates and Pillinger, 2019). The WHO and the UN's Food and Agriculture Organization (FAO) established the Codex Alimentarius Commission in 1963, which develops harmonised international food standards, guidelines and codes of practice to protect the health of consumers and ensure fair practices in food trade. The WHO and the International Labour Organization (ILO) work closely with respect to the health workforce (Yeates and Pillinger, 2019), occupational health standards and **social insurance**.

The WHO's role as the global standard–setting agency is frequently under attack from a variety of sources. Tobacco industry lobbying against the WHO and its activities in the area of tobacco control has been widely documented (see Fooks and Gilmore, 2013). The WHO's essential medicines policy, its work on rational use of medicines and access to medicines, as well as initiatives on R&D, have been lobbied by the pharmaceutical industry. In addition to the tobacco and pharmaceutical industries, the WHO has been the target of lobbying by the alcohol, sugar, soda and fast food industries.

### Health, the UN and the human and global social rights agenda

Various UN funds and programmes concern health issues, particularly in a development context, including the United Nations Children's Fund (UNICEF), the United Nations Population Fund (UNFPA) and the Joint United Nations Programme on HIV/AIDS (UNAIDS). UNAIDS (founded in 1994) coordinates the UN's activities around HIV/AIDS and is co-sponsored by 10 UN agencies and the World Bank.

Health, and rights related to health, is part of the UN's broader human rights agenda and agreements. The Convention on the Rights of the Child, hosted by UNICEF, is a global rights–based convention that has relevance to health. The Convention lies at the core of UNICEF's work. On a more practical level, UNICEF has worked on childhood immunisation programmes and procurement of medical supplies for children.

The UNFPA has been particularly active in the area of reproductive rights and family planning (see also **Chapter 10**, this volume). This is a politically challenging field, where commitments made as part of the Cairo Conference on Population and Development (1994) and the Beijing Conference on Women (1995) provided a framework for broader outlines and for action, which have since remained a reference point for global policy-making. **Sexual and reproductive health and rights** have re-emerged as a focus for global politics, especially as a result of the USA's focus on abortion and the Mexico City policy (known as the global gag rule) of declining funding for abortion.

The UN's relevance for global health policy-making is shaped by the **Sustainable Development Goals** (SDGs), where health targets are articulated under Goal 3. In contrast to the previous, more health-focused **Millennium Development Goals** (MDGs) that concentrated on poorer countries and on HIV/AIDS and malaria, the SDGs are applicable to all countries and have a broader health focus, including Target 3.8 for UHC.

UN Special Sessions and High-Level Meetings have become more important for health policies over the last decade. They were important for broader recognition and realisation of HIV/AIDS policies, and have consequently been sought to enhance global action on NCDs and UHC. In 2012 the UN General Assembly (UNGA) passed a resolution in support of universal coverage of healthcare with a follow-up meeting in 2019 (UN, 2012). The United Nations Department of Economic and Social Affairs (UNDESA) addresses a variety of social development issues, including follow-up from the Copenhagen Social Summit (1995) and the Madrid International Plan of Action on Ageing (2002). The UN hosts the secretariat for the Convention on the Rights of Persons with Disabilities, which is relevant to health systems and rehabilitation. While UN political declarations and statements are often considered to be of limited value, they provide legitimacy for global policies and frame priorities for future action and processes.

### Global health actors: public–private partnerships, NGOs and philanthropies

New global actors, institutions and initiatives have emerged in global health policy since the late 1990s. The G8 began to engage with debates and policies especially concerning access to medicines, and was important in shaping global **public–private partnerships** (PPPs) (see, for example, Labonté and Schrecker, 2007). The work of the G8 has enabled an increasing number of initiatives and new institutions, such as The Global Fund (Kirton et al, 2007). The G8's focus on health is an example of **venue shifting** and engagement by key governments, although since the **global financial crisis** (GFC) of 2007–09 and the emergence of the G20, the role of the G8 has been less prominent.

Collaboration between the public and private sectors in international development has grown in importance since the 1980s. At the beginning of the 21st century, a new form of global health-related public–private partnership (GHPPP) emerged, with the formation of GHPPPs as independent legal entities outside the auspices of the UN. The first GHPPP to emerge was the Global Alliance for Vaccines and Immunizations (GAVI) in 2000, which was used as a model in the formation of subsequent health partnerships, such as The Global Fund to Fight AIDS, Tuberculosis and Malaria ('The Global Fund'). GHPPPs are, by design, issue-specific vertical programmes (Ollila, 2005). Such programmes can create problems in coordination, accountability and resource allocation for national health systems and wider international development policies. New broader initiatives include the Drugs for Neglected Diseases initiative (DNDi), which seeks to enhance research on drugs for neglected diseases and the Coalition for Epidemic Preparedness Innovations (CEPI), which focus on vaccines, or Unitaid and the Medicines Patent Pool, which are involved in ensuring access to medicines.

Although MDG 8 and SDG 17 actively advocate for countries to promote PPPs, there is little scientific evidence supporting the effectiveness of such partnerships in promoting health. Rather, there are clear risks to agreements with industries whose business interests have a high potential to clash with health promotion priorities (Parker et al, 2019).

**International non-governmental organisations** (INGOs), missionary organisations and other non-governmental actors have played an important role in global health policies and service provision in many countries over a century. INGOs have also played an important role in emergency and humanitarian aid; the Red Cross and the Red Crescent, two major INGOs, are particularly crucial in this regard. While large service providers are not necessarily the most prominent in agenda setting at the global level, INGOs such as Médecins Sans Frontièrs (MSF) are particularly notable for their active role in both agenda setting and service provision at the local level. The role of HIV/AIDS-related organisations and action groups and MSF has been widely acknowledged in raising issues of HIV/AIDS and access to medicines on the global health policy agenda. The NCD Alliance of NGOs has called for an improved focus on NCDs. The role of patient organisations in global health has increased, possibly as a result of more industry funding. While the role of churches and religious organisations has been pronounced in matters of sexual and reproductive health, it has been more limited in campaigns around other health issues. The International Baby Food Action Network contributed substantially to the development of global guidelines on the advertising of infant foods.

The Bill & Melinda Gates Foundation's (BMGF) global health programme has become significant because of the volume of funds it raises and its influence in shaping health policy options, including for the WHO. While global private foundations, such as the Rockefeller Foundation, have been involved with global policy-making for a long time, the magnitude of BMGF financing is considerably larger, and extends from financing R&D, government programmes, NGOs and lobbying to global public–private partnerships and IGOs. The role of private philanthropies and **philanthrocapitalism** in the politics of engagement is a broader global health policy issue (see, for example, Birn, 2014). Further questions can be raised in this regard relating to corporate sponsorship, **corporate social responsibility** schemes and different schemes of private sector financing of healthcare (see, for example, Yeates and Pillinger, 2019, pp 189–95, on Global Skills Partnerships in relation to health workforce training).

Global NGOs also include representative associations for health professionals and health-related industries. For example, the International Federation of Pharmaceutical Manufacturers & Associations representing the pharmaceutical industry is classed as an INGO. Global health-related regulations and guidance are particularly important for health industries, whose profits are affected by global policy decisions. Industry lobbying and sponsorship is a concern for global health policy-making; the concern is that it exerts unwarranted influence on health financing and policy space for health. In addition to global humanitarian organisations, IGOs other than the WHO have a substantial health role. For example, the International Organization for Migration has become a prominent global service provider for migrants' health.

## Financing of global health

Financing for global health shapes how and what is addressed as part of global health policies as well as which agencies or actors are active in global health. In contrast to normative UN specialised agencies, such as the WHO, ILO and FAO, which at least in principle draw some of their core funding from membership fees, most global health financing and funds draw from philanthropic, charitable and/or development funding. Development funding for global health shifted in the 1990s to **international financial institutions** (IFIs), and again in the 2000s, more towards PPPs and new forms of 'innovative' financing.

The role of development financing for global health is expected to decline; however, the pandemic may change this. It is also known that commercial and private sector funding usually forms only a very limited share of funding for GHPPPs. In 2020 the private sector – including philanthropies – accounted for less than 6 per cent of Global Fund funding (The Global Fund, 2020). Airline taxes have been used in funding Unitaid, but the utilisation of taxes for global and/or national health policy support remains strongly contested by TNCs and some governments.

International financial institutions, such as the World Bank and the International Monetary Fund (IMF), influence global health policy (see **Chapter 2**, this volume). World Bank and IMF guidance on broader public sector reforms and poverty reduction measures define the scope for national health policy options and available resources. Rowden (2009) emphasised how the IMF's neoliberal blueprint shaped global health policies: it has, he argued, systematically undermined public health policies. The IMF's mandate is to ensure the stability of the international monetary system, and its role in the provision of loans in times of economic crises means it exerts significant influence over the determinants of health and health policies in the recipient country. Decisions concerning public spending, economic reforms, terms of lending and debt repayment and aid allocation all affect health policies, health systems and health outcomes.

The World Bank influences global health through direct funding of health programmes as well through broader guidance on macroeconomic policies. It has engaged with health issues as part of its population, health and nutrition agenda, which initially began as a lending programme to fund population measures (Wolfson, 1983). It first engaged with global health policy guidance in the 1990s through its landmark World Development Report *Investing in health* (World Bank, 1993). Its emphasis on health reforms, user fees and further engagement with the private sector and NGOs in service provision was at odds with the WHO's focus on primary healthcare. On the other hand, its analysis of the economics of tobacco control proved important and supportive for its negotiations over the FCTC. In the 2000s, the World Bank had a lower profile in health, and in 2012, Jim Yong Kim, a past strong critic of World Bank policies from a health perspective, was appointed as the new World Bank Director. Since then, it has been supportive of UHC, although there remain concerns about its support for a substantial private sector role in achieving that coverage. Otherwise, it has increased engagement with novel financing mechanisms. This culminated in 'pandemic bonds', which gained criticism on the grounds that they were too beneficial for investors and overly cumbersome in addressing actual health and other needs arising from pandemics (Stein and Sridhar, 2017; Jonas, 2019).

## Global health policy space and policies for health

Policy space for global health is shaped by both positive and negative global commitments. The FCTC is an example of a global legal agreement that creates positive policy space at a national level. Global health policies are also influenced by broader human rights obligations, which can be invoked to support action across sectors. Policy space is affected by active engagement and lobbying by TNCs on global health issues. Such engagement has raised critical interest in the commercial determinants of health, corporate political involvement and the role of TNCs in shaping public health policy (Fooks and Gilmore, 2013; Moodie et al, 2013).

International trade agreements have become a concern for national and global health policy space (see also **Chapter 3**, this volume; on policy space, see Koivusalo et al, 2009). Attention has focused on the interface between national pharmaceutical policies and trade-related commitments in global and **bilateral** trade agreements and their provisions on trade-related aspects of intellectual property rights. The World Trade Organization's (WTO) agreement on Trade-Related Intellectual Property Rights (TRIPS) changed the context of pharmaceutical R&D and production as a result of the establishment of product patents and requirements for trademark protection. Prices of medicines are known to fall substantially as a result of competition, and this creates strong incentives for the pharmaceutical industry to try to extend monopoly rights that would maintain higher prices. The TRIPS agreement also allows what are known as 'flexibilities', which permit governments to issue compulsory licensing on defined grounds to allow production of medical goods for government use or to stimulate competition in the production of these goods.

The interpretation of whether and when governments could use these flexibilities became a matter of contention before the Doha round of trade negotiations. The Doha *Declaration on the TRIPS agreement and public health* (Doha WTO Ministerial, 2001) was a major watershed in this respect as it confirmed that TRIPS should be interpreted in a way that supports public health priorities. However, bilateral trade agreements often include 'TRIPS+' provisions, which stipulate further requirements that may compromise the intended effects of the Doha Declaration (Shadlen et al, 2020). The COVID-19 pandemic may also become important in revealing and requiring new limits for the application of trade and investment agreements and the enabling of broader use of the TRIPS flexibilities to ensure access to vaccines for all.

Other concerns for policy space and trade agreements relate to public services and procurement, health services financing, regulatory cooperation and precautionary measures. Policy space concerns also apply to investment **liberalisation** and protection, which have become part of modern trade agreements (see **Chapter 3**, this volume). Trade agreements also apply to the cross-border mobility of people and professionals (see **Chapter 9**, this volume).

If globalisation and transnational corporate and financial interests affect global health policy space, this is also the case for **populist** and nationalist regimes and policies, which seek to restrict the applicability of global regulation. So-called 'plutocratic populists' (see Hacker and Pierson, 2020) tend to align more with key corporate players in support of global neoliberal or libertarian positions (see, for example, Slobodian, 2020).

## Global health policy agendas and debates

Global health policy agendas represent more elaborated policy priorities rather than merely gravitating towards common global health concerns. This section outlines three overlapping global agendas.

### From Health for All to UHC

While initially the WHO focused on the control of infectious diseases, by the late 1970s a new philosophy had emerged in its emphasis on the role of national healthcare infrastructures, various societal sectors and multidisciplinary expertise in improving public health. This new thinking was prompted by failures in the malaria eradication programme (Siddiqi, 1995; Koivusalo and Ollila, 1997), and emerging scientific debates that emphasised the importance of population health (Milio, 1988). This new philosophy was embodied in the joint WHO–UNICEF international conference on primary healthcare in Alma Ata in the Soviet Union (now Kazakhstan) and the ensuing Declaration of Alma Ata by the WHO and UNICEF in 1978. However, UNICEF shifted soon after the conference to selective healthcare with 'vertical' approaches to health, and the WHO showed varying commitment to it too.

The launch of the World Bank's *World development report* in 1993 followed sharply increased World Bank lending for health from the late 1980s, and anticipated its growing dominance in shaping global health agendas during the 1990s. The World Bank's focus on healthcare reforms originated from broader public sector reforms and efforts to control healthcare costs through healthcare reforms that had been proposed by the Organisation for Economic Co-operation and Development (OECD). In general, healthcare reforms involved an increased role for private healthcare provision, separation of the purchaser and provider of services, and renewed payment and revenue collection mechanisms, including incentives for providers as well as patients to change their patterns of health service usage and provision (Mills et al, 2001).

Meagre funding, high costs of healthcare and more disease-based global financing made it clear that global health needed to focus on health systems. The UNGA resolution on UHC (UN, 2012) was a key contribution to the evolving discussion on healthcare reforms and policy as it emphasised social equity in access to healthcare and UHC. The role of public health beyond purely curative services to a broader focus has always been a challenge for UHC, which tends to focus more on the financing of services. Although the model health system for realising and organising the Health for All strategy and primary healthcare draws from the model of public provision, as in the UK's National Health Service (NHS), the dominant global model for UHC fits more with an insurance-based health system.

Access to and rational use of pharmaceutical medicines has been central to global health policy agendas for many decades. The underlying concerns have remained the same: financial and physical access to pharmaceuticals, and proper quality, proper information about, and proper use of pharmaceuticals in practice. In the 1990s the traditional emphasis on the rational use of pharmaceuticals was joined by a new emphasis on access to medicines, for two reasons: first, the concern over HIV/AIDS and the availability of new drugs for the treatment of HIV/AIDS for all; and second, the establishment of the WTO and increasing consideration of pharmaceuticals as a key trade-related issue in the TRIPS agreement and in bilateral trade negotiations. Problems of guiding R&D, medicines shortages and high prices of medicines, including new medicines for cancer, rare diseases and antimicrobials, now affect **middle–** and **high–income countries** (CEWG, 2012; WHO, 2018).

Articulation of the right to access pharmaceuticals has ushered in a more **universal** rights-based discourse to global health policy and has challenged

TNCs' commercial rights. At the same time, however, this has shifted the focus of global health policy towards single–disease approaches, giving rights to access pharmaceuticals for some diseases while neglecting others. Although focusing on the specific needs of developing countries is important for global social solidarity, it can also obscure the differences between corporate and public policy needs within countries and the common health policy interests across countries.

### Social equity: social determinants of health and Health in All Policies

The need to address health through the policies and actions of multiple social sectors is reflected in the WHO Constitution, the WHO Health for All Strategy (1978) and the WHO Ottawa Charter for Health Promotion (1986). The more recent agendas on Health in All Policies (HiAP) and on social determinants of health (SDH) focus on addressing health implications of other policies for health, health systems and the distribution of health.

HiAP is a public policy approach for promoting and protecting health, health equity and the functioning of health systems. It was developed during the Finnish presidency of the EU in 2006 to strengthen the implementation of Article 168 of the Lisbon Treaty on protecting human health. It has since been further developed for the purpose of policy-making. For example, Canada and southern Australian states have further developed HiAP to serve health promotion efforts across sectors. HiAP includes health promotion and protection, health systems and accountability for health consequences (Leppo et al, 2013).

Evidence from practising the HiAP approach is that its implementation is easier when synergies between the various policy actors can be found, for example between education, environment and health. Conversely, its implementation is more complicated and difficult when there are intrinsic conflicts between the aims of the actors, as between, for example, public health actors and commercial policy interests in unhealthy products. A key global challenge to health arises from corporate lobbying to become involved as partners in global partnerships and multistakeholder arrangements (see also **Chapter 4**, this volume).

SDH are defined as the conditions in which people are born, grow, live, work and age, including socioeconomic status, education, neighbourhood and physical environment, employment, and social support networks, as well as access to healthcare (see **Box 13.1**). The agenda on SDH is inspired by the understanding that there is an unjustifiable gap in health between rich and poor people, which is best addressed through focused action on SDH. It is not only concerned with improving overall health, but also with socially equitable access to healthcare and reducing health inequalities.

SDH rose to the global agenda as a result of the work of the WHO's Commission on the Social Determinants of Health. The Commission's report, *Closing the gap in a generation*, was explicit about the need for international action and monitoring (WHO, 2008). It is also evident in the UN resolution on UHC and in various commitments to social equity. However, the follow-up of action and guidance for addressing SDH has been hampered by meagre resources.

At the global level, SDH have been elaborated by an emphasis on the commercial and political determinants of health. Commercial determinants of health are 'factors that influence health which stem from the profit motive' (West and Marteau, 2013), whereas political determinants of health emphasise the importance of health as a political choice and the politics involved in this (see, for example, Bambra et al, 2005; Kickbush, 2015).

## Health security and health protection

Health security and health protection rely on public health capacities, regulation and surveillance; they also influence regulation in other policy areas. Health security can be interpreted either narrowly as a focus on biosecurity and biohazards, or more broadly, including epidemic control, capacity building, broader **social security** measures and health protection as part of health security. It can also be understood in the broader context of human security, first introduced by the UNDP in the 1990s.

Global health security has become a more prominent field of study in the context of international relations, which has also lead to a concern of securitising infectious disease (see, for example, Rushton, 2011). The COVID-19 pandemic has revealed weaknesses in global health governance, which relate to the relationship between health and other policy concerns in the core areas of global normative health policies. Prior to that, the Ebola crisis in 2014 led to broader criticism over the WHO's capacity in health security. However, since 2014 the WHO has been a key actor on Ebola oversight and control, which is reflected in its prominent role in the COVID-19 pandemic and its advocacy of the test, trace and isolate strategy. While some countries may have blamed the WHO, it has redeemed its relevance and role as *the* global health agency, demonstrating unexpected resilience and an active presence for the **low-income** and poorest **countries** as well as for high-income ones.

The focus on health protection aligns with action on antimicrobial resistance and global environmental challenges, from air pollution to biodiversity and climate change. Environmental health issues are frequently dealt with under One Health, which works together with veterinary and plant health, and is particularly relevant to food safety, the control of zoonoses and combating antibiotic resistance (when bacteria change after being exposed to antibiotics and become more difficult to treat) (see **Box 13.2** and **Figure 13.2**). One Health is a collaborative, multisectoral and transdisciplinary approach to be distinguished from social or political environmental and health movements and project organisations.

## Box 13.2: One Health

The WHO works with the FAO on food safety and plant health and the World Organization for Animal Health on multisectoral responses to food safety hazards, zoonoses and public health threats from the human–animal–ecosystem interface (WHO, 2020b).

*Figure 13.2: One Health*

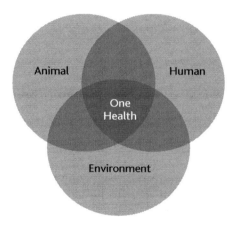

Source: WHO (2017)

Air pollution is an example of a globalised health protection issue. It is now a more prominent problem in middle-income and poor countries. Not only does it adversely impact on health in large cities, but it can also move across borders (Landrigan et al, 2018). Climate change has similarly become a global health policy issue. Again, this is not only because of its adverse impacts on health, but also because of the potential benefits to health from appropriate, timely action. Climate change impacts are strongly related to air quality, nutrition and the production of food within and between countries; changing diets globally can improve nutrition as well as influence climate change (Aleksandrowicz et al, 2016). Global biodiversity and sustainability requirements are important parts of the emphasis on planetary health measures that seek to adapt global and national health policies to the requirements for planetary health and sustainability (see **Chapter 7**, this volume).

# Conclusion

A global dimension to health policy is, in many ways, much more explicit than in other areas of social policy. While all health policies are grounded in cultural values and priorities, the biomedical and clinical aspects of health provide a more universal basis for common dialogue across borders. A set of commonly agreed global commitments and a legal framework exist in health, even if in a rather limited form. Global health policies can result from conscious choices and efforts to tackle health problems through an emphasis on the wider determinants of health, as illustrated by the FCTC. On the other hand, global health policies emerge as a response to health crises and more specific disease threats, such as HIV/AIDS or pandemics.

A key challenge for global health governance and health policies is to engage with national and global regulation and redistribution for health, where corporate actors and interest groups may influence health policy priorities groups. Global pandemics also remind us of the importance of global health cooperation and engagement with normative policies at the heart of global health policy.

The need to engage with the underlying SDH is recognised both in the context of a focus on UHC as well as with respect to interlinkages between health, poverty and inequalities. To address the SDH and ensure access to healthcare for all, global health policies will need to focus more on the redistribution of resources both between and within countries.

Finally, just as in other policy areas, global health policy formation is not merely a matter of technical concern or biomedical facts, but is embedded in values, power relations, politics and institutional and cultural priorities.

## Summary

- Global health policy is an arena for public policy decisions and debates on how global policies support health systems, social, environmental and political determinants of health and health protection and security.
- Global health policy tends to be defined as predominantly a development issue, where global health policy applies to the Global South and/or as a remedy to impacts from broader trade and commercial policies.
- Despite the pandemic, global cooperation to address crucial health systems issues, determinants of health and regulatory needs in the context of global health policies and globalisation, including the erosion of the WHO's resource base (which affects its capacity to undertake public health and regulatory work) has weakened.
- Private foundations and NGOs play a stronger role in agenda-setting; commercial actors and their forums also play a stronger role in global policy-making.

## Questions for discussion

- How are global health policies both different from and similar to other areas of global social policy?
- What kinds of legal instruments are available for global health policy?
- How do the health agendas and priorities of different IGOs compare with one another?

## Follow-up activities

- Investigate the ways in which any of the global health agendas are reflected within your country of choice. Think about which other global policy actors and principles have a tangible bearing on health policy formation in the country you have chosen. What kind of global health policy issues are brought up in the daily news?
- Consult the websites of national or international NGOs involved in trade, environmental and social justice campaigns. To what extent do they raise health as an issue of global concern rather than one of national or local concern? What are the key health-related agendas, and how do these relate to global health policy?

## Further resources

You can gain access to global policy documents directly from IGOs' web pages. Global health statistics are also easily available from the WHO and UN websites, annual flagship reports of UN organisations and the World Health Statistics report. The UN website provides human rights-related materials, including Special Rapporteurs' reports. Twitter is a good source for current social media discussion and global health debate, but podcasts and videos are expanding. **International organisations**, universities and health foundations have websites and Twitter accounts, which provide updates and reactions to policy decisions. The following journals regularly carry articles and features on global health policy: *Bulletin of the World Health Organization, Globalisation and Health, Global Social Policy, Lancet Global Health, BMJ Global Health* and *Global Public Health*.

## References

Aleksandrowicz, L., Green, R., Joy, E.J.M., Smith, P. and Haines, A. (2016) 'The impacts of dietary change on greenhouse gas emissions, land use, water use, and health: A systematic review', *PLoS ONE*, 11(11), e0165797, doi:10.1371/journal.pone.0165797.

Bambra, C., Fox, D. and Scott-Samuel, A. (2005) 'Towards a politics of health promotion', *Health Promotion International*, 20, 187–93.

Birn, A.E. (2014) 'Philanthrocapitalism, past and present: The Rockefeller Foundation, the Gates Foundation, and the setting(s) of the international/ global health agenda', *Hypothesis*, 12(1), e8, doi:10.5779/hypothesis.v12i1.229.

CEWG (Consultative Expert Working Group) (2012) *Research and development to meet health needs in developing countries: Strengthening global financing and coordination*, Geneva: World Health Organization.

Cueto, M., Brown, T.M. and Fee, E. (2019) *The World Health Organization: A history*, Cambridge: Cambridge University Press.

Dahlgren, G. and Whitehead M. (1991) *Policies and strategies to promote social equity in health*, Stockholm: Institute for Futures Studies.

Deacon, B., Stubbs, P. and Hulse, M. (1997) *International organisations and the future of social welfare*, London: SAGE Publications.

Doha WTO (World Trade Organization) Ministerial (2001) *Declaration on the TRIPS agreement and public health*, WT/MIN(01)/DEC/2 (www.wto.org/english/thewto_e/minist_e/min01_e/mindecl_trips_e.htm).

Fidler, D.P. and Gostin, L. (2006) 'The new international health regulations: An historic development for international law and public health', *Journal of Law, Medicine and Ethics*, 34(1), 85–94.

Fooks, G.J. and Gilmore, A.B. (2013) 'Corporate philanthropy, political influence, and health policy', *PLoS ONE*, 8(11), e80864, doi:10.1371/journal. pone.0080864.

Global Fund, The (2020) *Pledges and contributions*, Geneva: The Global Fund.

Hacker, J. and Pierson, P. (2020) *Let them eat tweets: How the right rules in an age of extreme inequality*, New York: Liveright Publishing.

Jonas, O. (2019) 'Pandemic bonds designed to fail in Ebola', *Nature*, 572, 285 (https://doi.org/10.1038/d41586-019-02415-9).

Kickbush, I. (2015) 'The political determinants of health – 10 years on', *British Medical Journal*, 350, 1–2.

Kirton, J., Roudev, N. and Sunderland, L. (2007) 'Making G8 leaders deliver: An analysis of compliance and health commitments, 1996–2006', *Bulletin of the World Health Organization*, 85(3), 192–9.

Knight, L. (2008) *UNAIDS: The first 10 years, 1996–2006*, Geneva: UNAIDS (https://data.unaids.org/pub/report/2008/jc1579_first_10_years_en.pdf).

Koivusalo, M. and Ollila, E. (1997) *Making a healthy world: Agencies, actors and policies in international health*, London: Zed Books.

Koivusalo, M., Labonté, R. and Schrecker, T. (2009) 'Globalization and policy space for health and social determinants of health', in R. Labonté, T. Schrecker, C. Packer and V. Runnels (eds) *Globalization and health: Pathways, evidence and policy*, London: Routledge, 105–30.

Koplan, J.P., Bond, C., Merson M., Reddy, K., Rodriguez, M., Sewankambo, N. and Wasserheit, J. (2009) 'Towards common definition of global health', *Lancet*, 373, 1993–5.

Labonté, R. and Schrecker, T. (2007) 'Foreign policy matters: A normative view of the G8 and population health', *Bulletin of the World Health Organization*, 85(3), 185–91.

Landrigan, P., Fuller, R., Acosta, N.J., Adeyi, O., Arnold, R., Basu, N.N., et al (2018) 'The Lancet Commission on pollution and health', *Lancet*, 391, 462–512.

Leppo, K., Ollila, E., Peña, S., Womar, M. and Cook, S. (eds) (2013) *Health in All policies: Seizing opportunities, implementing policies*, Helsinki: Ministry for Social Affairs and Health, United Nations Research Institute for Social Development (UNRISD), THL (Finnish Institute for Health and Welfare), WHO Observatory.

Milio, N. (1988) 'Making healthy public policy: Developing the science of art: an ecological framework for policy studies', *Health Promotion*, 2(3), 236–74.

Moodie, R., Stuckler, D., Monteiro, C., Sheron, S., Neal, B., Thamarangsi, T., et al (2013) 'Profits and pandemics: Prevention of harmful effects of tobacco, alcohol, and ultra-processed food and drink industries', *Lancet*, 381, 670–9.

Mills, A., Bennett, S. and Russell, S. (2001) *The challenge of health sector reform: What must governments do?*, New York: Palgrave Macmillan.

Ollila, E. (2005) 'Global health priorities – Priorities of the wealthy?', *Globalization and Health*, 6, 1–6.

Parker, L.A., Zaragoza, G.A. and Hernández-Aguado, I. (2019) 'Promoting population health with public–private partnerships: Where's the evidence?', *BMC Public Health*, 19, 1438.

Rosen, G. (1993) *A history of public health* (expanded edn), Baltimore, MD: Johns Hopkins University Press.

Rowden, R. (2009) *The deadly ideas of neoliberalism: How the IMF has undermined public health and the fight against AIDS*, New York: Zed Books.

Rushton, S. (2011) 'Global health security: Security by whom? Security for what?', *Political Studies*, 59, 779–96.

Rushton, S. and Williams, O. (2012) 'Frames, paradigms and power: Global health policy-making under neoliberalism', *Global Society*, 26(2), 147–67.

Shadlen, K.C., Sampat, B.N. and Kapczynski, A. (2020) 'Patents, trade and medicines: Past, present and future', *Review of International Political Economy*, 27(1), 75–97.

Siddiqi, J. (1995) *World health and world politics*, London: C. Hurst & Co.

Slobodian, Q. (2020) *Globalists: The end of empire and the birth of neoliberalism*, Cambridge, MA: Harvard University Press.

Stein, F. and Sridhar, D. (2017) 'Health as a "global public good": Creating a market for pandemic risk', *British Medical Journal*, 358, j3397.

UN (United Nations) (2012) *Global health and foreign policy*, A/RES/67/81, Resolution adopted 12 December 2012, New York: UN.

West, R. and Marteau, T. (2013) 'Commentary on Casswell: The commercial determinants of health', *Addiction*, 108(4), 686–87.

WHA (World Health Assembly) (2019) *Programme budget 2020–21*, Geneva: WHO (www.who.int/about/finances-accountability/funding/A72_R1-en.pdf?ua=1).

WHO (World Health Organization) (2008) *Closing the gap in a generation*, Report of the Commission on Social Determinants of Health, Geneva: WHO (www.who.int/social_determinants/en).

WHO (2010) *The WHO global code of practice on the international recruitment of health personnel*, World Health Assembly Resolution 63.16, Geneva: WHO (www.who.int/hrh/migration/code/code_en.pdf).

WHO (2017) *One health picture*, Geneva: WHO (https://twitter.com/WHO/status/918504092464504834/photo/1).

WHO (2018) *Access to medicines, vaccines and pharmaceuticals: Pricing of cancer medicines and its impacts*, Technical report, Geneva: WHO.

WHO (2020a) 'Assessed contributions 2020–2021' (www.who.int/about/finances-accountability/funding/2020-21_AC_Summary.pdf?ua=1).

WHO (2020b) *One health*, Geneva: WHO (www.who.int/news-room/q-a-detail/one-health).

Wolfson, M. (1983) *Profiles in population assistance: A comparative review of the principal donor agencies*, Development Centre Studies, Paris: OECD.

World Bank (1993) *World development report 1993: Investing in health*, New York: Oxford University Press.

Yeates, N. and Pillinger, J. (2019) *International health worker migration and recruitment: Global governance, politics and policy*, London: Routledge.

# 14

# Global education policy

Susan Robertson and Roger Dale

## Overview

This chapter examines the expansion of global education policy-making over the past three decades, broadly driven and given shape by the globalising of neoliberalism, on the one hand, and greater engagement with the idea of education as a human right, on the other. Our argument is elaborated through the analysis of four education policy issue areas. The first focuses on the first attempt to globalise education policy via the United Nations Universal Declaration of Human Rights. The second global policy issue examines how the Organisation for Economic Co-operation and Development has used and promoted large-scale assessments such as the Programme for International Student Assessment to reframe the goals and activities of national education systems. The third policy issue is the emergence and promotion of public–private partnerships as a mode of governance in national settings, giving rise to ongoing processes of the privatisation of public services. The fourth policy issue is the growth of education as a services sector to be incorporated into, and governed by, the global trading system.

**Key concepts**
Scale; multilateralism; neoliberalism; commodification

## Introduction

Over the past three decades there has been an expansion of global education policy–making. This is the outcome of interactions among an array of international, **multilateral**, corporate agencies and **civil society** actors, who have entered into the education sector in various capacities: as policy shapers, providers, financiers, owners of infrastructures and regulators.

Given that education is a profoundly national and sub–national activity, it might come as a surprise that education systems around the world are increasingly governed through global policies. This involves not only obvious forms of global activity, but also, as Sassen argues, significant units within sub/national state architectures that have recalibrated their spatial horizons *towards* the global (2006), creating new interdependencies between the institutions of **global governance** and national states (see **Chapter 1**, this volume). Understanding why and how this is happening is important, not least because education is a key pillar of the **social contract** between states and civil society as well as a key institution of welfare systems. Such developments bring new challenges for governing, especially for **intergovernmental organisations** (IGOs), particularly when they lack strong regulatory capacities.

In this chapter we draw on Mittelman's (2000) conceptualisation of **globalisation** as a syndrome of related, although contradictory, processes and activities, that have set in train a historic transformation in the economy, in politics and in cultural milieus (Mittelman, 2000, p 7). A key feature of the current manifestation of globalisation is its ideational base – that of **neoliberalism** – mobilised in the 1980s by critics of bureaucratic state power (Peck, 2013), and as an alternative to **Keynesianism** (Harvey, 2007) (see **Chapter 1**, this volume). We also take Santos's point, that globalisation is 'a process by which a given entity reaches the globe by enlarging its own ambit and by doing so, develops the capacity or the prerogative of naming as "local" all rival entities' (quoted in Dale and Robertson, 2004, p 149). Santos has in mind large ideational projects promoted by actors with interests that have transformed societies, their economies and education projects around the world. In education, ideational projects that shape policy include education as a human right, the idea of school choice, **public–private partnerships** (PPPs), and education as a services sector involving internationally tradable commodities (see also **Chapter 3**, this volume).

## From national education systems to global (post-national) learning regimes

We began this chapter by noting that over the past three decades there has been an expansion of global education policies. However, early global policies can be traced back to the end of the Second World War and the view that the global community should take responsibility for building a new kind of society. This had three significant consequences. First, there was widespread acknowledgement of the *collective* responsibility of the world for ensuring the human rights of all of its inhabitants. This is most clearly inscribed in the establishment of the United Nations (UN) system, and a UN Charter. Second, education as a 'human right' was enshrined in the 1948 Universal Declaration of Human Rights (UDHR), which all UN countries are signatories to. The UDHR (see **Box 14.1**) states that everyone has the right to education, and that the state has a duty to provide education for free. Third, a large number of new nations emerged in the 1950s and 1960s, now with formal responsibility for their own education systems and policies. This was seen by their former colonial masters, along with the USA and Russia, as an opportunity to maintain and increase their spheres of interest internationally.

---

**Box 14.1: Education and the Universal Declaration of Human Rights (1948), Article 26**

(1) Everyone has the right to education. Education shall be free, at least in the elementary and fundamental stages. Elementary education shall be compulsory. Technical and professional education shall be made generally available and higher education shall be equally accessible to all on the basis of merit.

(2) Education shall be directed to the full development of the human personality and to the strengthening of respect for human rights and fundamental freedoms. It shall promote understanding, tolerance and friendship among all nations, racial or religious groups, and shall further the activities of the United Nations for the maintenance of peace.

(3) Parents have a prior right to choose the kind of education that shall be given to their children.

---

They did this through conceptualising the problem for the newly formed states as 'traditional' societies moving towards being modern. It was argued that the 'stages of growth' (Rostow, 1960) could be accelerated by the development of education systems. Of crucial and lasting significance was the identification of human capital theory (see Schultz, 1971), which posited that the key variable shaping successful economies was investment in education. Education was thus harnessed to the project of nation–building, and economic development followed the same dual objectives – of making *citizens* and making *economies*. These two different understandings of 'education' in global education policy, one humanitarian and the other economic, are the basis of a fundamental division between the multilateral agencies, and can be seen in how each IGO frames global policy problems and their solutions.

## Globalisation of education through 'development'

The United Nations Educational, Scientific and Cultural Organization (UNESCO) and the UDHR were the first two key elements of global education policy-making in the immediate aftermath of the Second World War. UNESCO was formed following an establishment conference in Britain in 1945, and its constitution ratified in 1946. Its mandate was formed out of the view that intellectual and educational cooperation was essential for the construction of a peaceful, democratic and civilised international society (Mundy, 1999).

Yet UNESCO's project was full of tensions and contradictions. Issues surfaced from the 1950s onwards, such that UNESCO was beset by global geopolitical dynamics: the onset of the Cold War, the rise of McCarthyism in the USA and demands by the newly independent states for membership and representation in UNESCO's **governance** arrangements (Hoggart, 1976). Not surprisingly, these independent states found UNESCO's single destiny and world culture approach deeply problematic, not least because UNESCO's presumption was that the destiny of the new states would continue to be determined by their old colonial masters. In this moment, the image of UNESCO as a world forum and international public sphere also provoked fears among governments, notably the USA, which called for censorship of UNESCO's **cosmopolitan** aims. UNESCO also faced an ongoing crisis of mission as well as financing (Mundy, 1999). This limited its capacity to govern education futures with any authority.

This created a window for entry of the World Bank as a provider of development finance to the newly independent states (Mundy and Verger, 2015, p 10). The World Bank's activities in education began in 1960 with very little investment in education. By 1965 it was spending the same amount as UNESCO. Some 50 years on, the World Bank was spending 16 times as much on education as UNESCO (Mundy and Verger, 2015). By the 1980s, it had replaced UNESCO as the lead global agency for education (Jones, 1992). It was also during this time that the World Bank began producing a series of education strategy papers that set the frame for global education policies aimed at national education systems (Klees, 2010). Significant changes in the goals and the modalities of 'aid' resulted, with global education policies increasingly dominated by powerful countries of the **Global North**.

The first example was a shift to aid policies informed by neoliberalism (often called the **Washington Consensus**) (Williamson, 1993). The Consensus involved the following key ideas: privatisation, **liberalisation**, deregulation and fiscal discipline, to be implemented through **structural adjustment programmes** (SAPs). SAPs favoured the use of **conditionalities** to implement 'free' market policies, although these were to be later severely criticised, and the World Bank faced its own crisis of legitimacy (Mundy and Verger, 2015, pp 11–12). Nevertheless, various strands of those policies continued in the so-called 'Post-Washington Consensus', which included support for education as a means to produce **human capital** as the basis of economic growth. Such policies also spawned international markets and privatisation policies in education.

It can be argued that the Education For All (EFA) goals (see **Box 14.2**), first launched in 1990 in Jomtien (Thailand), represented the first significant move towards a global human rights–based approach to education that honoured the promise of the UDHR (Chabbott, 1998). However, the EFA goals were not met by 2000, and at the World Education Forum (held in Dakar in 2000) governments, development agencies, civil society and the private sector agreed to work together to reach the EFA goals by 2015 and adopted the Dakar Framework for Action (World Education Forum, 2000).

The Dakar Framework for Action (World Education Forum, 2000) mandated that UNESCO coordinate the partners, with **member states** viewing UNESCO as the most democratic IGO in its representation, and because of distrust of the World Bank (Edwards et al, 2017). However, it became clear that UNESCO did not have the capacity to deliver the goals, and the lead role was taken over by the World Bank, which had oversight of the Fast-Track Initiative that funded education policy and programmes. Edwards et al (2017, p 46) argue that UNESCO recovered a degree of legitimacy by taking on the oversight of the Global Monitoring Report (GMR), which was launched in 2000 to monitor progress towards realising the EFA goals (see GMR, 2020; see also **Box 14.2**).

The GMR has come to be relied on by a wide range of actors. GMR data show, for example, declining rates of non-participation in primary and secondary schooling in all regions of the world, especially Sub-Saharan Africa and Central and South Asia (see **Figure 14.1**). This data seems to confirm progress towards universal education. However, the World Bank often disputes the GMR's usefulness. These frictions remind us of the ideational differences and tensions among the education IGOs.

## Box 14.2: Education For All (EFA)

The EFA movement is a global commitment to provide quality basic education for all children, youth and adults. At the World Education Forum in Dakar in 2000, 164 governments pledged to achieve EFA and identified six goals to be met by 2015. Governments, development agencies, civil society and the private sector are working together to reach the EFA goals.

The Dakar Framework for Action mandated UNESCO to coordinate these partners, in cooperation with the four other convenors of the Dakar Forum: United Nations Development Programme (UNDP), United Nations Population Fund (UNFPA), United Nations Children's Fund (UNICEF) and the World Bank. As the leading agency, UNESCO focuses its activities on five key areas: policy dialogue, monitoring, advocacy, mobilisation of funding, and capacity development.

In order to sustain the political commitment to EFA and accelerate progress towards the 2015 targets, UNESCO has established several coordination mechanisms managed by UNESCO's EFA Global Partnerships team. Following a major review of EFA coordination in 2010–11, UNESCO reformed the global EFA coordination architecture.

Source: www.unesco.org/new/en/education/themes/leading-the-international-agenda/education-for-all

The shift from EFA in 1990 to the **Millennium Development Goals** (MDGs) launched in 2000 (to be realised by 2015) and, most recently, the **Sustainable Development Goals** (SDGs) launched in 2015 (to be realised by 2030) can be read as a shift from a 'multilateral' agency to a 'global agency' approach. Over time the number of goals and indicators has increased (from 8 to 17 goals – education is now SDG 4). Bull and McNeill (2019) argue that this entails a shift from 'market multilateralism' to 'governance by goal setting'. Importantly, the range of actors and agencies involved in shaping the goals and indicators and their realisation has expanded to include large for-profit actors that have a direct commercial stake in shaping a new kind of education system.

While the SDG framework is seen as laudably ambitious, there is considerable slippage in meaning between the broad values outlined in the goal statements and the global indicators selected to evaluate progress (Unterhalter, 2019, p 39). Bull and McNeill (2019, p 471) argue that the SDGs are also different in important respects from the MDGs, beyond the addition of more goals: the SDG process was more open to **non-state actors**, including business; the SDG goals apply to all countries of the world and not just low- and **middle-income countries**; and the SDGs include greater emphasis than the MDGs on the means of implementation (notably by global partnerships, now SDG 17). This goal reinforces the use of PPPs to coordinate the delivery of education. More than this, it brings in a range of other actors/partners not previously recognised as having a part to play in global education policy-making (Yeates, 2017).

## The OECD's Programme of International Student Assessment

The clearest challenge to education policy as a national affair is found in the OECD's Programme of International Student Assessment (PISA). PISA is formally 'an international study which aims to *evaluate education systems worldwide* by testing the skills and knowledge of 15-year-old students' (OECD, 2006; emphasis added). By 2018 PISA had involved 600,000 students in 79 countries, representing 32 million 15-year-olds (OECD, 2018). It is a huge and ambitious project that represents the apogee of the relationship between globalisation and education.

*Figure 14.1: Global number of out-of-school children, adolescents and youth, 2000–18*

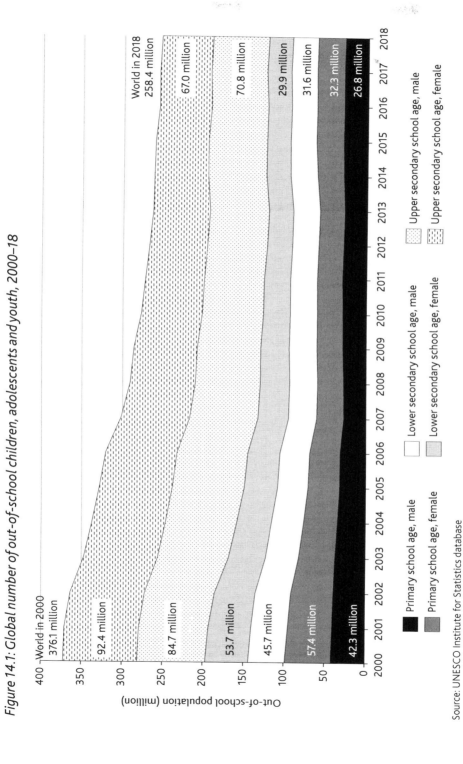

Source: UNESCO Institute for Statistics database

In approaching PISA as an example of the operation of a key facet of global education policy, we note that the basis of its intervention is not so much providing *responses* to the new challenges of 'globalisation' but in *framing* and *defining the nature of* those new challenges. That is, the OECD's PISA programme specifies and formulates the nature of the problems, it argues, are faced by national systems. In the case of PISA, they do this by evaluating education *systems* testing the competences of 15-year-old students in the areas of literacy, science and mathematics.

In 2018, the OECD added into PISA a global competence framework (OECD, 2016, 2018) aimed at overcoming what it described as growing social inequalities within and across nations, conflict as a result of mass **migrations**, and the ubiquity of digital technologies in the lives of young people. The move to assess cultural attributes such as global competences has been challenging for the OECD, with many participating countries paying for data collection, but not collecting it. Assessing diverse values and beliefs using a one-size-fits-all survey is deeply controversial (Auld et al, 2019).

The OECD has also expanded its suite of PISA portfolios, to include PISA for Development (PISA-D). PISA-D is an adaptation of the pre-existing PISA test, specifically designed for **low-income countries**. The OECD's expansion into low-income countries is particularly interesting, especially given that it legitimates itself as an IGO. In this case, low-income countries do not have membership of the OECD. However, the OECD argues that developing countries have pressed for data on student learning to enable them to show how they might realise the SDGs (Auld et al, 2019, p 198).

PISA rests on two basic principles. The first is a focus on student competences, on what students are able to *do* with the knowledge they accumulate. The second is in making national education systems comparable in terms of a single metric, which is used to order and hierarchically rank countries' education systems against each other. PISA sets a common *global* benchmark for all its member states, no matter how different their socioeconomic position, current education policies or cultural background.

PISA is also a very particular kind of instrument, which uses ordinal judgements that tend towards numerical commensuration. In doing so, they present themselves as an objective process of quantification, for example, the top 5 or 10, or 25 countries on the OECD's PISA lists of rankings. Robertson (2018) has called this vertically represented ordinal system 'vertical vision'. Ordinal systems have their own spatial dynamics. This is because only one entity can occupy one space at a time – despite, in some cases, very marginal differences between entities. Small differences are amplified, and large differences are scaled back.

PISA does not *prescribe* any particular policy, but rather provides a common framework of analysis that any policies might be expected to take into account. In this sense it is most usefully seen as a 'meta-policy', that is, it is a policy that frames the possibilities and expectations of, and sets limits to, what can count as policy. However, this does not mean that PISA somehow escapes, or overrides, existing differences between national conceptions of education. Nevertheless, the nature of such a common base cannot be neutral, or indeed be able to treat all existing systems in the same way, since, being developed and carried out by the OECD, PISA is obviously not ideologically neutral, but rather evaluates education from an economic perspective and promotes, according to this paradigm, related learning techniques. From this viewpoint, PISA is much closer to the pre-existing Anglo–American understanding of education than that of continental Europe (Martens and Niemann, 2010, p 1). Meyer and Benavot (2012, p 6) express these views more trenchantly, arguing that PISA is:

> ... well on its way to being institutionalized as the main engine in the global accountability regime, which measures, classifies and ranks students, educators and school systems from diverse cultures and countries using the same standardized benchmarks. The OECD, in turn, begins assuming a new institutional role as arbiter of global educational governance, simultaneously acting as diagnostician, judge and policy advisor to the world's school system.

They see PISA as:

> ...advancing a new mode of global educational governance in which state sovereignty over educational matters is replaced by the influence of large-scale international organizations, and in which the very meaning of public education is being recast from a project aimed at forming citizens and nurturing social solidarity to a project driven by economic demands and labour market orientations. (Meyer and Benavot, 2012, pp 9–10)

One important mechanism through which PISA works is to shift the burden of education accountability to *outputs* (such as achievement levels) rather than *inputs* (such as funding, or curriculum). It therefore defines what counts as evidence (the scores of 15-year-olds on tests of mathematics, literacy and science), irrespective of national locations. This makes it truly transnational, and the forms of governance it promotes both acknowledge and respond to this mission. PISA is not directly concerned with what is taught in a country's schools. Rather, it is,

> ... as a tool of expectation management [that] PISA fosters a transformation of what had been ill-defined issues (eg, curriculum contents) into seemingly well-defined attainment goals. It delivers,

at the same time, a parameter for holding schooling accountable – for delivering according to the expectations embedded into its questionnaires. (Hopmann, 2008, p 425)

However, it is also important to consider how PISA has been received and interpreted by its members, and to ask about its impact on national education policies and practices. A study by Breakspear (2012) of the 'normative impact' of PISA suggests that 'on the ground' it becomes essentially a 'problem framing' discourse, which is differently interpreted as it comes into contact with situated national education systems. This suggests that the acceptance of/adherence to PISA's common problematic – the discursive framing of educational quality via accountability – is more prominent in PISA's aims than in its outcomes, as delivered through national education systems.

In an interesting, and different, perspective on the matter, Takayama (2018) argues that the success of many Asian education nations in the PISA league tables to the point that they become 'reference societies' has also altered the negative views of Asian societies regarding their education systems. He uses this to also reveal the historically racist representations of Asia that the West has held since the inception of the UN system described earlier. Similarly, Waldow et al (2014) also show the way in which PISA success stories enable them to become referent nations, and that this projection is not only discursively powerful, but that the idea of greatness also carries with it social power. The role of the media is central in intensifying attention, in turn ensuring PISA's global visibility and reach. Grey and Morris (2018) argue that framing, new values and mediatisation work together to position PISA as a global education policy in its own right.

## Globalising public–private partnerships in education

In this third set of global education policies, we introduce public–private partnerships (PPPs) (Robertson et al, 2012). PPPs have largely replaced the privatisation policies and programmes associated with the 1980s Washington Consensus mentioned earlier. In reality, PPPs continue to pursue similar goals and outcomes. At the broadest of levels, PPPs are defined as a 'cooperative institutional arrangement between public and private sector actors … where they jointly develop products and services and share risks, costs and resources which are connected to these products' (Hodge et al, 2010, p 4).

In the education sector, policies promoting PPPs have resulted in a range of combinations of engagement among state, for-profit and not-for-profit civil society actors. The claim is these kinds of arrangements promote greater competition and efficiencies in education systems, increasing the quality of learner outcomes, and enabling governments to avail themselves of greater budgetary flexibility (Patrinos et al, 2009). Opponents of PPPs argue that these policies foster greater privatisation in the education system, and are part of a rapidly growing corporate industry in education (Williamson and Hogan, 2020).

The significance of PPPs, and the changing relationship between the public and the private sectors in education governance, rests on two things: (1) that areas like education are viewed as sectors that can yield profits for private companies; and (2) that state–driven Keynesian policies created monopolies leading to inefficiencies and lack of innovation. For neoliberals, the appropriate role for the state is to create and preserve an institutional framework that ensures the conditions for the market to work efficiently, even in the areas for which the state is held responsible. PPPs now include: (1) the management of school districts (Ball, 2007; DiMartino and Butler Jessen, 2018); (2) the delivery of education provision, such as through charter schools, school vouchers (cf Lubienski, 2013) or low–fee private schools (Tooley, 2013); and (3) deals with commercial firms around exclusive rights regarding textbooks, testing services, tutoring, quality assurance and inspection services (cf Scott and DiMartino, 2009; Verger et al, 2016).

The education sector has also attracted the attention of global private equity firms, with significant investments in reform initiatives and online platforms servicing schools and higher education (Williamson and Hogan, 2020). Not surprisingly, for–profit firms tend to view education itself as simply another sector from which to make a profit, and the students and their families as consumers of education. A specialist (increasingly corporate) industry has sprung up around PPPs, particularly in developed economies that have taken PPPs the furthest (for instance, Australia, the UK and USA), and one that services the UN system (Robertson et al, 2012). This industry, which is increasingly exporting its expertise globally, includes a rapidly growing number of private actors, from foundations, specialist PPP firms, global consultancy firms, banks, local consultants, think–tanks, dedicated websites, rapid response teams and specialist law firms, which increasingly act as market–oriented sources of authority and 'establish rules, norms and institutions that guide the behaviours of the participants, and affect[s] the opportunities available to others' (Cutler et al, 1999, p 4).

A central assumption of PPPs is that 'education is a consumer good, and that the student is the principal consumer through parents' (World Bank, 2001, p 1). What follows from this assumption is that in order for parents/guardians (and students) to choose, the education sector needs to be organised so that it operates according to the logic of a 'free' market. This includes information on the nature of the education offered by various providers including: its quality; incentives that ensure the right kind of performance; regulatory guarantees to protect the interests of private investors and ensure fair competition among providers; and an evaluation system that is able to feed back into the information system, creating a virtuous circle (IFC, 2001; Robertson and Verger, 2012). The role of the state in the governance of education is seen as important, first, to ensure against the market failing, and second, to respond to concerns from critics about the inequities that arise when choice, markets, competition and standards policies are at work. In relation to market failure, the World Bank argues that the role of the state in PPPs is to provide oversight of the contract and ensure the quality of the outcomes. That is:

> … government guides policy and provides financing while the private sector delivers education services to students. In particular, governments contract out private providers to supply a specified service of a defined quantity and quality at an agreed price for a specific period of time. These contracts contain rewards and sanctions … in which the private sector shares the financial risk in the delivery of public services. (Patrinos et al, 2009, p 1)

Yet what is clear is that it is difficult for governments to write and provide oversight of contracts in the education sector because education itself is a complex service to provide (cf Ball, 2007, 2012), creating the real possibility of market failure. In relation to equity and opportunity, Scott (2013, p 6) argues there has been an elision between the idea of choice and equity, and civil rights. In other words, PPP advocates appropriate the language of civil rights, yet distil the most individualistic aspects of civil rights aspirations while neglecting broader communitarian components. It is around the individualising of education aspirations and the outcomes of decisions that we are able to see some of the negative outcomes of PPPs for social equity. Because education is a 'positional good' – meaning, as Brighouse and Swift (2006, p 472) argue, a good whose value derives from its scarcity – policies that intensify competition for desired places increase tendencies to either 'rig' the competition in such a way that it favours particular groups or encourages education providers to select those students (known as 'creaming') who will ensure success on high-stakes testing.

Given the issues, how is it that PPPs have been promoted as desirable policy tools? The legitimacy of PPPs lies in a promise to resolve the intractable problems facing the development community. This includes *access* to quality education, a key part of the EFA, MDG and SDG agendas. Yet, as evidence shows, PPPs have not favoured the very poor, and nor have they (in the case of the IFC) favoured low-income countries, despite the fact that it is argued that PPPs are pro-poor in effect (Harma and Rose, 2012). Others are critical of the way those promoting PPPs use them to exploit the poor in order to make profits (Riep and Macacek, 2016).

Clearly, alignments between global, national and local policies and practices around PPPs provide the means, motivations and mechanisms through which ~these policies are advanced globally. But we can also see that they are dependent on the activities and efforts of the policy entrepreneurs, whose framing, commissioning and selecting of evidence supports their ongoing project. By also deepening and extending the activities of those with a growing private set of interests in the education sector, PPPs become embedded in policy lexicons and industry practices.

## International trade in education services

In our final section we look at the way education has been drawn into nations' 'trade' accounts as a services sector. From the early 1980s a number of countries – notably the UK, Australia and New Zealand – began to view their (largely higher) education institutions as able to directly contribute to the economy through the recruitment of full fee-paying international students (Welch, 2002). This shift in how education was viewed and valued can be traced to neoliberal ideologies referred to above, which were beginning to permeate and reshape education sectors more generally. It was also fuelled by an emerging middle class in Asia, parts of Africa and Latin America, and their desire for higher education qualifications.

By the late 1980s, countries like Australia and New Zealand began to position themselves strategically to capture more of this market, and to market or export their educational services more aggressively. Indeed, by the beginning of the 2000s, the export of education services had risen to become a greater foreign exchange earner than the wine industry in New Zealand (Robertson and Kedzierski, 2016). The premium attached to the English language as the medium of instruction, and the possibilities this opens up for global mobility, has enabled key English-speaking countries to consolidate their positions as exporters of education services. The result has been a spectacular increase in the volume of student movement, particularly from the Asian region to OECD countries, although new undercurrents are emerging with movements of students now to China (Robertson and Kedzierski, 2016). In 2019, the OECD (2019, p 228) reported that English-speaking countries continue to be the most attractive to international students – Australia, Canada, the UK and the USA together receive more than 40 per cent of all mobile students in the OECD and partner countries. Students from Asia also form the largest group of international students enrolled in tertiary education programmes at all levels.

Prior to the **global financial crisis** (GFC) in 2007–09 the USA stood apart from this model of trade in education generated through the recruitment of full fee-paying foreign students. The USA's interest in the student mobility market related to the recruitment of (largely) science and technology graduate students – typically funded by scholarships awarded by US institutions – to boost its research and innovation efforts. Following graduation, a good percentage of these international students, many from China and India, stayed in the USA working on research and development in and around the universities (Robertson and Kedzierski, 2016). If US universities entered into the fee-paying undergraduate market, it was largely via the development of branch campuses overseas. Lane and Kinser (2014) chart the growth of what in trade language is termed the 'commercial presence' of foreign universities, mostly in East Asia and the Middle East.

Trade in education services, either through sending students or hosting branch campuses, is an important 'industry' in a growing number of countries, including Australia, New Zealand, the UK, the USA, Germany, the Netherlands and Canada. But there are new kids on the block looking to take a share of this market. Countries here include Singapore, China and Malaysia, as well as other European countries aside from the UK. All are jockeying for a share of the market (Robertson and Kedzierski, 2016), using trade deals to strengthen and lock in their position. However, the COVID-19 global pandemic has sent ripples through the higher education sector, with students unable to travel because of borders being closed.

At the global level, the idea that education might be a tradable service was given impetus by the view in the 1980s and 1990s within the USA's Department of Trade, and among influential lobby groups, such as the US Coalition of Service Industries, that education might be regarded as part of a services sector, and that a growing services sector would compensate for the USA's declining share in the production of goods (Kelsey, 2008). These views were crucial in shaping the General Agreement on Trade in Services (GATS), which was launched by the World Trade Organization (WTO) in 1995 (see also **Chapter 3**, this volume). The WTO replaced the General Agreement on Tariffs and Trade (GATT) that had guided international negotiations and agreements through the post–Second World War period. In contrast to the GATT, where the negotiations took place over pluri-lateral codes, the WTO has a much stronger capacity to enforce rules. For example, the member countries (164 in 2016) commit themselves to all of the codes already negotiated.

The GATS represented a significant, and controversial, global policy for the education sector. First, while our discussion here refers to higher education, *all* sectors of education (from early years learning to schooling and higher education) were to be included in negotiations and obligations. Second, membership of the WTO means a commitment to the progressive liberalisation of the economy – in this case, to opening up education sectors to other countries and their trade departments. Third, four 'modes' were included in the negotiations on education as a tradable services sector: *cross-border supply* – meaning providing services such as testing or distance education over national borders; *consumption abroad* – such as enabling students to study abroad; *commercial presence* – enabling a foreign investor to establish a commercial presence (such as a foreign university); and *presence of natural persons* – for instance, the ability to move labour, such as academics, between countries (Robertson et al, 2002, p 486). In short, these modes are an attempt to bind a country into long-standing decisions that make it difficult to withdraw from. The controversial elements of this global policy were that it reinforces the view that education is a tradable good, and that it enables those countries that were well positioned in the market to both extend and protect their interests.

The WTO negotiations around education services became both difficult and protracted, and by 2003, they had largely stalled because of opposition by protestors. However, this did not mean those countries and the interested providers simply stopped pushing ahead on liberalising education sectors and opening them to more commercial interests and foreign investors. Rather, as Sell (2009) shows, there has been a tendency to strategically **venue shift** to other sites across different scales of governance in order to advance their agendas.

A first wave of scalar strategies includes, in the European context, the European Commission's Services Directive launched in 2006, the strategic targeting of national governments and agencies by investors to open up new spaces for market activity, the use of the Services Directive to claim tax exemptions, making it more viable to enter national education sectors, and the proliferation of **bilateral** and preferential trading agreements. From 2011 onwards, spurred on and legitimated by the 2008 GFC and poor economic development, a second wave of trade strategies emerged that included mega–trade agreements such as the Trans–Pacific Partnership (TPP), the Comprehensive Economic Trade Agreement (CETA), the now defunct Transatlantic Trade and Investment Partnership (TTIP), and the Trade in Services Agreement (Robertson et al, 2017).

The TTIP is being morphed into a different negotiating strategy, CETA has been concluded, and the TPP continues with a slightly different grouping of members. All agreements include the progressive liberalisation of education sectors, their lock-in to privatisation trajectories, and complex international **dispute settlement mechanisms** (cf Robertson et al, 2017). This makes education very much a key part of global economic and trade governance (see **Chapter 3**, this volume). There are longer term consequences for education being transformed in this way. This includes closing down education policy reform options by committing governments to binding future measures; the potential for 'regulatory hopping' by investors; and the implications (such as lack of transparency) of multiple, overlapping agreements for governing education.

## Conclusion

We conclude this chapter by restating the argument we put at the beginning, that there has been an expansion of global education policies over the past 30 years. At the same time, we showed a nascent set of global policies in place in the immediate aftermath of the Second World War. Over time it is possible to see that the range and scope of global policies has changed, as well as the scales on which these actors operate. Actors include multilateral agencies, corporations, aid agencies, foundations, teacher unions and civil society actors that are located beyond the state and have entered into the education sector in various capacities: as policy shapers, providers, financiers, owners of infrastructures and regulators. In this regard the sub/national state has been joined by a range of global actors involved in shaping education policy and its regulation.

Yet such significant transformations have not gone unchallenged. For example, Education International – the global teachers union – has spearheaded a global campaign to resist the privatisation of education around the globe. It has commissioned a range of investigations into the role of the for–profit sector, and raised concerns about the exploitation of the poor, the diversion of state resources into profits and the reconceptualisation of education as a commodity. We can also see struggles over who has the power to shape education futures. In its initial phase, the formulation of the various SDGs was significantly more expansive so that different constituencies had their voices heard (Unterhalter, 2019). However, as the SDGs were translated into targets and indicators, there has been a significant narrowing into what can be measured. It is in these moments of narrowing that we see changes in how notions of learning replace education, who is viewed as a legitimate actor in the education sector, and whether and how education might be constituted as a services sector.

In our final conclusions we reflect on the global pandemic caused by COVID–19 that emerged in 2020, resulting in border and education closures. The broader context of the pandemic needs to be set against the rise of authoritarian **populist** regimes and surging nationalisms. Are the days of global education policy over, as some observers have been quick to declare? We think not. Rather, COVID–19 has accelerated the involvement of the ed–tech corporate giants in the delivery of education via platforms and various learning products, while revealing a widening gap between those with resources and those without, both within and between countries.

## Summary

- Globalisation has changed both the forms and objectives of education policy, and the conceptual means through which they have to be approached. This does not mean national states no longer make education policy, but it does limit and shape their options.
- The main actors in these processes are major IGOs, such as the OECD, the World Bank and UNESCO, and international non-governmental organisations such as global firms and foundations, global teachers' unions, and key national states.
- Education has become a key part of the global trading system.
- There is an overall trend in the direction of greater private sector involvement in education as exemplified through the influence of PPPs, and the inclusion of for-profit actors in delivering the SDGs.

- The dual aims of education – promoting human rights and promoting economic growth – are increasingly heavily weighted in the direction of the latter.
- COVID-19 has created the conditions that amplify private sector involvement in education, particularly via the ed-tech giants, their platforms and education products.

## Questions for discussion

- The **international organisations** that are most successful in promoting global education policy do not have 'education' as their main purpose. What can be inferred by this regarding the nature and purpose of global education policy?
- What are the implications of constructing education as part of trade policy rather than as public services policy?
- Can you see examples of forms of resistance to the commodification and privatisation of education in local communities?

## Follow-up activities

- There is an enormous amount of literature on PISA, EFA, SDGs, GMR, PPPs and trade agreements. This literature can be searched in any number of ways – by country, by year of publication, by educational output – that will give more substance to, or challenge, what is written in this chapter.
- A GMR is published annually. Find out what have been the themes over time, and how the problem of education is represented over time.

## Further resources

A very good open access overview of actors and ideational projects in globalising of education policies in low-income countries can be found in Robertson et al's (2007) *Globalisation, education and international development*. Robertson et al's (2012) edited collection on PPPs takes an in-depth view on opening education systems to non-state actors, including philanthropic foundations, and how these change the overall governance of the sector. Mundy et al's (2016) *The handbook of global education policy* is invaluable for its coverage of a range of issue areas in the developed and developing world. See www.ei-ie.org for further information on Education International and its activities. See also **Chapter 3** in this volume, by Chris Holden, which discusses trade in relation to global social policy.

## References

Auld, E., Rappeleye, J. and Morris, P. (2019) 'PISA for development: How the OECD and World Bank shaped education governance post 2015', *Comparative Education*, 55(2), 197–219.

Ball, S. (2007) *Education PLC: Understanding private sector participation in public sector education*, New York: Routledge.

Ball, S. (2012) *Global education Inc: New policy networks and the neo-liberal imaginary*, London and New York: Routledge.

Breakspear, S. (2012) *The policy impact of PISA: An exploration of the normative effects of international benchmarking in school system performance*, OECD Education Working Papers, No 71, Paris: OECD Publishing.

Brighouse, H. and Swift, A. (2006) 'Equality, priority and positional goods', *Ethics*, 116, 471–97.

Bull, B. and McNeill, D. (2019) 'From market multilateralism to governance by goal setting: SDGs and the changing role of partnerships in a new global order', *Business and Politics*, 21(4), 464–86.

Chabbott, C. (1998) 'Constructing educational consensus: international development professionals and the World Conference on Education for All', *International Journal of Educational Development*, 18(3), 207–18.

Cutler, A.C., Haufler, V. and Porter, T. (1999) *Private authority and international affairs*, New York: New York University Press.

Dale, R. and Robertson, S. (2004) 'Interview with Boaventura de Sousa Santos', *Globalisation, Societies and Education*, 2(2), 147–60.

DiMartino, C. and Butler Jessen, S. (2018) *Selling school: The marketing of public education*, New York: Teachers College Press.

Edwards, D.B., Okitsu, T., da Costa, R. and Kitamura, Y. (2017) 'Organizational legitimacy in the global education policy field: Learning from UNESCO and the Global Monitoring Report', *Comparative Education Review*, 62(1), 31–63.

GMR (Global Monitoring Report) (2020) *Inclusion and education: All means all*, Paris: GMR.

Grey, S. and Morris, P. (2018) 'PISA: Multiple "truths" and mediatised global governance', *Comparative Education*, 54(2), 109–31, doi:10.1080/03050068. 2018.1425243.

Harma, J. and Rose, P. (2012) 'Is low-fee primary education affordable for the poor? Evidence from rural India', in S. Robertson, K. Mundy, A. Verger and F. Menashy (eds) *Public–private partnerships in education: New actors and modes of governance*, Cheltenham: Edward Elgar, 243–58.

Harvey, D. (2007) *A brief history of neoliberalism*, Oxford: Oxford University Press.

Hodge, G., Greve, C. and Boardman, A. (2010) 'Introduction: The PPP phenomenon and its evaluation', in G. Hodge, C. Greve and A. Boardman (eds) *International handbook on public–private partnerships*, Cheltenham: Edward Elgar, 3–16.

Hoggart, R. (1976) *An idea and its servants: UNESCO from within*, London: Chatto & Windus.

Hopmann, S. (2008) 'No child, no school, no state left behind: Schooling in the age of accountability', *Journal of Curriculum Studies*, 40(4), 417–56.

IFC (International Finance Corporation) (2001) *Handbook on PPPs and education*, Washington, DC: IFC.

Jones, P. (1992) *World Bank financing of education*, London: Routledge.

Kelsey, J. (2008) *Serving whose interests? The political economy of trade in services agreements*, London and New York: Routledge.

Klees, S. (2010) 'Aid, development, and education', *Current Issues in Comparative Education*, 13(1), 7–28.

Lane, J.E. and Kinser, K. (2014) 'Transnational education: A maturing phenomenon', *Forum* (Summer), 8–10.

Lubienski, C. (2013) 'Privatising form or function? Equity, outcomes and influence on American charter schools', *Oxford Review of Education*, 39(4), 498–513, doi:10.1080/03054985.2013.82185.

Martens, K. and Niemann, D. (2010) *Governance by comparison – How ratings and rankings impact national policymaking in education*, Bremen: TranState Working Papers No 139.

Meyer, H.-D. and Benavot, A. (eds) (2012) *PISA, power, and policy: The emergence of global educational governance*, Oxford: Symposium Books.

Mittelman, J. (2000) *The globalization syndrome*, Princeton, NJ: Princeton University Press.

Mundy, K. (1999) 'Educational multilateralism in a changing world order: UNESCO and the limits of the possible', *International Journal of Educational Development*, 19, 27–52.

Mundy, K. and Verger, A. (2015) 'The World Bank and global governance in a changing world order', *International Journal of Educational Development*, 40, 9–18.

Mundy, K., Green, A., Lingard, B. and Verger, A. (2016) *The handbook of global education policy*, Oxford: Wiley.

OECD (Organisation for Economic Co-operation and Development) (2006) *The Programme for International Student Assessment (PISA)* (www.oecd.org/pisa/pisaproducts/39725224.pdf).

OECD (2016) *Global competency for an inclusive world*, Paris: OECD.

OECD (2018) *PISA: Preparing our youth for an inclusive and sustainable world. The OECD global competence framework*, Paris: OECD.

OECD (2019) *Education at a glance 2019*, Paris: OECD.

Patrinos, H., Barrera-Osario, F. and Guáqueta, J. (2009) *The role and impact of public–private partnerships in education*, Washington: World Bank.

Peck, J. (2013) *Constructions of neoliberal reason*, Oxford: Oxford University Press.

Riep, C. and Macacek, M. (2016) *Schooling the poor profitably*, Brussels: Education International.

Robertson, S.L. (2018) 'Governing through quantification: On the contradictory dynamics of "flat Earth", "ordinalisation" and "coldspot" education policies', ECER Keynote Address, Bolzano, Italy, 5 September.

Robertson, S.L. and Kedzierski, M. (2016) 'On the move: Globalising higher education in Europe and beyond', *The Language Learning Journal*, 44(3), 276–91.

Robertson, S.L. and Verger, A. (2012) 'Governing education through public–private partnerships', in S.L. Robertson, K. Mundy, Verger, A. Verger and F. Menashy (eds) *Public–private partnerships in education*, Cheltenham: Edward Elgar, 21–42.

Robertson, S.L., Bonal, X. and Dale, R. (2002) 'GATS and the education service industry: The politics of scale and global reterritorialization', *Comparative Education Review*, 46(4), 472–96.

Robertson, S.L., Tidy, J. and Ayuso-Arcan, S. (2017) *What educators need to know about global trade agreements*, Brussels: Education International.

Robertson, S.L., Mundy, K., Verger, A. and Menashy, F. (2012) *Public–private partnerships in education*, Cheltenham: Edward Elgar.

Robertson, S.L., Novelli, M., Dale, R., Tikly, L., Dachi, H., and Ndibelema A. (2007) *Globalisation, education and international development: Ideas, actors and dynamics*, London: Department for International Development.

Rostow, W. (1960) *The stages of economic growth: A non-communist manifesto*, Cambridge: Cambridge University Press.

Sassen, S. (2006) *Territory, authority, rights*, Princeton, NJ: Princeton University Press.

Schultz, T.W. (1971) *Investment in human capital: The role of education and of research*, New York: Free Press.

Scott, J. (2013) 'A Rosa Parks moment? School choice and the marketization of civil rights', *Critical Studies in Education*, 54(1), 5–18.

Scott, J. and DiMartino, C. (2009) 'Public education under new management: A typology of educational privatization applied to New York City's restructuring', *Peabody Journal of Education*, 84(4), 432–52.

Sell, S. (2009) 'Cat and mouse: Forum shifting in the battle over intellectual property enforcement', Paper presented to the American Political Science Association Meeting, 3–6 September, Toronto.

Takayama, K. (2018) 'The constitution of East Asia as a counter reference society through PISA: A postcolonial/de-colonial intervention', *Globalisation, Societies and Education*, 16(5), 609–623, doi:10.1080/14767724.2018.1532282.

Tooley, J. (2013) 'Challenging education injustice: "Grassroots" privatisation in South Asia and sub-Saharan Africa', *Oxford Review of Education*, 39(4), 446–63 (http://dx.doi.org/10.1080/03054985.2013.820466).

Unterhalter, E. (2019) 'The many meanings of quality education: Politics of targets and indicators in SDG4', *Global Policy*, 10(1), 39–51.

Verger, A., Fontdevila, C. and Zancajo, A. (2016) *The privatization of education: A political economy of global education reform*, New York and London: Teachers College Press.

Waldow, F., Takayama, K. and Sung, Y.-K. (2014) 'Rethinking the pattern of external policy referencing: Media discourses over the "Asian Tigers'" PISA success in Australia, Germany and South Korea, *Comparative Education*, 50(3), 302–21, doi:10.1080/03050068.2013.860704.

Welch, A. (2002) 'Internationalizing Australian universities', *Comparative Education Review*, 46(4), 433–71.

Williamson, J. (1993) 'Democracy and the "Washington Consensus"', *World Development*, 21(8), 1329–36.

Williamson, B. and Hogan, A. (2020) *The edtech pandemic shock*, Brussels: Education International.

World Bank (2001) *Handbook on public–private partnerships*, Washington, DC: World Bank.

World Education Forum (2000) *The Dakar framework for action: Education for all: Meeting our collective commitments*, Paris: UNESCO.

Yeates, N. (2017) *Beyond the nation state: How can regional social policy contribute to achieving the Sustainable Development Goals?*, UNRISD Issue Brief No 5, November, Geneva: United Nations Research Institute for Social Development (UNRISD) (www.unrisd.org/ib5).

# 15

# Global social security policy

## Lutz Leisering

### Overview

The idea that every person on the globe should be covered by social protection seems to be self-evident, but it is rather recent. This chapter explains the meaning of the terms 'social protection' and 'social security', and how social security has evolved historically. Global social security has a complex history, with distinct histories in the Global North, in the Global South, and in global arenas with international organisations as key actors, and these histories are intertwined. Social protection programmes account for the bulk of social spending in Northern welfare states, but have only recently expanded in the Global South. The chapter depicts the key policies and institutional models of global social security, the current state of social security worldwide, and the ways international organisations influence domestic policies.

### Key concepts

Social security; social protection; social insurance; universalism; inclusion; international organisations; global campaigns; human rights; development; poverty

## Introduction

In 2016, the World Bank and the International Labour Organization (ILO) launched the Global Partnership for Universal Social Protection to Achieve the Sustainable Development Goals, in short, USP2030 (Rutkowski and Ortiz, 2016), with a view to ensuring 'full coverage of all people across the life cycle'. The USP2030 marks a new stage in the long struggle for protecting individuals against the vicissitudes of life. **Social security** is a response to the socioeconomic insecurities that people experience in modern society and capitalism, ensuing from industrialisation, marketisation, urbanisation, **migration** and individualisation.

This chapter enquires: what is social security? How did the idea and practice of social security rise historically in the **Global North** and **South**? What are the key policies and institutional models of global social security? In what ways do **international organisations** (IOs) influence domestic policies? What issues are at the forefront of social security policies, with what contestations? And what are the new challenges faced by global social security policies?

'Social security' denotes welfare programmes, mainly income security and social services, but it is also an *ideal*, carrying visions of a good society (Kaufmann, 2012). Since the early 2010s, the term **social protection** has almost superseded the older term 'social security'. In this chapter I mostly use the term 'social security', which is still in use, because the historical rise of social protection revolved around this term, and security, rather than protection, is a fundamental normative idea of modernity. The term 'social protection' has been defined in very different ways (see Devereux and Sabates–Wheeler, 2004, pp 3–4, for a discussion), sometimes equated with 'social security' (see, for example, UN, 2018, p 5), sometimes defined in a broader way, including labour rights and anti-discrimination. While some authors confine the concept of social protection to the poor (see, for example, Devereux and Sabates–Wheeler, 2004), social security also encompasses income maintenance and social services for the better–off.

## What is social security? Four normative models

Social security policies involve redistribution, and this may give rise to contestation: who deserves benefits, on what grounds, and through what kinds of welfare programmes? Accordingly, there are different models of social security with different normative orientations (see **Table 15.1**).

*Table 15.1: Four normative models of social security*

|  | Social insurance | Social assistance | Universal programmes | Allowances |
|---|---|---|---|---|
| **Examples** | Old-age pension insurance, unemployment insurance, health insurance | Social assistance, social cash transfers, social safety nets, poor relief | National health service, universal pensions, universal child benefit, Universal Basic Income | Benefits for public sector employees, compensation of war victims |
| **Normative basis** | Achievement (wage labour/ contributions) | Need | Citizenship | Desert |
| **Addressees** | Workers | Poor people | Citizens | Deserving people |

All four models can be found in both the Global North and South, and countries tend to combine several models in practice, often adding up to a multitiered and multidimensional overall architecture of social security. There are affinities between models and IOs. The ILO is the champion of contributory **social insurance**, having promulgated this model across the globe since its foundation in 1919. Since the 2000s, it has increasingly opened up to non–contributory programmes, especially **means–tested social assistance**. The World Bank emphasises private provision, confining public social security to basic social security, that is, to social assistance, social cash transfers and 'social safety nets' (World Bank, 2018). Since around 2005, a consensus has emerged among IOs that social cash transfers are desirable instruments of social security (von Gliszczynski, 2015; Leisering, 2019). **Universal** programmes are advocated by non–governmental organisations (NGOs), such as HelpAge International (HAI), but also by the United Nations Children's Fund (UNICEF). Social movement organisations like Attac and the Basic Income Earth Network call for a universal basic income (UBI), but to date, there are only limited UBI experiments, and no country has fully adopted UBI nationally (Gentilini et al, 2020). However, universalism in the broader meaning of covering every person – not necessarily under one programme, and not necessarily by non–means–tested programmes – is a basic principle of human rights law and of the USP2030.

Generally, to assess the coverage, adequacy and normative principles of social protection, we need to look into the overall architecture of social security in a country rather than just individual programmes. The ILO's 'staircase' model is an example of a multitiered and multidimensional design of social protection (see **Figure 15.1**). The Social Protection Floors (SPFs) (see **Box 15.4** later) serve as the bottom tier.

*Figure 15.1: The International Labour Organization's 'staircase' model*

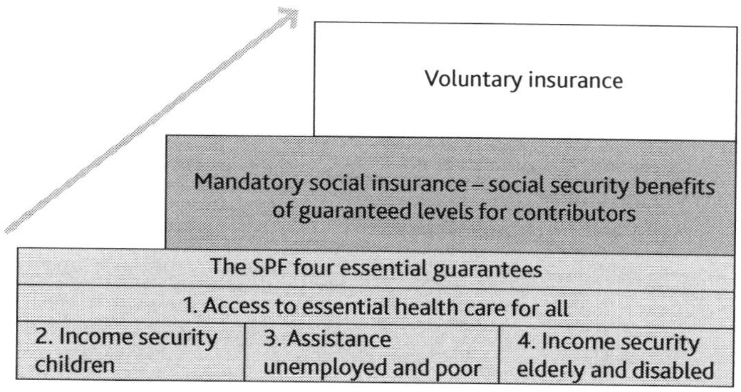

Source: www.social-protection.org/gimi/ShowTheme.action?id=2505

## The worldwide rise of social security

*Spread and expansion of programmes*

Overall, social security has a history of proliferation and expansion since the beginning. Imperial Germany's Chancellor Otto von Bismarck pioneered social insurance in the 1880s, as a response to the newly emerging 'worker question' in industrialising Germany. Social insurance soon spread to other European countries in the ensuing decades, making its way from Northern to Southern Europe. In the interwar years (1919–39), varieties of social insurance also spread in Latin America, the USA and the Soviet Union. Asia and the Pacific came later, and African countries came last, with most adoptions taking place after the Second World War (Schmitt et al, 2015). After the Second World War, European welfare states reached 'growth to limits' (Flora, 1986). While in the Global North, social insurance was the pathway to extending social security coverage, in the Global South the rise of social cash transfers since the early 2000s has been a key means by which coverage has been extended (Leisering, 2019).

This expansion was rarely interrupted by periods of far-reaching retrenchment, such as in the early 1930s under the Great Recession in Germany and in the first decades of economic **liberalisation** in China, from 1978 to 2000. In the course of economic liberalisation since the 1980s, social security was retrenched, especially in the Global South under the World Bank's **structural adjustment programmes** (SAPs). Northern welfare states also experienced retrenchment, but even during the decades of **austerity** since the 1990s, they have largely remained stable (Greve, 2020), and total social spending has not gone down. Despite the dominance of **neoliberalism**, social security expanded significantly during the 2000s in many **middle-income countries**, such as China, Turkey, Brazil and Iran, facilitated by the massive economic growth during that decade. Overall, then, social security has expanded to different degrees in different dimensions. **Box 15.1** depicts four ways of measuring the expansion of social security.

### Box 15.1: Measuring social security – four indicators

*Statutes:* What programmes were legislated, and when? Measuring the incidence of statutes says little about the coverage of programmes and their implementation, however. Notably, in the Global South, social insurance is largely confined to a minority of urban workers in formal employment, and implementation can be seriously defective.

*Coverage:* There are many ways of measuring this, for example as the proportion of the population who formally have access to benefits, or the number of social risks covered.

However, it leaves open the kind of benefits, and whether the level of payment is enough to live on. There may be a trade-off between extending coverage and raising benefit levels. Data on coverage is more easily available than data on benefit levels.

*Social spending:* This is a measure of 'welfare effort', but leaves open how the money is spent. While in Northern welfare states, social spending makes up 20–35 per cent of **gross domestic product** (GDP), most of which goes on social security, regional averages in the Global South range from 5 per cent to 13 per cent of GDP, with outliers at around 2 per cent and 20 per cent.

*Quality of provision and services:* Measuring quality has high data requirements. For Northern welfare states, Esping-Andersen's (1990, pp 47–54) 'decommodification index' measures coverage, rules of eligibility and access and benefit levels for the average formal worker and for the key social risks. This measure is not applicable to Southern countries with extensive informal sectors.

**Figures 15.2** and **15.3** provide data on the current state of social security, with particular reference to coverage and social spending. Broadly, European countries and **member states** of the British Commonwealth rank highest, Latin America comes next, followed by Africa (Hickey et al, 2019) and South Asia. In Africa, only 17.8 per cent of the population receive at least one social protection cash benefit, with significant variation across countries. Asia and the Pacific as a whole rank only slightly higher than Africa. Regarding old age security, almost all countries in the world have programmes, but often with very low coverage and benefits. Coverage is lowest in Africa (27.1 per cent of older people), Southern Asia (39.2 per cent) and Arabic (24.0 per cent) countries (with generally scarce data on the latter; see Jawad et al, 2019), while Northern countries, including Eastern Europe and Central and Western Asia, achieve almost 100 per cent. Southeast Asia and the Pacific, as well as Latin America and the Caribbean, occupy the middle ground (88.3 per cent and 75.4 per cent, respectively) (ILO, 2021).

## Impacts

Social security programmes reduce poverty significantly, in both the North and South. In the South, **relative poverty** (the lowest quintile of the income distribution) is reduced by 14 to 36 per cent (depending on the world region) in urban areas and by 3 to 20 per cent in rural areas; only former Soviet Union member states are more successful due to the legacy of state social insurance (UN, 2018, p 22). Data from the mid-2010s on social safety nets (that is, social cash transfers plus some other non–contributory provisions) show that 36 per cent of

*Figure 15.2: Effective social protection coverage, by regions and population groups (%)*

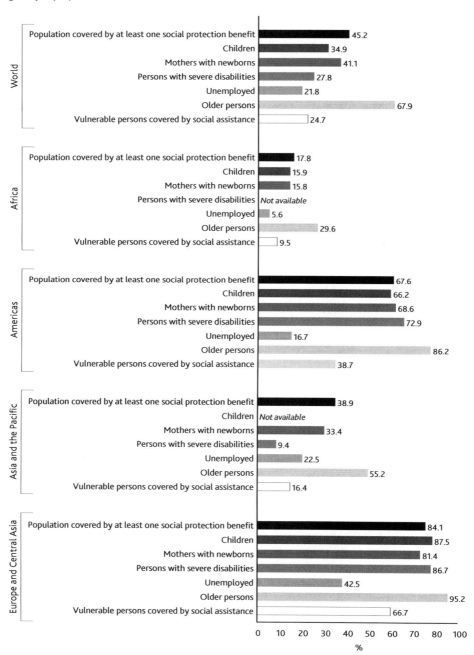

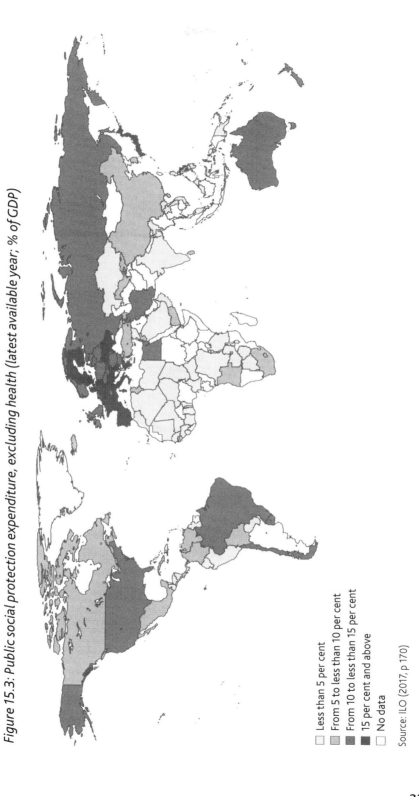

*Figure 15.3: Public social protection expenditure, excluding health (latest available year; % of GDP)*

☐ Less than 5 per cent
▨ From 5 to less than 10 per cent
▩ From 10 to less than 15 per cent
■ 15 per cent and above
☐ No data

Source: ILO (2017, p 170)

extremely poor households have been lifted out of **extreme poverty** worldwide, as measured by the US$1.90/day threshold (World Bank, 2018, p 60); however, inequality was only reduced by 2 to 4 per cent (UN, 2018, p 12; World Bank, 2018, p 61). In some countries, social insurance is actually regressive, effecting a redistribution from the bottom to the top or middle. Moreover, 'inclusion errors' (including non-poor people) and 'exclusion errors' (excluding poor people) are common under social cash transfer programmes.

Social security is not just a response to social problems. In Northern welfare states, where 'cradle to grave' provision is strong, social security may strengthen individual autonomy and empower people in the labour market (what Esping-Andersen, 1990, calls 'decommodification'), in the family (what Esping-Andersen, 1999, p 45, calls 'de-familialisation') and in social relationships ('de-clientelisation'). Individual entitlements to welfare provisions make older people and women less dependent on their families. Social security entitlements contribute to 'social citizenship' (Marshall, 1950), which enables people to make better use of their political and civil rights. The rise of social cash transfers in the Global South has turned millions of older people, children, people with disabilities and other groups from objects of charity into individual rights holders (Leisering, 2019).

### Emerging ideas of the 'social'

The first use of the term 'social security' is commonly attributed to US President Franklin Delano Roosevelt in 1934. The term figured explicitly in the name of the USA's Social Security Act of 1935, which was part of the New Deal in the Great Depression. However, while the term was new, it did not express ideas previously unknown in Europe (Kaufmann, 2012, p 135). In common US usage, 'social security' means old age insurance pensions.

In international arenas, the term 'social security' emerged in the 1940s as part of the 'welfare internationalism' of the decade, which reflected visions of a new post-Second World War order (Kaufmann, 2012, Chapter 4). The Atlantic Charter of 1941 mentioned the term, and the ILO used it officially from 1942 (Berten, 2020). Since its foundation in 1919, the ILO has acted as the guardian of social insurance and, since the 1940s, of the broader idea of social security (Rodgers et al, 2009, Chapter 4; Maul, 2019). In India, China and South Africa the term was also used as early as the 1940s, while it entered Brazilian social law as late as 1988 (Leisering, 2021a).

Social security is not only about welfare programmes; it is also an idea and a vision that signalled an opening to a universalistic inclusion of people, beyond the confines of the earlier concept of social insurance (see Leisering, 2021a). William Beveridge, in his 1942 report, designed a 'plan for social security' – 'it is a plan all-embracing in scope of persons and of needs' (Beveridge, 1942, p 9).

The idea of social security has found its strongest expression in international declarations that have established social security as a human right (see **Box 15.2**). However, the International Covenant on Economic, Social and Cultural Rights (ICESCR) (1966) has only one sentence on this right, which is much less than for other rights. Moreover, only one instrument is named explicitly – social insurance – and the ILO was tasked with defining standards of provision for it (Davy, 2013). The Covenant made the realisation of social rights subject to the availability of resources in any given country, and countries were permitted to achieve full realisation gradually (ICESCR, Article 2; see **Box 15.2**). A General Comment on the right to social security (General Comments are explications of the meaning of human rights articles) was published by the United Nations (UN) as late as 2008, indicating how little attention this right had received.

---

### Box 15.2: The right to social security in the United Nations' human rights declarations and conventions

- Universal Declaration of Human Rights, 1948:
  - Article 22: Everyone, as a member of society, has the right to social security and is entitled to ... the economic, social and cultural rights indispensable for his dignity and the free development of his personality.
  - Article 25: (1) Everyone has the right to a standard of living adequate for the health and well-being of himself and of his family, including food, clothing, housing and medical care and necessary social services, and the right to security in the event of unemployment, sickness, disability, widowhood, old age or other lack of livelihood in circumstances beyond his control.
- International Covenant on Economic, Social and Cultural Rights, 1966:
  - Article 2: Each State Party to the present Covenant undertakes to take steps, individually and through international assistance and co-operation ... to the maximum of its available resources, with a view to achieving progressively the full realization of the rights....
  - Article 9: The States Parties to the present Covenant recognize the right of everyone to social security, including social insurance.
  - Article 11: (1) The States Parties to the present Covenant recognize the right of everyone to an adequate standard of living for himself and his family, including adequate food, clothing and housing, and to the continuous improvement of living conditions.... (2) The States Parties to the present Covenant, recognizing the fundamental right of everyone to be free from hunger....

---

- Convention on the Elimination of All Forms of Discrimination against Women (1979): Article 11(e).
- Convention on the Rights of the Child (1989): Articles 26, 27.
- International Convention on the Protection of the Rights of All Migrant Workers and Members of Their Families (1990): Articles 27(1) and 61(3).
- Convention on the Rights of Persons with Disabilities (2006): Article 28.
- General Comment No 19: The Right to Social Security (Article 9), Committee on Economic, Social and Cultural Rights, UN (2008).
- *The Cairo Declaration on Human Rights in Islam* (1990): Articles 13 and 17(b) refer to social security but without using the term; see also Article 17(c).

Conceiving of social security as a human right marks a crucial difference to earlier forms of welfare, provided by family and kin, charity and under clientelist social relationships such as quasi-feudalism or patronage by local politicians and oligarchs. But what does the right to social security mean, exactly? The meaning of the right to social security has changed considerably. Today we take an individualised understanding of social rights for granted, but in historical perspective it is rather recent. Article 9 of the ICESCR was interpreted by UN member states in collective terms well into the 1990s, either developmental or socialist (Davy, 2013). A developmental understanding emphasises macroeconomic policies to advance national prosperity through economic growth, assumed to benefit growing sections of the population in the middle and long term – the 'trickle-down' effect. Individual entitlements to welfare benefits responding to individual needs in the here and now were seen as secondary or residual. A developmental understanding of social rights reflects the idea of 'growth-mediated security', which is driven by economic markets, while individual entitlements reflect the idea of 'support-led security' (Drèze and Sen, 1991, p 22). In socialist countries, social security was embedded in the socialist organisation of production, which also indicates a collective understanding of social rights. The individualistic interpretation of social rights as individual entitlements to benefits came to prevail as late as the 1990s. Moreover, social human rights only became a powerful frame in **global social policy** discourses from the 1990s and 2000s.

The idea of social security has gained strength by virtue of its linkages to broader and more powerful ideas. The argument that social security has a collective utility for society as a whole, beyond individual welfare, has been the strongest driver of the historical expansion of social security (Kaufmann, 2012, Chapter 11): a political utility (contributing to social peace), a social utility (strengthening social cohesion) and an economic utility, namely creating a productive labour force and fostering economic growth.

# The emergence of social security as a global social policy field (since the 1990s)

Social security as a field of global policy with a distinct policy community fully emerged as late as the 1990s. This was part of what Deacon et al (1997, p 3) called the 'socialisation' of global politics since the 1990s, namely that 'social' issues have moved up on global agendas. While the term 'socialisation' includes collective measures like global and regional funds and the regulation of trade and migration to fight (collective) poverty and exploitation, it also includes the rise of individualised notions of need and related remedies, especially a concern for individual poverty and individualised welfare benefits. This has brought social security to the forefront of political agendas, through calls for 'social security for all' (ILO, 2001, 2003) to be a new global consensus (Leisering, 2020).

Global social security has fully unfolded as an identifiable policy field: with a distinct policy community, with shared problem definitions (poverty, risk/insecurity, vulnerability), consensual lead ideas (such as universalism and inclusiveness) and distinct models of social security (especially social insurance and social assistance). In operational terms, this new policy field is underpinned by vast quantitative global datasets, indicator systems and numerical tools (Berten and Leisering, 2017) – an 'epistemic infrastructure' (Berten, 2020). In a world with around 200 countries that differ widely in socioeconomic and sociocultural terms, numbers enable global policy-makers to compare heterogeneous countries and to assess the state of social security worldwide.

Three characteristics of the new policy field stand out: new actors, a high level of consensus and linkages to other policy fields.

First, after decades of domination of global social policy by the ILO (Maul, 2019), since the 1990s a broader political space has opened up in terms of discourses and actors. Actors from other fields of global politics, especially the World Bank, UNICEF, HAI and the G20, brought in new ideas that challenged the ILO's dominance. The World Bank put the issue of global poverty on the agenda, culminating in the first individualised measurement of global poverty in the *World development report* of 1990, the US$1/day threshold (Hulme, 2015; see also **Chapter 8**, this volume). The ILO had only been implicitly concerned with poverty. In 1994, the World Bank also stepped into the field of old age pensions that had been previously dominated by the ILO (see **Box 15.4**).

Second, the emerging global politics of social security are characterised by extensive cooperation underpinned by a high degree of consensus among policy actors. Since the 1990s, 'neoliberal' policies of retrenching or reorienting public social security in economic terms have given rise to fierce controversies, leading many scholars to conceive of a sharp opposition between neoliberal and progressive policies, epitomised by the World Bank and the ILO, respectively (see Deacon, 2007). However, such views have been questioned (in health, see Kaasch, 2013).

Rather, there is remarkable consensus regarding lead ideas (see below) and broad models of welfare programmes. Major IOs share 'umbrella models' (Leisering, 2019, p 110) that define a broad space in which each IO (and each country) may devise its preferred more specific model. The multipillar model of old age security, the concept of social cash transfers, and even the older concept of social insurance are key examples of umbrella models.

For social cash transfers (and beyond), von Gliszczynski (2015; see also Leisering, 2019, pp 266–7) identifies two discourse coalitions that 'speak' to each other and that have shaped global debates since the 1990s: the economic development coalition, centring on the World Bank and other development banks like the Inter-American Development Bank and the Asian Development Bank, conceives of social security as a social investment to improve resilience among people living in poverty, and favours residual provisions and conditional transfers. Human rights are neither rejected, nor promoted. The **human development** coalition, by contrast, focuses on human capabilities and need, and refers to human rights to legitimise policies, but also emphasises that social protection also needs to be judged in terms of its impact on economic development. This coalition tends to favour unconditional benefits or universal cash transfers, and advocates for basic tiers of public social security as well as higher ones. Actors include NGOs like HAI and FIAN International, UN organisations like UNICEF, the United Nations Development Programme (UNDP), the ILO, and national development agencies like the German Corporation for International Cooperation.

Cooperation between IOs with different agendas is frequent. Calling on 'all stakeholders' is a typical way of initiating global policies, as found in many global campaigns (see **Box 15.3**). In 2012, cooperation between IOs began to intensify through the establishment of the Social Protection Inter-Agency Cooperation Board (SPIAC-B), which responded to a request from the G20 Development Working Group. The ILO and the World Bank were key actors in SPIAC-B, supported by NGOs like HAI, Save the Children, and UN agencies such as UNDP, the Food and Agriculture Organization (FAO), UNICEF and the World Health Organization (WHO).

Third, social security has been increasingly linked to other policy fields, especially to development policy, demonstrating the collective utility of social security. The poor were 'discovered' to be active agents of development rather than passive recipients of it, and this helped make a case for supporting them through public benefits. As described, social security policy also connects to human rights politics. Furthermore, social security is increasingly linked to global environmental policy through issues like climate change (see **Chapter 7**, this volume) and migration (see **Chapter 9**, this volume). Since the other fields tend to have more political clout than social security, framing social security issues by reference to them helps to strengthen claims associated with it.

The 'socialisation of global politics' (cf Deacon et al, 1997, p 3) was not only about public welfare; it included increasing attention to private welfare, as promoted by the World Bank. While the ILO had excluded private provision from the concept of social security early on (Berten, 2020), the World Bank forcefully made a case for private provision as a major pillar of old age security (see **Box 15.4**), and the OECD (Adema, 1999) developed measures of social security that included private provisions, called 'net total social expenditure'. In the ensuing global campaign by the World Bank, more than 30 countries (partially) privatised their pension systems in one way or another (Orenstein, 2008). The results of the reforms were mixed, however; by the mid-2000s privatisation had slowed down or was even reversed (Orenstein and Deacon, 2014).

## How do international organisations influence domestic policies?

Considering the extreme socioeconomic and sociocultural diversity of the countries in the world and the absence of a world–state and a global democracy (see **Chapters 5** and **6**, this volume), key questions are, how is *global* social security policy possible at all, and what does it mean? The agents of global social policy are diverse, and include many national and transnational actors (see **Chapter 2**, this volume). Since the 1990s, **intergovernmental organisations** (IGOs) have increasingly become the subject of research, especially in terms of the extent to which IGOs and other IOs influence domestic policies, and how.

IOs face two challenges. First, legitimacy: how can they create political support for their ideas and policy models in the countries they address (and by other IOs)? Second, applicability: how can models of social security be designed in a way to make them applicable in many or all countries of the world despite very diverse national conditions and welfare traditions? World Society theory helps to explain the influence of IOs (see **Box 15.3**).

---

**Box 15.3: International organisations as conveyors of world culture**

According to the World Society theory (see **Chapter 5**, this volume), IOs present themselves as 'objective disinterested others' or 'rationalised others', that gain legitimacy by pursuing universal, world cultural values such as universalism, individualism, rationalism and the belief in social progress rather than sectional interests (Meyer, 2009, pp 186, 188). States subscribe to these ideas in order to pose as good states, even if they cannot or do not want to implement the global norms. Therefore, 'decoupling'

---

between talk and action is frequent (Meyer, 2009, p 182). For example, states adopt the world cultural language of 'rights' even if the notion of individual rights is foreign to local welfare traditions and will guide policy-making only in a superficial way. Moreover, some groups or even states reject the imposition of global ideas and models.

What instruments do IOs use to influence domestic policies? Since they largely lack coercive powers that characterise states, they mostly use soft power. Instruments include knowledge, money, **soft law** and expertise (see **Chapter 2**, this volume). Indeed, the World Bank calls itself the world's 'knowledge bank'. IOs develop general ideas as well as institutional models of welfare. In the field of social security, models of welfare programmes are key avenues of the global diffusion of ideas. These models are not simply imposed on or copied by countries. Rather, IOs emphasise country-led development. To this end, they do not promote 'bespoke' specific models, but rather, general 'umbrella' models. IOs can also influence domestic social security policies through creating extensive quantitative datasets and indicators of social security that are used to benchmark national policies against international practices.

Money is a powerful influence. It can fund the incubation and development of new ideas and models that are then taken up in mainstream debate. It also finances loans that may be linked to social security and social security–related conditions. The World Bank and the IMF exercise considerable power in this way. Law comes in mostly as 'soft' law, including standard setting (a key remit of the ILO), declarations of human rights (by the UN and **world–regional organisations**), and global **conventions**. These may come with monitoring procedures (for example, in the case of ICESCR or ILO social security conventions and **recommendations**) but normally lack 'hard' (that is, enforceable) sanctions. Expertise is the key resource being offered in the vast amounts of 'technical assistance' that go into social security extension projects in the Global South. Who is offering what sort of advice to these countries is a major source of contestation.

IGOs run global campaigns (see **Box 15.4**) to canvass their ideas and influence the course of national social security policy development. To be effective, they seek to rally a broad range of stakeholders and forge alliances. Campaigning includes holding international conferences, installing websites, undertaking regional missions, referring to global norms and reporting on national experiences. In a broad sense, the ICESCR can also be considered a campaign, because the efforts of ratifying countries are closely observed through a monitoring mechanism. Countries are required to write regular reports, which may elicit critical shadow reports by NGOs and give rise to reforms. Many campaigns share a bias towards poverty, vulnerable groups and basic security, combined with a broader, but little-specified, reference to universalism, inclusiveness and equality.

## Box 15.4: Global social security campaigns by international organisations

*International Covenant on Economic, Social and Cultural Rights (1966; ratifications from 1976):* This has a monitoring mechanism administered by the UN Committee on Economic, Social and Cultural Rights. The so-called 'States Party Reports' under the mechanism are accessible online.

*The World Bank's campaign for reforming old age security (from 1994; World Bank, 1994; analysed by Orenstein, 2005, 2008):* Through this campaign, the World Bank moved into a field dominated by the ILO, and opened up the concept of social security beyond public welfare. In view of extending the share of private provisions, it proposed a multipillar model of old age security with basic and higher tiers, and with private and (smaller) public programmes.

*Decent work (ILO, 1999):* This initiative synthesises key concerns of the ILO in view of making progress in implementation. The inclusion of social security as one of four pillars of Decent Work (along with employment creation, rights at work and social dialogue) reflects the importance attached to social security. Decent Work includes designing tools for assessing and comparing the achievements of states, but this has been subject to controversies in the ILO, and remained unfinished till the present day. Decent Work has been incorporated into the 2030 Agenda for Sustainable Development.

*Millennium Development Declaration, with the Millennium Development Goals (2000/01):* This was the first comprehensive global declaration in view of practical action, and the first overarching document that articulated poverty as the global problem No 1. The MDG process involved country reports and stock taking within a specified time frame (2015). The declaration was superseded by the 2030 Agenda for Sustainable Development.

*Global Campaign on Social Security and Coverage for All (ILO, 2003):* This ILO campaign was foreshadowed in 2001 (ILO, 2001, pp 1, 13–15, 56–68) and launched in 2003 (ILO, 2003). The campaign reflects the full recognition by the ILO of the need to fill the gap left by social insurance. The call sought to develop a 'broad partnership' of many stakeholders. Rather than promoting specific models of social security, the ILO envisaged an open process of 'experimentation and social dialogue' (that is, communication between employers, trade unions and states) and observance of national experiences.

*Social Protection Floors (SPFs; ILO Recommendation No 202, 2012):* This recommendation goes back to the Coalition for a Global Social Floor, set up in 2007, which was led by the ILO and supported by the UN Department of Economic and Social Affairs (UNDESA), UNICEF, HAI and others. The Social Floor then became one out of nine initiatives launched by the UN in 2009 in response to the **global financial crisis** (GFC) of 2008. The SPFs include four basic guarantees (see **Figure 15.1**). The recommendation does not proclaim a global norm, but delegates legislation, programme design and the definition of benefit standards to the states – what started as 'Social Protection Floor' ended up as 'Social Protection Floors' (Deacon, 2013). Moreover, the SPFs are about 'guarantees' rather than rights, and even the design of these guarantees is left to the states. The SPFs have a poverty bias by addressing 'poverty, vulnerability and social exclusion' and basic security only, with a brief reference to 'higher levels of protection' in the strategic section. The SPFs have been incorporated into the 2030 Agenda for Sustainable Development.

*The 2030 Agenda for Sustainable Development, with the Sustainable Development Goals (SDGs; UN, 2015):* The SDGs are the most comprehensive and most recent collection of goals set by IOs for global development. The 2030 Agenda incorporates the SPFs and Decent Work, and is to be put into practice through a 'global partnership' of many stakeholders. Social protection does not figure as a goal in its own right, but is mentioned as an instrument in several of the 17 SDGs, figuring as the core instrument for achieving SDG 1, 'End poverty in all its forms everywhere'. Social protection is also mentioned in SDG 3 on health, SDG 5 on domestic work and paid care, and SDG 10 on inequality, and can also contribute to other goals even if not explicitly mentioned, in particular to SDG 2 on hunger and food and to SDG 4 on education. Social protection in the SDGs is biased towards basic security and the poor, only complemented by broad references to universalism and inclusiveness.

*UHC2030: International Health Partnership. Global Compact for progress towards universal health coverage (WHO, 2017):* The UHC2030 draws on a long tradition of calls for 'Health for All', going back to the Declaration of Alma Ata of the WHO in 1978. In accordance with the principle of 'progressive realisation' of UN human rights law, the UHC2030 calls for 'progressive universalism' (UHC2030, 2019).

*USP2030: Universal Social Protection to achieve the Sustainable Development Goals, A global partnership for universal social protection to achieve the SDGs (Rutkowski and Ortiz, 2016; USP2030, nd):* The USP2030 is the most comprehensive initiative towards universalism in social protection. Launched by the ILO and the World Bank, a broad range of stakeholders is included under this 'global partnership'. 'Universal' means 'cash transfers for all who need it' (USP2030, nd), that is, the term is not restricted to non-means-tested programmes, and universalism refers to social protection regimes, not necessarily to universal programmes.

IOs articulate lead ideas to express key values and goals and generate legitimacy for their policies among states and other IOs. The most general lead ideas are remarkably consensual. 'Universalism' (most explicitly articulated in USP2030 and UHC2030) and 'inclusiveness' (see, for example, UN, 2018) are the main overarching terms that IOs have recently come to use. These are normatively indistinct terms that blur or gloss over fundamental normative choices, such as those depicted in **Table 15.1**. On the one hand, these broad visions enable consensus among diverse actors (among countries as well as among IOs), but on the other hand, they 'dilute' the content of the human right to social security (Leisering, 2020). In particular, they focus on coverage and divert attention from the question of benefit standards. The two lead ideas lend themselves to a poverty bias and a basic security bias (see **Box 15.4**).

Advancing policies is also about articulating frames that support the acceptance and take-up of a designated model or regime among global or national actors. The most powerful frames of social security policies are about the collective utility of social security. Reference to economic growth is not restricted to neoliberal views, but cuts across political camps. Human rights are another influential frame in global discourses about social security, although not quite as influential as economic development (see the distinction of two global discourse coalitions on p. 330).

## Key issues and points of contestation

Despite the widespread calls for a one-world perspective, key policy issues continue to differ between the Global North and South, even if there is an overlap.

Countries in the Global North are experiencing an increase in non-standard employment biographies, characterised by unemployment, low pay, short-term working contracts, platform work or work from home, liable to erode the contribution base of social insurance. This has triggered various reforms with no clear direction, and has fuelled calls for an unconditional UBI. These changes in employment as well as demographic change and fiscal straits have put the financial sustainability of social security programmes on political agendas since the 1980s, especially in relation to old age pensions. Cost control and retrenchment, however, have, in turn, raised issues of social sustainability since the 2000s, that is, new inequalities and poverty ensuing from politics of retrenchment.

In the Global South, the persistence of informal labour is a key challenge. How can informal workers be reached by social security? While some actors like the ILO seek to extend the coverage of social insurance, others see social cash transfers for the poor as a new social model for the South. Alternatives like micro insurance, micro credit or crop insurance for farmers are also debated and practised.

Another issue is: public or private welfare, and in what mix? Actors from the economic development coalition advocate for a larger share of private welfare, and global insurance corporations have established the 'InsuResilience Global

Partnership' to campaign for 'inclusive insurance', which would cover not only the middle classes, but also the poor.

The design of social security programmes also raises a number of issues that are hotly debated. First, should receipt of social cash transfers be made conditional on 'good' behaviour by recipients, or some other factor? 'Conditional cash transfers', which are especially widespread in Latin America, impose behavioural conditions on receiving families, especially participation of the children in education and health check-ups. Conditions may enhance **human capital**, but also curtail the human right to social security. A means test for social cash transfers is also a common condition. Proponents of means testing argue that it is an efficient use of limited resources, while critics argue that means testing is liable to vast inclusion and exclusion errors, is costly to administer and stigmatises claimants.

Second, to what extent, and how, should the design of social security programmes take account of economic imperatives? Is social security primarily designed to meet current need, or should measures seek to encourage (or push) claimants to participate in the labour market (Midgley et al, 2017)? References by the World Bank and global insurance corporations to 'resilience' tend to signal an economic orientation: enhancing the ability of claimants to cope with future risks rather than meeting current needs.

Third, what kind of benefits and what welfare goods are to be given priority with what mix: cash, in-kind or assets? While cash benefits have proliferated, benefits in-kind and subsidies to food are still common in some countries, especially in India. Asset-based social policy is an alternative to (consumption-based) social security. Land, in particular, can serve as social security, as does housing. Micro credit is a contested variety of asset-based social policy.

## Conclusion

What future for global social security? Most IOs agree that the COVID-19 crisis has exposed new social risks, and that it should be taken as an opportunity to reform social security. Beyond the immediate imperative of expanding social cash transfers and extending coverage, social security policies are facing three structural challenges: tackling soaring economic inequality; coping with transnational processes and crises; and entrenching social security in domestic politics in the South. Each of these challenges reveals inherent limitations of global social security policies.

### *Expanding social cash transfers*

Social cash transfers have played a major role in cushioning the impact of the COVID-19 crisis across the Global South. However, these were only transitory stopgap measures (Gentilini et al, 2021; Leisering, 2021b). Despite the campaigns for extending coverage, social cash transfer programmes are far from covering all poor people. In particular, those of working age are rarely covered (Leisering, 2019). The vast size of the informal sector remains a structural limitation of social security in the Global South. Besides coverage, a crucial priority for reform would be to set adequate benefit standards. Global calls for 'universal' or 'inclusive' social protection presently tend to boil down to meagre benefits or residual universalism. However, raising benefit levels would require more far-reaching redistribution, for which political support will be difficult to secure.

## Soaring economic inequality

Social cash transfers, which target the poor, are not sufficient. The 'missing middle' – those who fall between social cash transfers and social insurance (UN, 2018, pp 14, 52; Packard et al, 2019, pp 7, 14) – highlights the structural deficits of social security regimes. This missing middle was hit badly by the COVID-19 crisis. The key challenge is to establish a comprehensive institutional and organisational architecture of a social security regime as a whole, rather than focusing on the design of single programmes and on basic social security for the poor and vulnerable.

Social security policies will need to address the whole range of inequalities beyond extreme poverty. Economic inequality has been soaring since the 1990s in many middle-income countries in tandem with the extension of economic liberalisation (see **Chapter 8**, this volume). Gini coefficients of income inequality close to 0.6 and more have become much more prevalent (Leisering, 2021a). Reducing such inequalities significantly is beyond the remit of social security. Social security is geared to alleviating insecurity and poverty within capitalism rather than challenging the structural inequalities inherent in capitalism. In other words, social security is a reformist strategy rather than a socially transformative one. Pellissery et al (2015) hold that durable and structural inequalities – in their case, the caste system in India – are beyond the reach of social security policies. However, Midgley (2020) has argued that social protection has a role to play in reducing inequality, and Devereux and Sabates-Wheeler (2004) have developed the ambitious concept of 'transformative social protection'. Most IOs agree that the COVID-19 pandemic has produced a 'new poverty' that reaches well beyond the people conventionally seen as poor to include significant sections of the urban workforce (Leisering, 2021b). One question here is how far will it be possible to forge a global alliance of actors pressing for global redistribution to fund the extension of coverage in the Global South?

## Transnational processes and crises

The nation-state continues to be the legal and economic guardian of the right to social security. However, a variety of social and economic processes and crises transcend the boundaries of the nation-state, such as the cross-border migration of **refugees** or workers, **remittances**, climate change and other ecological problems, pandemics, and an increasingly diverse and fluid global labour force in an age of digitalisation, with new forms of work like platform work (Packard et al, 2019). These diverse transnationalisms present very important global (and national) policy issues such as the degree of portability of social security rights between countries (see Yeates, 2018; see also **Chapter 9**, this volume).

New sources of solidarity and collective action beyond the nation-state are called for (see **Chapter 1**, this volume). During the COVID-19 crisis, donors and IOs carried almost 100 per cent of the cost of the emergency cash transfers in **low-income countries** (in 2020), and 63 per cent in lower-middle-income countries (Gentilini et al, 2021). However, these were only stopgap measures. While many IOs called for a new departure in global social security in response to the COVID-19 crisis to prepare for future shocks, their ideas promulgated through policy papers have lacked new concepts (Leisering, 2021b). More broadly, **global governance** in respect of social security is rather limited, relying as it does on 'soft' power. The institutions of global and regional **governance** would need to be strengthened considerably to make signatory governments' formal adherence to global conventions on social security a reality for their populations.

### Entrenching social security in national politics

In the absence of a world-state and in the face of a thin world culture, social policy-making largely remains a domestic issue. While social policy is a key issue in Northern democracies that can win or lose elections, national politics in many Southern countries need to be 'socialised' in the first place (Leisering, 2019, p 325). For example, in many countries of the South, social security has only recently made it on to national agendas. Establishing domestic (not externally imposed) 'social' discourses, political parties, **epistemic communities** and so on, with social remits, are all key ingredients of 'getting the politics right' (Niño-Zarazúa et al, 2012). It will also matter that social security politics has something to offer to the middle classes in the Global South in order to create political support for public welfare beyond the dominant focus on anti-poverty policy.

National state traditions and traditions of welfare co-determine if and how ideas like social security catch on and take root (Kaufmann, 2012). It is open to question if Southern countries will develop a welfare state with a universal and generous social security regime – and if so, which ones. In the North, only a few countries – in Western and Northern Europe and some member states of the Commonwealth – have achieved this (Kaufmann, 2012).

## Summary

- Social protection has spread since the late 19th century under the influence of labour movements and, since 1919, the ILO. Social security became almost universal after the Second World War in some countries of the Global North. However, a wide range of IOs has only fully emerged as social security actors since the 1990s.
- The global (and national) politics of social security often revolves around individual programmes, but assessment of whether social security coverage is adequate (or not) and the nature of provision overall (whether universalist, residualist) needs to take a broader view, by looking at the 'architecture' of the regime as a whole.
- Social security has helped to reduce poverty in the Global South, mainly from the 2000s. Yet huge coverage gaps of social security remain, and social spending and benefit levels are low.
- In the North, the development of post-Second World War social security regimes has had a major impact on social cohesion and standards of living, even if not all countries there ever achieved a fully universal and generous regime. Established social security regimes have proved resilient in the face of retrenchment initiatives.
- Since the 2000s, IOs have called for universal and inclusive social protection, running campaigns like 'Social Security for All'. However, universalism and inclusiveness are very broad ideas that act as a platform of consensus in a diverse world; they tend to dilute the content of the right to social security.
- It is an open question whether social security regimes will become much more comprehensive in many Southern countries. It has helped, however, that initiatives to expand social cash transfers in Latin America and elsewhere have been presented by domestic coalitions as social policy rather than as aid by IOs and donors, with all its insinuations of colonialism and charity.

## Questions for discussion

- Is a Universal Basic Income a good idea? Discuss the pros and cons.
- What is different and what is similar between social security in the Global South compared to the Global North?
- To what extent and in what ways can IOs influence domestic social security policies? Discuss how different circumstances (such as financial crises, pandemics, civil conflict) open up opportunities or limit IOs' influence.

## Follow-up activities

- Construct a Social Protection Floor for a country of your choice, using the ILO Social Protection Floors Cost Calculator: www.social-protection.org/gimi/gess/SPFCalculReport. action (for information on ILO tools, see: www.ilo.org/global/about-the-ilo/newsroom/news/WCMS_613784/lang--en/index.htm).
- Assess the social protection systems and policies in countries of your choice using the Inter-Agency Social Protection Assessments (ISPA): https://ispatools.org
- Browse through the States Party Reports under the ICESCR: https://tbinternet.ohchr.org/_layouts/15/treatybodyexternal/TBSearch.aspx?Lang=en&TreatyID=9&DocType ID=29

## Further resources

The *World social protection report 2020–22* (ILO, 2021) gives an in-depth overview of social security worldwide, with lots of data, tables and diagrams. The handbook by Schüring and Loewe (2021) has concise chapters on virtually all aspects of social protection.

Two books depict the historical and ideational background of the rise of social protection in global arenas – Kaufmann (2012, Chapters 4 and 5) – and in middle-income countries, Leisering (2021a). Rodgers et al (2009, Chapter 4) and Maul (2019) zoom in on the history of the ILO, the key global proponent of social protection. Schmitt (2015) and Midgley and Piachaud (2011) explore the historical relationship between social security and colonialism.

There are many case studies of social assistance and social cash transfers, but two books provide a comprehensive picture: Leisering (2019) covers the entire Global South as well as global discourses and the concepts of IOs; Bahle et al (2011) analyse the Global North.

Orenstein (2008) provides the classic account of a transnational social security campaign (the World Bank's campaign for privatising pensions during the 1990s and 2000s), while Leisering (2020) makes sense of the range of campaigns by IOs for universalising social protection (such as 'Social Security for All'), which started in the 2000s and have gathered momentum since the 2010s.

The websites of the ILO, World Bank, UNDP, UNICEF, FAO, HAI, USP2030, UHC2030, www.social-protection.org, https://basicincome.org and others provide lots of analyses, documents and data.

# References

Adema, W. (1999) *Net social expenditure*, OECD Labour Market and Social Policy Occasional Papers, No 39, Paris: OECD Publishing.

Bahle, T., Hubl, V. and Pfeifer, M. (2011) *The last safety net: A handbook of minimum income protection in Europe*, Bristol: Policy Press.

Berten, J. (2020) 'Laboratories of social knowledge: How international organizations constructed social policy through numbers, 1919–2015', PhD thesis, Bremen: Bremen University.

Berten, J. and Leisering, L. (2017) 'Social policy by numbers: How international organisations construct global policy proposals', *International Journal of Social Welfare*, 26(2), 151–67.

Beveridge, W. (1942) *Social insurance and allied services*, London: HMSO.

Davy, U. (2013) 'The rise of the "global social": Origins and transformations of social rights under UN human rights law', *International Journal of Social Quality*, 3(2), 41–59.

Deacon, B. (2007) *Global social policy and governance*, London: SAGE Publications.

Deacon, B. (2013) *Global social policy in the making: The foundations of the social protection floor*, Bristol: Policy Press.

Deacon, B., with Hulse, M. and Stubbs, P. (1997) *Global social policy: International organizations and the future of welfare*, London: SAGE Publications.

Devereux, S. and Sabates-Wheeler, R. (2004) *Transformative social protection*, IDS Working Paper 232, Brighton: Institute of Development Studies.

Drèze, J. and Sen, A.K. (1991) 'Public action for social security: Foundations and strategy', in E. Ahmad, J. Drèze, J. Hills and A.K. Sen (eds) *Social security in developing countries*, Oxford: Clarendon Press, 3–40.

Esping-Andersen, G. (1990) *The three worlds of welfare capitalism*, Cambridge: Polity Press.

Esping-Andersen, G. (1999) *Social foundations of postindustrial economies*, Oxford: Oxford University Press.

Flora, P. (ed) (1986) *Growth to limits: The western European welfare states since World War II*, Berlin: de Gruyter.

Gentilini, U., Grosh, M., Rigolini, J. and Yemtsov, R. (eds) (2020) *Exploring universal basic income: A guide to navigating concepts, evidence, and practices*, Washington, DC: World Bank.

Gentilini, U., Almenfi, M., Blomquist, J., Dale, P., De la Flor Giuffra, L., et al (2021) *Social protection and jobs responses to COVID-19. A real-time review of country measures*, Version 15, 14 May, Washington DC: World Bank.

Greve, B. (2020) *Austerity, retrenchment and the welfare state: Truth or fiction?*, Cheltenham: Edward Elgar.

Hickey, S., Lavers, T., Nino-Zarazúa, M. and Seekings, J. (eds) (2019) *The politics of social protection in Eastern and Southern Africa*, Oxford: Oxford University Press.

Hulme, D. (2015) *Global poverty: Global governance and poor people in the post-2015 era* (2nd edn), New York: Routledge.

ILO (International Labour Organization) (1999) *Decent work*, Report of the Director-General, International Labour Conference, 87th Session, Geneva: ILO.

ILO (2001) *Social security: A new consensus*, Geneva: ILO.

ILO (2003) *Global Campaign on Social Security and Coverage for All*, Geneva: ILO.

ILO (2017) *World social protection report 2017–19: Universal social protection to achieve the Sustainable Development Goals*, Geneva: ILO.

ILO (2021) *World social protection report 2020–22: Social protection at the crossroads – In pursuit of a better future*, Geneva: ILO.

Jawad, R., Jones, N. and Messkoub, M. (eds) (2019) *Social policy in the Middle East and North Africa: The new social protection paradigm and universal coverage*, Cheltenham: Edward Elgar.

Kaasch, A. (2013) 'Contesting contestation: Global social policy prescriptions on pensions and health systems', *Global Social Policy*, 13(1), 45–65.

Kaufmann, F.-X. (2012) *European foundations of the welfare state*, New York: Berghahn Publishers.

Leisering, L. (2019) *The global rise of social cash transfers: How states and international organizations constructed a new instrument for combating poverty*, Oxford: Oxford University Press.

Leisering, L. (2020) 'The calls for universal social protection by international organizations: Constructing a new global consensus', *Social Inclusion*, 8(1), 90–102.

Leisering, L. (ed) (2021a) *One hundred years of social protection: The changing social question in Brazil, India, China, and South Africa*, Cham: Palgrave Macmillan

Leisering, L. (2021b) 'Social protection responses by states and international organizations to the COVID-19 crisis in the global South: Stopgap or new departure?', *Global Social Policy*, 21(3), 396–420 (https://doi.org/10.1177/14680181211029089).

Marshall, T.H. (1950) 'Citizenship and social class', in T.H. Marshall, *Citizenship and social class and other essays*, Cambridge: Cambridge University Press, 1–85.

Maul, D. (2019) *The International Labour Organization: 100 years of global social policy*, Oldenbourg: de Gruyter.

Meyer, J.W. (2009) 'The nation-state', in G. Krücken and G.S. Drori (eds) *World society: The writings of John W. Meyer*, Oxford: Oxford University Press, pp 173–205.

Midgley, J. (2020) *Inequality, social protection and social justice*, Cheltenham: Edward Elgar.

Midgley, J. and Piachaud, D. (eds) (2011) *Colonialism and welfare: Social policy and the British imperial legacy*, Cheltenham: Edward Elgar.

Midgley, J., Dahl, E. and Wright, A.C. (eds) (2017) *Social investment and social welfare: International and critical perspectives*, Cheltenham: Edward Elgar.

Niño-Zarazúa, M., Barrientos, A., Hickey, S. and Hulme, D. (2012) 'Social protection in Sub-Saharan Africa: Getting the politics right', *World Development*, 40(1), 163–76.

Orenstein, M.A. (2005) 'The new pension reform as global policy', *Global Social Policy*, 5(2), 175–202.

Orenstein, M.A. (2008) *Privatizing pensions: The transnational campaign for social security reform*, Princeton, NJ: Princeton University Press.

Orenstein, M.A. and Deacon, B. (2014) 'Global pensions and social protection policy', in N. Yeates (ed) *Understanding global social policy* (2nd edn), Bristol: Policy Press, 187–208.

Packard, T., Gentilini, U., Grosh, M., O'Keefe, P., Palacios, R., Robalino, D. and Santos, I. (2019) *Protecting all: Risk sharing for a diverse and diversifying world of work*, Washington, DC: World Bank.

Pellissery, S., Pampackal, A.J. and Bopaiah, P. (2015) 'Caste and distributive justice: Can social policy address durable inequalities?', *Social Policy & Administration*, 49(6), 785–800.

Rodgers, G., Swepston, L., Lee, E. and van Daele, J. (2009) *The International Labour Organization and the quest for social justice, 1919–2009*, Geneva: International Labour Organization.

Rutkowski, M. and Ortiz, I. (2016) *Universal social protection to achieve the SDGs: Launch of the new global partnership for universal social protection to achieve the Sustainable Development Goals*, New York: United Nations, World Bank Group and International Labour Organization.

Schmitt, C. (2015) 'Social security development and the colonial Legacy', *World Development*, 70, 332–42.

Schmitt, C., Lierse, H., Obinger, H. and Seelkopf, L. (2015) 'The global emergence of social protection: Explaining social security legislation 1820–2013', *Politics & Society*, 43(4), 503–24.

Schüring, E. and Loewe, M. (2021) *Handbook on social protection systems*, Cheltenham: Edward Elgar.

UHC2030 (Universal Health Coverage) (2019) *Moving together to build a healthier world: Key asks from the UHC movement*, UN High-Level Meeting on Universal Health Coverage (www.uhc2030.org/fileadmin/uploads/uhc2030/Documents/UN_HLM/UHC_Key_Asks_final.pdf).

UN (United Nations) (2015) *Transforming our world: The 2030 Agenda for Sustainable Development*, UN General Assembly Resolution A/RES/70/1, 25 September, New York: UN.

UN (2018) *Promoting inclusion through social protection: Report on the world social situation 2018*, New York: UN.

USP2030 (Universal Social Protection) (no date) *Universal social protection 2030: Vision* (www.usp2030.org/gimi/USP2030.action).

von Gliszczynski, M. (2015) *Cash transfers and basic social protection: Towards a development revolution?*, Basingstoke: Palgrave Macmillan.

WHO (World Health Organization) (2017) *UHC2030 International Health Partnership: Global Compact for progress towards universal health coverage*, Geneva: WHO (www.uhc2030.org/fileadmin/uploads/uhc2030/Documents/About_UHC2030/mgt_arrangemts___docs/UHC2030_Official_documents/UHC2030_Global_Compact_WEB.pdf).

World Bank (1994) *Averting the old age crisis: Policies to protect the old and promote growth*, New York: Oxford University Press.

World Bank (2018) *The state of social safety nets 2018*, Washington, DC: World Bank.

Yeates, N. (2018) 'Social security in a global context', in J. Millar and R. Sainsbury (eds) *Understanding social security* (3rd edn), Bristol: Policy Press, 141–58.

# Glossary

**Absolute poverty**   A state of being in which household income does not meet the level required to maintain basic living standards. It is often measured using a poverty line based on the expenditure deemed necessary to buy a minimum standard of nutrition and other necessities.

**Asylum–seeker**   A person who has been forced to leave their home country and is seeking protection in another. Once asylum has been granted, an asylum-seeker becomes a refugee.

**Austerity**   Policies enacted by a government seeking to reduce public expenditure, often to reduce the public debt. Most commonly this involves cuts to public spending, resulting in the reduction or elimination of certain government services or benefits.

**Bilateral, bilateralism**   A political or economic relationship or agreement occurring between two countries.

**Brain drain**   The loss of skilled labour arising from outward migration.

**Bretton Woods**   A place in New Hampshire, USA, where the Bretton Woods Conference was held in 1944. The Conference established the Bretton Woods system of monetary arrangements between countries, and created the International Monetary Fund and the World Bank. The latter two organisations are often referred to as the 'Bretton Woods institutions'.

**Business association**   A membership organisation that supports business interests.

**Capability approach**   An approach to human welfare that conceives of wellbeing as the freedom of an individual to be or to do the things that they value, based on 'capabilities' and 'functionings'. In the analysis of poverty it looks beyond income measures to consider quality of life and has influenced both the Human Development Index and the measurement of multidimensional poverty.

**Care economy**   A term used to encompass economic activities that fit within the concept of human services and that have a strong personal or emotional dimension, for example, child rearing, childcare, healthcare, elder care, social work and education.

**Civil society**   An ecosystem of active citizenship, where non–governmental organisations or groups seek to achieve social change by partaking in public discourse and advocacy.

**Climate justice**   A term used to encompass concerns about the unequal harmful effects of climate change, and fairness within policy–making and implementation.

**Commercial determinants of health**   Strategies and approaches used by the private sector to promote products and options that are detrimental to health.

**Communicable disease**   An illness that is caused by an 'infectious agent' that can be transmitted directly or indirectly between individuals.

**Comparative advantage**   An economic idea that all countries will gain if every country specialises in industries in which it is most efficient, or the least inefficient.

**Complex multilateralism**   A process in which both governments and non-governmental actors (corporations and civil society) collaborate within the international institutional architecture to achieve policy goals.

**Conditionality**   In international governance, the setting of policy conditions for aid, whereby an aid-recipient government is required to carry out certain policies in exchange for grants or low-interest loans. Within social protection systems, it is sometimes used to refer to conditions attached to the receipt of cash benefits.

**Convention**   An agreement between countries, often within an intergovernmental organisation, that is legally binding.

**Corporate social responsibility** (CSR)   A management concept whereby businesses incorporate social considerations into their operations.

**Cosmopolitan citizenship**   Citizenship that recognises the multiple identities of citizens, that is, the identities that link individuals to a new place of residence while recognising cultural or migrant heritage. It also respects the rights of all citizens regardless of nationality.

**Cosmopolitanism**   The idea that all human beings are members of one 'universal' community.

**Cultural diffusion**   The process by which cultures vary among human populations and the spread of the ideas, beliefs, practices and objects of one culture to another.

**Decarbonisation**   The removal or reduction of carbon emissions from a sector, economy or nation.

**Deglobalisation**   The reversal of processes of globalisation.

**Demand–side policy**   A macroeconomic policy concerned with consumers, governments and businesses' demand for goods and services, that is, what economic actors buy in markets. Keynesian theorists favour demand-side macroeconomic policies as part of an effective response to recessions.

**Diaspora**   A community of people dispersed throughout the world from their original location.

**Dispute settlement mechanism**   A set of procedures put in place at the global level to resolve trade or investment disputes between parties.

**Distributional justice**   A concept of justice concerning the socially just allocation of resources.

**Domestic work and care**   Closely associated with the concept of social reproduction, it includes cooking, cleaning, laundry etc, for a household, and care for children, the elderly and infirm.

**Domestic worker**   A person who carries out paid work within the scope of a private household involved in tasks such as cleaning and cooking.

**Economism**   The belief in or commitment to prioritising economic growth and competitive economic success as the best way to strengthen societies.

**Emigration**   The act of leaving a country to live in another on a temporary or permanent basis.

**Epistemic community**   A network of knowledge-based experts.

**Extreme poverty**   A measure of absolute poverty. The World Bank measures extreme poverty globally using its international poverty line, which is based on the expenditure deemed necessary to buy a minimum standard of nutrition and other necessities in low-income countries, currently set at US$1.90 a day.

**Fair trade**   A counter-argument to free trade economic theory, arguing that trade should take whatever form most benefits the poorest and least-developed countries.

**Feminisation**   The increased presence of women, whether numerically within a given population (for example, migrant flows, labour force) or by means of greater attention to the needs, perspectives and rights of women (for example, as the result of feminist scholarship).

**Foreign direct investment** (FDI)   The process of investing in a business operation overseas to produce a good or to provide a service.

**Free trade**   International trade that is driven solely by market activity, without government interventions such as tariffs, quotas or other restrictions. Pure free trade rarely exists, but the concept is often used in support of liberalisation processes.

**Gender equality**   The ideal whereby a person's rights, resources and opportunities are not impacted by their biological sex or gender.

**Gini coefficient**   A measure of inequality that represents inequality in a single number between 0 and 1 (100), where 0 represents perfect equality and 1 (100) represents maximum inequality.

**Global Compact**   A United Nations voluntary initiative based on corporations committing to abide by human rights, labour, environmental and anti-corruption principles.

**Global constitutionalism**   An approach to global governance whereby global institutions set rules and regulations that bind all countries and populations, in a manner that is analogous with state-level constitutions.

**Global financial crisis** (GFC)   A severe financial and economic crisis, the impacts of which are worldwide in reach. The term is most commonly used to refer to the crisis that occurred in 2007–09.

**Global governance**   Governance arrangements at the global level involving states, intergovernmental organisations and international non-state actors, including both international non-governmental organisations and transnational corporations.

**Globalisation**   The increasing interconnectedness between economies, cultures and populations, brought about by increased international trade, cultural exchange and advancing technologies.

**Global justice**   An approach that considers the distribution of benefits and risks across the whole global population.

**Global North**   A category used to define countries by their socioeconomic and political characteristics, equated with richer, 'developed' countries.

**Global social governance**   Global governance arrangements that specifically address issues of social policy.

**Global social justice**   The global moral and political standards of how people ought to live and relate to one another within a framework of fair institutions and social relations.

**Global social policy** (GSP)   A transnational approach to the study and practice of social policy, which considers the global aspects of social policy-making and implementation and of social welfare in all their dimensions.

**Global South**   A category used to define countries by their socioeconomic and political characteristics. Usually equated with poorer, 'developing' countries.

**Global union federation** (GUF)   An international federation of national trade unions. It can be organised along the lines of specific industry sectors or occupational groups.

**Governance**   The process of governing, controlling, managing or regulating the affairs of an entity or system.

**Gross domestic product** (GDP)   A measure of a country's economic activity within its borders. It is most commonly thought of as the value of all the goods and services produced within a country in a given year, but is also equal to the income earned from that production and the total amount spent on final goods and services.

**Gross national income** (GNI)   Similar to gross domestic product (GDP), GNI is the estimated measure of a country's economic activity within a set time period. GNI is the total income earned by a country's people and businesses regardless of where it was earned. It is thus gross domestic product plus net receipts from abroad.

**Gross national product** (GNP)   Similar to gross national income (GNI), GNP is the estimated measure of a country's economic activity within a set time period. It includes within the total all the income of a country's residents and businesses, whether it flows back to the country or remains abroad.

**Hard law**   Refers to legal obligations that are binding and can be enforced within a legal system.

**High-income country**   A country defined by the World Bank as one where the gross national income per capita exceeds US$12,695 (threshold correct as of July 2021).

**Human capital**   The skills, experience and knowledge of an individual.

**Human development** A development approach that seeks to increase the quality of human life, rather than solely to develop the economy in which human beings live. It is related to the capability approach to development.

**Human Development Index** (HDI) A statistical composite index that ranks countries according to their average achievements in key social and economic dimensions (life expectancy, education, and per capita income).

**Immigration** The act of entering one country from another to live there on a temporary or permanent basis.

**Informal economy** Economic activities that are not covered by formal state arrangements such as taxation or regulation (excluding illicit economic activities).

**Intergovernmental organisation** (IGO) An organisation or entity that comprises two or more sovereign states that are bound by a treaty to work together on social, economic or political issues.

**International financial institution** (IFI) A financial institution that has been established by, and has a broad membership of, sovereign states, created to support sustainable development, reduce poverty and to promote international cooperation and coordination. The International Monetary Fund and the World Bank are the main IFIs.

**International governance** Governance processes that facilitate cooperation between states, including through intergovernmental organisations.

**International non-governmental organisations** (INGOs) Non-state organisations such as non-profit organisations, civil society organisations and lobby groups that operate in more than one country or at the global level.

**International organisation** (IO) An international body that promotes cooperation and coordination among its members. The term is sometimes used to refer to intergovernmental organisations, but in this book it is used more broadly to encompass both intergovernmental organisations and international non-governmental organisations.

**International system** The politics and interrelatedness of all the world's states.

**International treaty** A legally binding agreement between two or more countries.

**Keynesianism** A macroeconomic theory developed by John Maynard Keynes that posits that aggregate demand is the most important determinant of economic activity, and that government intervention is sometimes necessary to stabilise the economy.

**Labour standards** The rules, norms and regulations that govern working conditions.

**Lesson drawing** The act of examining policies and programmes in a different jurisdiction to draw logical and empirical conclusions to help develop domestic policies.

**Liberalisation** (of trade)    The removal or reduction of restrictions or barriers to trade (such as tariffs and quotas).

**Low carbon economy**    An economy with very low carbon emissions.

**Low-income country**    A country defined by the World Bank as one where the gross national income per capita is below US$1,046 (threshold correct as of July 2021).

**Managed migration**    Discourses and schemes used to control the migration of workers and their families for the benefit of the countries of origin *and* destination.

**Means test**    An assessment of incomes and assets of social assistance claimants to ascertain eligibility.

**Member states**    The members of an intergovernmental organisation.

**Methodological nationalism**    An approach that considers the nation–state as the primary unit of analysis and focuses on the social ties, activities and interactions within it.

**Methodological transnationalism**    An approach that looks at social ties, activities and interactions that cut across nation–states.

**Middle-income country**    A country defined by the World Bank as one where the gross national income per capita is between US$1,046 and US$12,695. There are two sub-categories within this group: lower-middle income countries (gross national income [GNI] per capita between US$1,046–4,095) and upper-middle income countries (GNI per capita between US$4,096–12,695) (thresholds correct as of July 2021).

**Migration**    The movement of people from one country to another, or from one area of a country to another.

**Millennium Development Goals** (MDGs)    United Nations development objectives consisting of eight goals for measures that should be achieved by 2015. They were replaced by the Sustainable Development Goals (SDGs) in 2015.

**Multilateral, multilateralism**    A political or economic relationship or agreement occurring between three or more countries.

**Multilevel governance**    Concept used to describe different vertical and horizontal jurisdictional levels of governance, to encapsulate (for example) local, regional, national, international and global levels of governance and the interaction and overlaps between them.

**Neoliberal, neoliberalism**    An economic approach that embraces free market capitalism and economic liberalisation, and espouses the deregulation of markets and the reduction of state involvement in the economy.

**Non-state actors**    Organisations or individuals involved in policy-making that are not affiliated with, or directed by, government actors, for example corporations and civil society organisations.

**Normative power**    Power that is achieved through an evaluation or value judgement, that is, power that does not utilise material or physical incentives.

**Path dependency**   The process by which policy choices and decisions are dependent on those made in the past, rather than on current conditions. It is used to help explain continuity in welfare state development.

**Philanthrocapitalism**   The philosophy and practice of applying capitalist objectives, methods, criteria or profits to philanthropic projects.

**Policy diffusion**   The process by which an innovation is communicated through certain channels or networks, over time. It is a special type of communication in that the messages are concerned with new ideas.

**Policy transfer**   An umbrella concept that encapsulates the different theories (for example, lesson drawing, policy diffusion) that examine how policies can cross jurisdictional boundaries.

**Populist, populism**   A political stance that juxtaposes the idea of 'ordinary people' against 'the elite'. It is often used as a political strategy by nationalist or right-wing politicians.

**Procedural justice**   A concept of justice concerning fairness within administrative and legal processes determining, for example, dispute resolution and resource allocation.

**Protectionist, protectionism** (trade)   The protection of domestic industries against foreign competition; (childhood and youth studies) the protection of and support for human welfare and development.

**Public–private partnerships** (PPPs)   An arrangement between two or more public and private bodies to address a public policy issue. Often it refers to the financing of a government project (such as a hospital building and management) by a private actor.

**Purchasing power parity** (PPP)   A theoretical exchange rate that compares currencies by using a 'basket of goods' approach. It is used to compare standards of living between countries.

**Quota** (in trade)   A governmental trade restriction that limits the number (or value) of a product that can be imported into the country.

**'Race to the bottom'**   A phrase used to describe government policies of deregulation and tax reduction in order to remain or become economically competitive with other countries.

**Recognition justice**   A concept of justice concerned with the achievement of the conditions of mutual recognition, including of people's different identities and of existing inequalities.

**Recommendations**   International instruments adopted by intergovernmental organisations that are not legally binding and that serve as guidelines to help member states formulate policies.

**Refugee**   A displaced person forced to leave their home country and who cannot return there safely. Until they have been permitted to remain in a country of destination, they are known as an 'asylum-seeker'.

**Relative poverty**   A state of being in which someone does not have enough to fully participate in the society in which they live and cannot afford what other people take for granted. It is measured in comparison to the standards of living of others within the same country or community, and is often operationalised as an income of less than 50 or 60 per cent of median income.

**Remittance**   A payment transferred through cash or in-kind.

**Selective**   The provision of targeted services or benefits to those in greatest need.

**Sexual and reproductive health and rights** (SRHR)   A concept that goes beyond reproductive health and rights to include the notion of sexual health. Also includes sexual orientation and gender identity.

**Social assistance**   Means-tested and tax-financed regular benefits to poorer social groups.

**Social contract**   The moral or political obligations that the population of a state are owed by their government.

**Social determinants of health** (SDH)   Non-medical factors created by the social conditions in which people are born, grow, work, live and age that influence health outcomes.

**Social insurance**   A government scheme that insures workers against the risks of working life, such as industrial accidents, sickness, unemployment and old age, funded mainly by contributions from employers and employees.

**Social protection**   An umbrella term for government schemes such as social insurance, social assistance and labour rights.

**Social reproduction**   Refers in feminist discourse to the maintenance and reproduction of people on a daily and intergenerational basis, encompassing sexuality and biological reproduction, and work and care performed in the household and in the wider economy.

**Social security**   An umbrella term for government schemes such as social insurance and social assistance. Similar to the term 'social protection', but does not include labour rights.

**Soft law**   Agreements, principles and declarations that are not legally binding.

**Structural adjustment programme** (SAP)   A loan-based programme provided by the International Monetary Fund and the World Bank to a government that is subject to conditionalities, specifically, a set of economic reforms including reducing government spending, privatisation and trade liberalisation, that the government must enact.

**Supply-side policy**   An economic policy aimed at reducing costs. Supply-side policies often aim to reduce labour market regulations, such as those concerned with working conditions or wages. They are often associated with neoliberal economists.

**Supranational institution**   A multilateral organisation or association in which member states pool some degree of sovereignty and cede authority to a higher body.

**Sustainable development**  A development approach that seeks to meet the immediate needs of development without compromising the ability of other countries and/or future generations to meet their needs. Usually refers to environmental sustainability, but may also refer to social and economic sustainability.

**Sustainable Development Goals** (SDGs)  A collection of 17 global development goals set by the United Nations system. They superseded the Millennium Development Goals (MDGs) in 2015, and are intended to be achieved by 2030.

**Tariff**  A tax imposed by one country on goods and services imported from another country.

**Trade union**  An association of employees who group together to maintain and improve their working conditions.

**Transnational advocacy coalition**  A coalition of global actors who coordinate to suggest policy ideas and influence the policy-making process.

**Transnational corporation** (TNC)  A large business enterprise that operates in more than one country. It may have a sophisticated division of labour involving operations in many different countries.

**Universal, universalism**  Refers to all members of a designated community.

**Universal health coverage** (UHC)  Refers to a system where all individuals and communities have access to health services. Says nothing about the composition of that coverage, whether for-profit or not-for-profit.

**Venue shifting**  When policy actors move a policy discussion from one forum to an alternative forum, where the final policy decision is more likely to reflect their interests and result in favourable outcomes for them (also known as 'forum shifting').

**Venue shopping**  When policy actors select the most appropriate and beneficial forum for them to pursue their policy ideas and goals (also known as 'forum shopping').

**Veto point**  A juncture in the policy-making process where policy actors are able to block attempts at policy change.

**Washington Consensus**  A set of economic policy recommendations for developing countries that were considered the 'standard' reform package required to rebuild and regenerate a struggling economy. The recommendations followed free market principles that focused on privatisation, liberalisation and macro stability.

**World-regional organisation**  An organisation that operates at a sub-global but supra-state level, such as the European Union.

**Zoonosis**  Any disease or infection that is transmitted from vertebrate animals to humans.

# Index

Note: Page numbers in bold refer to boxes.

Soviet bloc 51

Soviet Union 29, 287, 322, 323
  *see also* Russia

Spain 82, 234

Stanford school of global analysis *see* World
  Society theory

state-owned enterprises (SOEs) (China) 50

Stockholm, Sweden 256, 258

Stockholm Environment Institute 264

structural adjustment programmes (SAPs) 83,
  170, 258, 300, 322, 352
  *see also* World Bank, IMF

Sub-Saharan Africa 143, 163–5, 173, 188,
  217, 301
  *see also* individual sub-Saharan African
  countries

supranational institutions 7, 8, 10, 28, 54,
  193, 352
  *see also* intergovernmental organisations
  (IGOs)

sustainable development 13, 38, 253, 254,
  255–8, 260, 261, 263, 265, 269, 270,
  279, 353

Sustainable Development Goals (SDGs) 13,
  14, 15, 16, 31, 37, **38**, 41, 159, 170,
  178, 194, 214, 215, **222**, 235, 253,
  255, 267–9, 282, 319, 353

Sweden 175, 256

Swedish International Development
  Cooperation Agency 258

Switzerland 56, 262

**T**

Taiwan 12

tariffs 49, 50, 51, 52, 54, 60, 177, 353

Task Force on Youth Policies and Programmes
  (UN) 234

tax, taxation 36, 51, 53, 68, 69, 76–80, 81,
  82, 83, 91, 115, 120, 125, 172, 177,
  178, 196, 277, 284, 311

Thailand 56, 301

Thatcher, Margaret 53

tobacco control 55, **56**, 278, 281

trade *see* global trade, international trade

trade unions 30, 58, 67, 70–1, 72, 76, 79,
  93, 193, 195, 198, 209, 216, 217, 333,
  353

Trade Adjustment Assistance (TAA) 60

Trade in Services Agreement *see* General
  Agreement on Trade in Services
  (GATS)

Trade-Related Aspects of Intellectual Property
  Rights (TRIPS) 41, 52, 55, 56, 57,
  285, 286, 287

Trade Union Advisory Committee to the
  OECD (TUAC) 69, 71, 73, 74–5

Transatlantic Trade and Investment
  Partnership (TTIP) 57, 311
  *see also* global partnerships

transitions discourse (young people) 229,
  230, 231, 232, 236–40, **236–7**, 246

transnational actors 9, 100, 331

transnational advocacy coalitions 57, 353
  *see also* advocacy coalitions

transnational corporations (TNCs) 9, 10, 11,
  26–7, 40, 41, 42, 53, 55, 58, 71, 72,
  76, 114, 276, 278, 284, 285, 288, 353

transnational feminist networks (TFNs) 198,
  207, 208, 209, **210**, 217, 219, 221,
  222, 223, 224

transnational tobacco companies (TTCs) 55,
  **56**

Trans-Pacific Partnership (TPP) 57, 311
  *see also* global partnerships

trickle-down effect 328

TRIPS+ 286

Trump, Donald 6, 32, 34, 41, 50, 57, 148,
  176, 212, 222

Turkey 322

**U**

UEAPME *see* European Association of Craft,
  Small and Medium-Sized Enterprises

UHC2030: International Health Partnership
  **334**
  *see also* global partnerships

Ukraine 56

UN Water 264, 271

UN Women 191, 192, 198, 208, 209, 215,
  218, 221, 223

UNAIDS *see* Joint United Nations
  Programme on HIV/AIDS

unemployment 58, 59, 75, 229, 235, 238,
  277, 320, 327, 335
  benefits 60, 73, 75,
  insurance 79